Press Bias
and Politics

Recent Titles in the
Praeger Series in Political Communication
Robert E. Denton, Jr., General Editor

Press Bias and Politics

How the Media Frame
Controversial Issues

Jim A. Kuypers

Praeger Series in Political Communication

Westport, Connecticut
London

Library of Congress Cataloging-in-Publication Data

Kuypers, Jim A.
   Press bias and politics : how the media frame controversial issues / Jim A. Kuypers.
     p. cm.—(Praeger series in political communication, ISSN 1062–5623)
   Includes bibliographical references and index.
   ISBN 0–275–97758–7 (alk. paper)—ISBN 0–275–97759–5 (pbk. : alk. paper)
   1. Journalism—Objectivity—United States. 2. United States—Politics and government—1989– I. Title. II. Series.
PN4888.O25K89 2002
302.23'0973—dc21   2002022468

British Library Cataloguing in Publication Data is available.

Library of Congress Catalog Card Number: 2002022468
ISBN: 0–275–97758–7
    0–275–97759–5 (pbk)
ISSN: 1062–5623

First published in 2002

Praeger Publishers, 88 Post Road West, Westport, CT 06881
An imprint of Greenwood Publishing Group, Inc.
www.praeger.com

Printed in the United States of America

The paper used in this book complies with the
Permanent Paper Standard issued by the National
Information Standards Organization (Z39.48–1984).

10 9 8 7 6 5 4 3 2 1

To my family,
whose love and support
are constant

Contents

Series Foreword

Those of us from the discipline of communication studies have long believed that communication is prior to all other fields of inquiry. In several other forums I have argued that the essence of politics is "talk" or human interaction.[1] Such interaction may be formal or informal, verbal or nonverbal, public or private, but it is always persuasive, forcing us consciously or subconsciously to interpret, to evaluate, and to act. Communication is the vehicle for human action.

From this perspective, it is not surprising that Aristotle recognized the natural kinship of politics and communication in his writings *Politics* and *Rhetoric*. In the former, he established that humans are "political beings [who] alone of the animals [are] furnished with the faculty of language."[2] In the latter, he began his systematic analysis of discourse by proclaiming that "rhetorical study, in its strict sense, is concerned with the modes of persuasion."[3] Thus, it was recognized over twenty-three hundred years ago that politics and communication go hand in hand because they are essential parts of human nature.

In 1981. Dan Nimmo and Keith Sanders proclaimed that political communication was an emerging field.[4] Although its origin, as noted, dates back centuries, a "self-consciously cross-disciplinary" focus began in the late 1950s. Thousands of books and articles later, colleges and universities offer a variety of graduate and undergraduate coursework in the area in such diverse departments as communication, mass communication, journalism, political science, and sociology.[5] In Nimmo and Sanders's early assessment, the "key areas of inquiry" included rhetorical analysis, propaganda analysis, attitude change studies, voting studies, government and the news media, functional and systems analyses, technological changes, media technologies, campaign techniques, and research techniques.[6] In a survey of the state of the field in 1983, the same authors and Lynda Kaid found additional, more specific areas of concerns such as the presidency, political polls, public opinion, debates, and advertising.[7] Since the first study, they have also noted a shift away from the rather strict behavioral approach.

A decade later, Dan Nimmo and David Swanson argued that "political communication has developed some identity as a more or less distinct domain of scholarly work."[8] The scope and concerns of the area have further expanded to include critical theories and cultural studies. Although there is no precise definition, method, or disciplinary home of the area of inquiry, its primary domain comprises the role, processes, and effects of communication within the context of politics broadly defined.

In 1985, the editors of *Political Communication Yearbook: 1984* noted that "more things are happening in the study, teaching, and practice of political communication than can be captured within the space limitations of the relatively few publications available."[9] In addition, they argued that the backgrounds of "those involved in the field [are] so varied and pluralist in outlook and approach, . . . it [is] a mistake to adhere slavishly to any set format in shaping the content."[10] More recently, Nimmo and Swanson have called for "ways of overcoming the unhappy consequences of fragmentation within a framework that respects, encourages, and benefits from diverse scholarly commitments, agendas, and approaches."[11]

In agreement with these assessments of the area and with gentle encouragement, in 1988 Praeger established the series entitled "Praeger Series in Political Communication." The series is open to all qualitative and quantitative methodologies as well as contemporary and historical studies. The key to characterizing the studies in the series is the focus on communication variables or activities within a political context or dimension. As of this writing, over seventy volumes have been published and numerous impressive works are forthcoming. Scholars from the disciplines of communication, history, journalism, political science, and sociology have participated in the series.

I am, without shame or modesty, a fan of the series. The joy of serving as its editor is in participating in the dialogue of the field of political communication and in reading the contributors' works. I invite you to join me.

Robert E. Denton, Jr.

NOTES

1. See Robert E. Denton, Jr., *The Symbolic Dimensions of the American Presidency* (Prospect Heights, IL: Waveland Press, 1982); Robert E. Denton, Jr., and Gary

Woodward, *Political Communication in America* (New York: Praeger, 1985; 2d ed., 1990); Robert E. Denton Jr., and Dan Hahn, *Presidential Communication* (New York: Praeger, 1986); and Robert E. Denton, Jr., *The Primetime Presidency of Ronald Reagan* (New York: Praeger, 1988).

2. Aristotle, *The Politics of Aristotle*, trans. Ernest Barker (New York: Oxford University Press, 1970), p. 5.

3. Aristotle, *Rhetoric*, trans. W. Rhys Roberts (New York: The Modern Library, 1954), p. 22.

4. Dan Nimmo and Keith Sanders, "Introduction: The Emergence of Political Communication as a Field," in *Handbook of Political Communication*, eds. Dan Nimmo and Keith Sanders (Beverly Hills, CA: Sage, 1981), pp. 11–36.

5. Ibid., p. 15.

6. Ibid., p. 17–27.

7. Keith Sanders, Lynda Kaid, and Dan Nimmo, eds. *Political Communication Yearbook: 1984* (Carbondale, IL: Southern Illinois University, 1985), pp. 283–308.

8. Dan Nimmo and David Swanson, "The Field of Political Communication: Beyond the Voter Persuasion Paradigm," in *New Directions in Political Communication*, eds. David Swanson and Dan Nimmo (Beverly Hills, CA: Sage, 1990), p. 8.

9. Sanders, Kaid, and Nimmo, *Political Communication Yearbook: 1984*, p. xiv.

10. Ibid.

11. Nimmo and Swanson, "The Field of Political Communication," p. 11.

Acknowledgments

There are so many people to whom I owe gratitude. I offer thanks to all who have helped me with this project, most notably Bob Denton and Andy King. Further, I offer distinctive gratitude to my family, Marvin and Joany Floyd and Rebel and Watson Kuypers. I wish to add a special thanks to Dick Sheldon of Dartmouth College, for his friendship and encouragement.

Chapter One

Understanding Media Manipulation of Controversial Issues

When men understand what each other mean,
they see, for the most part, that controversy is either superfluous or
hopeless.[1]

—John Henry Newman

Race relations, homosexual activism, partial-birth abortion, the death
penalty, women in combat, affirmative action, federal funding for stem-
cell research—the list goes on. Controversial issues are, by their essential
nature, unsolvable to everyone's satisfaction. Such issues are open to
discussion—debatable, questionable—and generally in dispute by contending groups. Our tolerance for one position over another is usually a
matter of degree. We hear about controversial issues every day; we discuss them with family, friends, coworkers, and others. Although we often look to friends for information on these issues, we look to experts as
well. We seek the opinions of politicians, prominent social figures, religious leaders, and academic and technical experts. Yet it is not often that
we consider the messenger who brings us our information about controversial issues. Controversial issues are news, and for news we look to
the press.

Recent surveys show that 77% of Americans read their daily local papers, and this on average of five days a week.[2] The consumption of print
news takes on greater importance when we see that 54% of Americans
turn to an additional print source for news. Furthermore, there is a direct
correlation between reading print sources for news and educational and
income level. In short, the higher an individual's education and income,
the more likely that individual will look to print sources for news. News

sources are not limited to local papers, however. According to Ted Smith and colleagues, "Major national newspapers ... are read by ... about one-third of all adult Americans. People with high levels of education and income are ... approximately twice as likely as those with low levels to read a major national newspaper. Less than one-fourth (24%) of those Americans whose education is limited to high school read a national paper, while more than one-half (55%) of those with a college degree do the same.[3] What makes this large readership all the more worthy of study "is that newspaper reading is strongly associated with political involvement."[4] It seems clear that to better grasp how Americans come to view controversial issues we need to understand the influence of the press upon our acquisition of information.

The purpose of this book is to understand and chart the potential effects the printed press—and by extension, broadcast media—have upon the messages of political and social leaders when they discuss controversial issues. Although much has been written about how the media focus public attention on certain issues over others, there exists scant literature that explores how media reportorial practices take into account the original utterances of those being reported upon. This book explores how press reports modify the original meaning of that which they report upon; as case studies I use two high-profile controversial issues: race and homosexuality. In examining the relationship of press reports to our understanding of these issues, this book asks and answers rather broad-based questions about press influences on our public debates: Guided by the press, how do we perceive controversial issues? In what terms are these issues discussed by the press, and do these terms limit options for discussion in the public sphere? Is the press neutral, or does it encourage us to view controversial issues in a certain way? How does the press construct a notion of tolerance for a particular position?

As the above questions suggest, the idea behind this book is to make readers more knowledgeable consumers of news media products. One should be able to say after reading this book: "I know now what will happen when the media reports on almost any given controversial topic. I know now how the information will be meditated by those in the press." Armed with this knowledge, readers will be better able to make critical assessments of the news.

BACKGROUND INFORMATION

The manner in which I examine the influence of the press on our understanding of controversial issues is a combination of rhetorical analysis, journalism theory, and modified social scientific inquiry (framing analysis).[5] Ultimately, this book is a rhetorical analysis of the interaction of a political or social leader's speech and the subsequent press coverage;

thus this section will briefly cover the concepts of rhetoric and rhetorical situations before moving to the areas of media agenda-setting, agenda-extension, and framing analysis.

Rhetoric and Rhetorical Situations

For the purposes of this book, I define rhetoric as the strategic use of communication, oral or written, used to achieve specifiable goals. Thus, public pronouncements on controversial issues may be counted as rhetoric. Public speaking does not exist in a vacuum. That which politicians and other public figures say in public is in response to a situation of some sort. This is to say, the person speaking has determined that something needs to be done, has crafted a response announcing a plan of action or hoped for interpretation, and then has made comments or given a speech. Because of this, when analyzing the words, or utterances, of a speaker, it is important to understand the situation surrounding the problem a speaker is addressing.

One way of understanding such a situation was provided by communication theorist Lloyd Bitzer.[6] His classic definition of a rhetorical situation is worth noting: "a complex of persons, events, objects, and relations presenting an actual or potential exigency which can be completely or partially removed if discourse, introduced into the situation, can so constrain human decision or action as to bring about the significant modification of the exigency."[7] An "exigence is an imperfection marked by some degree of urgency; it is a defect, an obstacle, something to be corrected."[8] The audience consists of those individuals capable of modifying the exigence. In short, they have the power to change the situation, to solve or modify the problem. Constraints influence both audience members and speakers and are composed of "persons, events, objects, relations, rules, principles, facts, laws, images, interests, emotions, arguments, and conventions."[9] Constraints act to limit and influence what a speaker may say as well as how an audience interprets what it hears.

The above concepts (exigency, audience, and constraints) are intertwined and mutually influence each other. The three taken together require some type of discourse to fuel their interaction and possible modification. The discourse, or *utterance* in Bitzer's terminology, "participates naturally in the situation, is in many instances necessary to the completion of situational activity, and by means of its participation with situation obtains its meaning and its rhetorical character."[10]

A *situation* is not the same as *context*, however. Context, a necessary component of human communication, is more than the historical facts surrounding a rhetorical situation. Context is, in part, constituted by the various interpretive communities that apprehend what a speaker says.

In this vein, Gregory Bateson provides a useful definition of context: "a collective term for all those events which tell the organism among what *set* of alternatives he must make his next choice."[11] Viewed in this manner, contexts may have broad influences upon our understanding of any particular speech or utterance. Rhetorical situations, on the other hand, are not to be understood at a general level but rather through the speaker's interaction with audience, exigency, and constraints. Contexts help shape the general level of interpretive precision that produces a speaker's utterance (and its subsequent interpretation); it is this utterance that enters into the rhetorical situation. Rhetorical situations are a part of the larger context; they "come into existence, then either mature and decay or mature and persist. . . . Situations grow and come to maturity; they evolve to just the time when a rhetorical discourse would be most fitting."[12] Contexts allow for the general interpretation of utterances; rhetorical situations provide moments for a "fitting" utterance through which modification of an exigence may be achieved.

For example, consider the impeachment proceedings against President Clinton in 1998. The larger contexts that could have influenced utterances within the rhetorical situation included the upcoming congressional elections, the ongoing Starr investigations, and the historical or cultural understandings of Americans concerning the distinction between private and public acts. As distinct from contexts, the rhetorical situation is modified by utterances that are shaped by the above contexts. The utterance, however, can have a bearing upon which contexts subsequently wax or wane in influence.

In order for the words of a speaker to modify an exigency successfully, they must "fit" not only the particular situation into which they enter but also the contexts which influence the situation. In fact, the creation of a stable context through which to view the situation is often the first step for the successful modification of an exigency that occurs in a situation impacted by multiple contexts. Yet the audience capable of enacting change—frequently voters—more often than not hears a speaker's words through the mediating influence of the press. Because of this, the role and influence of the press in transmitting information to the public must be examined.

The Agenda-Setting and Agenda-Extension Functions of the Press

Understanding the agenda-setting function of the press helps explain how press reports interact with political discourse and public perceptions of that discourse.[13] A famous statement still circulating in schools of communication and journalism was made by Bernard C. Cohen, who observed that the press "may not be very successful in telling its readers what to think, but it is stunningly successful in telling its readers what to think about."[14] If the second part of Cohen's statement is accepted as accurate, and I think it should, then it behooves us to consider speeches on controversial issues in relation to the press, not because the press represents public opinion (although many members of the public might think so), but because the press is a good indication of the issues and ideas that informed voters and opinion leaders will be talking about. These individuals are aware of the issues, ideas, and responses that circulate in the press not because they represent popular opinion, but because they are a good indicator of that which still needs to be addressed in public policy or that they should be talking about. Studies into the agenda-setting function of the press confirm that the media "have a great deal of influence" upon political decision making and that they are especially influential in telling the general population what to think about.[15]

For example, Maxwell E. McCombs and Donald L. Shaw argued that voters learn about an issue "in direct proportion" to the attention given that issue by the press, and that voters tend to share what the media defines as important.[16] Further, these researchers asserted that the mass media provide voters with the "major primary sources of national political information."[17] These findings were later corroborated by Sheldon Gilberg and colleagues. Their study found that the press has the potential to set our government's agenda, even at the highest levels.[18] That the press has the power to set an agenda should come as no surprise. McCombs and Shaw explain: "the press is an independent force whose dialogue with other elements of society produces the agenda of issues considered by political elites and voters. Witness the major role of the elite press as a source of information among major decision makers. Through its winnowing of the day's happenings to find the major events, concerns, and issues, the press inadvertently plays an agenda-setting influence role."[19] Often, the longer an issue remains in news focus, the more the public perceives it as a crisis. Michael B. Salwen highlighted the importance of this consideration when he suggested that policy makers "will address issues only when these issues are perceived as crises by the public."[20] These and similar studies paint a convincing picture: the mass media shape not only what the public "perceives" as "political reality" but also how political elites understand what voters and opinion leaders are thinking about. It is in this manner, then, that a conversation develops among the press, its sources, and the public audience that determines "what is *accepted* as the public agenda."[21]

Many studies testing agenda-setting theory have as their focus the president of the United States. For example, Gilberg and his colleagues asserted that the president is in a "strategic position to influence the agenda" of the press because he is the major source of news at the national level.[22] Although they found that the press had a significant influence upon President Jimmy Carter's second State of the Union address, they were unable to determine whether Carter's address influenced subsequent press issues. A later study by McCombs and colleagues found evidence of "presidential influence on subsequent press coverage."[23] However, although the president is occasionally able to influence coverage of issues, other politicians and social leaders are not in the same position of authority. The implications of this for the study of press influence upon political utterances should be clear, particularly in light of the degree to which the public relies upon the press for information, especially concerning issues of national importance. These national issues are generally not part of an individual's common experience; therefore, the "news media exercise a near monopoly as sources of information and orientation."[24] Although many politicians surely know more, the media tell them what we, *the public*, know.

Whereas agenda-setting serves to focus public attention upon an issue, agenda-extension occurs when the media move beyond a neutral reporting of events, and it is to this concern that we now turn. During the decade of the 1980s, communication and mass media researchers exploring the agenda-setting functions of the press began to discover an evaluative component to media news. These researchers postulated that the media do more than tell the public what to think about; they also tell the public *how* to think about any given topic. These studies revealed two other aspects of agenda-setting which relate to the public evaluation of political leaders; these aspects are called priming and framing. One way of understanding priming and framing is that the media provide the contextual cues "by which to evaluate the subject matter" under consideration.[25]

Shanto Iyengar and Adam Simon have studied the effects of network news coverage during the Gulf War, and provide examples of the differences among agenda-setting, priming, and framing. They defined priming as the "ability of news programs to affect the criteria by which political leaders are judged."[26] Specifically, priming involves the correlation among patterns of news coverage and the manner in which the public evaluates the performance of politicians. These effects upon evaluation are strongest in the area of performance and weakest in the area of affecting judgment on personality. Priming is intimately linked with agenda-setting because the "more prominent an issue in the national information stream, the greater its weight in political judgments."[27] In analyzing the news coverage of the Gulf War, Iyengar and Simon found that the "amount of coverage accorded to the Gulf's situation and the proportion of respondents nominating it as the nation's most important problem were highly correlated" (agenda-setting).[28] In terms of the role that priming played, they found foreign policy "performance assessments tended to override economic assessments in their impact on . . . ratings of George Bush during the Gulf crisis."[29]

These findings highlight the relationship between those issues political leaders announce as important and the perceived importance of those issues to the American people. Priming works because "by calling attention to some aspects of national life while ignoring others, network news programs determine the standards by which presidents [and political leaders] are judged."[30] Iyengar and Kinder, drawing from basic psychological theory, explain that this occurs because public attention is highly selective and that the public relies primarily upon information that is easily accessible. Judgments about political matters are in part due to what standards come to individuals' minds but also are due to those "considerations that are, for whatever reason and however briefly, accessible."[31] Mainstream news outlets are quick and accessible sources for news.

News coverage that implies politicians' responsibility for a situation at the national level encourages viewers to attach more importance to their performance on that particular situation when evaluating their overall performance. In addition, this "effect appears to be stronger for problems that are relative newcomers to the American political agenda, problems for which the public's understanding is still in formation."[32] Thus, when announcing new public policy initiatives, when public knowledge is in flux and new knowledge is constantly being injected into the public's evaluative consciousness, the effects of priming could be considerable. However, when issues are on-going—abortion, affirmative action, etc.—the effects of priming may not be as strong.[33]

Framing moves beyond priming because it involves the relationship between qualitative aspects of news coverage—contextual cues—and how the public interprets the news. William Gamson asserted that a "frame is a central organizing idea for making sense of relevant events and suggesting what is at issue."[34] Facts remain neutral until framed; thus, how the press frames an issue or event will affect public understanding of that issue or event. On this point Gamson argued that facts "take on their meaning by being embedded in a frame or story line that organizes them and gives them coherence, selecting certain ones to emphasize while ignoring others."[35] Framing, then, is the process whereby communicators act to construct a particular point of view that encourages the facts of a given situation to be viewed (or ignored) in a particular manner, with some facts made more noticeable than others. When speaking of political and social issues, frames actually define our understanding of any given situation.

According to political scientist Doris Graber, this type of "manipulative journalism raises philosophical, ethical, and news policy questions."[36] Graber calls this manipulative journalism agenda-building, the "process whereby news stories influence how people perceive and evaluate issues and policies."[37] This clearly moves beyond agenda-setting, and involves the influencing of public opinion. What Graber describes as agenda-building I call agenda-extension.[38] Graber and I are not alone in reporting upon press effects beyond agenda-setting. Agenda-setting researchers in the mid-1990s began to investigate second level agenda-setting effects.[39] Simply put, agenda-setting can be described as the role the media play in focusing the public's attention on a particular object or issue over another object or issue, primarily by how much attention the media gives to that object or issue. Second level agenda-setting posits that the media can focus attention on particular attributes within a particular object or issue. The notion of second level effects blends in well with research examining priming since the media would be elevating one attribute over another in the mind of the public. Since a particular attribute on an issue would be foremost in the public eye, it seems likely that the public would use that particular attribute to evaluate a politician's actions. Anne Johnston, in a review of media scholarship, discovered that work in agenda-setting research has well documented the agenda-extension process.[40] The public becomes primed to evaluate the president, for example, by how well he handles the issue covered by the press. The more the press covers an issue, the more the public will evaluate the president's success or failure in relation to the content of media coverage.

Johnston stated that news stories provide their audiences with more than the important subjects to think about; they also provide "contextual cues or frames in which to evaluate those subjects."[41] Issues are often framed by how station managers, producers, editors, and reporters tell the story of the issue. Gladys Engel Lang and Kurt Lang discovered this type of agenda-extension operating during the Watergate hearings. They demonstrated that agenda-extension begins when media gatekeepers decide to publish a particular story.[42] Although this is the first step in all news reporting, the move toward agenda-extension occurs when a second step is taken, the decision concerning how much attention to give to the story. As pointed out by Graber, it is at this "point where ordinary agenda-setting activities can most readily turn into deliberate agenda-building [agenda-extension]."[43] By continually focusing on an issue, the media may thrust it into the forefront of national thought. And at the point when an issue emerges, its media frame becomes crucially important. Lang and Lang noted that the Watergate coverage was first put into the framework of the election campaign, thus leading the public to think of it as partisan politics as usual. As soon as the media switched frames, moving from the framework of the 1972 presidential campaign to the framework of continual Washington corruption, the nation became obsessed. It is at this point that agenda-extension goes beyond second level agenda-setting in that it posits that the media not only focus attention on particular attributes of an issue, making some portions more salient than others, it does so in such a manner that a particular political agenda is advanced. Simply put, second level agenda-setting examines *what* attributes are stressed, agenda-extension allows us to see *how* those attributes are stressed to influence audience reaction.[44]

Although it can be successfully argued that providing contextual cues for interpretation is a necessary part of media responsibility, when the media places its partisan context over that of the people or government, the potential for public manipulation increases.[45] For example, Graber conducted a content analysis of television news coverage of the 1984 presidential campaign that sheds light upon this media manipulation.[46] Her focus was on how the news was framed. She found that there was a ratio of three to one of bad over good news for the United States during this period. This news primarily focused on foreign policy and economic concerns. Graber posited that this bad-news coverage should have derailed President Reagan's reelection bid but did not. While the networks had framed the news so as to stress the bad aspects of American news, they also primed the population to evaluate President Reagan's performance on foreign policy and economic considerations. Thus, frames do allow for multiple interpretations. As Graber noted: "[V]arious media effects are modulated by the sensitivity of audiences to particular issues, and that effects vary with background, demographic characteristics, and experiences of individual audience members."[47] Reagan was able to overcome the negative effects of priming because there were good stories mixed in with the bad that had a "leavening" effect. Graber, like Iyengar and Simon, also noted that priming effects are linked with policy and not with personality.

The very real power of frames to influence the way in which the public interprets certain issues is well documented by Paul M. Sniderman and colleagues. Using mandatory testing for HIV (human immunodeficiency virus) as their controlled frame, these researchers found that the effect "of framing is to prime values differentially, establishing the salience of the one or the other. [A] majority of the public supports the rights of persons with AIDS [acquired imuno-deficiency syndrome] when the issue is framed to accentuate civil liberties considerations—and supports ... mandatory testing when the issue is framed to accentuate public health considerations."[48] Another powerful example of frames is provided by Thomas Nelson and colleagues. Using a local news story about a Ku Klux Klan march as the controlled frame, these researchers presented audiences with either one of two stories: "One framed the rally as a free speech issue, and the other framed it as a disruption of public order. Participants who viewed the free speech story expressed more tolerance for the Klan than those participants who watched the public order story."[49] When one considers the pervasiveness of the mass media in America, one must conclude that the potential power of framing is great indeed.

Another way of using frame analysis to understand news stories has been advanced by Zhongdang Pan and Gerald M. Kosicki. These researchers suggested that each news story will have a theme that "functions as the central organizing idea" of the story, and that these themes provide readers with cues that prompt them to understand and interpret a news story in a specific manner.[50] The cues within themes are "structurally located lexical choices of codes constructed by following certain shared rules and conventions."[51] These codes and lexical choices are the tools that news-makers use to construct news discourse and the psychological stimuli the audience processes when reading the news. For Pan and Kosicki, themes function as frames, and the cues within themes may be likened to framing devices. In this way, the framing of news stories is reduced to lexical choices made by the journalists—words in a vocabulary. The words chosen by a news reporter, then, reveal the way he categorizes that which he is reporting upon. One way of understanding frames is to consider how word choice often "signifies the presence of a particular frame."[52]

For example, look to descriptions of Yugoslavian President Slobodan Milosevic given by American reporters during the NATO bombing of Serbia. President Milosevic was described as an "evil dictator," "a cruel and determined enemy," and "a brutal dictator" to name only three. Comparisons with Hitler were frequently made as well: "Adolf Hitler had a 'final solution.' Slobodan Milosevic has 'ethnic cleansing.' Each leader's term gives a brilliant, if not positive, spin to his massacres."[53] If one were to describe Milosevic as the "Yugoslavian leader," "Yugoslavian president," or the "Yugoslavian commander in chief," the connotations about Milosevic's legitamacy would be quite different.[54] The lexical choices made act to frame the news story so that it facilitates a dominant reading of that story. Pan and Kosicki pointed out that framing analysis allows researchers to provide information about how an issue is discussed in the news and "how the ways of talking about the issue [are] related to the evolution of the issue in political debates."[55]

In order to make generalizations about a frame's influence on political debates, one must be able to identify frames at a general level of analysis. The work by Robert M. Entman, who comparatively analyzed the narratives within news stories about the downing of KAL 007 in 1983 and Iran Air 655 in 1988, is especially instructive.[56] Entman chose these particular incidents because they could have been reported on in a similar fashion; thus, any differences in the information that comprised the frames would be easier to detect. For Entman, "frames reside in the specific properties of the news narrative that encourage those perceiving and thinking about events to develop particular understandings of them."[57] The specific properties that reside in the narrative accounts of events are composed of key words, metaphors, concepts, symbols, and visual images. Understood in this manner, frames are manufactured by particular words and phrases that consistently appear within a narrative and "convey thematically consonant meanings across . . . time."[58] Framing thus elevates the salience of some ideas over others, while making some ideas virtually invisible to an audience.

For Entman, the framing process begins with the interaction of sources and journalists. Once established, the frame guides audience and journalist thinking. Entman called this initial interaction "event-specific schema." Once in place, event-specific schema encourage journalists to "perceive, process, and report all further information about the event in ways supporting the basic interpretation encoded in the schema."[59] In his study of the coverage of the two destroyed planes, Entman used news items appearing in *Time, Newsweek, CBS Evening News,* the *Washington Post,* and the *New York Times.* He found that the Soviet downing of KAL 007 was framed as a moral outrage, whereas the American downing of Iran Air 655 was framed as a technical problem. Entman's findings also demonstrated that frames have the capacity to obscure contrary information that may be presented in a particular news story. As Entman asserted, "for those stories in which a single frame thoroughly pervades the text, stray contrary opinions . . . are likely to possess such low salience as to be of little practical use to most audience members."[60] Because of this, Soviet explanations that included technical information were pushed aside for information that supported the interpretation of the event as a moral outrage. In the case of the United States downing of Iran Air 655, Iranian evidence of U.S. negligence was pushed aside for information that supported the interpretation of the event as a technical difficulty. Accordingly, while it was perfectly acceptable for political elites to describe the downing of KAL 007 as a brutal attack, it was far less likely for them to describe it in terms of a tragedy; the frame had been set: the Soviets were evil and at fault. To think of the plane's destruction in terms of tragedy runs against the frame and would mitigate the culpability of the Soviets.[61]

It is important to note that Entman focused on those frames he considered politically important—those elements within frames most likely to "promote a common, majority response to the news events as measured in public opinion polls."[62] Viewed in this manner, framing is a reciprocal process between political elites and journalists. In established frames, political elites often find it difficult, if not foolhardy, to resist the frame's pervasive influence; however, in the development of *new* event-specific schemata elites have great influence in establishing the initial frames.

THE ASSUMPTIONS OF THIS BOOK

In *Presidential Crisis Rhetoric and the Press in a Post–Cold War World* (1997) I employed a new approach to analyze both the press and the Clinton administration's handling of three international crisis situations. Using case studies of Bosnia, Haiti, and the alleged North Korean nuclear build-up in 1993, I examined contemporary presidential crisis communication and the agenda-extension function of the press. I found that the press often advanced an oppositional frame to that used by the Clinton administration, and that in part this frame was based upon an idealized, or utopian, form of Anglo-American Liberalism (i.e., pushing to the extreme radical notions of egalitarianism and freedom). The press frames were found to limit the options of President Clinton, even when the press supported a particular presidential strategy.

I am inclined to believe that instead of an objective Fourth Estate, the media have evolved into a partisan collective which both consciously and unconsciously attempts to persuade the public to accept its interpretation of the world as true. Such press practices are not without their difficulties. According to journalism ethicist Louis Day, media practitioners should "strive to keep their personal preferences and opinions out of news stories. . . . [They should be] concerned with facts and impartiality in the presentation of those facts."[63] Unfortunately for Americans, such press practice is not the norm. As Irving Kristol stated, "There is a comfortable symbiosis between our national newsmagazines, our half-dozen or so newspapers that claim national attention, and our national television networks. They are all liberal, more or less, and feel that they share the journalistic mission of 'enlightening' . . . the American public."[64] Impartiality is often ignored for various reasons (economic, political, institutional). However, by not striving to be objective, by establishing an agenda, the press steps out of its socially mandated role of a responsible Fourth Estate and instead assumes its own political persona in opposition to the elected government and the will of the people. Strong evidence exists that this relationship is unidirectional; that is to say, press content affects public concern, but public concern does not affect that which the news focuses upon.[65] If my assumptions hold true, then, the press no longer acts in a socially responsible manner, but instead sets itself up as an independent advocate for particular political ends.

According to Mitchell Stephens, objectivity involves both impartiality and the reflection of the "world as it is, without bias or distortion of any sort;"[66] in short, the news as a true image of the world. This is a laudable goal but difficult to put into practice. Yet by framing an issue, the press has a decision to make: 1) frame it according to the needs of the readers; 2) frame it according to the needs of the press; or 3) frame it so as to accurately impart the meaning of those speaking or writing upon that issue. The last of these choices seems to adhere best to the requirements of a socially responsible press. But what is a socially responsible press?

Reportorial Practices and Social Responsibility

If we are to accuse the press of being biased, we need first to establish how we expect the press to behave. The press "takes on the form and coloration of the social and political structures within which it operates ... [and] it reflects a system of social control whereby the relations of individuals and institutions are adjusted."[67] For America, this claim has come to mean a free and democratic press, a press concerned with democratic ideals. Originally, however, the press in America operated quite differently. Early American newspapers were a small, cottage affair that actually began as a sideline for many printers. The largest papers in the country were read by a few thousand people at most, and this was the norm until the rise of the penny press in the 1830s. These early presses did not need to be objective in the sense that we use the term today, for they had a limited, partisan audience of readers: Whigs, Democrats, Republicans, French, German, etc. Even at the onset of the twentieth century the presses were not entirely objective. Joseph Pulitzer made his fame and fortune on sensationalistic stories printed using yellow headlines; today we call his brand of reporting yellow journalism. William Randolph Hearst competed with Pulitzer for readership. He took a strong stand concerning American and Spanish relations that eventually helped "inform" the citizenry that we needed to go to war after the *USS Maine* exploded.

The late nineteenth and early twentieth century papers were primarily weekly editions; the major source of news was still local and face to face. These papers, however, still reflected the viewpoint of individual owners, not a contemporary objective viewpoint. For example, Benjamin Flowers published the *Arena*, a weekly protest magazine; Samuel McClure published *McClure's Magazine*. These and other weekly papers and magazines were used to call attention to certain social conditions that existed in the country at that time. In short, objective reporting rarely existed. The purpose was often sensational stories that sold papers. Yet, at the beginning of the twenty-first century, we expect the press to be objective.[68] We use a general notion of objectivity to judge norms of reportorial practice that exist today. But from where did we acquire our notion of an objective press? We often hear members of the press justifying their requests for information or their actions with the well-worn phrase: "The public's right to know." This phrase represents well the perspective underpinning the social responsibility theory of the media, from which we derive our current notions of objective reporting.

A socially responsible press was conceived as "a partner in the search for truth" with a rational and enlightened citizenry who would look to the press to provide the necessary information to "make up their own minds as to policy."[69] It was assumed that this partnership necessitated minimal or no government control. As this perspective grew in importance, Americans have come to view the press as a Fourth Estate in this country. We see, however, concerns about source control—press ownership—emerge by the mid-1920s when the media of this country had come to be dominated by a few wealthy and powerful people. Shortly after World War II, the Commission on Freedom of the Press, the so-called Hutchins Commission, took up the issue of press ownership and responsibility. The report of the commission, *A Free and Responsible Press*, advocated a norm of "social responsibility" for future press practices. The basic premise of the commission was that "the power and near monopoly position of the media impose on them an obligation to be socially responsible."[70] This idea behind the commission's report is the bedrock upon which the contemporary notion of social responsibility is erected, and is well summed by Theodore Peterson: "Freedom carries concomitant obligations; and the press, which enjoys a privileged position under our government, is obliged to be responsible to society for carrying out certain essential functions of mass communication in contemporary society."[71]

The socially responsible view of the press underscores the common citizen's right to enough information to make educated decisions in a democratic society; it also stresses a journalist or editor's moral responsibility to ensure that the requirements for an informed citizenry occur. Six basic press functions exist under the theory of social responsibility: (1) give service to the political system by providing information, discussion, and debate; (2) help to enlighten the general public so that it might self-govern; (3) act as a defender of civil rights by assuming a role as government watchdog; (4) act as a conduit through which the economic sector might be served by bringing together buyers and sellers through advertisements; (5) provide entertainment; and (6) maintain financial independence so that reporting will not be influenced by special interests.[72] Since 1947 various extensions of this report have taken into account three aspects of contemporary media: (1) communication technology; (2) economic pressures; and (3) societal change. Social responsibility theory attempts to incorporate all three of these important considerations.

The Hutchins Commission, anticipating that the press would need guidance in realizing the above six functions, listed the following standards for press performance. First, the press must provide "a truthful, comprehensive, and intelligent account of the day's events in a context which gives them meaning."[73] Second, the press must serve as a "forum for the exchange of comment and criticism."[74] Third, the press must project "a representative picture of the constituent groups in society."[75] Fourth, the press must assume responsibility for "the presentation and clarification of the goals and values of the society" in which it operates.[76] Finally, the press must provide "full access to the day's intelligence."[77] Michael Ryan argued that "Objective journalists refuse to serve or to support any political, social, economic, or cultural interests, even those that appear to some observers as laudatory (e.g., those that oppose gun control, abortion, or the status quo; that give voice to marginalized groups; that support gun control, abortion, or the status quo; or that ignore marginalized groups)."[78] Ryan also stated that those who reject this type of reportorial practice instead "attempt to redefine journalistic practice to reflect their views of what is 'good,' and that, for them, means requiring that journalists start with personal agendas (e.g., to improve democracy, to adopt perspectives of marginalized groups, to expand freedom). All favor a 'progressive' journalism that requires deliberate ideological intervention."[79]

Communication and political science scholars have incorporated the above social responsibility standards into their work. Graber has maintained that there exist four basic functions of the press: surveillance, interpretation, socialization, and manipulation. Surveillance corresponds to the "information and news providing function of mass communication."[80] Interpretation corresponds to what Dominic A. Infante and colleagues have called correlation, "how the mass media select, interpret, and criticize the information they present to the public."[81] Socialization "involves the learning of basic values and orientations that prepare individuals to fit into their cultural milieu."[82] Finally, manipulation refers to "the deliberate manipulation of the political process."[83] This final function reported by Graber corresponds to what Infante and colleagues called mobilization: "the ability of the media to promote national interests and certain behaviors, especially during times of national crisis."[84]

Graber's conception of manipulation is important to this study since she presumes that the media maintains an agenda; moreover, her conception suggests an active role for the media in shaping the news, and consists of two distinct forms. The first of these involves writing "stories that expose misconduct in government and produce reforms" and the second involves presenting "sensational information that attracts large media audiences and enhances profits."[85] The first form of manipulation concerns us in this study. By deciding what needs to be changed or fixed in our society, the press has distinctly moved away from its perceived tradition of objective news reporting, placing one foot within the realm of social responsibility and one foot within the realm of social activism. We must remember, however, that the "mass media are an important influence on politics because they regularly and rapidly present politically crucial information to huge audiences."[86] Like Graber, I maintain

that agenda-extension is a "widely used strategy for manipulating politics."[87] I further maintain, however, that an activist press is a danger to
a democratic society.

The press in this country is increasingly being charged with bias and
partisan reporting.[88] This study will help to determine the nature of the
bias operating in the national and regional press. That bias exists in news
coverage is a rather uncontested assumption; however, the type of bias
operating is not generally agreed upon. I have encountered two camps,
the apologists and the realists. The apologists, well represented by the
recent work of Dan Hahn, state that they do not believe the more significant biases of the press to be political (conservative or liberal). They
instead suggest what they feel are "those more important, more real,
biases." These are biases toward what makes money; a bias toward the
visual; a bias in favor of the contemporary and immediate; a bias in
support of the status quo; a bias in favor of the assumptions of American
society; bias toward fairness and balance; bias in favor of bad news; and
bias toward certain ways of covering stories.[89]

The realist position is represented by the work of Thomas Patterson.
In a review of his work at Dartmouth College, Patterson outlined the
political disposition of journalists in five countries, including the United
States. Patterson's research documented the willingness of reporters to
allow their personal ideologies—left-leaning in all countries—to influence their reportorial practices.[90] Another source which documents the
left-leaning political bias in mainstream American news media is
published regularly by the Media Research Center.[91] I will be using in-
sights generated by both the apologists and the realists to better determine how media coverage helps or hinders transmission of the original
meaning of public pronouncements on controversial issues, specifially
the issues of race and homosexuality.

The effects of press agenda-setting can be seen in poll data. For example, 43% of the public agreed with the statement that the press "plays
the most influential role in determining which issues and events are considered important these days," whereas only 22% said "political leaders
in Washington" play the more influential role.[92] Poll data also demonstrates the political leanings of the press. Some rather startling data has
emerged which strongly suggests a robust liberal leaning among members of our national press. For example, whereas 89% of Washington
reporters voted for Bill Clinton in 1992, only 7% voted for George Bush.
As an aside, only 4% were registered Republican, whereas 50% said they
were Democrat.[93] This lop-sided registration and voting record continues
when one moves beyond Washington: 44% of reporters polled nationwide considered themselves Democrats; 34% as independents; only 16%
identified themselves as Republicans.[94] In addition, self-descriptions of
political leanings indicate a substantial liberal bias in the press corps of

this country. Since 1980, polls of journalists have revealed a pronounced liberal leaning among both journalists and editors. One study found over 56% of the press considered themselves to be very to somewhat liberal, with only 18% considering themselves somewhat to very conservative. These studies will be discussed more fully in the final chapter of this book, but suffice it to say now that no poll of journalists to date remotely suggests anything but a heavy liberal political adherence among American journalists.[95] Contrast these journalistic self-descriptions with self-descriptions of voters in 1994. Only 14% thought of themselves as liberal to some degree; 26% thought of themselves as conservative to some degree; and 22% stated that they did not know.[96]

Of course, just because reporters and editors say they are Democrats, vote for Democrats, and say they are liberal does not mean that they cannot engage in neutral reportorial practices. However, admissions coming from the press corps itself show remarkable candor about willingness to engage in partisan politics as reportorial practice. Take, for example, former CBS News correspondent Bernard Goldberg in a *Wall Street Journal* opinion piece in 1996: "There are lots of reasons fewer people are watching network news, and one of them, I'm more convinced than ever, is that our viewers simply don't trust us. And for good reason. The old argument that the networks and other 'media elites' have a liberal bias is so blatantly true that it's hardly worth discussing anymore. No, we don't sit around in dark corners and plan strategies on how we're going to slant the news. We don't have to. It comes naturally to most reporters."[97] Evan Thomas, *Newsweek* Washington Bureau Chief from 1986 to 1996, plainly stated, "There is a liberal bias. It's demonstrable. You look at some statistics. About 85 percent of the reporters who cover the White House vote Democratic, they have for a long time. There is a, particularly at the networks, at the lower levels, among the editors and the so-called infrastructure, there is a liberal bias. There is a liberal bias at *Newsweek*, the magazine I work for."[98] Perhaps most convincing is this statement by legendary anchor Walter Cronkite: "Everybody knows that there's a liberal, that there's a heavy liberal persuasion among correspondents."[99]

My assumption is that, viewed as a whole on the national level, the press in this country operate under a norm of liberal bias (the full details of which will be discussed in the final chapter). I, like many of the reporters and scholars cited above, believe this to be the case. However, what is not generally agreed upon is the extent to which the liberal leanings of the press affect news coverage. It is my belief that this bias has great influence on how the news is framed. Thus this book illuminates *how* public utterances by political leaders on controversial issues are manipulated by press accounts. The influence of the press has a direct bearing upon the leadership ability of politicians and social leaders as they interact with the general public. Since the press is the vehicle through which the bulk of public pronouncements are disseminated to the general public, the leadership ability of many politicians and social leaders is directly linked to press accounts of what they say. The present study is concerned with the persona of the press, and contends that the press will not frame a particular utterance on race and homosexuality in such a manner that the original meaning of the speaker remains intact. In this light, then, the book will work toward a broader, sociological perspective of understanding the relation of the press to those it reports upon. By this I mean that our understanding of controversial issues is linked with media framing of those same issues.

HOW THE ASSUMPTIONS WILL BE PROVEN

Looking for bias within press accounts of events is not an easy task. Bias is not highlighted as such, and newspapers certainly do not advertise their political leanings on the front page. However, by using framing analysis, one may discover how the press frames an issue and then look at that frame for bias. Rarely is the entire original source of a report included within that news story. Moreover, when original utterances are included, for example, snippets of a politician's speech, only press-chosen sentences are included. This means that even the original utterances of political actors are manipulated by the press. The way to begin looking for press bias, then, is to examine the original utterances of political actors. Thus each analysis chapter in this book will begin with a framing analysis of a speech of a politician or social leader; after this, the press accounts of those speeches will be analyzed. The purpose of each speech varies, but each includes comments on either the issue of race or homosexuality. I follow the work of Entman here, in that to frame is to take "some aspects of a perceived reality and make them more salient in a communicating text, in such a way as to promote a particular problem definition, causal interpretation, moral evaluation, and/or treatment recommendation for the item described."[100] Frames define problems, diagnose causes, make moral judgments, and suggest remedies. They operate by making some information more salient than other information; therefore, they "highlight some features of reality while omitting others."[101] Thus I will be looking for where the frames of the original speaker converge or contend with those used by the press. On the issue of race I examine "The Confederate Battle Flag: A Symbol of Racism?" by Charles Davidson; "Initiative on Race," by William J. Clinton; and "Remarks at the Million Man March," by Louis Farrakhan. On the issue of homosexuality I examine "Armstrong Williams Show Interview Remarks," by Trent Lott; "Speech Before the Wisconsin Legislature," by

Reggie White; and "Remarks by the President at Human Rights Campaign Dinner," by William J. Clinton.

To be as inclusive as possible, press reports on these speeches were gathered using Lexis/Nexis, and included all printed press reports, national and regional, during a two-week period following the speeches.[102] I examined the speeches for narratives, and looked for the various framing devices that were used by the speakers: key words, metaphors, concepts, and symbols. Having accomplished this, I then repeated the analysis on the press articles. This study does not differentiate between new stories, news analysis, editorials, and opinion pieces. In her study of the relationship of the press and presidents during six crisis periods, Brigitte Lebens Nacos found "distinctive patterns" in the manner in which the press covered the various crises, one of which was a strong relationship between editorial positions and the content of political news coverage.[103] This strongly suggests that editors exert a greater degree of control over news items during times of crisis, and I believe this holds true on controversial issues as well. I am not asserting that the press is intentionally ignoring responsible norms of objectivity; that is something we may not know without asking members of the press. Be that as it may, the media may attempt some objectivity but still frame in such a manner that prevents readers from making a "balanced assessment" of a particular event.[104] By including editorials in the general pool of news articles, one can determine if editorial position correlates with the content of news stories and news analysis stories. In each chapter the following general questions are answered: How did the speakers frame the issue? How did the press, responding to the speakers, frame the issue? And at what time, if at all, did the frames converge to present a unified contextual whole? The focus will be on the overall impression given by the press when viewed as a collective whole.

It is my general contention that the mainstream press in America operate within a narrow range of liberal beliefs. This hurts the democratic process in general by ignoring or even dismissing non-mainstream left positions and vilifying many moderate and the vast majority of right-leaning positions. Because of this, only a narrow brand of liberal thought is supported by the press; all other positions are denigrated. Those with more conservative views will certainly feel the brunt of the press's bias. However, those who embrace moderate political beliefs will be hurt when they step to the right of the press position. The press will actively help certain politicians and social leaders on the left who espouse the same view of the country that the press has adopted. However, those who step beyond this narrow brand of liberal reporting, moving even further to the left, will be ignored or denigrated. In this manner, then, the American press acts to shut out the full range of political voices in the country.

NOTES

1. John Henry Newman, "Faith and Reason, Contrasted as Habits of Mind" (Epiphany, 1839) *Oxford University Sermons* (1843) no. 10.

2. Ted J. Smith, III, S. Robert Lichter, and Louis Harris and Associates, Inc., *What the People Want from the Press.* (Washington, DC: Center for Media and Public Affairs, 1997), 16.

3. Ibid., 20.

4. "Studies using N.E.S. data found this to be true . . . as have studies using *The Civic Culture* data . . . *Times-Mirror* Center data . . . and a Wisconsin-based dataset. . . ." Roderick Hart, "Citizen Discourse and Political Participation: A Survey," *Mediated Politics: Communication in the Future of Democracy,* ed. W. Lance Bennet and Robert M. Entman (Cambridge University Press, 2001), 407–432.

5. In many ways this present volume is an extension my earlier work, Jim A. Kuypers, *Presidential Crisis Rhetoric and the Press in a Post–Cold War World* (Westport, CT: Praeger, 1997).

6. For a comprehensive and nuanced explication of Bitzer's notions of rhetorical situation, audience, and public knowledge see Marilyn J. Young, "Lloyd F. Bitzer: Rhetorical Situation, Public Knowledge, and Audience Dynamics," *Twentieth-Century Roots of Rhetorical Studies,* ed. Jim A. Kuypers and Andrew King (Westport, CT: Praeger, 2001), 275–301.

7. Lloyd F. Bitzer, "The Rhetorical Situation," *Rhetoric: A Tradition in Transition,* ed. Walter Fisher (East Lansing: Michigan State University Press, 1974), 252. The initial publication of "The Rhetorical Situation" may be found in *Philosophy and Rhetoric* 1 (1968): 1–14.

8. Lloyd F. Bitzer, "Functional Communication: A Situational Perspective," *Rhetoric in Transition: Studies in the Nature and Uses of Rhetoric,* ed. Eugene E. White (University Park: Pennsylvania State UP, 1980), 23.

9. Ibid., 26.

10. Bitzer, "Rhetorical Situation," 215. The conception of rhetorical situation advanced here does not ignore revisionist modifications of Bitzer's work. I do, however, advance my own understanding of Bitzer's work as a guide for understanding public communication. For two examples of revisionists at work see William L. Benoit, "Genesis of Rhetorical Action," *Southern Communication Journal* 59.4 (1994): 342–355, and Craig R. Smith and Scott Lybarger, "Bitzer's Model Reconsidered," *Communication Quarterly* 44.2 (1996): 197–213.

11. Gregory Bateson, *Steps to an Ecology of Mind: Collected Essays in Anthropology, Psychiatry, Evolution, and Epistemology* (San Francisco: Chandler Publishing Company, 1972), 289.

12. Bitzer, "Rhetorical Situation," 258.

13. I consider agenda-setting to be a function of the media. To be fair, other scholars of communication are not certain whether to call it a function, a theory, or a hypothesis. Maxwell E. McCombs and Donald L. Shaw, two of the most distinguished researchers in this area, consider it a function. See "The Agenda-Setting Function of Mass Media," *Public Opinion Quarterly* 36 (1972): 176–187. McCombs has spent most of his career supporting this assertion, and I borrow freely from his ideas in this area. See the present volume's bibliography for ad-

ditional examples of his research in this area. Also see W.J. Severin and J.W. Tankard, *Communication Theories*, 2nd ed. (New York: Longman, 1988). For a detailed explanation of agenda-setting as theory, see R.D. Wimmer and J.R. Dominick, *Mass Media Research*, 2nd ed. (Belmont, CA: Wadsworth, 1987).

14. Bernard C. Cohen, *The Press and Foreign Policy* (Princeton: Princeton University Press, 1963), 13.

15. Judith S. Trent and Robert V. Friedenberg, *Political Campaign Communication: Principles and Practices*, 2nd ed. (New York: Praeger, 1991), 107. For an organized background reader on the function of agenda-setting see, James W. Dearing and Everett M. Rogers, *Agenda-Setting* (Thousand Oaks, CA: Sage Publications, 1996).

16. McCombs and Shaw, 177.

17. Ibid., 185.

18. Sheldon Gilberg et al., "The State of the Union Address and the Press Agenda," *Journalism Quarterly* 57 (1980): 584–588.

19. Maxwell E. McCombs and Donald L. Shaw, "Agenda-Setting and the Political Process," *The Emergence of American Political Issues: The Agenda-Setting Function of the Press*, ed. Donald L. Shaw and Maxwell E. McCombs (St. Paul, MN: West Publishing Co., 1977), 151.

20. Michael B. Salwen, "News Media and Public Opinion: Benign Agenda-Setters? Opinion Molders? Or Simply Irrelevant?" *Florida Communication Journal* 18.2 (1990): 17.

21. McCombs and Shaw, 152.

22. Gilberg et al., 585.

23. Reported in Maxwell E. McCombs and Sheldon Gilberg, "News Influence on Our Pictures of the World," *Perspectives on Media Effects*, ed. Jennings Bryant and Dolf Zillman (Hillsdale, NJ: Lawrence Erlbaum Associates, Publishers, 1986), 14.

24. Ibid., 11.

25. Trent and Friedenberg, 109.

26. Shanto Iyengar and Adam Simon, "News Coverage of the Gulf Crisis and Public Opinion: A Study of Agenda-Setting, Priming, and Framing," *Communication Research* 20.3 (1993): 368.

27. Ibid., 368.

28. Ibid., 375–376. They found r =.85. This is a very high degree of correlation. Not to belittle their results, it must be mentioned, however, that America was at war. It makes sense that the majority of Americans would consider an event involving the lives of American soldiers as being among the nation's most important problems.

29. Ibid., 376.

30. Shanto Iyengar and Donald R. Kinder, "More than Meets the Eye: TV News, Priming, and Public Evaluations of the President," *Public Communication Behavior*, ed. George Comstock, Vol. 1 (Orlando, FL: Academic Press, 1986), 136.

31. Ibid., 139.

32. Ibid., 162.

33. Zhongdang Pan and Gerald M. Kosicki, "Priming and Media Impact on the Evaluation of the President's Performance," *Communication Research* 24.1 (1997): 3–30.

34. William A. Gamson, "News as Framing: Comments on Graber," *American Behavioral Scientist* 33 (1989): 157.

35. Ibid., 157.

36. Graber, Doris A. *Mass Media and America Politics* 3rd ed. (Washington, DC Congressional Quarterly Press, 1989), 278.

37. Ibid., 287.

38. I do this to distinguish it from the agenda-building theory discussed by others. Michael B. Salwen, drawing from the work of Roger W. Cobb and Charles D. Elder, described agenda-building as a theory that explains how the "public can participate in the democratic process in a limited way by influencing national agendas." This theory essentially stresses grassroots genesis of political ideas and change. See Salwen, 16–23; see also Roger W. Cobb and Charles D. Elder, *Participation in American Politics: The Dynamics of Agenda-Building* (Baltimore: Johns Hopkins University Press, 1983).

39. For examples of studies exploring agenda-setting second level effects see, in chronological order, Maxwell McCombs, "The Future Agenda for Agenda Setting Research," *Journal of Mass Communication Studies* 45 (1994): 171–181; Maxwell McCombs and Taara Bell, "The Agenda Setting Role of Mass Communication," *An Integrated Approach to Communication Theory and Research*, ed. Michael Salwen and Don Stacks (Mahway, NJ: Erlbaum, 1996): 93–110; Maxwell McCombs and George Estrada, "The News Media and the Picture in Our Heads," *Do the Media Govern? Politicians, Voters, and Reporters in America*, ed. Shanto Iyengar and Richard Reeves (Thousand Oaks, CA: Sage, 1997): 237–247; Maxwell McCombs, Donald L. Shaw, and David Weaver, *Communication and Democracy: Exploring the Intellectual Frontiers in Agenda-Setting Theory* (Mahwah, NJ: Lawrence Erlbaum Associates, Publishers, 1997); Esteban Lopez-Escobar, Juan Pablo Llamas, Maxwell McCombs, and Federico Rey Lennon, "Two Levels of Agenda Setting among Advertising and News in the 1995 Spanish Elections," *Political Communication* 15 (1998): 225–238.

40. Anne Johnston, "Trends in Political Communication: A Selective Review of Research in the 1980s," *New Directions in Political Communication: A Resource Book*, ed. David L. Swanson and Dan Nimmo (Newbury Park, CA: Sage Publications, 1990), 329–362.

41. Ibid., 337.

42. Gladys Engel Lang and Kurt Lang, "The Media and Watergate," *Media Power in Politics*, ed. Doris A. Graber (Washington, D.C.: Congressional Quarterly Press, 1984), 202–209.

43. Graber, *Mass Media*, 288.

44. For example, Russell J. Dalton et. al. found in their study of the 1992 elections that "a newspaper's presidential endorsement had little impact on its news coverage of the issue themes of the campaign" (476). Agenda-setting allows these findings; however, it can only examine the type of issues reported on and their frequency of occurence in articles. Agenda-extension allows for the examination of how the papers covered particular "issue themes," thereby allowing examination of differences of how the issues were framed (were Bush's themes, for example, characterized as positive or negative when compared to Clinton's). Thus, using an agenda-extension perspective allows the researcher to comparatively analyze news content for bias. For a good example of using agenda-setting

to determine coverage of candidates' issues see, Russell J. Dalton, Paul Allen Beck, Robert Huckfeldt, and William Koetzle, "A Test of Media-Centered Agenda Setting: Newspaper Content and Public Interests in a Presidential Election," *Political Communication* 15 (1998): 463–481. Of note is that these researchers found that no bias was seen in the papers covered simply because the papers covered the issues brought up by the candidates, irrespective of the paper's editorial endorsement of a particular candidate. This type of logic is a limitation of agenda-setting research. Using an agenda-extension perspective, one moves beyond frequency of reporting to examine the manner in which the papers reported the issues—thus one may look for bias.

45. I am inclined to believe this manipulation includes lack of press coverage. Numerous examples of press "black outs" of controversial events potentially damaging to President Clinton have been documented and are available through the MediaWatch Archive, <http://www.mrc.org/news/mediawatch/archive. html> free of charge.

46. Doris A. Graber, "Framing Election News Broadcasts: News Context and Its Impact on the 1984 Presidential Election," *Social Science Quarterly* 68 (1987): 552–568.

47. Ibid., 566.

48. Paul M. Sniderman, Richard A. Brody, and Philip E. Tetlock, *Reasoning and Choice: Explorations in Political Psychology* (Cambridge, England: Cambridge UP, 1991), 52.

49. Thomas E. Nelson, Rosalee A. Clawson, and Zoe M. Oxley, "Media Framing of Civil Liberties Conflict and its Effects on Tolerance," *American Political Science Review* 91.3 (1997): 567.

50. Zhongdang Pan and Gerald M. Kosicki, "Framing Analysis: An Approach to News Discourse," *Political Communication* 10.1 (1993): 55–75.

51. Ibid., 59.

52. Ibid., 62.

53. Ben Kauffman, "As You Were Saying . . . Evil Euphemisms Must Not Pass Our Lips Unexamined," *Boston Herald* (2 May 1999): A28.

54. In all fairness to the press, a majority of the papers examined did use these terms. However, enough pejorative examples of naming exist to color the otherwise neutral descriptions.

55. Pan and Kosicki, 65.

56. Robert M. Entman, "Framing U.S. Coverage of International News: Contrasts in Narratives of the KAL and Iran Air Incidents," *Journal of Communication* 41.4 (1991): 6–27.

57. Ibid., 7.

58. Ibid., 7.

59. Ibid., 7.

60. Ibid., 21.

61. For a more detailed explanation of this see Jim A. Kuypers, Marilyn J. Young, and Michael K. Launer, "Of Mighty Mice and Meek Men: Contextual Reconstruction of the Iranian Airbus Shootdown," *Southern Communication Journal* 59.4 (1994): 294–306.

62. Entman, "Framing U.S. Coverage," 8.

63. Louis A. Day, *Ethics in Media Communication* (Belmont, CA: Wadsworth Publishing Company, 1991), 32.

64. Irving Kristol, "America's 'Exceptional Conservatism,' " *Neo-conservatism: The Autobiography of an Idea* (New York: Free Press, 1995): 383.

65. Roy L. Behr and Shanto Iyenger, "Television News, Real-World Cues, and Changes in the Public Agenda," *Public Opinion Quarterly* 49 (1985): 38–57.

66. Mitchell Stephens, *A History of News: From the Drum to the Satellite* (New York: Viking Penguin, 1988), 264.

67. Fred S. Siebert, Theodore Peterson, and Wilbur Schramm, *Four Theories of the Press* (Urbana: University of Illinois Press, 1956): 12.

68. According to *What the People Want from the Press*, a "large majority (82%) of the population shares the belief that first and foremost the media should provide news and information" (12).

69. Siebert, Peterson, and Schramm, 3.

70. Ibid., 5.

71. Ibid., 74.

72. Ibid., 74.

73. Ibid., 87.

74. Ibid., 89.

75. Ibid., 91.

76. Ibid., 91.

77. Ibid., 91.

78. Michael Ryan, "Journalistic Ethics, Objectivity, Existential Journalism, Standpoint Epistemology, and Public Journalism," *Journal of Mass Media Ethics* 16.1 (2001): 4.

79. Ibid., 14.

80. Graber, *Mass Media*, 11.

81. Dominic A. Infante, Andrew S. Rancer, and Deanna F. Womack, *Building Communication Theory*, 2nd ed. (Prospect Heights, IL: Waveland Press, 1993), 397.

82. Graber, *Mass Media*, 11.

83. Ibid., 12.

84. Infante, Rancer, and Womack, 399.

85. Graber, *Mass Media*, 12.

86. Ibid., 29.

87. Ibid., 277.

88. Ted J. Smith III, S. Robert Lichter, and Louis Harris and Associates, Inc., *What the People Want from the Press* (Washington, D.C.: Center for Media and Public Affairs, 1997).

89. Dan Hahn, *Political Communication: Rhetoric, Government, and Citizens* (State College, PA: Strata Publishing, 1998).

90. See also, Thomas Patterson and Wolfgang Donsbach, "News Decisions: Journalists as Partisan Actors," *Political Communication* 13 (1996): 455–468.

91. The Media Research Center's searchable Web site is located at <http://www.mrc.org/>.

92. Times Mirror Center for the People and the Press, February 1994 survey of 1,207 people. <http://www.people-press.org/>.

93. Roper Center poll for the Freedom Forum. Survey of 139 Washington

bureau chiefs and Congressional correspondents, April 1996. <http://www.ropercenter.uconn.edu/>.

94. Freedom Forum-sponsored poll of 1,400 journalists across the country, 1992. <http://www.freedom forum.org/>

95. The People, Press and Politics (Pew Research Center for the People & the Press, July 1985).

96. Reported in David C. King, "The Polarization of American Political Parties and Mistrust of Government." Working Paper, <http://www.ksg.harvard.edu/prg/king/polar.htm>.

97. *Wall Street Journal* (13 February 1996).

98. *Inside Washington*, (12 May 1996).

99. Walter Cronkite at the Radio and TV Correspondents Association dinner, 21 March 1996.

100. Robert M. Entman, "Framing: Toward Clarification of a Fractured Paradigm," *Journal of Communication* 43 (1993): 52. Italicized in original.

101. Ibid., 53.

102. In order to limit the imposition of my own preconception onto the various news articles I read, I engaged this study using a blind reading. This is to say, although the news articles were read in chronological order, authorship, paper identification, and type of story (news, news analysis, editorial, or opinion essay) remained unknown to me until after the analysis has been completed. Additional information detailing specific methodological issues are given in each analysis chapter.

103. Brigitte Lebens Nacos, *The Press, Presidents, and Crises* (New York: Columbia UP, 1990).

104. Entman, "Framing: Toward Clarification," 56.

Chapter Two

Charles Davidson: "The Confederate Battle Flag: A Symbol of Racism?"

How could the war be fought over slavery when both sides had slaves?

—Senator Charles Davidson

[He] ought not to have used the Bible for what was essentially his own racist view.

—*News & Record*

On 9 May 1996, Alabama State Senator Charles Davidson distributed by his own hand copies of a speech he intended to deliver to the Alabama Senate.[1] The speech was written in support of a proposal to resume flying the Confederate battle flag atop the State Capitol building.[2] Because the proposal was tabled prior to his being able to orally deliver the speech, Senator Davidson presented copies to interested parties on the steps of the capital, including journalists and fellow senators. His professed purpose for writing the speech was to "set the record straight" about Confederate history and the proper interpretation of the Confederate battle flag. The speech received intense scrutiny from the press; however, subsequent press accounts of the speech's content and purpose contrast greatly from the original speech.

In this chapter I first examine Senator Davidson's speech, reviewing the major themes and arguments; in short, I will be looking for how he frames the issue of reflagging the capitol building. I next analyze the press coverage of the speech. In the summary of this chapter I will answer three questions: How did Senator Davidson frame the issue? How did the press, responding to Senator Davidson's speech, frame the issue?

And at what time, if at all, did their frames converge to present a unified contextual whole?[3]

SENATOR DAVIDSON'S SPEECH

"Our South," is the focus of Senator Davidson's speech. "Our South" is also a term that allows us to identify Senator Davidson's primary audience: Southerners. The speech focuses quite clearly on the hypocrisy of those who argue against flying the Confederate battle flag, and by extension, denigrate the South. Senator Davidson argues that those against flying the flag base their reasons in historical inaccuracies that have been transmitted through the media (news and entertainment) and the educational system. These inaccuracies promote myths and propaganda that serve to drive a wedge between black and white Southerners. Thus "Our South" includes those who are not offended by the flag, those who have been misled by media and the educational system, and those who actively fight the flying of the flag. In other words, the speech is aimed at all Southerners, including those who besmirch the honor of the flag.

Senator Davidson relies heavily upon historical evidence to back his assertions.[4] In addition, he cites poll data that 92% of all Southern people are not offended by the Confederate battle flag, and that nationwide 68% of blacks are not offended.[5] A good portion of his speech, however, centers around dispelling myths that have accrued around the flag: "the Confederate battle flag has no more to do with the Ku Klux Klan than the Christian cross which the Klan carries and burns or the flag of the United States that the Klan says the pledges of allegiance to, yet the news media and Hollywood constantly try to connect our Confederate flag to the Klan in their propaganda. However, the news media never ask preachers if they are Klan members . . . or link the American Legion to the Klan because they carry the U.S. flag."[6] Davidson calls this press behavior "anti-Confederate bigotry."

Senator Davidson's stated purpose for giving this speech is to "set the record straight" by reminding Southerners of the "truth concerning our Confederate ancestors and history."[7] Early in his speech he implores those hearing his words to "listen with an open mind and a Christian heart." He also states: "It is my hope and fervent prayer that truth will replace fiction; that tolerance will replace intolerance; that peace will replace violence; that love will replace hate; and that unity will replace division."[8] He identifies, and sets out to refute, three main lies promoted by the entertainment industries, news media, and detractors of the flag: (1) that slavery was linked exclusively to racism; (2), that slaves were mistreated in the Old South; and (3), that the war between the states was fought over slavery. By far the bulk of the speech, 40%, is devoted to this third point, whereas the introduction, conclusion, and the remaining two lies each receives approximately 20% of the speech's total time.

"The First Lie Concerns Slavery and Its Link to Racism"

Senator Davidson provides a dense etymology of the word *slave*, and demonstrates that there were white slaves in Europe and in the English colonies in America. He also points out that blacks were only slaves in the English colonies for about 100 years, and that only about 5% of slaves ever taken from Africa came to the Colonies. His main point is that all races have owned slaves of other races at some time in history. To better understand the history of the American slave trade Davidson injects Biblical reasoning. Jews were once slaves, and they owned slaves as well. Yet no one calls Abraham racist or evil. Comparatively speaking then, one ought not to call George Washington, Thomas Jefferson, or Jefferson Davis racist or evil either. To do so is hypocrisy, according to Davidson. Almost every nation in the world owned slaves at some point, including African nations. It follows that if one were to call the Confederate battle-flag racist because it flew over slave-holding states, then one must call most flags of the world racist, including the flag of the United States. Davidson drives this point home when he states, "What hypocrisy and bigotry to criticize only white Southerners or the Confederate states for owning slaves. Almost every nation in the world owned slaves, especially the black masters in Nigeria, where most American blacks have their roots. Accordingly, if flags of nations that owned slaves are to be labeled 'racist,' then almost all the flags in the world are 'racist,' especially the African flag of Nigeria which dealt so overwhelmingly in slave trading."[9]

Davidson also points out what might seem to some a rather striking bit of information: some Southern blacks owned slaves. He states, "free blacks owned slaves, white and black, in the Old South. That's right, even blacks and Indians owned slaves in the Old South. While 7% of Southern whites owned slaves, 2% of free blacks in the South owned slaves. For example, in 1860, the U.S. Census reported that around 10,000 free blacks owned some 60,000 black slaves."[10]

Senator Davidson is clear to point out that he is sharing what those living in the Old South believed when discussing what the Bible says regarding slavery: "Our ancestors in the Old South were fundamental Christians, which means they believed that the Bible, Old and New Testaments, were the opinions of Almighty God, who does not change, and not the opinions of man. On the other hand, the abolitionists from up North were humanists. They believed that God changed with the times and that the Bible was merely the opinions of men and not necessarily the opinions of God. I shall read to you a little of what God says in the

Bible concerning slavery and thus what our ancestors in the Old South believed."[11] It follows that what he is about to share with listeners is a 150-year-old cultural understanding of slavery.

In explaining the antebellum view of slavery, Davidson brings up the division between Southern antebellum fundamentalism and Northern abolitionist humanism. He cites Old Testament verse to demonstrate what the Southerners of the time would have believed: "People who are bitter and hateful about slavery are obviously bitter and hateful against God and his word, because they reject what God says and embrace what mere humans say concerning slavery. This humanistic thinking is what the abolitionist embraced, while Southerners and most Northerners embraced what God said in the Bible. [The humanistic] argument is not with me or the South or the United States but rather . . . with God. They have made themselves out to be greater than God, for they add to God's word when they call something evil that God obviously allows. This is what the humanistic abolitionists did, teaching the doctrines of men as if they were the doctrines of God."[12]

"The Second Lie Is That Slaves Were Mistreated in the Old South"

Slavery's legacy is with us today. Slavery is, by its very nature, an abhorrent practice. We have all heard that slaves, beyond the practice of slavery, were mistreated in the South. Senator Davidson claimed not that abuse never occurred, rather that the treatment of Southern slaves was linked to the Christian beliefs of slave owners. Given the religious nature of these Southerners, says Davidson, they would follow the admonitions of Jesus: "masters, grant to your slaves justice and fairness, knowing that you too have a master in heaven."[13] There were also laws in place to protect servants and slaves from abuse. Davidson noted that just as the Old South had laws protecting slaves and servants from abuse, so too we have laws today protecting wives and children from abuse. According to Davidson, to "say that slaves were mistreated in the Old South is to say that the most Christian group of people in the entire world, the Bible belt, mistreated their servants and violated the commandments of Jesus their lord."[14] That a few physically abused their slaves and servants does not mean that everyone did; because a few abuse their wives and children does not mean that all do.

In an era when emotions run high during discussions about race, these are controversial thoughts. Davidson does, however, offer a long list of examples for listeners to consider. For instance, he also provides contemporary data about the social difficulties faced by numerous black Americans today, and constrasts it to black slaves in the Old South: the "incidence of abuse, rape, broken homes and murder are 100 times greater, today, in housing projects, than they ever were on the slave plantations in the Old South."[15] Davidson asserts that the institution of slavery as practiced in the Old South, "was a family institution . . . just like it says in the Bible in Galatians 4:1 'as long as the son is a child he does not differ at all from a slave although he is the heir of every-thing.' "[16] Davidson never suggests that slavery was an easy institution, that slaves were never abused, or that slavery ought to be practiced today. Rather, he argues that slavery in the Old South was not as we have been taught: "Slaves were treated better in the Old South than anywhere else. Just as white European slaves were primitive, barbaric pagans who practiced human sacrifice, incest, witchcraft, and idolatry; yet were converted to Christianity, learned trades and skills and became a civilized people under black, oriental and white masters, so also did black African barbaric, pagans become civilized, Christians with skills and trades under slavery in the Old South."[17]

Davidson asserts that it is hypocrisy to say that all slaves were mis-treated in the Old South. As support, he offers an illustration of Southern family structure among slave owners: "A typical family plantation had one family of whites living next door to one family of blacks. They had the same last name, worked in the fields and on the farm, side by side, played together, prayed together, raised each others children, took care of each other in sickness and all in all, loved one another, just like family. It was here on the family plantation that blacks learned trades and skills. . . ."[18] Davidson also speaks to the history of forced black migration to the American colonies, saying it was not "Southern whites who cap-tured black African slaves." Davidson reminds listeners that black Af-ricans captured and sold each other to slave traders, and it was "the northern American states that sailed in the slave trade, flying under the U.S. flag, not the Confederate flag. Black Africans captured and sold other blacks as slaves, they were already slaves of black Africans before they ever set foot on a Spanish, Portuguese, English or New England Yankee slave ship."[19]

Davidson points to the strong merchant fleets of the northern states: Massachusetts, Rhode Island, New York, and New Jersey—all of which sailed under the flag of the United States. He firmly states that not "one Southern ship sailed to Africa to bring back slaves and no ship ever sailed under the Confederate flag to bring back slaves." Rather the slave trade was big business to the "rich New England Yankees."[20]

"The Third Lie Is That the War for Southern Independence . . . Was Fought over Slavery"

Senator Davidson devotes 40% of his speech to discussing this lie. He points out that all thirteen colonies contained slaves, yet few consider the 4th of July or the American flag racist. This being the case, one ought not consider the Confederate battleflag racist. According to Davidson, the hypocrisy of those who say the war was fought over slavery emerges if one considers several key pieces of evidence. During the war between the states, many northern states owned slaves—Delaware, Maryland, Kentucky, Missouri, West Virginia, even Washington, D.C. Furthermore, many well-known northern citizens owned slaves; for instance, Ulysses S. Grant and Abraham Lincoln's father-in-law. These slaves were not freed during the war. Davidson asks, "How could the North be fighting the war to free Southern slaves when they would not free their own? What hypocrisy! Even worse, Lincoln and the U.S. Congress offered to pass a constitutional amendment for the South, guaranteeing permanent slavery in the slave states, if only the Southern states would return to the union. The South refused the offer. Is the U.S. flag a symbol of slavery because the North owned slaves during the war? No, then neither is the Confederate battle flag. How could the war be fought over slavery when both sides had slaves?"[21]

Davidson also points out that during the war, the Confederacy offered to free all Southern slaves in return for the Union army withdrawing. The Union refused this offer. In highlighting Northern attitudes toward blacks, Davidson offers seldom-taught information concerning the racial attitudes of President Lincoln and other northern leaders. For example, "President Abraham Lincoln stated that he had 'no purpose, directly or indirectly to interfere with the institution of slavery in the states where it exists. I believe I have no lawful right to do so, and I have no incli-nation to do so.' "[22] Davidson also shares the comments of Ulysses S. Grant, who during the war said that if he " 'thought this war was to abolish slavery, I would resign my commission, and offer my sword to the other side.' A war over slavery? Not hardly!" says Davidson, who added:

The term "free" state meant free from blacks. Northerners did not want to live with blacks, slave or free, and many Northern states and territories actually passed laws prohibiting free blacks from entering into them. Abraham Lincoln, himself, stated the opinion of the Northern people at a meeting with a group of black leaders during the war, when Lincoln said to them "there is an unwilling-ness on the part of our people (Northern whites) to live with you free colored people. Whether this is right or wrong, I am not prepared to discuss, but a fact with which we must deal. Therefore I think it best for us to separate." Whereupon, Abraham Lincoln and the United States Congress purchased land, passed laws and started shipping free Northern blacks out of the [U.S.] down to poverty stricken Haiti. At the end of the war . . . Union General Benjamin Butler asked Abraham Lincoln what was he going to do with all the recently freed Southern blacks? Lincoln replied "I think we should deport them all."[23]

If not to free black Americans, then why was the war fought? Local self-government for the South versus centralist government by the North.

The centralist government won and local self-government lost. Davidson is quite clear in stressing the Southern view of the war: the *"Confederate battle flag is the symbol of the right of the local people and the states to govern themselves and is flown in memory and honor of our Confederate ancestors and veterans who gave their lives for less government, less taxes and Southern independence."*[24] Taxation without representation is a common theme in Southern accounts of secession. Davidson explains that the northern industrial states were "constantly trying to raise taxes on Southerners through high taxes on imported goods, in order to protect the inefficient big businesses up North who could not compete with manufactured goods from England and France with whom the South traded cotton in exchange for . . . manufactured products. The South did not have factories so had to import most finished products."[25] Davidson sums up the reason for the war between the states; not slavery, but economics and political self-determination were at the heart of secession and the war:

Within Lincoln's first month in office, the U.S. Congress had passed the Morrill Tariff, which was the highest import tax in U.S. history, which more than doubled the import tax rate, from 20% to 47%. . . . This oppressive tax is what pushed Southern states to legally withdraw from the voluntary union, and not slavery. It was to collect this oppressive import tax to satisfy his Northern industrialist supporters that Abraham Lincoln invaded our South and not to free any slaves. Lincoln's war cost the lives of 600,000 Americans.[26]

All Southerners fought in the war: whites, blacks, Indians, Jews, Catholics, Protestants, rich, and poor. For Davidson, "the Confederate battle-flag represents all Southerners and even northern Confederates from states like Ohio, Illinois, Indiana, and others who supported the South . . . Nowhere in the history of movements of independence and self government have a people been so united in purpose and dedicated to the cause of independence. No, not even in 1776 did the 13 colonies receive such support of and sacrifice by the people and that war was fought over a 3% tax on tea!"[27]

He sums his thoughts best when he states that the "Confederate battle-flag represents all Confederates, regardless of race or religion and is the symbol of less government, less taxes, and the right of a people to govern themselves. It is flown in memory and honor of our Confederate ancestors and veterans who willingly shed their blood for Southern independence."[28]

THE RESPONSE OF THE PRESS

The press coverage of Senator Davidson's speech was limited, with a total of thirty-nine articles used for this chapter: twenty-four news articles, thirteen opinion essays, and two editorials. The majority of news articles were published during the three days following the speech, with opinion and editorial essays found consistently throughout the period examined. Senator Davidson's speech was a complex one, yet the basic frames are obvious: hypocrisy of those arguing against flying the Confederate battle flag and the flag's true meaning of states' rights. Yet the press did not choose to highlight these frames. Nor did the press choose to describe the speech in a manner that would allow readers to judge for themselves what Senator Davidson had said. Rather, the press advanced an extremely narrow yet consistent interpretation of the speech. Simply put, the press framed the entire speech as a defense of slavery. One sees this most readily when looking at the headlines used to introduce each of the stories about the speech. Of course, headlines cannot be used exclusively to determine how the press frames an issue. However, they can be used as one way of gaining insight into the framing devices used within the story that follows. Given the extremely narrow focus of the press stories, the headlines used in Davidson's case are even more revealing than is usually the case. These headlines clearly show that the press focused upon one section of Davidson's speech, the section where he explains the Old South view of slavery.

Davidson Defends Slavery

What follows, in chronological order, are the headlines given for Senator Davidson's speech:

"U.S. House Candidate Uses Bible To Defend Slavery" (10 May 1996)

"Candidate Uses Bible To Defend Slavery" (10 May 1996)

"Candidate Praises Slavery" (10 May 1996)

"Around the South: Candidate Praises Slavery" (10 May 1996)

"House Candidate Uses Bible to Defend Southern Slavery" (10 May 1996)

"Bible Backed Slavery, Says a Lawmaker" (10 May 1996)

"Senator Not Just Whistling 'Dixie' with Speech Defending Slavery" (10 May 1996)

"Lawmaker: Bible OKs Slavery" (10 May 1996)

"Alabama State Senator: Slavery Good for Blacks" (10 May 1996)

"Candidate Cites Bible on Slavery" (10 May 1996)

"Slavery Stance Draws Fire" (11 May 1996)

"Candidate Withdraws After Slavery Defense" (12 May 1996)

"Candidate Who Upheld Slavery Quits Race" (12 May 1996)

"Candidate Ends Bid over Slavery Issue" (12 May 1996)

"Candidate Who Backed Slavery Quits" (12 May 1996)

"Candidate Quits After Speech on Slavery" (12 May 1996)

"Elections" (12 May 1996)

"Heflin Chastises State Senator in Speech at ASU" (12 May 1996)

"Slavery Defender Embarrasses State, Party" (12 May 1996)

"Davidson Drops Out of GOP Contest" (12 May 1996)

"Slavery Defense Derails Candidacy" (12 May 1996)

"Out of His Cotton Pickin' Mind" (13 May 1996)

"Candidate Uses Bible to Justify Blacks' Slavery" (13 May 1996)

"It Defies Common Sense, Decency to Justify Slavery" (14 May 1996)

"Southern Denial Defies Decency" (14 May 1996)

"Bible's 'Slaves' Were a Far Cry from South's" (14 May 1996)

"Wasted Davidson Donors Should Get Refunds" (14 May 1996)

"Revisionist History of Slavery Reveals a Pervasive Racism" (14 May 1996)

"In Biblical Terms, An Abomination" (15 May 1996)

"Defense Knocks Out House Hopeful" (15 May 1996)

"Modern Biblical Blasphemy" (15 May 1996)

"Senator's Denial of Slavery's Harm, Racism Is Absurd" (16 May 1996)

"American Education Distorts and Devalues Black History to the Point of Ignorance" (16 May 1996)

"Wrong to Imply Christianity Condones Slavery" (19 May 1996)

"Does the Bible Justify Slavery? Yes It Does—and Therein Lies the Pitfall of
Mixing the Bible with Politics" (26 May 1996)

"What Does Koch Think Is a Sin?" (2 June 1996)

"Times Are Right for a Return of a Tradition: Slavery" (2 June 1996)

"Food for Thought Gives Bellyache and the Giggles" (3 July 1996)[29]

Even a cursory reading reveals the frame used by the various papers
and writers these headlines represent. Davidson's speech was only about
defending slavery.

The opening sentences from the articles introduced by the above headlines clearly frame the speech as a defense of slavery. Consider, for example, these four lead sentences from among articles appearing during
the first day of coverage: (1) "A white state senator running for Congress
wrote a speech in which he argued that slavery is justified by the Bible
and was good for blacks."[30] (2) "A state senator running for the U.S.
House wrote a speech saying the Bible justifies slavery and that the institution, as practiced in the Old South, was beneficial to blacks."[31] (3)
"A state senator running for the U.S. House said he was trying to correct
historical inaccuracies about slavery when he wrote a speech saying that
the practice is justified by the Bible and was good for blacks."[32] (4) "An

Alabama State Senator running for Congress has written a speech arguing that slavery was justified by the Bible and that it was good for blacks."[33] The speech has been clearly labeled as a defense of slavery. No mention of any other topic covered by Davidson is included.

The framing of Davidson's speech as a defense of slavery was constant throughout all the news coverage. For example, the Associated Press (AP) stated that "Davidson's slavery defense came in a speech he planned to deliver in the state senate last week supporting a proposal to resume flying the Confederate battle flag atop the Capitol. In the speech, the freshman senator quoted Bible passages about slavery and wrote that Southern farmers taught slaves about the Bible and converted them to Christianity."[34] The Associated Press then highlighted this frame by providing this Davidson quote: " 'Those bitter about slavery,' Davidson wrote, 'are obviously bitter and hateful against God and his word, because they reject what God says and embrace what mere humans say concerning slavery.' "[35] Editorially speaking, the *Montgomery Advertiser* stated that "State Sen. Charles Davidson, long a defender of the Confederate Battle Flag, has come out of the closet. It's not just southern pride that he is intent on defending, but slavery as well. That's right, slavery."[36] Another example shows the same trend: "A Republican congressional candidate dropped out of the race Saturday amid criticism over his defense of slavery in the Old South. [His] slavery defense came in a speech he planned to deliver in the state Senate last week supporting a proposal to resume flying the Confederate battle flag atop the Capitol."[37]

Next we see the same frame developed in opinion articles and editorials. For example, Bob Ingram wrote: "After his pro-slavery remarks last week. . . ."[38] Howard Kleinberg pushed the same frame as well: "but along came Alabama state Sen. Charles Davidson, who last week defended slavery as being accepted by God and . . . says it was a good thing for Southern blacks."[39] Another common example is provided by the "Campaign Brief" distributed by the Capitol Hill Publishing Corp: "After defending slavery as 'beneficial' to blacks. . . ." And, "In remarks prepared in support of a proposal to fly the Confederate flag atop the State Capitol, Davidson said the Bible justified slavery and that the institution was 'beneficial' to blacks."[40] Rod Watson guessed at Davidson's biblical knowledge: "Davidson scoured the Bible in a bid to justify slavery. Not many others would be ignorant enough to publicly call slavery the good old days for blacks."[41] An editorial by the *Charleston Gazette* invented its own logic for Davidson's speech: "Sen. Charles Davidson, running for Congress, said the Confederate flag should fly atop the Alabama Capitol because the Bible condones slavery."[42]

On the Trail of the Associated Press

The snippets of sentences that the press chose to print supported the frame they wished to advance. Moreover, the few quotes of Davidson's speech that were provided lent support to the press's frame, rather than helping to explain Davidson's point of view. These quotes were from wire reports, which are important sources for papers when writing news stories. Much of what comes over the wires is not reported in daily papers. That which is reported is often rewritten by reporters on a paper's staff. Wire reports explain how so many papers across the country picked up the Davidson story. This also helps to explain the narrow focus on certain parts of Davidson's speech. Consider, for example, that all but one of the following Davidson quotations appeared in the initial AP wire reports:

- "The truth is that nowhere on the face of the earth, in all of time, were servants better treated or better loved than they were in the Old South by white, black, Hispanic and Indian slave owners." (Seen in eleven articles.)

- "You may acquire male and female slaves from the pagan nations that are around you." (Seen in ten articles.)

- Slaves should "regard their own masters as worthy of all honor." (Seen in nine articles.)

- "The incidence of abuse, rape, broken homes and murder are 100 times greater, today, in the housing projects than they ever were on the slave plantations in the Old South." (Seen in seven articles.)

- Those upset by slavery are "obviously bitter and hateful against God and his word, because they reject what God says and embrace what mere humans say concerning slavery." (Seen in seven articles.)

- "People who are bitter and hateful about slavery are obviously bitter and hateful against God and his word. . . ." (Seen in four articles.)

- "This humanistic thinking is what the abolitionists embraced, while Southerners and most Northerners embraced what God said in the Bible." (Seen in one article.)

- The Confederate Battle Flag "is the symbol of less government, less taxes and the right of a people to govern themselves." (Seen in one article.)

- "Fundamentalist Christians would believe what the Bible said about slavery, and nowhere is slavery condemned." (Seen in one article.)

- "I am sure that those converted black Southerners are most grateful today." (Seen in one article.)

- "Just because a few men abuse their wives or children does not make marriage or having children a cruel, hateful endeavor. The same is true for slavery." (Seen in one, non-AP article.)

The above AP-distributed quotes from Davidson's speech were strategically used to frame Davidson as defending or justifiying slavery in almost every article in which they appeared. However, the reliance upon only the AP-provided quotes lead to certain difficulties. For example, after the spate of original quotations, many editorials, opinion pieces, and news stories began to misquote Davidson, based upon what AP writers had *summarized* Davidson as saying. Furthermore, some press reports began to *borrow* from earlier AP reports, using AP phrases as their own. One example of this is this sentence: "In the speech, the freshman senator quoted Bible passages about slavery and wrote that southern farmers taught slaves about the Bible and converted them to Christianity."[43] This sentence is used six times during the following day. Many of the reporters used this sentence without citing an AP source, thus leaving readers with the impression that it is the original thought of the journalist. In addition, AP-generated sentences ended up being ascribed to Davidson: "In remarks prepared in support of a proposal to fly the Confederate flag atop the State Capitol, Davidson had said the Bible justified slavery and that the institution was 'beneficial' to blacks."[44] Nowhere in his speech does Davidson ever use the word "beneficial." Another misquote is provided by the *Charleston Gazette*, which editorially stated: "Sen. Charles Davidson, running for Congress, said the Confederate flag should fly atop the Alabama Capitol because the Bible condones slavery."[45] *Hotline* provided this: "Davidson wrote 'that the Bible justifies slavery and that the institution as practiced in the Old south was beneficial to blacks.' "[46] As has already been shown, this is an AP-generated interpretation of what Davidson said; nowhere in Davidson's speech does he actually say this.

Resignation Results from Wrong Views

According to the press, Senator Davidson defends slavery, considers it a benign institution, and approves of it: this is his view according to the press. Having established that Davidson held these views through its frame, the press was in a position to demonstrate how these views, and thus Davidson, were wrong. This was accomplished primarily through quoting reactions from politicians and press-defined "black leaders." As news stories waned and opinion essays waxed, the press attacked Davidson and his (press-defined) views more directly. Consider, for example, Alabama State Representative Alvin Holmes, who was quoted as saying: " 'To have a state senator take such an outrageous, evil, racist, backwards, lying position toward blacks, the Republican Executive Committee should remove him as a candidate for Congress.' "[47] Later, after Senator Davidson dropped out of the race, Holmes was quoted as saying, "Sen. Davidson's statements were cruel to blacks and embarrassed Alabama. 'The sad part about it is that I think he actually believes that. His mind is warped to the point that he actually believes that the blacks loved slavery and fought in the Civil War.' "[48]

The press found numerous detractors to cite concerning Davidson's speech. Alabama State Representative and Legislative Black Caucus chairman Laura Hall was quoted as saying: "Davidson's views were outdated and 'sad. That may have been appropriate in the 1930s and 1940s, but not in 1996. . . .' "[49] Hall was also quoted as saying: " 'I respect his beliefs. It's sad to think we have anyone with that type of thinking in 1996.' "[50] The press also used quotes from Klanwatch "Researcher" Tawanda Shaw: " 'It was similar to the white supremacist literature we read every day. That's certainly not to accuse the senator of being affiliated with any white supremacist group. [M]ost of his speech was inflammatory, easily refuted and quite untrue.' "[51] Johnnie Carr, an "organizer" of the 1955 Montgomery bus boycott, was quoted as saying that Senator Davidson's "views were troubling for a congressional candidate. 'People are trying to get every twist they can to set back every advancement we have made.' "[52] Alabama Representative Tom Bevill (D) was quoted as saying he "was 'shocked, embarrassed and angered by the ridiculous and insulting comments made by Sen. Davidson. [He] should apologize to the people and remove himself from office.' "[53] Later, after Davidson had dropped out of the primary for the Republican nomination for the U.S. House seat, Bevill was quoted as saying: " 'I think he's done the right thing.' "[54] An Alabama House primary opponent of Davidson, Kerry Rich, was quoted as saying: " 'If Davidson believes what he said, he is nuts. [He] should step aside in this race, should resign from the Senate, and, most importantly, he should resign from the Republican Party.' "[55] Democratic U.S. Senator Howell Heflin was quoted as saying: Davidson's remarks were " 'demagoguery. It shocks our conscience. . . . We've made a lot of racial progress in Alabama. His remarks are not representative of the vast majority of Alabamians.' "[56]

These critics of Davidson were found in all the news stories that reported reactions to the stories of Davidson's speech. In addition, Republican leaders were quoted as well. The Alabama State Republican National Committeeman, Martha Foy (said to have "just read" the speech—no others were so reported), was quoted as saying the speech's "contents were not among any party literature she had ever seen. 'I find it just shocking he could have spent so much time on this.' "[57] Former finance chairman of the Alabama Republican party and former Gubernatorial candidate Winton Blount was reported as saying: " 'It is unfortunate Davidson holds a position in the state Senate that gives him publicity for his misguided views. I call on him to either apologize to the people of Alabama or resign his seat . . . and withdraw from the race for the House of Representatives.' "[58] The Executive Director of the Al-

abama Republican Party, Mike Burton, was quoted as saying "Davidson's comments [were] 'bizarre. He's the one that created the issue . . .
the whole history lesson is bizarre, and why an elected official would
come up with a speech, not deliver it and then release it, is bizarre.' "[59]
Later, after Davidson dropped out of the primary race, Burton was
quoted as saying, " 'I assume there's relief that he dropped out of the
race. [T]he Republican Party feels like he made a good decision by his
stepping aside. It was bizarre to me . . . I've never heard anything like
this. I have never heard people defend slavery in the same paragraph
that they defend the confederate flag.' "[60] The chairman of the Walker
county Republican Party, Mary Owen, was reported as saying that
" 'Sen. Davidson's speech was surprising, but it shouldn't reflect on the
party.' "[61] Milton Bethune, a black Republican Congressional candidate
was reported as saying: " 'The fact that he has dropped out of the race
is a step forward for the Republican Party and the state.' "[62]

Echoing those critics quoted in news stories, editorials, and opinion
essays were vicious in condemning Davidson. Editorially speaking, the
Montgomery Advertiser stated that Davidson has "dared use the Bible in
an attempt to justify slavery."[63] It continued, attacking Davidson and his
arguments:

There's nothing new in Davidson's arguments. They came essentially straight
from the pro-slavery apologists who floated such nonsense in the South during
the 1850s. What is amazing is that any apparently sane individual anywhere in
the world can seriously push this same nonsense almost 150 years later.

Why would anyone write such divisive trash today?

That image of slavery as something the slaves should welcome was wrongheaded in 1850; and it is repulsive and ludicrous today. There is extensive good
scholarship available that shows the abuse of slaves, their deliberate breeding by
slave owners, the breakup of families and the use of slave women as sex objects
were common.

HIS APPALLING COMPARISON [*sic*] with today's housing projects is especially misleading, and ignores the fact that one wrong in no way justifies another.

Davidson even floats the canard about the Civil War not being about slavery.

So, Sen. Davidson, if you think slavery is so great, why don't you give it a
try?[64]

Columnist Clarence Page paraphrased earlier press reports when he
wrote: "Slavery was good for blacks. It wasn't about race. It was justified
by the Bible. American slaves were better treated than anywhere else in
the world. Black slaves suffered less than free blacks suffer today from
abuse, rape, broken homes and murder. So says Alabama state Sen.
Charles Davidson. It is painfully obvious that he is not a historian [*sic*]."
Page attempts to draw analogies to instances of bigoted revisionism:
"Jews are plagued by the holocaust-denial industry. Blacks are plagued

by slavery deniers. Davidson seems just like the rest of them. Davidson and [Minister Louis] Farrakhan have a lot in common. Each uses distortions of history to relieve his constituency of guilt feelings."[65] In a similar vein, Gene Owens stated that "A number of people have come forward to deplore the senator's revival of a now-discredited mindset."[66] Owens's line of thought is reflected in the headline: "Revisionist History of Slavery Reveals a Pervasive Racism."[67]

Rod Watson wrote that Davidson "went on to deride movies like 'Roots' as misrepresentational and opined that conditions in black housing projects today are worse than on slave plantations. . . . [M]any who profess puzzlement as to where such ideas come from are the same ones who think U.S. education is just fine, thank you. Long after Davidson's 15 minutes of infamy have been forgotten, textbooks and schools will still be distorting or devaluing black history. . . ."[68] Howard Klienberg wrote, Senator Davidson "says he was completely misunderstood when he cited passages in the books of Leviticus and 1 Timothy in which slavery was sanctioned by God, but didn't really say what it was we were to understand."[69] One article had Davidson withdrawing from the race and apologizing "for saying that people opposing slavery 'are obviously bitter and hateful against God and his word, because they reject what God says and embrace what mere humans say concerning slavery.' "[70] Davidson actually apologized for having statements he had written construed by others as being racially motivated.

The press mentioned *once* that Davidson had "said the Confederate battleflag is not a symbol of slavery and racism, but 'is the symbol of less government, less taxes and [the] right of a people to govern themselves.' "[71] In addition, the press did report some defenders of Davidson's speech. The Director of the Alabama Historical Commission, Larry Oaks, was quoted—in one of thirty-nine articles—as saying that "the battleflag raises emotions that other flags of the Confederacy don't. 'Everything about the battle flag eventually gets back to race.' . . ."[72] The Chairman of the Confederate Heritage Fund, Roger Broxton, was reported as saying, "Davidson was trying to tell people that the Civil War was not over slavery but the South 'paying an unfair burden of taxes.' [S]lavery was not an issue in the Civil War because most Southerners were fundamentalist Christians. '[F]undamentalist Christians would believe what the Bible said about slavery, and nowhere is slavery condemned.' "[73]

The Abusive Ad Hominem

An ad hominem attack is one that appeals to prejudices or the emotions. An abusive ad hominem is a bit different: it avoids addressing an opponent's arguments through "an intentional effort to damage the opponent's character or reputation by name-calling and labeling."[74] Fifteen of the thirty-nine articles examined for this chapter contained some form of this name-calling, be it as direct quotes, or the editors and columnists themselves engaging in this behavior. Examples are rife: Alabama State Representative Alvin Holmes was quoted as saying: " 'To have a state senator take such an outrageous, evil, racist, backwards, lying position toward blacks, the Republican Executive Committee should remove him as a candidate for Congress. [And] His mind is warped to the point that he actually believes that the blacks loved slavery and fought in the Civil War.' "[75] Kerry Rich, one of Davidson's primary opponents, was quoted as saying: " 'If Davidson believes what he said, he is nuts.' "[76] The *Montgomery Advertiser*, editorially speaking, was especially abusive, calling Davidson "This yokel politician from Jasper...." The editorial continued: "What is amazing is that any sane individual . . . can seriously push this . . . nonsense.... Until now, Davidson was best known for promoting the canning of lawbreakers. Now we know whom he really wants to cane. [This point of view] was wrongheaded in 1850; and it is repulsive and ludicrous today. Perhaps Abraham Lincoln had the best response to idiots who defend slavery...."[77]

Editorials and opinion essays essentially had the same point of view. The *News & Record* editorially wrote: "A former Alabama candidate ought not to have used the Bible for what was essentially his own racist view. The South wants to see itself emerging from the War Between the States with clean hands, but some of its leaders keep washing them in the same old racist water, using the same old lie soap."[78] Bob Ingram, editorially writing for the *Montgomery Advertiser*, stated: "One of my favorite quotations suggests that it is far better to remain silent and let people think you are a fool than to open your mouth and confirm it. If you would like to mail that quote to state Sen. Charles Davidson [address was inserted here] be my guest. I can think of no one who is in greater need of committing it to memory. [H]e is not the sharpest knife in the drawer."[79] Howard Kleinberg, writing a commentary for the *Tampa Tribune*, stated, "It is not clear if Davidson also will retire from the Alabama Senate. He ought to; he's needed back at the plantation. 'Abomination' is a word used often in the Bible; it also best describes Ole Massa Davidson's values."[80] Rob Watson, writing in the "Viewpoints" section of the *Buffalo News*, began his essay with, "Forget for a moment the obvious question of how the Republican Party could ever have thought of running a racist like Alabama State Sen. Charles Davidson for Congress.... Since god has yet to send Davidson a revised copy [of the Bible], one can presume he still thinks owning slaves puts one on the stairway to heaven. [N]ot many others would be ignorant enough to publicly call slavery the good old days for blacks. That makes Davidson, bless his racist little heart, a walking, talking good ol' poster boy for that dreaded concept: multiculturalism."[81] The *Mobile Press Register's* Coleman wrote, "[This] is fresh evidence that their state is a bastion of racism.... I can only hope that the rest of the nation will see him for what he is: a reprehensible aberration who should be thrown out of office."[82] Columnist Clarence Page wrote: "It is painfully obvious he is not a historian [*sic*]. He denies that he is a racist. [T]here have always been 'experts' and pseudo-intellectuals who try in defiance of common sense and decency to justify the evil institution."[83]

SUMMARY

Let us now turn to answering the questions I posed in the introduction to this book. Two extremely different frames emerge when contrasting what Davidson wrote with what the press reported he wrote. There is no middle ground. The press focused on an extremely small portion of Davidson's speech, and placed those comments into a different frame than that which Davidson used. Although Davidson would try to respond with an apology for any misunderstanding, the press frame was so well defined that even those comments were seen as unimportant.

How Did Senator Davidson Frame the Issue?

There are several interrelated ideas revealed by Senator Davidson's framing of the issue. Overall, the purpose of Davidson's speech is dispelling myths about the Confederate battleflag caused by inadequate education and the misrepresentation in the media. He supplies listeners with information by attacking three myths surrounding the Confederate battleflag and the war between the states. This educational mission is supported by what Davidson sees: that the truth about the Old South is not known by many in the South and in the nation at large. The lack of knowledge is used by the media and certain political elites to drive wedges between whites and blacks, particularly Southern whites and blacks. Although only small percentages of Americans, white and black, are offended by the Confederate battleflag, Davidson sees its flying being turned into a divisive racial issue. He seeks to prevent this by focusing his remarks on three key myths.

When examining the first myth—the link between slavery and racism—Davidson frames his remarks in such a way that a specific problem emerges. Too many persons in America feel that the institution of slavery was perpetuated by whites on blacks; in particular that Southern whites prior to the war between the states were the only ones practicing slavery. Davidson points out that all peoples throughout history have owned slaves, and that each of the different races have owned slaves of other races. He also brings up the antebellum interpretation of the Bible.

His reasoning suggests that if we do not call Abraham racist, then we cannot call our own slave-owning founders racist, since they believed in the same God as Abraham. Indeed, even a small percentage of Southern blacks owned other black slaves. The problem, Davidson suggests, is with education. Along these lines Davidson points out that since the U.S. flag flew over all slave-holding American states, then one cannot call the Confederate battleflag a symbol of racism unless one is willing to do the same for the U.S. flag. This brings us to Davidson's frame of hypocrisy. Too many do call the battleflag racist without calling the U.S. flag the same.

The second myth demonstrates a different problem. Too many persons feel that all slaves in the South were mistreated, and that all Southerners were evil and cruel. Although Davidson never claims that slaves in the South were never abused, he does set out to share the general relationships and conditions in which Southern slaves found themselves. Their treatment is linked to the strong Southern belief in God, whose word is revealed through the Bible. In addition to the scriptural references for treatment of slaves, Davidson points out that there were laws that punished those who abused their slaves. He relays that the institution of slavery in the Old South was often a "family institution," with white and black families living side by side. He states that northern slave owners frequently abused their slaves, but that no one calls northerners racist. He points out that just because a few Southerners abused their slaves does not mean that all did, and drew an analogy with wife abusers today—just because a few do, does not mean all do. Davidson points out that it was the northern merchant marine that sailed to Africa to buy slaves: no Southern ships ever engaged in the slave trade. Thus he returns to the theme of hypocrisy: the northern states, whose ships brought the African slaves to the U.S. to sell them to Southern planation owners, are not the ones called abusive and racist; neither is the U.S. flag, under which the northern ships sailed, called a symbol of racism.

The third myth Davidson addresses reveals a new problem: that too many Americans think the war between the states was fought over slavery. This is an obviously important area for Davidson, and he devoted two-fifths of his speech to it. Again the theme of hypocrisy surfaces concerning those who embrace this myth. If all original thirteen colonies owned slaves, but none call the 4th of July or the American flag racist, then neither should the Confederate battleflag be called racist. More tellingly, if numerous Union states held slaves during the course of the war, then how could the purpose of the war be to free the slaves? If it was so fought, then why did the Congress fail to pass an Act to free all the slaves once the Southern legislators had gone home? If the war was to free the slaves, then why would the northern-controlled United States offer to pass a Constitutional amendment allowing permanent slavery if the Southern states would return to the Union? And why did the North not accept the South's offer to free all the Southern slaves if only the Union would withdraw? With this in mind, if the U.S. flag, flown by slave-owning states during the war is not considered racist, then it is hypocrisy to view the Confederate battleflag as racist.

Davidson also shows the problem in contemporary education by explaining why the war was fought: local self-government versus an all-powerful Federal government using unfair taxation. The South was upset over a 20% tariff on imported manufactured items, especially considering they had little industry and purchased most of their manufactured goods from Europe. Instead of freeing slaves when the Southern states seceded, the states of the Union passed the Morrill Tariff, which imposed a 47% tariff on European goods. As Davidson said, it "was to collect this . . . tax . . . that Abraham Lincoln invaded our South and not to free any slaves." Davidson points out at that all Southerners fought in the war. Only a small percentage of whites (7%) actually owned slaves, yet all Southerners fought. The vast majority of Southern blacks were slaves; yet many of them fought as well. In addition, many Jews, Catholics, and Indians fought as well. Those individuals of which the Confederacy was composed were diverse in color, but united in thought: local control. And that, for Davidson, is what the battleflag is all about.

How Did the Press, Responding to Senator Davidson, Frame the Issue?

In striking contrast to Davidson's framing of the issue, the press advanced its own frame immediately with the first reports. Summed simply, Davidson was framed a defender of slavery. This frame was so well established that all articles covered his speech from this angle. Headlines tended to suggest this frame, which in turn were supported by opening sentences, which in turn were supported by critics of Davidson. Many of those writing used only AP wire reports, which set the tone for the initial reports. The AP was very selective in the portions of Davidson's speech that it put out over the wires. Given that the press had framed Davidson as a defender of slavery, it only made sense to then cast him as a racist. This was accomplished through selective quotes, but also through editorials and most notably, opinion essays.

Davidson's wide-ranging views were reduced to a single-minded defense of slavery. This view was depicted as wrong. According to the press Davidson, now exposed, resigned from the Republican primary. Critics were brought in to rail against his view, and thus he ultimately resigned. Editorials and columnists called him a racist and left no room for dialogue.

Did the Frames Converge to Present a Unified Contextual Whole?

Simply put, no. Never did the frames converge. Moreover, the press never reported the fullness of Davidson's speech or its overriding frame of education and hypocrisy. In all, fourteen different critics were quoted by the press, yet only one person was reported who supported Davidson's interpretation of Southern history. Both of the editorials were negative. Of thirteen opinion essays, only one was neutral, and the other twelve pointedly negative. Davidson's speech has a total of 237 sentences. The press presented only eleven, or less than 5% of the speech. Moreover, consider that five of those eleven sentences appeared only one time, and you then have the press representing Davidson's speech relying upon only six sentences, or roughly 2.5% of the speech. Thus 2.5% of what Davidson said, without contextual support, was reported. The press provided its own context, and Davidson was villainized. This was consistent throughout the press reports. Whereas Davidson focused on the hypocrisy of those who condemn the flag and contemporary myths that drive wedges between whites and blacks, the press framed him as a racist defender of slavery who dared suggest that the war between the States was not fought over slavery and that the Bible, in the eyes of antebellum Southerners, allowed slavery. Some papers went so far as to state that Davidson was suggesting slavery was acceptable today.

Editorials and opinion essays matched the framing of general news articles, but with increased condemnation. However, the accusations and condemnation occur not through the quotations of others, but rather through the editors and journalists themselves. Although the papers do say that the speech was being given in support of flying the battle flag, they link support of the flag to a support of slavery since they do not provide Davidson's definition of the flag's symbolism. A common example of this practice would be for a paper to report that, "Sen. Charles Davidson, who is white, wrote the speech in support of his proposal to resume flying the Confederate battle flag atop the Capitol."[84] Following this the press would simply move into saying that Davidson "defended slavery as being accepted by God and . . . says it was a good thing for Southern blacks."[85] In this manner the press put its own interpretation over that expressed by the person they were supposed to report objectively upon. Readers are left with only one conclusion to draw: Davidson is a racist; or he is "nuts." Either way, his political career is irreparably damaged if not ruined. Only once was Davidson's assertion that the battleflag "is the symbol of less government, less taxes, and the right of a people to govern themselves" mentioned in a news article.

The press stressed that Davidson was engaging in poor history or a revisionist history—yet evidence to support these press assertions is not provided. Moreover, the press claimed that extensive good scholarship—

all contradicting Davidson—is available; however, these assertions simply stay assertions, since the press does not provide evidence to support their claims. In a sense, the very myths Davidson was trying to eradicate were being used as evidence against him. In this manner readers are denied the opportunity to make up their own minds about what Davidson said, even about the few sentences the press reported since they were presented out of context. For example, the press stated that slaves were routinely abused in the Old South, and that there were slave brothels and breeding houses. No evidence for these press claims are offered. There is evidence to the contrary, however; yet on this point the press remained silent.[86]

What is most striking about the reportorial practice is that only five articles offered any evidence that the authors read beyond the AP-generated quotes. This suggests that numerous reporters made judgments about Davidson without even having read his speech.[87] So, while others denigrate both Davidson and his speech, Davidson is unable to defend himself or his views due to the awesome power of the press-generated frame. Essentially, the press called him a racist, and once so labeled, the conversation ended. Even the mention of flying the flag is mired with the very myth that Davidson tried to explain; not even his belief about the flag is relayed for readers to think about. They are denied Davidson's point of view, except for his wish to continue flying the flag, which has now been linked to defending slavery and racism. Instead of the neutral environment needed for the free exchange of ideas, the press shut down Davidson's right to free speech and the public's right to know through the creation of a hostile environment. Davidson's ideas about the hypocritical double standards, his ideas about antebellum attitudes on slavery, and his ideas about the cause of the war between the states are never relayed for readers—many in his constituency—to ponder and ultimately to make their own judgment. The press did their thinking for them.

NOTES

1. Originally the speech was untitled. I have used the title provided by The League of the South's Web site <http://www.dixienet.org/>.

2. The Confederate battleflag is an adaptation of the Scottish Cross of Saint Andrew. For an excellent review of the history of the flags of the South, see the Heritage Preservation Association, <http://www.hpa.org/edu/csaflags.htm>.

3. It is of interest to note that Senator Davidson's speech made national papers; in all, a total of thirty-nine news articles about the speech were able to be included in this chapter. Using Lexis-Nexis, a search was performed with the key words of "Charles Davidson." Additional search terms included "slavery" or "race" or "confederate flag." Unlike the other analysis chapters in this book, the time period for inclusion of press reports was open in order to yield the maximum number of news articles. The range of articles ran from 10 May 1996

to 3 July 1996. All but five of the articles were published during a two-week period after the speech was released to the public.

4. In preparing this speech, Senator Davidson consulted with the Confederate Heritage Fund and former Stillman College History Professor Michael Hill concerning the accuracy of the historical acts (Charles Davidson, Phone Conversation).

5. There have been numerous surveys conducted whose data support Davidson's cited poll data. For example, a 1987 University of Alabama Capstone poll of Alabama residents found that 74.6% favored flying the battleflag over the state capital building. A 1988 University of Alabama Capstone poll of Alabama residents found that 77.3% opposed taking the flag down. A 1995 University of North Carolina poll of North Carolinians asked if "people who want to ban the display of the confederate flag" made the respondent feel "very uncomfortable": 27.6%; "somewhat uncomfortable": 26.9%; "not at all uncomfortable": 36.2%; "no answer": 9.3%. The same poll asked if "people who display the confederate flag outside their homes" made the respondent feel "very uncomfortable": 13.8%; "somewhat uncomfortable": 18.7%; "not at all uncomfortable": 61.7%; "no answer": 5.8%. A 1991 *Atlanta Journal and Constitution* Southern Culture Poll of Southern Residents asked if respondents felt the Confederate battle flag was "more a symbol of racial conflict": 24.2% or "of southern pride": 68%; 7.8% held no opinion. A 1992 Southern Focus poll (University of North Carolina, Chapel Hill) of Southerners found similar results with 19.6% saying the flag was a symbol of racial conflict and 71.8% saying it was a symbol of Southern pride; 8.6% held no opinion. The 1993 Southern Focus poll asked the same questions of citizens nationwide and found that 17.4% felt the flag to be a symbol of racial conflict and 66.7% felt it to be a symbol of Southern pride; 16% held no opinion. A 1994 Southern Focus poll asked respondents in the South if there should be "no official use of the Confederate flag by state and local governments—for instance, in state flags or over state buildings." 33.5% agreed with this statement and 50.9% disagreed; 15.5% held no opinion. A 2000 Gallup poll found that 59% of Americans felt the flag to be a symbol of Southern pride and 28% felt it to be a symbol of racism. Gallup poll can be found at <http://www.gallup.com/poll/releases/pr000509.asp>. All other polls found at the Southern Focus Poll Web site: <http://www.unc.edu/depts/csas/poll/poll.htm>.

6. Davidson, 1996, 1.

7. Ibid., 1.

8. Ibid., 1.

9. Ibid., 2.

10. Ibid., 4. A more detailed examination of the census material Davidson cites seems to support his presentation: "According to the 1860 census only three-quarters of one percent of Southerners could be classified as planters, owning twenty or more slaves. Less than 10% owned even one. Most Southerners were self-sustaining landowners, who raised most of what they needed. Selling a few hogs every year gave them enough money to buy what manufactured goods they needed. Thomas Jefferson's embargo against England almost destroyed New England, but was hardly felt by the South, because most Southerners didn't participate in the economy. Blacks were slave owners, too. Again, according to the 1860 census, some 12,000 slaves were owned by some 3,000 Black slave own-

ers." U.S. Civil War Centennial Commission, *The United States on the Eve of the Civil War As Described in the 1860 Census* (Washington, DC: U.S. Government Printing Office, 1963). The census is listing figures for Southern blacks. It is unclear if the figures cited by Davidson were for the South only, or for the entire United States. Either way, it is clear that free blacks owned black slaves in the United States prior to the war between the states.

11. Ibid., 2.

12. Ibid., 3.

13. Ibid., 3. Quotation found in Colossians 4:1.

14. Ibid., 3.

15. Ibid., 3.

16. Ibid., 4.

17. Ibid., 4.

18. Ibid., 4.

19. Ibid., 4.

20. Ibid., 4–5.

21. Ibid., 5–6.

22. Ibid., 6.

23. Ibid., 6.

24. Ibid., 6, emphasis mine.

25. Ibid., 8.

26. Ibid., 8.

27. Ibid., 8

28. Ibid., 8–9.

29. Each of these articles is listed in the bibliography.

30. Associated Press, "U.S. House Candidate Uses Bible to Defend Slavery," *Columbus Dispatch* (10 May 1996): A11.

31. Journal Sentinel Wire Reports, "Candidate Uses Bible to Defend Slavery," *Milwaukee Journal Sentinel* (10 May 1996): News 4.

32. Phillip Rawls, "House Candidate Uses Bible to Defend Southern Slavery," *Associated Press* (10 May 1996).

33. *New York Times* (10 May 1996): A20.

34. Associated Press, "Candidate Who Backed Slavery Quits," *Commercial Appeal* (12 May 1996): A2.

35. Ibid.

36. Editorial, "Slavery Defender Senator Embarrasses State, Party," *Montgomery Advertiser* (12 May 1996): F2.

37. Jessica Saunders, "Davidson Drops Out of GOP Contest," *Montgomery Advertiser* (12 May 1996): A1. (This is the writer for the AP.)

38. Bob Ingram, "Wasted Davidson Donors Should Get Refunds," *Montgomery Advertiser* (14 May 1996): A6.

39. Howard Kleinberg, "In Biblical Terms, An Abomination," *Tampa Tribune* (15 May 19967): Nation/World 11.

40. "Campaign Brief," *Hill* (15 May 1996): 15.

41. Rod Watson, "American Education Distorts and Devalues Black History to the Point of Ignorance," *Buffalo News* (16 May 1996): B3.

42. "Editorial," *Charleston Gazette* (20 May 1996): P4A.

43. Associated Press, *Montgomery Advertiser* (11 May 1996): A1.

44. "Campaign Brief," *Hill* (15 May 1996): 15.

45. "Editorial," *Charleston Gazette* (20 May 1996): P4A.

46. "Out of His Cotton Pickin' Mind," *Hotline* (13 May 1996): AL 04.

47. Rawls, "House Candidate Uses Bible."

48. Saunders. No paper mentioned that there exists substantial evidence of black Southerners fighting for the Confederacy. For example, see "On Black Confederates," at the Texas Calvary 37th Terrell's Web site: <http://www.37thtexas.org/html/BlkHist.html>. This site also provides photographs of monuments erected in the South to the memory of black Confederate soldiers: <http://www.37thtexas.org/html/Memoriam.html>. There exists evidence of other non-white Southerners fighting for the South as well. See John O'Donnell-Rosales, *Hispanic Confederates*, (Baltimore, MD: Clearfield Company, 2000).

49. Rawls, "House Candidate Uses Bible."

50. Ibid.

51. Ibid. Klanwatch was created by the Southern Poverty Law Center in 1981.

52. Ibid.

53. Associated Press, "Slavery Stance Draws Fire," *Montgomery Advertiser* (11 May 1996): A1.

54. Saunders.

55. Associated Press, "Slavery Stance Draws Fire."

56. Marc Egan, "Heflin Chastises State Senator in Speech at ASU," *Montgomery Advertiser* (12 May 1996): B1.

57. *New York Times* (10 May 1996): A20.

58. Associated Press, "Slavery Stance Draws Fire."

59. Ibid. Apparently Burton did not realize that the proposal was tabled by the Senate before Davidson could deliver his speech.

60. "Defense of Slavery Knocks Out House Hopeful," *The Hill* (15 May 1996): 15.

61. Associated Press, "Slavery Stance Draws Fire."

62. Saunders.

63. Editorial, "Slavery Defender Senator Embarrasses State, Party."

64. Ibid., F2.

65. Clarence Page, "It Defies Common Sense, Decency to Justify Slavery," *Orlando Sentinel* (14 May 1996): A9. This column also appeared in the *Phoenix Gazette, Seattle Post-Intelligencer*, and the *Fresno Bee* under different titles.

66. Gene Owens, "Bible's 'Slaves' Were A Far Cry From South's," *News & Record* (14 May 1996): A7.

67. Clarence Page, "Revisionist History of Slavery Reveals a Pervasive Racism," *Seattle Post-Intelligencer* (14 May 1996): A9.

68. Watson. Watson ignores that Senator Davidson was sixty-one years old at the time, and thus went to school long before the majority of his press-reported critics did so.

69. Howard Kleinberg, "In Biblical Terms." Of course, if Kleinberg had read the speech he would be able to answer this question for himself.

70. "In the News," *Arkansas Democrat-Gazette* (12 May 1996): A1.

71. Phillip Rawls, "Senator Not Just Whistlin' 'Dixie' With Speech Defending Slavery," *Montgomery Advertiser* (10 May 1996): A1. This quote, with the insertion, is in Davidson's original speech. However, it is uncertain whether the author of

this article was drawing from the speech or an interview with Davidson for this quotation. Thus Davidson's view of what the flag means is supplanted by what the press constructs it to mean: racism.

72. Rawls, "House Candidate Uses Bible."

73. Ibid. The Confederate Heritage Fund is one of the groups who provided research support for Senator Davidson.

74. James A. Herrick, *Argumentation: Understanding and Shaping Arguments* (Scottsdale, AZ: Gorsuch Scarisbrick, Publishers, 1995), 267.

75. Saunders.

76. Associated Press, "Slavery Stance Draws Fire."

77. Editorial, "Slavery Defender Senator Embarrasses State, Party." Lincoln was reported as saying in 1865: "I have always thought all men should be free; but if any should be slaves, it should first be those who desire it for themselves, and secondly those who desire it for others. Whenever I hear anyone arguing for slavery, I feel a strong impulse to see it tried on him personally." The editors ignored, however, the Lincoln quotes and other evidence provided by Davidson's speech: for example, "northern slaves were even exempt from Lincoln's emancipation proclamation! Furthermore, captured Southern slaves on the Mississippi river were forced to work on the plantations as slaves for the United States army, growing cotton for northern factories, rather than be set free. In his inaugural address of March 4, 1861, President Abraham Lincoln stated that he had 'no purpose, directly or indirectly to interfere with the institution of slavery in the states where it exists. I believe I have no lawful right to do so, and I have no inclination to do so.' President Abraham Lincoln brutally violated almost every article and amendment to the U.S. Constitution, throwing over 35,000 Northern citizens in prison as political prisoners, including state legislators, without cause or trial, as well as, violently closing dozens [of] opposition newspapers and suppressing freedom of speech."

78. Owens.

79. Ingram.

80. Kleinberg.

81. Watson.

82. "Out of His Cotton Pickin' Mind."

83. Clarence Page, "It Defies Common Sense."

84. Rawls.

85. Kleinberg.

86. For example, see the work of William Fogel, economist, and 1993 Nobel Prize Winner. Abuse of slaves was uncommon in the South. Moreover, there is not one documented case of an American slave-breeding institution. Most slave children sold were orphans. The Christian standards adhered to in the South, combined with the general Victorian standards of the day, provided for a low level of black slave women as sex objects. In addition, there is no evidence to support assertions that there were black slave brothels. See Robert William Fogel, *Without Consent or Contract : The Rise and Fall of American Slavery* (New York: Norton, 1989); Robert William Fogel and Stanley L. Engerman, *Time On the Cross: The Economics Of American Negro Slavery* (Boston: Little Brown, 1974).

87. One example stands out. Rod Watson wrote in passing that Davidson had

mentioned the popular movie series Roots, which was not contained in any of the AP reports used for this study. Rod Watson, "American Education Distorts And Devalues Black History To The Point Of Ignorance," *Buffalo News* (16 May 1996): B3.

Chapter Three

William J. Clinton: "Initiative on Race"

Can we be one America respecting, even celebrating, our differences, but embracing even more what we have in common?
—William J. Clinton

President Clinton seemed to be taking on the role of an artist commissioned to paint the beautiful American rainbow.
—Miguel Perez

On 14 June 1997, President William J. Clinton attended commencement at the University of California at San Diego. He used this opportunity to extend congratulations to the graduating class and to announce a new public policy initiative: One America in the 21st Century: The President's Initiative on Race. This initiative was designed to "prepare our country to live as one America in the 21st century."[1]

In this chapter I examine President Clinton's speech; specifically, I will be looking for how he frames his initiative on race.[2] I next analyze the press coverage of President Clinton's announcement, looking for how the press frames the initiative. Three questions are asked: How did President Clinton frame the issue? How did the press, responding to President Clinton's speech, frame the issue? And at what time, if at all, did their frames converge to present a unified contextual whole?[3]

PRESIDENT CLINTON'S SPEECH

Although proclaimed in the press as an announcement of his initiative on race, the president's speech was also a commencement address to a graduating class. Thus the president needed to relate his topic to the class while also announcing his initiative on race. He accomplished this by focusing on the "diversity" of the graduating class he was addressing: "I want to thank you for offering our nation a shining example of excellence rooted in the many backgrounds that make up this great land. You have blazed new paths in science and technology, explored the new horizons of the Pacific Rim and Latin America. This is a great university for the 21st century. Today we celebrate your achievements at a truly golden moment for America."[4] The president makes a brief series of assertions about this golden moment, then suggests that there still exist challenges for the class to face: "terrorism, organized crime and drug trafficking, the spread of weapons of mass destruction, the prospect of new diseases and environmental disaster."[5] He continues, stating that the class "must continue to fight the scourge of gangs and crime and drugs. [And] must prepare for the retirement of the baby boom generation so that we can reduce that child poverty rate. . . . [The class] must harness the forces of science and technology for the public good, the entire American public."[6]

The president hands these challenges to the class, and then shifts to the initiative on race: "I believe the greatest challenge we face . . . is also our greatest opportunity. Of all the questions of discrimination and prejudice that still exist in our society, the most perplexing one is the oldest, and . . . the newest: the problem of race. Can we fulfill the promise of America by embracing all our citizens of all races. . . . In short, can we become one America in the 21st century?"[7] The president frames his call for one America as unity through diversity. Two interanimated themes run through this frame: diversity as both strength and opportunity, and responsibility as keys to community.

Diversity as Strength

The One America goal was described as unattainable through money, power, or technology. The president states clearly that it "is something that can come only from the human spirit. . . ."[8] He cites Hawaii as the exemplar for his vision, explaining that it has "no racial or ethnic group" in the majority. Because of this, it is "a wonderful place of exuberance and friendship and patriotism."[9] California is on this path too, since in "three years . . . no single race or ethnic group will make up a majority of the state's population," which is, according the president, the same situation the remainder of America will find herself in fifty years.[10] With this line of reasoning, the president implies that where there is a clear majority, that majority is the cause of minority problems.

The president's central question to his audience and to the American public is simple: "Can we be one America respecting, even celebrating, our differences, but embracing even more what we have in common?"[11] According to the president, we hold our values in common, and these are not demonstrated "just in terms of the hyphen showing our ethnic origin."[12] The president's frame of unity through diversity is illustrated well when he states, "those who say we cannot transform the problem of prejudice into the promise of unity forget how far we have come, and I cannot believe they have ever seen a crowd like you."[13] Just prior to this the president had complimented the graduating class on its racial and ethnic diversity. Outside of Hawaii and California there are still problems, however. These problems exist not only between black and white Americans, but also between Americans of African and Hispanic descent, Americans of Asian and Middle Eastern descent, and a "resurgent anti-Semitism, a new hostility to new immigrants."[14] Although the president focuses primarily on blacks and whites, he does attempt to show that there are tensions among all races and major ethnic groups.

In spite of these tensions and problems, progress had been made because America now is more racially and ethnically diverse than ever: "More of us enjoy each other's company and distinctive cultures than ever before."[15] He also states that "as you have shown us today, our diversity will enrich our lives in non-material ways—deepening our understanding of human nature and human differences, making our communities more exciting, more enjoyable, more meaningful. That is why I have come here today to ask the American people to join me in a great national effort to perfect the promise of America for this new time as we seek to build our more perfect union."[16] This perfect union involves tearing down all the barriers the president sees: "the barriers in our lives, our minds, and our hearts."[17] He suggests that if Americans tear down the remaining barriers, then they can "draw strength from all our people and our ancient faith in the quality of human dignity, to become the world's first truly multi-racial democracy."[18]

Through Opportunity and Responsibility, One Community

Ultimately, the president is relating his plan for uniting Americans, for producing "One America." For the president, this is to be accomplished through a "strategy of opportunity for all, responsibility for all, and an American community of all our citizens."[19] The plan, and resulting actions, must be put in place by Americans realizing and incorporating the "realities and perception affecting all racial groups in America."[20]

The president directly links opportunity to participation in the economy: "full participation" in the "economy is the best antidote to envy, despair, and racism."[21] Thus, he would have citizens moving from welfare to work, and increase economic opportunities for those in both urban and rural settings. Although he does not provide a specific plan for this, he does say that education is the key to successfully increase economic participation by non-whites: "There are no children who, because of their ethnic or racial background, who cannot meet the highest academic standards if we set them and measure our students against them, if we give them well-trained teachers and well-equipped classrooms, and if we continue to support reasoned reforms to achieve excellence, like the charter school movement."[22] As part of this educational endeavor, the president wants to "make at least two years of college as universal at the dawn of the next century as a high school diploma is today."[23]

The president links this expansion of opportunity to affirmative action programs. Although admitting affirmative action has not been perfect, he asserts that it has worked well when correctly used. He presents the military as the best example of a successful affirmative action program: "Our armed forces are diverse from top to bottom—perhaps the most integrated institution in our society and certainly the most integrated military in the world. And, more important, no one questions that they are the best in the world. So much for the argument that excellence and diversity do not go hand in hand."[24] President Clinton links affirmative action programs directly with educational programs, and attributes recent drops in "enrollments" (as opposed to applications) to some states removing affirmative action programs from public universities. He implies that racism is to blame for continued poor performance among California's minority populations: "I know that the people of California voted to repeal affirmative action without any ill motive. The vast majority of them simply did it with a conviction that discrimination and isolation are no longer barriers to achievement."[25] Thus, even though the president states that the people of California voted to repeal affirmative action without any ill motive, it is racism that led to the drop in enrollments.

Educational opportunity is loosely linked with equal economic opportunity, thus the president mixes opposition to affirmative action programs with opposition to equal economic opportunity for minorities: "we should not stop trying to equalize economic opportunity. To those who oppose affirmative action, I ask you to come up with an alternative."[26] The president links education and economic responsibility by asserting that Americans must act responsible by continuing their education beyond high school. The president stresses the overall importance of education: "The new economy offers fewer guarantees, more risks, and more rewards. It calls upon all of us to take even greater responsibility for our education than ever before."[27] He almost implies that without affirmative action minorities will be unable to be responsible citizens since they will be unable to obtain a good education.

According to the president, through affirmative action comes economic opportunity and eventually one community; this community will be "based on respect for one another and our shared values."[28] The mutual respect the president desires will come about through a national conversation on racial issues: "We must begin with a candid conversation on the state of race relations today and the implications of Americans of so many different races living and working together as we approach a new century."[29] This envisioned conversation will begin with the formation of a Presidential panel that will travel the country seeking input from citizens. The purpose will be to "help educate Americans about the facts surrounding issues of race, to promote a dialogue in every community of the land to confront and work through these issues, to recruit and encourage leadership at all levels to help breach racial divides, and to find, develop, and recommend how to implement concrete solutions to our problems—solutions that will involve all of us in government, business, communities, and as individual citizens."[30]

Talk is not enough, however, and the president says that if "we do nothing more than propose disconnected acts of policy, it would be helpful, but it won't be enough."[31] Thus, he implies to the nation that talk comes first, and from the talk will come actual policy recommendations. He throws the importance of the national conversation into the future: "But if ten years from now people can look back and see that this year of honest dialogue and concerted action helped to lift the heavy burden of race from our children's future, we will have given a precious gift to America."[32] As an example of shared values the president tells of the reactions of Americans to the Oklahoma City bombing. That was the day that "we saw and wept for Americans and forgot for a moment that there were a lot of them from different races than we are. Remember the many faces and races of the Americans who did not sleep and put their lives at risk to engage in the rescue, the helping, and the healing. Remember how you have seen things like that in the natural disasters here in California. That is the face of the real America. That is the face I have seen over and over again. That is the America, somehow, some way we have to make real in daily American life."[33]

THE RESPONSE OF THE PRESS

The press coverage of President Clinton's speech was extensive with a total of 214 articles used for this chapter: 74 news articles, 112 opinion essays, and 28 editorials. The lion's share of news articles were published during the two days following the speech, with opinion essays and editorials found consistently throughout the ten days following the president's speech. Taken together, these articles reveal five distinct areas in which the press framed issues contained in President Clinton's speech: a general defense of affirmative action, press opposition to California's

Proposition 209, diversity, press criticism of the speech, and press praise of the speech.

Clearly President Clinton wished to address the issue of "One America." How could America come together and overcome lingering racial and ethnic tensions? The press answered this question by contextualizing the speech as having addressed the issue of affirmative action's assault on bigotry, prejudice, and overt racism. For example, the *Chicago Sun-Times* said that the president "assailed bigotry . . . and touted a new advisory board he has charged with addressing racial, religious and ethnic prejudice."[34] *Newsday* wrote that the president asked Americans to work for "racial reconciliation" and said that healing "the wounds of prejudice" was America's "greatest challenge."[35] This interpretation was reinforced by the article's headline: " 'One America': Clinton Outlines Need to Transcend Ethnic Prejudice." This interpretation was also stressed by the *Pantagraph*, which ran an article titled, "Clinton Attacks Racism," and suggested that President Clinton's speech "challenged the nation . . . to confront ingrained prejudices and stereotypes. . . ."[36]

Editorials and opinion essays followed this general pattern as well. Editorially speaking, *USA Today* stated, "Let's talk about race. That was the black and white, red and brown and yellow bottom line of President Clinton's kickoff . . . for a year-long examination of U.S. race relations."[37] The *Arizona Republic* editorially stated, "President Clinton attempts to lay bare the national psyche and minister to its soul."[38] The *Buffalo News*, editorially speaking, demonstrated well the frame of the press: "To his credit, President Clinton has chosen to spark a year-long conversation about racial healing, directly challenging Americans to face up to prejudices, stereotypes and hatreds that mar our lives together and keep some people away from opportunities to reach their potential. Clinton has underscored a critical topic for our diverse free society."[39]

The *Des Moines Register* suggested that white racism is the problem facing minorities: "Yet something is missing. Maybe it's jobs. Despite the robust economy, unemployment among African-Americans, especially those in low-income urban areas, often doubles, sometimes triples that of whites. For many African-Americans, and other minorities, race relations often boil down to myths and stereotypes whites have toward them."[40] Russell Baker wrote: the president "was also speaking in California, where people have recently been voting bleak anti-black, anti-immigrant passions. Endorsing affirmative action in this benighted territory, the President could show his critics that [he could take a stand]."[41] David Broder reported a study that found nearly three-fourths of whites told Gallup interviewers they thought blacks were treated the same as whites in their own city, but almost half the blacks said they had encountered unfair treatment in stores, restaurants or theaters, at work, on the road or in dealing with police—just within the past 30 days."[42] Rekha Basu wrote that President Clinton unveiled his initiative as "fresh evidence [that] the country's racial fissures keep piling up—from clashes over affirmative action to discrimination suits against corporations."[43] Arthur Dobrin and Warren Payton stated that the president was correct in "focusing on racial justice as one of America's greatest need[s]," and also stated that "he challenged Americans to come to grip with racism and its insidious effects upon all people in this country."[44]

General Frame of the Speech: In Defense of Affirmative Action

Having established a rather bleak picture of race relations as context, the press then relayed thoroughly the comments the president made regarding affirmative action. Although the press did present the speech as attacking racial hatreds, the overall frame described the president's speech as "vigorously defending affirmative action. . . ."[45] This portion of the general frame was well established the first day of press coverage and continued throughout the weeks following the speech. For instance, The *Arizona Republic* wrote that President Clinton had "passionately defended affirmative action as a way to overcome America's racial and ethnic tensions. Clinton's stand came in a broad speech on race relations in which he challenged Americans to push beyond the civil-rights laws of the 1960s and examine their own attitudes toward one another."[46] The *Atlanta Journal and Constitution* asserted that the president's speech "included a prickly political challenge to opponents of affirmative action programs."[47] These press assertions were backed by excerpts from the president's speech: "to those who oppose affirmative action, I ask you to come up with an alternative—I would embrace it if I could find a better way. . . ."[48] The press relayed often that the president had said that ending affirmative action through Proposition 209 had been "dramatic and devastating."

A typical example of this framing is seen in the *Atlanta Journal and Constitution*: "Calling on Americans to overcome their racial and ethnic divisions, President Clinton warned . . . that—three decades after the civil rights revolution—the nation faces a return to racial segregation in its colleges unless affirmative action policies are kept in place. In California, a state at the forefront of the movement against preferences, Clinton strongly defended affirmative action as a means of easing the nation's racial fault lines."[49] The *Detroit News* stated that in California, "a state that has repealed affirmative action programs, Clinton reiterated his support for such initiatives. 'Many affirmative actions students excel. . . . If we close the door on them, we will weaken our greatest universities, and we won't ever build the society we need in the 21st century. . . . ' "[50] The *Houston Chronicle* stated that President Clinton "defended affirmative action as

a tool for equality" and "called on affirmative action opponents to offer alternatives rather than abandon the concept."[51]

The *New York Times* began its coverage of the speech with this sentence: "Speaking in a state that has led the movement against racial preference programs, President Clinton today made a broad appeal for racial
reconciliation and vigorously defended affirmative action on college
campuses. 'We must not resegregate higher education,' Mr. Clinton
said."[52] Similarly, the *Washington Post* wrote that the president "Argues
for Affirmative Action," and that this arguing represented a "vigorous
defense of affirmative action."[53] The paper also stated that the president
called for a "renewal of affirmative action programs at America's Universities. . . ."[54] The *Plain Dealer* wrote that the president said: "that the
greatest challenge Americans face is creating an America where all people regardless of race or nationality have equal rights and opportunities.
He told the crowd affirmative action helps to achieve these goals."[55] The
St. Louis Post-Dispatch led with this headline, "President Kicks Off Anti-
Racism Campaign; Defends Affirmative Action, Opens 'Conversation'
for Next Century," and this lead sentence, "Declaring 'we must not resegregate higher education,' President Bill Clinton made an impassioned
defense of affirmative action . . . and kicked off a 12-month campaign for
improved race relations."[56]

The *Des Moines Register* stated in its lead sentence that the president
had "opened a year-long campaign against American racism . . . with a
vigorous defense of affirmative action in a place where it has been
erased," and then wrote that the president had "passionately defended
affirmative action . . . as a way to overcome America's racial and ethnic
divisions."[57] *The State Journal-Register* said that President Clinton "delivered an impassioned defense of affirmative action. . . ."[58] The *Record* suggested through its headline that a defense of affirmative action was the
"First Steps on the Path to Harmony" and followed with: "President
Clinton opened a year-long campaign against racism . . . with a defense
of affirmative action and a [call] for Americans to confront and erase
their most deeply held prejudices. 'Emotions may be rubbed raw, but
we must begin.' "[59] The *News and Observer* led with this sentence: "President Clinton passionately defended affirmative action . . . as a way to
overcome America[n] racial and ethnic divisions. Clinton's stand came
in a broad speech on race relations in which he challenged Americans
to push beyond the civil rights laws of the 1960s and examine their own
attitudes toward each other."[60] The *Palm Beach Post* stated that the speech
was attempting to heal "America's racial divide" but "included a prickly
political challenge to opponents of affirmative action. . . . [T]he president
denounced attempts . . . to end affirmative action, complaining that the
results so far have been 'dramatic and devastating' to minorities. 'Call it

what you will, but I call it resegregation,' Clinton . . . said."[61] Perhaps foreshadowing the strength of this frame, the reporter for this article put those words in the president's mouth; the president never said this in his speech.

The vigorous defense the press claims the president made is explained using the president's *assertions*: "He said affirmative action programs . . . were essential without an effective alternative to assure equal opportunity. Directly addressing the foes of affirmative action, Clinton said: 'I ask you to come up with an alternative. I would embrace it, if I can find a better way.' "[62] The standard quote used by the press to justify saying that the president had mounted a "vigorous" or "strong" defense of affirmative action was: " 'To those who oppose affirmative action, I ask you to come up with an alternative.' "[63] In addition, the press often coupled the above quote with the president asserting, " 'I know affirmative action has not been perfect in America . . . but when used the right way, it has worked.' "[64] Examples of using assertions as evidence abound. For example, being more thorough than most papers by citing the assertions the president made concerning minority enrollment drops, the *Atlanta Journal and Constitution* editorially stated: "Those who feared that the speech would be no more than a feel-good pep talk should have been reassured by Clinton's words on affirmative action. Speaking in a state that has recently repudiated affirmative action at the polls, the president offered an intelligent defense of this valuable tool against the consequences of racism. Noting that minority enrollment had dropped at California and Texas graduate schools after affirmative action programs were rescinded in those states, Clinton delivered an admonition the nation needs to hear: 'We must not resegregate higher education.' "[65] The *Pittsburgh Post-Gazette* editorially stated that the president "did offer a ringing endorsement of affirmative action. . . . Noting that black admissions at two law schools had dropped 80 percent and Hispanic admissions 50 percent since the University of California system banned race-based preferences, the president asked opponents of affirmative action to offer some alternative that would not result in the resegregation of higher education."[66]

Most papers used fewer examples of the president's assertions in order to establish his "vigorous" and "strong" defense of affirmative action. For instance, Rhonda Chriss Lokeman, writing for the *Kansas City Star* stated, "It didn't go unnoticed by affirmative action supporters—including this newspaper—that . . . Clinton publicly endorsed affirmative action and did so in California."[67] Louis Freedberg wrote that even though the speech was "short on specifics . . . one of its most notable aspects was its clear defense of affirmative action. 'For those who oppose affirmative action, I ask you to come up with an alternative. . . . ' "[68]

Press Opposition to Proposition 209

Closely related to the issues of affirmative action and diversity was press framing of California's Proposition 209. President Clinton did make reference to Proposition 209 in his speech, and the press relayed this section of the speech in full. For example, the *Atlanta Journal and Constitution* stated that "Republican opposition to affirmative action also fueled the ballot initiative in California which resulted last fall in the passage of Proposition 209, ending all racial and gender preferences in that state. Proposition 209 was one of the key reasons the White House chose the graduation ceremonies at the University of California, Dan Diego, as the site for his speech on racial reconciliation. 'I know that the people of California voted to repeal affirmative action without ill motive,' Clinton said. 'The vast majority of them simply did it with the conviction that discrimination and isolation are no longer barriers to achievement.' But the results have been that minority enrollments in law schools and graduate programs are 'plummeting for the first time in decades,' he said."[69] The *New York Times* illustrated the general press interpretation of Proposition 209:

Californians last year approved Proposition 209, which bans consideration of race and sex in state hiring, contracting and education. Although a Federal appeals court in San Francisco upheld the constitutionality of the initiative in April, its provisions have been stayed pending further court appeals. "Let me say, I know that the people of California voted to repeal affirmative action without ill motive," Mr. Clinton said. "The vast majority of them simply did it with the conviction that discrimination and isolation are no longer barriers to achievement." But he pointed to reports that the University of California has seen a significant drop in applications from minority students and, more recently, in the number accepted. "Minority enrollments in law school and other graduate programs are plummeting for the first time in decades," he said. "Assuming the same will likely happen in undergraduate education, we must not resegregate higher education. . . ."[70]

The *Denver Rocky Mountain News* similarly reported that "California, where [the president] decided to give his race-relations speech because of its ethnic mixture, just voted to abolish affirmative action—meaning, for example, that minorities will no longer get preference in public universities. Already, the number of blacks going to medical, law, and graduate schools in California is declining, Clinton noted. At the same time, the number of Asian Americans in those schools is rising out of proportion. 'We must not try to stop equalizing economic opportunity,' Clinton warned."[71] The *St. Louis Post-Dispatch* reported in a similar manner that "The president told the crowd how, without affirmative action, the number of blacks admitted to the University of California's law school tumbled 81 percent in one year, and Hispanic admissions fell 50 percent."[72]

Often the press would support an assertion of the president with an assertion of its own, thus lending more weight to the president's words. For example, the *Tampa Tribune* wrote that "Clinton said the results [of Proposition 209] has been minority enrollments in graduate programs are 'plummeting.' Indeed, the enrollment of minority students has dropped significantly since the University of California regents voted to end affirmative action for admissions in 1995. 'We must not resegregate higher education or leave it to the private universities to do the public's work,' he said. 'To those who oppose affirmative action, I ask you to come up with an alternative. I would embrace it if I could find a better way.' "[73] Although there are alternatives, the press mentions none; neither does it provide numbers in support of its assertions. The *Sun* demonstrated its support for affirmative action and opposition to Proposition 209 when it wrote: "The most important underlying issue—especially to the school's minority students—is that many of the Latino and African-American students who graduated yesterday were admitted under affirmative action policies that have since been scrapped by the board of regents of the UC system. And last year, that policy was codified in law by California voters in a referendum known as Proposition 209. 'I know that affirmative action has not been perfect in America—that's why two years ago we began an effort to fix the things that are wrong with it,' Clinton said. 'But when used in the right way, it has worked.' The audience applauded exuberantly."[74] The *Washington Post* added, "At the last minute, Clinton dropped some language today that might have seemed harsher. For instance, in an earlier draft, he called the impact of the California affirmative action repeal 'devastating' and added, 'I call it resegregation'—two lines that did not show up in the final version."[75]

The press framed passage of Proposition 209 as an attempt to take back the civil rights of minorities. Speaking of Proposition 209, Lovell Beaulieu said, "As parts of the country strive to turn back the clock on race-related programs and race-specific initiatives, the president of the world's greatest superpower leads her into battle. He may pull it off; then again, he may not. But even if he doesn't, the greatest defeat would have come if he did not try."[76] The *Austin American Statesman* summed it well: "Calling on Americans to overcome their racial and ethnic divisions, President Clinton warned on Saturday that—three decades after the civil rights revolution—the nation faces a return to racial segregation in its colleges unless affirmative action policies are kept in place."[77] The *New York Times* editorially wrote that "the President rightly implored Americans not to follow that path [Prop 209], which would only turn their public universities and private workplaces into segregated islands of privilege."[78] In similar style, the *Atlanta Journal and Constitution* wrote,

"Noting that minority enrollment had dropped at California and Texas graduate schools after affirmative action programs were rescinded in those states, Clinton delivered an admonition that the nation needs to hear: 'We must not resegregate higher education.' Ending affirmative action programs at colleges and universities could reverse decades of progress toward equal opportunity for all Americans."[79]

Press Construction of Diversity

Throughout the press coverage of the speech, one finds references to multiculturalism, diversity, and tolerance. Although the press never explicitly defined these terms, one can construct from the various accounts a composite definition which flows from the press usage. Miguel Perez captures the spirit of the press account well: "when he set out to spark a national discussion about racial and ethnic tensions in America, President Clinton seemed to be taking on the role of an artist commissioned to paint the beautiful American rainbow. This is not an easy job. Artists don't usually have the whole world looking over their shoulders as they stroke colors on a canvass. But Clinton took on the responsibility of painting the American mosaic in a public forum, capturing on a multimedia canvass all of the beautiful shade from the American palette of racial and ethnic groups."[80] The focus on outer appearances, on color, is found throughout press accounts. For example, the *Atlanta Journal and Constitution* editorially wrote that "Newcomers to Atlanta often are shocked to discover that race is prominent in virtually all policy discussions. It is Atlanta's strength and its perdition. Strength because we do live in and believe in a multicultural society inclusive of all. So when we look around boards and committees and choose, as Clinton did, one of these and three of those, we are building a stronger community."[81] Ann McFeatters wrote that the president said "in 50 years there will be no majority ethnic group in America (he meant that Anglos then will constitute only 50 percent, instead of 75 percent). . . . But California, where he decided to give his race-relations speech because of its ethnic mixture, just voted to abolish affirmative action—meaning, for example, that minorities will no longer get preference in public universities. Already the number of blacks going to medical, law, and graduate schools in California is declining, Clinton noted. At the same time, the number of Asian Americans in those schools is raising out of proportion."[82]

The *Detroit News* opened its coverage with this sentence: "President Clinton shared his vision Saturday for an America that celebrates its diversity rather than cowers to its differences." The paper explained that this celebration is important since the nation will soon be moving "into a period in which no one racial or ethnic group will be a majority."[83] Highlighting the racial composition of the UCSD student body, the *Plain*

Dealer gave the president praise: "Clinton's speech drew an enthusiastic, though not overpowering, reaction from a student body that is 28 percent Asian American, 27 percent Latino and 5 percent black."[84] The *Washington Post* argued against recent Supreme Court rulings in the area of affirmative action: The Supreme Court "has found in the areas of federal contracting and voting districts that racial classifications 'balkanize' society. A narrow but controlling majority believes that such policies 'embody stereotypes that treat individuals as the product of their race, evaluating their thoughts and efforts—their very worth as citizens—by the color of their skins.' Yet Clinton tried to stress in his speech to students at the University of California . . . why government-sponsored diversity might help society. 'Look around this crowd today,' he said. 'Don't you think you have learned a lot more than you would have if everybody sitting around you looked just like you? I think you have."[85]

The *Baltimore Sun* reported that the president "had uttered most of the sentiments and anecdotes before and drew on events of his own life in discussing the need for tolerance and diversity to a student body receptive to this message. 'I went to segregated schools, swam in segregated pools, sat in all-white sections at the movies and traveled through small towns in my state that still marked restrooms and water fountains 'white' and 'colored. . . . ' "[86] Editorially speaking, the *Atlanta Journal and Constitution* stated that "We have already seen why diversity is beneficial. Our military could not function without attracting people from the spectrum of American ethnic groups. Similarly, American businesses have seen the advantages of having diverse work forces to cater to diverse markets."[87] Gregory Freeman stated that "Clinton thinks America's diversity can be an asset. There's no question that diversity is an asset to American cities. Those cities without many different ethnic groups tend to be a bit white-bread, not nearly as interesting as those with a variety of people who brought with them their cultures, foods, and sounds."[88]

Even the president's proposed advisory board on race was hailed, not for diverse intellectual interests, but rather for different skin tones: Trevor Coleman wrote that "The diverse, seven-member advisory board consists of a nice cross-section of Americans. . . ."[89] Along these lines, the *Portland Press Herald*, editorially speaking, stated that "[The advisory] board's very composition sends a message. [I]t includes three white members, two blacks, one Hispanic, and one Korean-American, reflecting the broad racial diversity of this country. Race relations do not involve black and white alone. The day soon will come, in fact, when the United States has no single racial or ethnic majority. On that day, it will be important that this be a rainbow nation not only in fact but in spirit. The rainbow nation will be a better nation."[90]

The *Washington Post*, in a fashion similar to other papers, implied that diversity means only skin color: "Clinton tried to stress in his speech . . .

why government-sponsored diversity might help society. 'Look around the crowd today,' he said. 'Don't you think you have learned a lot more than you would have if everybody sitting around you *looked just like you*? I think you have.' "[91] Ruben Navarrette Jr. wrote, "Facing an audience of college students as multicolored as a coastal rainbow, he [the President] extolled the virtue of diversity and reiterated his support for [affirmative action]."[92] Although Navarrette felt the class to be a rainbow, the *Record* shows the focus on color as diversity through the question why an affirmative action class produced so few non-white graduates: "Clinton's words drew hearty applause from the mostly white graduating class, which included several Asian and Hispanic students but an obviously smaller number of black students. Only one black male graduate . . . could be easily seen in the sea of caps and gowns."[93] Although each article saw a different rainbow, each focused upon the *colors* comprising those rainbows.

In stressing the various skin colors that Americans possess, the press also highlighted President Clinton's assertion of an America with no racial majority in fifty years. For example, the *New York Times* wrote: "The President acknowledged that there was still 'old and unfinished business' between black and white Americans. But he sought to reframe the debate in the context of demographic changes that he said now pose 'many dilemmas of race and ethnicity.' Predicting that in half a century there would be 'no majority race in America,' Mr. Clinton posed a choice: 'Will we become not two but many Americas, separate, unequal, and isolated?' he asked. . . . 'Or will we draw strength from all our people and our ancient faith in the quality of human dignity to become the first truly multiracial democracy?' "[94] Along similar lines, the *St. Louis Post Dispatch* stated that "The President noted that the nation was becoming ever more multi-ethnic and in 50 years would no longer have a single, distinct racial majority."[95]

The importance of a multicultural attitude is asserted through the appeal to the fifty year projection of the racial mix in America. As did the lion's share of papers reporting this, the *Christian Science Monitor* asserts this speculation as fact, thus lending greater weight to the President's original speculation: "By 2050, the U.S. will be close to having no majority racial group. The key to integrating America by then, Clinton argued, lies in expanding economic and education opportunities."[96] Editorially speaking, the *Pittsburgh Post-Gazette* wrote: "Race continues to be the great fault line in American public life, and the legacy of slavery makes the black-white divide the most difficult to mend. Yet America's ethnicity is becoming increasingly complex. Hispanics may become the biggest minority group in the nation within a decade, and are already close to being the biggest ethnic group of any kind . . . in California. If current demographic trends continue, Asian Americans will also out-number African Americans within decades."[97]

Specific Framing of Criticism

Criticism of the president's message was reported by the press, but it was framed in very specific ways that minimized any oppositional criticism of the president's ideas or plans. The criticisms break down into three broad areas: Republicans were depicted as attacking affirmative action and President Clinton; the press and liberal activists were depicted as calling for more action; and true press criticism.

Republicans Attack Clinton and Affirmative Action. Although minimally, the press did report specific criticisms of President Clinton's speech, and these critics were depicted almost exclusively as Republicans. The *Atlanta Journal and Constitution*, for example, pointed out that affirmative action "programs have been a major dividing point between Democrats and Republicans since they were spawned during Lyndon Johnson's presidency. But those differences have been especially pronounced since the Republicans took control of Congress from Democrats after the 1994 election."[98] Echoing this press depiction, the *Arizona Republic* reported that before "Clinton even uttered a word . . . his plan had been dismissed by skeptics as empty feel-goodism. Rep. Richard Armey, R-Texas, said blaming dropping minority enrollments on the end of affirmative action is a 'misdiagnosis. It's actually evidence of the urgent need for school choice,' Armey said in a statement. 'Calling for quotas in college admission is simply passing the buck. We can't expect anyone to survive 12 years in substandard schools and then excel in college.' "[99]

The *Boston Globe* wrote that all "seven members of a newly named presidential advisory panel on race support affirmative action—a fact that prompted House Speaker Newt Gingrich of Georgia to dismiss the effort as the same 'tired old government liberalism.' At the same time, Gingrich vowed to push legislation to ban the racial preferences that make up most affirmative action programs."[100] The *Denver Rocky Mountain News* found the space to insert this single line: "House speaker Newt Gingrich is already attacking Clinton for not having on his advisory board anybody who . . . opposes affirmative action as the wrong remedy, so Clinton's path to dialogue already has some big boulders."[101] The *New York Times* said that "opponents of affirmative action were highly critical of the speech because of Mr. Clinton's adherence to racial preferences programs. While Speaker Newt Gingrich told reporters . . . that he would be willing to work with the President's newly appointed . . . advisory panel on race, he also criticized its makeup and purpose: 'I'm going to ask it to have hearings where folks who are different than the normal

set of liberals are allowed to come and testify—successful black busi-
nessmen and women, people who have risen on their own, people who
are multiracial,' Mr. Gingrich said."[102]

The *Palm Beach Post* reported Rep. Charles Canady (R–FL) saying " 'the
president is right to call on the American people to work together to
build one America. . . . But his call for unity is at odds with his support
for government policies that grant preferences based on race. Racial preferences are inherently divisive, and they send a powerful and perverse
message from the government to the American people that we should
continue to think and act along racial lines.' "[103] The *Milwaukee Journal
Sentinel* reported the comments of Sen. Mitch McConnell (R–KY): "Citing
President Clinton's call for a national dialogue on race, a group of Republican lawmakers Tuesday introduced legislation to bar federal government from granting preferences based on race or gender. 'The Federal
government must lead by example,' McConnell said. . . . 'we must promote a nation where our citizens are seen as individuals and not as mere
members of a group.' "[104]

Although the above criticism may seem thorough, few papers carried
such criticism, and any potential power was mitigated by the placement
of this criticism. Usually, criticisms from opponents of affirmative action
were found at the end of articles. For example, after twenty-one paragraphs in which all but one were Clinton quotes or supportive explanations, the *Houston Chronicle* wrote: "Ward Connerly, a member of the
University California Board of Regents and the chief proponent of Proposition 209, bristled at Clinton's defense of affirmative action. 'He's not
about to convince me that discrimination is right.' said Connerly, who
is black. Connerly . . . said it was not the opponents' responsibility to find
an alternative. [H]e was alarmed at the decline in minority enrollment
at some University of California law schools because it indicated that
racial preferences had been heavily used."[105] Another example of this
was provided by the *Orange County Register*, which also quoted Connerly: "[W]hile he supports Clinton's attempts to open a dialogue on
race, he is concerned the administration's remedy will be the very programs Californians have voted to end. 'We have concluded in this state
that this whole business of government sorting out jobs and contracts
and college admissions to achieve diversity is idiocy,' Connerly said,
with particular emphasis on the last word. 'And that seems to be the
way the president wants to take us. And with all due respect, I think
he's wrong.' "[106]

Speech Criticism from the Press: More Action. Actual reported opposition
to the president's speech was minimal in press coverage. The overwhelming majority of negative criticisms took the form of reporter-
generated criticism and criticism from liberal political activists. As the
Boston Globe wrote, before the president "recited a word of his speech,

he was already beset by criticism, from liberals who said he had betrayed minorities with his support of welfare overhaul and by conservatives who rejected his stand on affirmative action."[107] The *Washington Post* suggested that reaction "to the nationally televised speech broke predictably along ideological lines, with many liberals describing it as a positive first step and conservatives complaining it focuses more attention on skin color rather than fulfilling the Rev. Martin Luther King Jr.'s dream of a colorblind society."[108] Unlike reported conservative reactions, the criticisms from the press and "civil rights groups" were not given in opposition to the president's point of view, but rather asserted that the president had not gone far enough in promoting certain causes. For example, the *Morning Call* editorially wrote, "Reaction has included support from those who believe that the conversation is healthy, to scorn from others seeking an avenue for political attack."[109] The *New York Times* wrote that, "Aside from the conservatives' criticism, civil rights groups called his speech a first step that needed to be followed with actions that go beyond sentiment and talk. 'An immediate and appropriate follow-up to the President's speech would be an increased effort by the Administration to enforce existing Federal civil rights protections that are being violated' by anti-affirmative action measures like the university system's new rules, said Thomas A. Saenz, the Los Angeles regional counsel for the Mexican American Legal Defense and Education Fund."[110]

The *Los Angeles Times* summed well the criticism given by liberal groups:

Advocates for different racial and ethnic groups were cautious in their responses Saturday. While they applauded Clinton's decision to make race a paramount national concern, they also contended that his rhetoric is not yet matched with deeds, and some said they were concerned that the high-visibility effort could prove disappointing. "He needs to go beyond a dialogue," said Georgia Verdugo, regional counsel in Washington for the Mexican American Legal Defense and Educational fund. "There are a lot of things he could do," she added, mentioning stricter enforcement of civil rights laws as one example. In one respect, the president attempted to defuse the criticism, calling on Congress to increase funding to help the administration slash a backlog of legal cases involving discrimination. "I think he correctly pointed out that this is an area where dialogue is important, but we've got to come up with policies that promote inclusion," said Hugh B. Price, president of the National Urban League, who was generally complimentary of the president's effort. "He's got a lot of work to do, and the American people have a lot of work ahead. But I think he set the right tone." [The] executive director of the National Pacific American Legal Consortium in Washington, described Clinton's effort as a good start. "These are things that are tough to talk about, and we all need to hear them. . . . [T]he real test is what kind of action is taken at the end of the year."[111]

The press handling of criticism reveals an interesting frame. The president was right in what he said, but he did not go far enough in making "necessary" policy changes. For example, Norman Lockman stated that "The president has more faith in the application of raw facts and jaw-boning than I do. American racial myths and white backlash are too stubborn to succumb to or even generate rational discussion in neighborhood get-togethers. Its going to take tough new anti-discrimination policies to prevent retrenchment from gains made in the past few years."[112] The *Atlanta Journal and Constitution* reported that President Clinton "made no specific proposals to protect affirmative action and offered few details beyond urging a public discussion in the coming year."[113] The *Plain Dealer* quoted several individuals who relayed essentially the same idea. Rep. Elijah Cummings (Dem), for example, was quoted as saying, " 'I really do applaud the president for trying to do what he's doing. . . . But unless we are able to look at this whole race issue from an economic standpoint, I think we are going to continue to have problems with race in the country.' [Additionally,] Kweisi Mfume, president of the NAACP, called the speech 'a good first step on a long path toward racial reconciliation.' But he added: 'The real work ahead means more than just having direction, it means now a real need to have dialogue. And while the president clearly is the right person to call for that, it is the American people—who are black, white, Hispanic, and Asian—who must now find a way for that to occur.' Jasmine Gilham, 23, a black visual arts graduate [UCSD] . . . wished he had gone further. 'I would have liked to hear about the programs that he's actually going to implement,' she said."[114] Columnist Les Payne summed well this "good talk but little action" frame: "Thrusting himself right up there with President Abraham Lincoln and Martin Luther King Jr., Clinton apparently has suffered no drop in self-confidence. His revolution [One America Initiative] which he planned to spell out in more words though little action . . . seeks to prepare the 21st Century America for a 'multiracial, multiethnic society.' "[115]

The *Washington Post* began its framing of this subject with the line, "With lofty rhetoric flavored by moments of blunt talk but no grand initiatives. . . ."[116] Randall Kennedy sums both the promise and perils of the president's initiative on race: "The promise is a focused examination of racial issues that will clarify dilemmas so that at least we can know where and why we agree or disagree with one another. The peril is that Clinton and his aides will squelch the possibilities for an informative, intense, and perhaps surprising discussion and instead sponsor a series of scripted, pseudo-events devoid of the candor and contentiousness required for any serious attempt to grapple with the race question."[117] This line of thought—that the event will not involve real talk—was echoed by many in the press. The *Sacramento Bee* opined, "Some civil rights advocates have already voiced concerns that the president's race initiative will be a series of 'feel-good' events that accomplish little, while conservatives worry that Clinton will try to enshrine policies they feel have already failed."[118]

The *News and Observer* reported, "In a nod to civil rights leaders who have wondered whether his effort will go beyond speeches, Clinton said . . . 'If we achieve nothing more than talk, that will be too little. If we do nothing but propose disconnected acts of policy, that will be too little. But if . . . [this] year of honest dialogue and concerted action helped to lift the heavy burden of race from our children's future, we will have given a precious gift to America.' "[119] The *Richmond Times* wrote: "President Clinton's call for a national campaign against racism is a step in the right direction, but now he must prove that it isn't empty rhetoric. . . . 'Without some economic reform to go along with it, I don't think it's going to work,' said Regina Swinford, coordinator of a discussion group on race relations at the Richmond Peace Education Center. [Of the president's panel she stated] 'They'll do a lot of talking. . . . And then we can all feel better because we've done something, without really doing anything."[120] The *Austin America-Statesman* lent support to this frame: "Civil rights advocates voiced support for Clinton's efforts, though several said they are eager for the president to put substance behind his rhetoric. But Clinton made no specific proposals to protect affirmative action and offered few details beyond urging a public discussion in the coming year."[121]

The *Christian Science Monitor* cited "Sanford Cloud, the African-American head of the National Conference on Christians and Jews [as saying] 'Honest conversation is the important beginning. . . . But it's got to be dialogue that's followed by action—public policy decision making consistent with his goals.' It's a comment echoed across the board, and most say it means Clinton has to put some money where his mouth is if he's to be taken seriously." This paper then goes on to cite four additional minorities from across the country, all backing Cloud's point of view.[122] The *Los Angeles Times* stated that from "the left, critics such as civil rights leader Jesse Jackson and law professor C. Lani Guinier accuse Clinton of lacking a strong commitment to civil rights issues. 'I don't think the president has exercised forceful leadership,' said Guinier."[123] Louis Freedberg represents well the underlying premise of the press: "Many blacks are tired of pleas from whites for more dialogue. After all, it is not blacks, but whites, who must come to terms with their racism. Show us what you are going to do, they say, instead of just talking."[124] Editorially speaking, the *Pittsburgh Post-Gazette* stated: "Mr. Clinton's ability to make his principles fit his needs (remember the welfare law?) may hurt his efforts to lead a moral struggle against racism and in pursuit of equal opportunity. But on the issues of race, the president's credentials are lifelong and as close to pure as politics allow. The biggest question, therefore, is not how sincere is the president or how valuable is racial rapprochement, but how much can the president and his distinguished advisory panel accomplish with talk?"[125]

The *St. Louis Post-Dispatch* reiterated what much of the press had already reported of President Clinton's speech: "That's lofty rhetoric. It's a vital goal [One America]. But the President seems short on fresh initiatives to achieve it."[126] The *Washington Post* editorially stated that "No single symbolic act or landmark speech can bring about . . . results. Some symbolic acts and speeches meant to make things better can actually make them worse by reinforcing the idea that all people today may be defined as to both their moral and political status strictly on the basis of the color of their skin. There is no substitute for courageous, real leadership and concrete actions."[127]

Press Criticism of the Speech. There was genuine press-generated criticism of the president's ideas. What is most evident about this criticism is that it represents no unified frame of reference, but rather individual reactions. However, it is important to consider that these criticisms were extremely limited in scope. For example, of twenty-eight editorials, only three were overtly negative. Of 112 opinion essays, only twenty-five were overtly negative.[128] Yet even that number is misleading, since a lone essay by George Will represents fourteen of those negative essays, and another lone essay by Charles Krauthammer represents five. Thus nineteen of twenty-five negative opinion essays were written by the same authors. George Will wrote that "Mr. Clinton said that curtailing affirmative action will have a 'devastating' effect on minority enrollment in graduate schools. But if that is so, what does that reveal about how affirmative action depends on debasing academic standards? In reaffirming his support for affirmative action, he further vindicated opponents of it who argue that it inevitably stigmatizes the achievements of minorities. He said: 'It has given us a whole generation of professionals in fields that used to be exclusive clubs.' That blanket ascription of minority progress to minority preferences is condescending and false."[129] Charles Krauthammer wrote that the president's speech "gives emptiness a bad name. It is so full of touchy-feely, fuzzy wuzzy, multicultural pap that it caricatures the very pious race talk that Mr. Clinton pretends to decry and professes to transcend."[130]

Ken Hamblin wrote that "As a black man, let me bluntly reply to [President Clinton's] analysis. Mr. Clinton and the Democrats are exploiting the race issue to hold onto the majority of the African-American vote in the 1998 congressional elections."[131] The *Atlanta Journal and Constitution* editorially stated: "We don't think any of this [positive change] is likely to happen if the 'dialogue' continues in the way the president has begun it with his speech . . . and his appointment of a panel without ideological balance to examine racial issues. [The] president has started out defending old ways of dealing with old conflicts, as if nothing had changed in thirty years. Most disappointing is his insistence that we must continue affirmative action programs even though he admits they are flawed. [He] clings to outdated remedies that no longer fit the reality that he says he sees around him, policies that do serious damage to the very ideals of equality and fairness that he claims to support."[132] Editorially, the *Plain Dealer* said: "Clinton would have done more to advance race-related dialogue if, at some point during his much-anticipated speech, he had bothered to define exactly what it now means to be an American. And even a brief discourse on the values we 'really live by' would have proved illuminating, not only for race talk, but as a compass for an increasingly divided public. If Clinton . . . had touted the virtues of affirmative action while acknowledging the destructive nature of quotas, his speech would have been significant. If the speech had offered a formula for determining when a nation could and should end race- or sex-based affirmative action, it would have been ground-breaking. But Clinton did neither, and so we're left where we started: with no sense of direction or resolve."[133]

Ben Wattenberg wrote the harshest criticism of all: "so far it seems like an exercise in race-based, politicized, hypocritical Clintonesquery rooted in the view that a multiracial democracy comes about by getting Americans to check boxes about their race and by keeping score."[134] Debra Saunders, while generally giving praise to the president's efforts, did mention the following after noting that only 2% of UCSD's 1996 freshmen class were black: "When an end to preferences in grad school admission reduced the percentage of blacks at UC Berkeley's Boalt School of Law's entering class to 2 percent, Clintonia [*sic*] cried resegregation. So let us be candid: At UCSD, 2 percent is 'diversity,' and at Boalt, it's KKK. Clinton hailed diversity as an essential element in education. If that were true, students couldn't get a good education at Howard University."[135] Don Feder points out that "The American people are not ready for the 'honest dialogue' on race the president promised in his . . . speech. . . . Caucasians aren't ready . . . because they know they'll be called racists, the establishment's habitual response to whites who ask uppity questions. Minorities—who have been reared on a steady diet of entitlement thinking and playing racial blame games—are unprepared for a rational examination of this sensitive subject."[136] Linda Chavez wrote, "Clinton would have Americans believe that the country is about to return to the days of Jim Crow. The reality is . . . completely different. Under legal obligation to begin using race-neutral admissions criteria, the University of California law schools . . . experienced an 80 percent drop in black student enrollment for the coming fall. But what this means is that these schools have been using racial preferences to favor less-qualified applicants all along."[137] John Carlson opined: "The bottom line is this: The very people who stand up at the podium proclaiming that 'it's time to talk about race' are those least interested in admitting and acknowledging that most problems facing black people today are caused by other black people. That society suffers not from a shortage of black leaders and role models but from a frightening shortage of black fathers. That the overwhelming majority of those who terrorize and attack black people today are not white racists but black thugs. That drugs and crack are in the inner cities not because of the CIA but because of black street gangs. Far from telling the truth, the president and his followers are interested only in spinning it."[138]

Bold Praise of the Speech

Overwhelming the minuscule press criticism was the overt praise for the president and his ideas. This was done in news articles (primarily by quoting those sources with a positive word to share), opinion essays, and the bulk of editorials. Of the 112 opinion essays, sixty-two were overtly positive. Of the twenty-eight editorials, twenty-one were overtly positive. For instance, the *Baltimore Sun* wrote that Leroy W. Waren Jr., a member of the NAACP board, "praised Clinton for pointing out 'a very real and very serious problem.' "[139] The *Washington Post* wrote that "Rep. John Lewis (D-GA), a hero of the civil rights movement . . . said he was moved to tears. 'It was a very moving statement about race,' he said. '[Clinton] was not speaking just as some political figure but as a human being.' "[140] Highlighting the importance of the advisory board and the president's call for a national conversation on race, the *Washington Post* wrote, " 'I'm not suggesting that town meetings will solve the problems . . . but I am suggesting that a national conversation about race and ethnicity has not occurred in our history,' said John Hope Franklin . . . who is leading the panel."[141]

Papers also tended to cite local liberal activists. For example, the *Cincinnati Enquirer* found the "Rev. Darmon Lynch Jr., president of the Baptists Ministers Conference . . . [who] said his group is pleased with the president's decision to address racial issues.' " The *Enquirer* also quoted Chip Harrod, the executive director for the Cincinnati office of the National Conference of Christians and Jews: "We applaud the president, he said."[142] The *San Antonio Express-News* wrote that "Oliver Hill, president of the San Antonio branch of the [NAACP], applauded Clinton's defense of affirmative action as a method of overcoming racial and ethnic divisions."[143] The *Christian Science Monitor* quoted Robert Jackson, a Hartford, CT, plant manager, as saying, "this country has been in denial about the race problem. . . . With [Clinton] starting this, it's bound to get people to stop and think."[144] The *Record* (Bergen County, NJ) cited nine local "civil rights" or "community leaders," not one of which provided an oppositional point of view to the president's.[145] The *Courier-Journal* (Louisville, KY), cited five local citizens, none of whom took issue with the president, but rather supported his call for dialogue.[146] The *Richmond Times Dispatch* listed four local civil rights leaders, all saying the talk is good, but needs to be followed by action.[147] The *New York Times* listed ten New Yorkers, with only two suggesting skepticism at the outcome.[148]

Generally speaking, the framing of the press was positive, insisting upon readers understanding the speech as a positive step in fixing the racial woes of the nation. For instance, Matthew J. Glavin wrote, "It's a terribly useful initiative, one that ought to be conducted without a partisan political agenda."[149] The *Denver Rocky Mountain News* called the speech "one of [Clinton's] finest and potentially most important speeches. . . ."[150] Louis Freedberg wrote that the president's initiative "is the most ambitious attempt by any president to focus on race since President Johnson persuaded Congress to pass the Civil Rights Act of 1964."[151] The *Commercial Appeal* lead with this statement, "Memphians whose work focuses on race relations said they welcome President Clinton's idea for a national campaign against racism."[152] Editorially speaking, the *New York Times* wrote that "President Clinton put the nation's most important social problem where it belongs, at the top of the national agenda. His speech . . . was a sermon with little sanctimonious preaching. [I]t took political audacity to stand up for affirmative action. . . ."[153]

The *Capital Times* (Madison, WI) editorially stated that "Clinton displayed political courage and personal backbone [with his speech]. Sadly, if polls are to be believed . . . a great many Americans are unwilling to give him that credit."[154] The *Buffalo News*, editorially speaking, said, "To his credit, President Clinton has chosen to spark a year-long conversation about racial healing. . . . Clinton also wins credit for making clear his continued support of affirmative action. . . . Clinton has underscored a critical topic for our free and diverse society."[155] Rhonda Lokeman asserted "Clinton now deserves applause. . . ."[156] Arthur Dobrin and Warren Payton wrote that "the president is right in focusing on racial justice as one of American's greatest needs, and we heartily endorse his sentiment. . . ."[157] The *St. Louis Post-Dispatch* stated editorially: "His race-relations speech . . . was Bill Clinton at his best, using his own experiences and Southern roots to appeal to our best instincts against racism while scolding us for not doing enough to close the racial divide."[158]

This type of overwhelming press support continued throughout the two weeks following the president's speech. *USA Today* reported that "this is a defining moment for the civil rights movement."[159] The *Albuquerque Journal* editorially asserted that "If Clinton can reinitiate a dialogue that takes the nation to the next step of civil harmony, he will have earned a place in history."[160] Editorially speaking, the *Buffalo News* stated that "Clinton also wins credit for making clear his continued support of affirmative action while speaking in a state where it has been shot down in a public referendum. . . ."[161] Speaking of "the Southern black trinity: Christ, the Rev. Martin Luther King Jr., and President John F. Kennedy," Jonathan Capehart stated: "Now comes a man [President Clinton] who is carving out a frame where his likeness might one day be added."[162]

The *Baltimore Sun* provided an example of the press using UCSD students for positive presidential quotes: " 'As a minority, he spoke a lot of truth to me,' said Sang Bae . . . [who] was born in Korea. 'What I liked about his speech is that it was encouraging,' added Renee Moisa . . . [a] Mexican-American graduate. . . . 'UCSD has a history of rejecting racism and embracing diversity, and the president really spoke to our hearts,' said . . . Suhhil Plaha . . . from India."[163] The *Washington Post* also highlighted student comments. UCSD student Jane Lin was quoted as saying, " 'He talked in a way that involved the audience. He didn't lecture us. He made us think about what we can do.' "[164] And UCSD student Edie Tsao "praised the president for bringing his message of racial healing to a state that has rejected affirmative action. 'It shows he cares so much for us. . . . ' "[165] Of note is that all student examples come from minorities, although the bulk of the graduating class was white.

SUMMARY

Let us now turn to answering the questions I posed in the introduction to this book. Overall, the press frames matched well those used by President Clinton. The president framed his remarks to emphasize a "unity through diversity" that would be acheived through mutual respect and discussion. The press echoed this reasoning, but did offer critique by suggesting that the president did not go far enough in advancing programs and other government intervention to stop racism. In this sense the press acted to encourage the president to adopt specific policies.

How Did President Clinton Frame the Issue?

The frame used by the president is strong yet subtle in its presentation. The president essentially framed the issue as one of American unity through American diversity. In short, the phrase "unity through diversity" sums his speech well. Through this frame the president relayed several key problems. There are, he maintained, tension between persons of different races; although over 75% white, America is still a diverse country in terms of racial and ethnic groups, and this diversity should enrich the lives of every American. Thus, diversity should be promoted more than it has, since more diversity will bring less tension. This is so since the tensions between racial groups (primarily between blacks and whites) will be eased by promoting understanding of their differences.

The challenges of unity, of building "one community," can be overcome through educational and economic opportunities, and responsibility. According to the president, the problem of racial tension between Americans is a result of the lack of economic and educational opportunities for non-whites. Thus there is not equal opportunity; a direct result of lingering racism. Non-whites are not fully integrated in the economy. The key to economic success is educational attainment. Non-whites (except for Americans of Asian descent) are not fully integrated into schools, and this, too, is a result of lingering racism. The president points to the decline in minority enrollments at elite California schools after affirmative action is abolished. There is not enough responsibility being taken by Americans, either. Economically comfortable whites ignore the racial divide; poor minorities turn to crime and drugs. Moreover, the challenge of one community is not met since America is a fractured community. The races are not mingling, and instead look to those of their own race for their community support.

The president advances affirmative action as the solution to these problems. He sees this program as producing a fully-integrated American community similar to the military. However, affirmative action has been banned in some areas, so non-whites are being denied the opportunity to advance their educational and economic potential. The president suggests that evidence of this can be seen in the decline of minority enrollments in elite schools in states that banned race as a criteria for admission to their schools. According to the president, racism and discrimination emerge to replace withdrawn affirmative action programs, so minorities are being denied opportunities.

Affirmative action is linked with economic opportunity and the president links those who would oppose affirmative action with opposition to economic opportunities for non-whites. Affirmative action will lead to better education for nonwhites, and better education will lead to better economic opportunities. When minorities make more money, then all races and ethnic groups will interact more, thus becoming one community. To facilitate this interaction, the president proposes the national conversation on race.

How Did the Press, Responding to President Clinton, Frame the Issue?

The press advanced four sub-frames, each focusing on a separate issue, but each supporting the overall frame, unity though diversity: first, President Clinton's speech aggressively defended affirmative action; second,

Proposition 209 was framed as a destroyer of diversity through its abolition of affirmative action programs; third, the press advanced a definition of what a diverse and multicultural America should look like; finally, the press relayed criticism of the president's speech, but in such a manner that the speech was actually supported.

Overwhelmingly, the strongest frame used by the press depicted the president's speech as a defense of affirmative action. Bigotry, prejudice, and racism, the "bog of our racial discontent" remains a vivid problem in America, and these are the root causes of all minority problems. Affirmative action will solve these problems if given a chance to work. It will overcome the country's "racial and ethnic tensions" and her "fault lines." Ending affirmative action will have devastating effects on minorities since the country will be unable to resolve these problems. Affirmative action will solve these problems by forcing white Americans to interact with non-whites, thereby appreciating each other's differences.

Related to the defense of affirmative action was the framing of Proposition 209 as destroying the civil rights and economic gains made by non-whites over the past forty to fifty years. If fully implemented, Proposition 209 would deny non-whites the opportunity to advance economically since it would end the practice of taking race, ethnicity, and gender into account in school admissions and government jobs in order to rectify past discrimination. Republicans were depicted as the leaders in destroying affirmative action and, by extension, equal opportunity for all Americans. For no affirmative action would mean a return to segregation in higher education, and ultimately in the work places in America.

Diversity was framed in a positive light in almost every press report in which it is mentioned. However, diversity was implicitly defined to be based on skin color: the American rainbow. The press spoke for all Americans, saying "we believe in a multicultural society. . . ." This multiculturalism, too, was based only on skin color, as evidence when one paper, speaking of the president's advisory board, said that it was right for the president to choose "one of these and three of those. . . ." We see this in the general press response to the president's choice for his advisory board members. One paper wrote that the board represented a "nice cross-section of Americans." This representative cross-section was in skin color only, however. In the mind of the press, all schools, all public places, must represent the national statistical breakdown of the races and ethnic groups in order to be diverse: "at the same time, the number of Asians in those schools [that have abolished affirmative action] is rising out of proportion."

The press suggested that America should celebrate its diversity. However, the celebration is generally for skin color as evidenced by the press's focus on the composition of the students the president addressed and the president's comments about the students: "would you have learned as much if everybody sitting around you looked just like you?..." Another example of this is the columnist who stereotypically links skin color to production of certain music and varieties of food: cities without different ethnic groups are "white-bread" and thus boring; cities with ethnic groups that provide "food" and "sound" make a city interesting, however. The press also echoed uncritically the president's usage of the military as a model of a diverse institution. One paper went so far as to say that the "military could not function without attracting people from the spectrum of American ethnic groups," thus ignoring the fact that the military possesses a distinct culture that is forcefully imposed on all who enter.

The press framed criticism of the president's speech in such a way that actual oppositional criticism was minimized. In general, criticism of the speech took the form of praise for the ideas and criticism for not taking definitive action in the name of diversity. Liberal groups, called "civil rights groups" and "advocates for different racial and ethnic groups," were quoted as saying that the president stopped short of action and intimated that problems—racism and prejudice—still exist in the form of educational and economic discrimination, so why not take action? Ultimately, though, this is a white problem, since only whites can be racists: "Many blacks are tired of pleas from whites for more dialogue. After all, it is not blacks, but whites, who must come to terms with their racism. Show us what you are going to do, they say, instead of just talking."[166] The Des Moines Register demonstrated that racism is only a white problem as well: "Yet something is missing. Maybe it's jobs. Despite the robust economy, unemployment among African-Americans, especially those in low-income urban areas, often doubles, sometimes triples that of whites. For many African-Americans, and other minorities, race relations often boil down to myths and stereotypes whites have toward them."[167] Editorially speaking, the St. Louis Post-Dispatch stated that the president "can at least put forth programs that offer hope to those blacks affected by lingering racism. The problems run deep: Both business disinvestment and middle-class flight have devastated cities and left behind poor people with few means of escape. Addressing these social conditions would amount to an attack on racism. It would deprive outsiders of an excuse for making the most stereotypical judgment about the behavior of minorities and the poor living in impoverished cities." The answer provided by the press: "a much better and lasting response to both the legacy of slavery and racism is a genuine commitment to diversifying America's educational and economic opportunities."[168]

Upon Republican shoulders was placed the primary burden for criticizing the president's speech; usually by being shown as saying that the policy was "divisive." They were depicted as being aggressively against racial preferences and affirmative action, and thus by extension, against equal opportunity for non-whites. Primarily because of this, the president's "plan" would face "some big boulders." However, the importance of Republican criticism was often minimized by its placement near the end of news stories. In addition, the press framed the main problems of criticism being from the Republicans and not liberal civil rights groups. Liberal criticisms were justified in that they were acting for minority rights; conservative criticisms were cast as boulders on President Clinton's path to racial reconciliation. Although Republicans were shown to disagree with the president, they were usually given only a small portion of the article space. When a paper did include actual Republican criticism, it usually did so by including only one of the Republicans mentioned earlier in this chapter, and by using only one quote. So while nationwide the variety of criticisms were extremely limited, within any one paper they were even more so.

In general, there was bold praise from the press, and the president's speech was lifted up as a positive and strong policy statement. The president had begun a positive discussion on a serious topic. Racism and prejudice were depicted as major problems facing non-whites in America, so what the president intended was timely and appropriate. The press offered its own praise through numerous opinion essays and editorials, but it also found a multitude of different "civil rights leaders" at the national and local levels that echoed well the positive assertions of the press. Readers were led to believe that the president had taken the first positive step toward combatting racism and prejudice. Standing up for affirmative action, which was in danger of being destroyed by those who were either blind to this prejudice or engaged in it, was a valiant first step by the president.

Did the Frames Converge to Present a Unified Contextual Whole?

The frames of the president and press blended well. The president stressed unity though American diversity and the press echoed word for word this primary frame for viewing the speech. The president asserted that there existed tensions among the different races in America. Suggesting that affirmative action would reduce this tension by fighting lingering white racism, the president also asserted that it would help non-whites achieve a good education and higher economic status. This parity with whites would insure tranquility. The press framed the president's speech as aggressively defending affirmative action. Moreover, the press frame of affirmative action as good was so strong that those against affirmative action or supporting Proposition 209 were cast as opponents of equal opportunity, and even as prejudiced. The president had suggested diversity as an American strength, and the press did so as well. And, like the president, the press highlighted a notion of diversity that relied solely upon skin color for its character, not upon ideas. Additionally, the press wrote in such a manner to suggest that diversity means complete intermingling, but then implied that each racial and ethnic group is a separate culture, which suggests a separate existence.

While on the one hand the press wanted distinctive racial and ethnic communities—thus self-segregated—to avoid "white bread" cities, it was unwilling to admit that this cultural distinctiveness comes with the price of forgoing unity through common American values. True criticism of the ideas within the president's speech was insignificant; when presented, the salience of the criticism was minimized due to the overwhelming positive praise given to the speech. Although criticism from liberal activists was relayed, it was in the context of praise for the president's speech and condemnation for not going further by enacting new programs to combat prejudice and racism. In this manner the overwhelming majority of criticism actually supported the presidential and press frames.

NOTES

1. Originally available at: <http://www.whitehouse.gov/Initiatives/One America/about.html>.

2. The White House writes of this initiative: "President Clinton's vision of One America in the 21st Century is to have a diverse, democratic community in which we respect, even celebrate our differences, while embracing the shared values that unite us. To reach that goal, the president has asked all Americans to join him in a national effort to deal openly and honestly with our racial differences. The year-long effort combines thoughtful study, constructive dialogue, and positive action to address the continuing challenge of how to live and work more productively as One America in the 21st Century." Obtained from <http://www.whitehouse.gov/Initiatives/OneAmerica/over-view.html>.

3. Using Lexis-Nexis, a search was performed with the key word of "Clinton." Additional search terms included "initiative on race" or "one america" or "san diego," or "race." The range of articles ran from 15 June 1997 to 25 June 1997 inclusive. The search produced 214 articles.

4. William J. Clinton, "Remarks by the President at University of California at San Diego Commencement," *White House Virtual Library* (14 June 1997): 2 <http://www.whitehouse.gov/>.

5. Ibid.

6. Ibid.

7. Ibid.

8. Ibid.

9. Ibid. The press failed to mention the movement for independence, the successful grassroots movement to stop homosexual marriages, or the other ethnic and racial tensions that exist there.

10. Ibid., 3.

11. Ibid.

12. Ibid.

13. Ibid.

14. Ibid.

15. Ibid., 4.

16. Ibid., 4–5.

17. Ibid., 9.

18. Ibid., 9–10.

19. Ibid., 5.

20. Ibid. The president had earlier discounted the views of many white Americans: "I know for many white Americans, this conversation may seem to exclude them or threaten them. That must not be so. I believe white Americans have just as much to gain as anybody else. . . . And, by taking responsibility, our children can be judged as Martin Luther King hoped, 'Not by the color of their skin, but by the content of their character.' " (5)

21. Ibid. This seems to imply that more money can solve racism.

22. Ibid.

23. Ibid. This is already the case. Later when he cites lowered enrollments in elite graduate programs, he ignores that the students have already been beneficiaries of affirmative action at college, thus avoiding the question, at what point does one stop providing affirmative action? Also, this might imply that higher education would intentionally stop students from entering based on race—an absurd proposition given the commitments of college educators.

24. Ibid., 6. When considering the military, it should be noted that it is its own monoculture. Diversity in the military exists only in looks which, it will be shown later, is how the press defines diversity. The military is officially a color-blind institution.

25. Ibid.

26. Ibid.

27. Ibid., 7.

28. Ibid.

29. Ibid.

30. Ibid., 8.

31. Ibid.

32. Ibid.

33. Ibid., 9.

34. Lee Bey, "Jackson: Action Must Follow Words," *Chicago Sun-Times* (15 June 1997): 28.

35. William Douglas, " 'One America': Clinton Outlines Need to Transcend Ethnic Prejudice," *Newsday* (15 June 1997): A3.

36. "Clinton Attacks Racism," *Pantagraph* (15 June 1997): A1. Headlines often foreshadowed the interpretations found in the news article that followed. For example, the *Plain Dealer* provided readers with this headline: "Clinton Pleads for an End to Prejudice. . . ." The *Sacramento Bee* with, "Clinton: Cast Off Racism." Other headline examples include: "President Kicks off Anti-Racism Campaign" and "Clinton Opens Fight against Racism in U.S."; found in, *St. Louis Post Dispatch* (15 June 1997): A1 and *Des Moines Register* (15 June 1997): 1, respectively.

37. "Inclusion, Not Rejection, Will Spur Racial Harmony," *USA Today* (16 June 1997): A18.

38. Editorial, "A New Racial Dialogue; Talk, But Let's Be Honest," *Arizona Republic* (20 June 1997): B4.

39. Editorial, "Clinton Picks the Right Subject for Dialogue on America's Future," *Buffalo News* (18 June 1997): C2.

40. Lovell Beaulieu, "What Bill Clinton Could Do About Race Relations in America," *Des Moines Register* (15 June 1997): Opinion 1.

41. Russell Baker, "We've Got to Talk," *New York Times* (17 June 1997): A21.

42. David Broder, "On Race Issues, America Has Work to Do," *Buffalo News* (16 June 1997): B3. The specific study mentioned was not referenced.

43. Rekha Basu, "An Experiment in Race Relations," *Des Moines Register* (16 June 1997): Today 1.

44. Arthur Dobrin and Warren Payton, "The Path to Racial Justice is Via Education," *Newsday* (18 June 1997): A40.

45. Allison Mitchell, "Defending Affirmative Action, Clinton Urges Debate on Race," *New York Times* (15 June 1997): A1.

46. Allison Mitchell, "Clinton Goes to California to Launch Initiative on Race," *Arizona Republic* (15 June 1997): A19.

47. Scott Shepard, "A 'Conversation About Race'; Analysis; Affirmative Action Divide Is Apparent," *Atlanta Journal and Constitution* (15 June 1997): A12.

48. Shepard, "A 'Conversation'."

49. Julia Malone, "Clinton Says Race Programs Needed; He Uses California Speech to Defend Affirmative Action," *Atlanta Journal and Constitution* (15 June 1997): A1.

50. Larry Bivins, "Clinton Tells America to Destroy Racism's Final Walls— 'in Our Hearts,'" *Detroit News* (15 June 1997): A1.

51. Nancy Mathis, "Clinton Calls for Dialogue on Race; Despite Raw Emotions, President Insists, 'We Must Begin,'" *Houston Chronicle* (15 June 1997): A1.

52. Alison Mitchell, "Defending Affirmative Action."

53. Peter Baker, "Clinton Sounds Call for Dialogue on Race; President Argues for Affirmative Action," *Washington Post* (15 June 1997): A1.

54. Joan Biskupic, "Call to Renew Preferences Faces Resistance; Courts, Many White Voters Skeptical About Affirmative Action at Colleges," *Washington Post* (15 June 1997): A8.

55. April McClellan-Copeland, "Clinton Pleads for an End to Prejudice: President Comes Out Strongly in Support of Affirmative Action," *The Plain Dealer* (15 June 1997): A1.

56. "President Kicks Off Anti-Racism Campaign: Defends Affirmative Action, Opens 'Conversation' for Next Century," *St. Louis Post-Dispatch* (15 June 1997): A1.

57. "Clinton Opens Fight against Racism."

58. "President Addresses Racial Healing," *State Journal-Register* (15 June 1997): 3.

59. Sonya Ross, "First Steps on the Path to Harmony; Clinton Sets Agenda on Race," *The Record* (15 June 1997): A1.

60. "Dialogue on Race Begins," *News and Observer* (15 June 1997): A1.

61. Scott Shepard, "Clinton's Talk Seen as Risky Rescue of Affirmative Action," *Palm Beach Post* (15 June 1997): A4.

62. Ross.

63. Julia Malone, "Clinton Says Race Programs Needed."

64. "Clinton Opens Fight against Racism."

65. Editorial, "Plain Speaking on Race," *Atlanta Journal and Constitution* (17 June 1997): A8.

66. Editorial, "The Great Debate: Clinton Challenges the Country to Address the Racial Divide," *Pittsburgh Post-Gazette* (17 June 1997): A10.

67. Rhonda Chriss Lokeman, "Clinton Right on Race; President Uses Office to Issue Call for Healing," *Kansas City Star* (18 June 1997): C8.

68. Louis Freedberg, "GOP Trying to Ban Affirmative Action; Bill Introduced in Response to Clinton Initiative on Race," *San Francisco Chronicle* (18 June 1997): A1.

69. Shepard, "A 'Conversation'."

70. Mitchell, "Defending Affirmative Action."

71. Ann McFeatters, "Clinton Calls for Racial Unity; Who Will Listen?" *Denver Rocky Mountain News* (15 June 1997): A57.

72. "President Kicks Off Anti-Racism Campaign."

73. "Clinton Focuses on Racial Divide," *Tampa Tribune* (15 June 1997): Nation/World1.

74. Carl M. Cannon, "President Urges 'One America'; in College Address, Clinton Opens Discussion of Race. . . ." *Baltimore Sun* (15 June 1997): A1.

75. Peter Baker.

76. Beaulieu.

77. Julia Malone, "Clinton Warns Against Return to Segregation; Campaign Against Racism," *Austin American-Statesman* (15 June 1997): 1B.

78. Editorial, "Opening a Conversation on Race," *New York Times* (16 June 1997): A14.

79. Editorial, "Plain Speaking on Race."

80. Miguel Perez, "Clinton's Call for Dialogue Left Out Much of America," *The Record* (20 June 1997): L09.

81. Editorial, "An Atlanta Journal-Constitution Editorial; Crossing the Color Line," *Atlanta Journal and Constitution* (15 June 1997): F5.

82. McFeatters.

83. Bivins.

84. "Clinton Praised for Speech, Told Real Work Lies Ahead," *The Plain Dealer* (15 June 1997): A16.

85. Biskupic, "Call to Renew Preferences Faces Resistance."

86. Cannon.

87. Editorial. "Plain Speaking on Race."

88. Gregory Freeman, "Clinton Does Nation a Favor by Talking on Race Relations," *St. Louis Post-Dispatch* (17 June 1997): B10.

89. Trevor Coleman, "Clinton Picks a Strong Leader for His Racial Advisory Board," *Detroit Free Press* (16 June 1997).

90. Editorial, "Clinton Starts Reaching Across Lines of Race; A Year of Words Must Produce Results to Have Any Meaning," *Portland Press Herald* (17 June 1997): A8.

91. Biskupic. Emphasis mine.

92. Ruben Navarrette Jr., "Clinton Must Extend Talk on Race Relations Past Affirmative Action," *Arizona Republic* (20 June 1997): B5.

93. Ross. At the time of the president's speech, the University of California at San Diego student body was 45% white; 28% Asian; 27% latino; and 5% black, which would then fit in well with the reporter's observation. Yet the reporter makes it seem as if the numbers are not enough, perhaps because they do not represent accurately the national figures on racial makeup of the country?

94. Mitchell, "Defending Affirmative Action."

95. "President Kicks off Anti-Racism Campaign."

96. Nicole Gaouette, " 'Honesty' Key to Racial Harmony," *Christian Science Monitor* (16 June 1997): 3.

97. Editorial, "The Great Debate."

98. Shepard, "A 'Conversation'."

99. Mitchell, "Clinton Goes to California." These same quotes were also found in, William Douglas, " 'One America,' Speech Gets Conditional Praise; Policy: Critics from Left and Right React to the President's Plan," *Orange County Register* (15 June 1997): A16; Scott Shepard, "Clinton's Talk Seen as Risky"; Walter F. Roche Jr., "Warnings Accompany Praise for Speech: President Is Lauded, but Action Is Sought on Economic Matter," *Baltimore Sun* (15 June 1997): A7; "Clinton Focuses on Racial Divide," *Tampa Tribune* (15 June 1997) A1; Sonya Ross, "First Steps on the Path to Harmony,"; Sonya Ross, "Clinton Attacks Racism," *Chattanooga Free Press* (15 June 1997): A1; Anita Snow, "Clinton Attacks Racism," *Las Vegas Review-Journal* (15 June 1997): A1.

100. Brian McGrory, "Clinton Sets a Dialogue about Race; Pledges to Draft Specific Plan Over Next Year," *Boston Globe* (15 June 1997): A1. Gingrich's essay may be found in the *New York Times* (15 June 1997): D4 and the *Orange County Register* (17 June 1997): B9.

101. McFeatters.

102. Mitchell, "Defending Affirmative Action."

103. Shepard, "Clinton's Talk Seen as Risky."

104. "Some in GOP Oppose Racial Preference: Measure Would Bar Government from Giving Weight to Race or Gender," *Milwaukee Journal Sentinel* (18 June 1997): A8. Similar reporting by Holly Yeager, "GOP Bill Goes after Affirmative Action: In Slap at Clinton, Measure Would Halt Federal Preferences," *San Francisco Examiner* (18 June 1997): A1.

105. Mathis.

106. "Speech Gets Conditional Praise."

107. McGrory.

108. Peter Baker.

109. Editorial, "Valley Must Join Dialogue on Race," *Morning Call* (17 June 1997): A14.

110. Mitchell, "Defending Affirmative Action."

111. Jonathan Peterson, "Clinton Calls for 'National Effort' to End Racism," *Los Angeles Times* (15 June 1997): A1. Price's comment's given in "Clinton Attacks Racism," *Pantagraph* (15 June 1997): A1.

112. Norman Lockman, "Pollyanna Approach Better Than Hiding from Problem," *Montgomery Advertiser* (15 June 1997): F3.

113. Julia Malone, "Clinton Says Race Programs Needed."

114. "Clinton Praised for Speech." Comments by Cummings and Mfume found also in Walter F. Roche Jr., "Warnings Accompany Praise for Speech." Cummings comments also found in Sonya Ross, "First Steps on the Path to Harmony." Comments by Jasmine Gilham may be found in Peter Baker, "Clinton Sounds Call for Dialogue."

115. Les Payne, "It's a Strange Time for a Race Revolution," *Newsday* (15 June 1997): G6.

116. Peter Baker.

117. Randall Kennedy, "Where Do We Go from Here? Clinton Must Resist the Impulse to Control the Debate to Come," *Washington Post* (15 June 1997): C1.

118. Laura Mecoy, "Clinton: Cast Off Racism," *Sacramento Bee* (125 June 1997): A1.

119. "Dialogue on Race Begins."

120. Carrie Johnson, "Virginians: It's First Step: Words Need to Give Way to Concrete Action, They Say," *Richmond Times Dispatch* (15 June 1997): A18.

121. Julia Malone, "Clinton Warns Against Return to Segregation."

122. Gaouette.

123. Ronald Brownstein, "Clinton Continues Attack on Prop. 209 with TV Interview," *Los Angeles Times* (16 June 1997): A3.

124. Louis Freedberg, "President Clinton's Ultimate Challenge," *San Fransico Chronicle* (15 June 1997): 9.

125. Editorial, "The Great Debate."

126. Editorial, "A President Confronts Race," *St. Louis Post-Dispatch* (18 June 1997): B6.

127. Editorial, "Conversation About Race," *Washington Post* (17 June 1997): A16.

128. Although the numbers reported in the summary section show that there were a total of thirty-eight negative opinion essays, thirteen of those were classified as being negative because they assailed the president for not going far enough with policy suggestions. They did not, however, directly assail the arguments provided by the president.

129. George F. Will, "There's More to It Than Just Black and White," *Baltimore Sun* (18 June 1997): A11.

130. Charles Krauthammer, "Clinton's Fuzzy-Wuzzy 'Candor,'" *Cincinnati Enquirer* (20 June 1997): A14. Krauthammer also writes that it "is the proponents of affirmative action who want a single characteristic (and one irrelevant to academic qualification), namely race, to trump all the other. Assigning by race is the ultimate in unidimensionality, a sin that the president pretends to find in those who would judge applicants by every measure except race."

131. Ken Hamblin, "Clinton Exploits Race for Votes," *Denver Post* (15 June 1997): E3.

132. Editorial, "Clinton Race Initiative Offers Nothing New," *Atlanta Journal and Constitution* (17 June 1997): A8. This is a *rare example* of an editorial going against regular news content.

133. Editorial, "Clinton Offers Only Platitudes to Heal Racism," *Plain Dealer* (17 June 1997): B9.

134. Ben Wattenberg, "Mr. Clinton's 'Silly Little Boxes,' " *Baltimore Sun* (19 June 1997): A17.

135. Debra J. Saunders, "The Let's-Talk President Says Little," *San Francisco Chronicle* (17 June 1997): A21.

136. Don Feder, "Honest Dialogue on Race Impossible," *Boston Herald* (18 June 1997): 29.

137. Linda Chavez, "Clinton Muddies Race Waters," *Denver Post* (18 June 1997): B9.

138. John Carlson, "Candor Missing from Clinton's Speech on Race," *News Tribune* (18 June 1997): A9.

139. Roche, "Warnings Accompany Praise for Speech."

140. Peter Baker.

141. Ibid.

142. Kristen Delguzzi, "Clinton Plan Applauded: Focus on Racial Divide Pleases Local Leaders," *Cincinnati Enquirer* (15 June 1997): A19.

143. "Clinton Urges Nation to Bridge Racial Divisions," *San Antonio Express-News* (15 June 1997): A1.

144. Gaouette.

145. Don Stancavish and Matthew Mosk, "Can the Rhetoric, Observers Say," *The Record* (15 June 1997): A14.

146. Leslie Scanlon, "Race Relations Always a Focus of Louisville-Area Pastors," *Courier-Journal* (15 June 1997): A15.

147. Johnson.

148. Steven A. Holmes, "Many Uncertain About President's Racial Effort," *New York Times* (16 June 1997): B10.

149. Matthew J. Glavin, "Crossing the Color Line," *Atlanta Journal and Constitution* (15 June 1997): 5F.

150. McFeatters.

151. Freedberg, "President Clinton's Ultimate Challenge."

152. Mickie Anderson, "Memphians Cheer Clinton Race Focus: 'Ought to Be Some Soul Searching,' " *Commercial Appeal* (15 June 1997): A15.

153. Editorial, "Opening a Conversation on Race."

154. Editorial, "Break Through Race Cynicism," *Capital Times* (Madison, WI) (17 June 1997): A10.

155. Editorial, "Clinton Picks the Right Subject for Dialogue on America's Future," *Buffalo News* (18 June 1997): C2.

156. Lokeman.

157. Arthur Dobrin and Warren Payton, "The Path to Racial Justice Is Via Education," *Newsday* (18 June 1997): A40.

158. Editorial, "A President Confronts Race."

159. DeWayne Wickham, "Blacks Should Seize Lead in Clinton Race Initiative," *USA Today* (17 June 1997): A13.

160. Editorial, "Clinton Timing Apt in Resuming Dialogue," *Albuquerque Journal* (18 June 1997): A8.

161. Editorial, "Clinton Picks the Right Subject."

162. Jonathan Capehart, "Black & White: Three Views; Bill Gaining Spot in Black History," *Daily News* (New York) (21 June 1997): 31. I spoke with numerous Southerners and the only trinity I have consistently heard being spoken of by

blacks and whites is the Father, Son, and Holy Ghost. Where Capehart comes by this reference is not noted in his article.

    163. Cannon.
    164. Peter Baker.
    165. Mecoy.
    166. Freedberg, "President Clinton's Ultimate Challenge."
    167. Beaulieu.
    168. Editorial, "A President Confronts Race."

Chapter Four

Louis Farrakhan: "Remarks at the Million Man March"

Clean up, Black man, and the world will respect and honor you.
—Minister Louis Farrakhan

Like [Mark] Fuhrman and David Duke, Farrakhan is a racist. He is a bigot. His own demons, his own hatred, will drive him back into the shadows of public discourse.

—Dan Schnur

On 16 October 1995, Minister Louis Farrakhan spoke to a large gathering of Americans—primarily black men—gathered in front of our nation's capitol.[1] The subject of his speech was atonement and reconciliation. The speech was the culminating moment of the march and was delivered over the course of approximately two-and-a-half hours. The Cable News Network (CNN) reported that over 2.2 million households tuned in to watch parts of the speech. Commentators have put forth numerous reasons for the march, but the basic reason, according to the man who called it into being, Louis Farrakhan, was for atonement and reconciliation.

FARRAKHAN'S SPEECH

After a traditional salutation, Farrakhan highlights the historic moment of the occasion by making reference to those Americans of African ancestry who died during the times of slavery and times of community strife: "We are standing in the place of those who couldn't make it here today. We are standing on the blood of our ancestors."[2] The lack of a distinct legislative agenda differentiated this march from others at the nation's capital, and Farrakhan sidestepped the obvious political associations with such a large gathering by saying that the assembled men did not come at his request, but rather at God's request. Although politics are involved later in the speech, Farrakhan highlights early the complex blending of religious belief and political persuasion in his message to black men and the rest of America. Reacting to earlier criticism from the press and some black leaders, however, Farrakhan firmly establishes that he gave the call for this event, and that one cannot separate the idea from the messenger who presents it to the people.

Farrakhan assumes a divide between blacks and whites in America and states clearly that overcoming this divide cannot be done by focusing on cosmetic differences. Blacks, and Americans in general, are "wounded" and there is a "hostility now in the great divide between the people. Socially the fabric of America is being torn a part," and every race seems to be against every other race.[3] The solution to this problem must move beyond skin color, and Farrakhan encourages those listening to him to do just this. Ultimately, he wants to overcome the divisions he believes were imposed upon different racial and ethnic groups, but primarily upon blacks. Three complimentary frames reveal how he wishes to move beyond these divisions: responsibility for the plight of black Americans, visions of government, and atonement.

Construction of Responsibility

Farrakhan's notion of responsibility exists on two distinct, yet interanimated levels: the personal and the governmental. The personal level involves blacks accepting responsibility for what God tells them to do and for what black Americans do to each other. The governmental level involves the (white) government accepting responsibility for the lack of black unity and prosperity, and it involves white responsibility for the "plot" to keep black Americans divided. On both levels, and for blacks and whites, it involves accepting responsibility for white supremacy. Farrakhan implores black men to listen to God and accept responsibility for the state of their lives and their communities; importantly, with this responsibility comes accepting that God is now calling upon black Americans to examine their lives and to change from downtrodden to uplifted. He speaks directly to the death and destruction existing within many urban black communities across the country, and relays how he heard one black man tell him that he had atoned "to the mothers for the death of the babies caused by our senseless slaughter of one another." He continues, stating, "Black men, we got to stop what we're doing where it is. We cannot continue the destruction of our lives and the destruction of our community."[4] From the ashes of this destruction Farrakhan issues a call for cultural renewal. He states that the violence in black communities acts to feed the mind of white supremacy. Moreover, the production of degenerate films and immoral rap music contributes to the same. Farrakhan states simply: "Clean up, Black man, and the world will respect and honor you. But, you have fallen down like the prodigal son and you're husking corn and feeding swine."[5]

The problems facing black communities are constructed in part as a pain that blacks have endured. Farrakhan tells blacks to ask God why this was allowed. If one asks God, and listens, then one is ready to grow: "You are ready now to accept the responsibility, oh, not just of the ghetto. God wants to purify you and lift you up, that you may call America and the world to repentance."[6] Ultimately, though, Farrakhan makes it clear that every black man must accept a personal portion of responsibility for the condition of blacks in America today: "Who is it that has to atone? [Audience]: Me. Who went wrong? [Audience]: Me. Who got to fix it? [Audience]: Me. Who should we look to? [Audience]: Me."[7]

In constructing his notion of white responsibility, Farrakhan tells the story of Willie Lynch.[8] The purpose of this story is to explain the divisions that black Americans must overcome. It also acts to ground Farrakhan's later arguments about white America's responsibility for the black condition. Stating that black Americans are a fractured people, Farrakhan begins to recite the 1712 speech of Willie Lynch, allegedly a white slave holder who is said to have delivered this address on how to control black slaves:

Gentlemen: I greet you here on the bank of the James River in the year of our Lord one thousand seven hundred and twelve. First, I shall thank you, The Gentlemen of the Colony of Virginia, for bringing me here. I am here to help you solve some of your problems with slaves. Your invitation reached me on my modest plantation in the West Indies where I have experimented with some of the newest and still the oldest methods for the control of slaves. Ancient Rome would envy us if my program was implemented. As our boat sailed south on the James River, named for our illustrious King, whose version of the Bible we cherish, I saw enough to know that your problem is not unique. While Rome used cords of wood as crosses for standing human bodies along its old highways, in great numbers you are here using the tree and the rope on occasion.

I caught the whiff of a dead slave hanging from a tree a couple of miles back. You are losing valuable stock by hangings, you are having uprisings, slaves are running away, your crops are sometimes left in the fields too long for maximum profit, you suffer occassional fires, your animals are killed off.

Gentlemen, you know what your problems are: I do not need to elaborate. I am not here to enumerate your problems. I am here to introduce you to a method of solving them.

In my bag here, I have a fool proof method for controlling your Black slaves. I guarantee everyone of you that if installed correctly, it will control the slaves for at least 300 years. My method is simple, any member of your family or any overseer can use it.

I have outlined a number of differences among the slaves: and I take these differences and make them bigger. I use fear, distrust, and envy for control purposes. These methods have worked on my modest plantation in the West Indies and it will work throughout the South for you also. Take this simple little list of differences, and think about them. On top of my list is "Age" but it is only there because it starts with an "A": the second is "Color" or shade, there is intelligence, size, sex, size of plantations, status on plantation, attitude of owners, whether the slaves live in the valley, on a hill, East, West, North, South, have fine or coarse hair, or is tall or short. Now that you have a list of differences, I shall give you an outline of action—but before that, I shall assure you that distrust is stronger than trust, and envy is stronger than adulation, respect, or admiration. The Black Slave, after receiving this indoctrination shall carry on and will become self-refueling and self-generating for hundreds of years, maybe thousands.

Don't forget you must pit the old Black male vs. the young Black male and the young Black male vs. the old Black male. You must use the dark skin slaves vs. the light skin slaves and the light skin slaves vs. the dark skin slaves. You must use the female vs. the male, and the male vs. the female. You must also have your caucasion servants and overseers distrust all Blacks, but it is necessary that your Black slaves trust and depend on us. They must love, respect, and trust only us.

Gentlemen, these kits are your keys to control. Use them. Have your wives and children use them. Never miss an opportunity. My plan is guaranteed, and the good thing about this plan is that if used intensely and properly for one year, the slaves themselves will remain perpetually distrustful.

Thank you Gentlemen.[9]

Farrakhan says that the mind-set that evolved from Lynch's process resulted in blacks, "as a people" being torn apart and separated. Because of this, many blacks "are still under the control mechanism of our former slave masters and their children."[10] A first step toward reunification has been taken, however, because his call for the march has overcome many of the divisions within black communities. Thus one sees the young and the old, the rich and the poor, and the light skinned and the dark skinned, all together in peace.

Partial responsibility for the divisions facing black Americans involves the role that the U.S. government, supported by a lingering white supremacy, has in the situation blacks find themselves in today. Farrakhan does not use this construction of responsibility to say that all whites are racists and that all black problems result from white supremacy. Although there are elements of finger-pointing, Farrakhan's conceptualization is more complex, and offers listeners the opportunity to incorporate personal responsibility into their process of atonement: "the real evil in America is not white flesh, or black flesh. The real evil in

America is the idea that undergirds the set up of the western world. . . . [W]hite supremacy."[11]

Strong words—white supremacy—yet Farrakhan gives a specific admonition to his black audience members and by extension, to nervous whites who might be listening: "Now wait. . . . Before you get angry. You don't even know why you behave the way you behave."[12] Speaking directly to President Clinton and the United States Congress, Farrakhan states that "White supremacy is the enemy of both White people and Black people because the idea of White supremacy means you should rule because you're White, that makes you sick. And you've produced a sick society and a sick world. The founding fathers meant well, but they said, 'toward a more perfect union' "[13] Earlier, Farrakhan described the original draft of the Great Seal of the United States, pointing out that its representation of the peoples forming the new republic were all of European descent; Farrakhan concludes that originally only Whites were seen as constituting the United States. Using the notion of a more perfect Union, Farrakhan stresses that blacks and other minorities should be viewed as constituting the United States as well: "So . . . we're going to do away with the mind-set of the founding fathers. You don't have to repudiate them like you've asked my brothers to do me. You don't have to say they were malicious, hate-filled people. But you must evolve out of their mind-set."[14] The movement out of white supremacy is not for the benefit of blacks alone, and here Farrakhan shows well how a notion of white supremacy harms whites, and by extension, America:

[Because of white supremacy you are] not well. And in the light of today's global village, you can never harmonize with the Asians. You can't harmonize with the dark people of the world. . . . White supremacy has to die in order for humanity to live.

Listen . . . white supremacy caused . . . some White folk to try to rewrite history and write us out.

White supremacy caused you to take Jesus . . . and make him White. So that you could worship him because you could never see yourself honoring somebody Black because of the state of your mind. You see . . . you really need help. You'll be all right.

Any great invention we made you put white on it, because you didn't want to admit that a Black person had that intelligence, that genius. You try to color everything to make it satisfactory to the sickness of your mind.[15]

According to Farrakhan, this notion of white supremacy has "poisoned the bloodstream" of every major social and political institution in America. Although a strong statement, seemingly damning to whites, Farrakhan stresses that all whites are not villains. They are, however, trapped in a mentality that hurts them since it ultimately prevents them from coming closer to God: "White people have to come out of that idea, which has poisoned them into a false attitude of superiority based on the color of their skins. The doctrine of white supremacy disallows whites to grow to their full potential."[16]

Although whites are exhorted to accept responsibility for white supremacy, blacks must help this process along; and in so acting, Farrakhan advances a notion antithetical to contemporary notions of diversity— a modified form of separatism. He asks those listening to him to consider the quickly growing economies of Asia, and how the Asians are not complaining about the white race. Farrakhan states that Asians do not complain, rather they simply act: "He just relocates the top banks from Wall Street to Tokyo. He don't say, I'm better than the white man. He just starts building his world and building his economy and challenging white supremacy. They just do their thing. And white folk have to readjust their thinking, because they thought that they could master [everything] and nobody else could, but the [Asians] are mastering it."[17] As they master those elements that whites thought only they could master, the effect is to disrupt the process of white supremacy.

Farrakhan explains some of the more recent problems facing blacks in America today. He specifically names Jesse Helms, Mark Furhman, Newt Gingrich, Bob Dole, and Supreme Court decisions as some of the problems, but identifies others as well: "fratracidal [sic] conflict, drugs and dope and violence and crime. But we've had enough now. This is why you're in Washington today."[18] These problems call for more than government action, they call for blacks to look to themselves and to turn to God. Thus, responsibility for the condition of blacks in America is given not solely to whites to bear, but to both blacks and whites.

To overcome the remnants of white supremacy, Farrakhan suggests that blacks "don't have to bash white people," rather all they have to do "is go back home and turn our communities into productive places [and] decent and safe place[s] to live. And if we start dotting the Black community with businesses, opening up factories, challenging ourselves to be better than we are, White folk, instead of driving by, using the "N" word, they'll say, look, look at them. Oh, my God. They're marvelous. They're wonderful. We can't, we can't say they're inferior anymore."[19]

Movement Toward a More Perfect Union

In order to build unity, blacks must confront their relationship with the government. Farrakhan believes black Americans often see the branches of government as "entrenched in their evil, intractable and unyielding [ways, and that] their power produces an arrogance." In this arrogance, governments will be "blind" and "do all manner of evil to the person who points out their wrong."[20] He implores America's government to confess its crimes against black Americans, and then asks: "And why should I confess? The Bible says confession is good for the soul. [W]hen the soul is covered with guilt from sin and wrongdoing, the mind and the actions of the person reflect the condition of the soul. So, to free the soul or the essence of man from its burden, one must acknowledge one's wrong, but then one must confess."[21]

Some of the wrongs Farrakhan points to involve the killing of "prophets": Martin Luther King Jr., Malcolm X, and W.E.B. DuBois. For these sins, and for causing and continuing the divisions that plague black communities and other Americans, Farrakhan expects the government to atone. Atonement "means penance, expiation, compensation and recompense made or done for an injury or wrong."[22] It is in a spiritual, not retributive manner, that Farrakhan calls for the government to atone: "[Y]ou're not liberated until you can forgive. You're not liberated . . . until we can ask God for forgiveness and then forgive others. . . ."[23] Farrakhan thus asks the government to atone, and to change. This change involves evolving out of the limiting mind-set of white supremacy, and is accomplished by moving toward a more perfect union.

Farrakhan traces the idea of moving toward perfection to the U.S. Constitution: the country moves ever toward a completion always in the future. This understanding of a perpetual motion toward perfect union is used by Farrakhan to allow others to stop the finger-pointing and accept the political process in the United States as one in transition— imperfect, but moving toward perfection.[24] In this light, Farrakhan moves beyond calling the government evil. The marchers are not there to "tear down America." Rather, Farrakhan states: "We are gathered here to collect ourselves for a responsibility that God is placing on our shoulders to move this nation toward a more perfect union."[25]

A more perfect union of the country necessitates a union of the differences within the black communities across the nation:

There's a new Black man in America today. A new Black woman in America today. [F]rom this day forward, we can never again see ourselves through the narrow eyes of the limitation of the boundaries of our own [differences]. We are forced by the magnitude of what we see here today, that whenever you return to your cities and you see a Black man, a Black woman, don't ask him what is your social, political or religious affiliation, or what is your status? Know that he is your brother. You must live beyond the narrow restrictions of the divisions that have been imposed upon us.[26]

Atonement

Atonement for all Americans is the major frame throughout Farrakhan's speech. First, there is atonement for black America and second, there is atonement for the U.S. government and white America. Farrakhan speaks to President Clinton, and by extension, to all Americans, saying that blacks are "a wounded people," but that "America is also wounded."[27] The solution involves atonement, which is one of eight steps involved in a cycle Farrakhan identifies with working toward a more perfect union. So, black or white, this is the road all must follow in order for the nation to move beyond polarized black and white racial visions, and to overcome white supremacy. The eight stages to atonement are point out the fault, acknowledge the fault, confess the fault, repent, make amends, forgiveness, reconciliation, and perfect union. Taken together, these steps are intended to bring those that follow it into "perfect union with God."

The first step to perfect union is to point out the wrong. After the fault has been pointed out, one takes the second step, to acknowledge the fault and to accept the criticism. Farrakhan states: "To acknowledge means to admit the existence, the reality or the truth of some reality. It is to express thanks, appreciation, or gratitude."[28] The third step is confessing the wrong. The importance of this confession is biblically stressed as beneficial to the soul. The soul is the "essence of a person's being" and by extension, the nation's: "And when the soul is covered with guilt from sin and wrongdoing, the mind and the actions of the person reflect the condition of the soul. So, to free the soul . . . from its burden, one must acknowledge one's wrong, but then one must confess. First, you confess to God. [T]hen . . . go to the person or persons whom your faults have ill-affected and confess to them. But, if we want a perfect union, we have to confess the fault."[29] The fourth step is repentance. To repent one must feel actual "remorse or contrition or shame for the past conduct which was and is wrong and sinful. It means to feel contrition or self-reproach for what one has done or failed to do."[30] Farrakhan links this action with breaking the cycle of sin: "But to stop it where it is, and Black men, we got to stop what we're doing where it is. We cannot continue the destruction of our lives and the destruction of our community. But that change can't come until we feel sorry."[31]

The fifth step is action, the actual atonement. Amends of some sort must be made, and thus one must actually do something to make up for past sins: "penance, expiation, compensation, and recompense made or done for an injury or wrong."[32] Farrakhan asks audience members to "resolve today that we're going back home to do something about what's going on in our lives and in our families and in our communities."[33] The sixth step is forgiveness. Farrakhan eloquently states that "so many of us want forgiveness, but we don't want to go through the process that leads to it. And so, when we say we forgive, we forgive from our lips, but we have never pardoned in the heart."[34] By only giving lip service to forgiveness, we allow the injury to remain. Farrakhan pleads with his audience on this spiritual point: "My dear family. My dear brothers. We need forgiveness. God is always ready to forgive us for our sins. Forgiveness means to grant pardon for, or remission of, an offense or sin. It is to absolve, to clear, to exonerate and to liberate."[35] The importance of this, for both white and black America, is made clear: "[Y]ou're not liberated until you can forgive. You're not liberated from the evil effect of our own sin until we can ask God for forgiveness and then forgive others. . . ."[36] The seventh stage is "reconciliation and restoration." The burning question for those listening is restoration to what? Farrakhan answers, "To our original position. To . . . become friendly, peaceable again, to put hostile persons into a state of agreement or harmony. . . ."[37] Once you reach this unimpaired relationship, one then moves to the final, eighth stage, perfect union with God, and by extension, with each other. The eighth stage is for all Americans, although Farrakhan specifically addresses his black audience who live with cultural memories of racial oppression and slavery: "Oh, brothers, brothers, brothers, you don't know what it's like to be free. Freedom can't come from white folks. Freedom can't come from staying here and petitioning this great government. We're here to make a statement to the great government, but not to beg them. Freedom cannot come from no one but the god who can liberate the soul from the burden of sin"[38]

Actions to Take

In addition to the specific call to atone, Farrakhan asks his audiences to take other actions. Although blacks must accept blame for their ruptured communities across America, both blacks and whites must accept the responsibility to challenge white supremacy. How does one do this? Whites can do so by recognizing what they have done, and atoning. White America begins this process by addressing "the evil of slavery because that's the root of the problem."[39] Blacks can indirectly challenge white supremacy by "building his world and building his economy and challenging white supremacy."[40] This line of reasoning provides a strong call to action for Farrakhan's black audience: "Black man, you don't have to bash white people, all we gotta do is go back home and turn our communities into productive places."[41] There are actions not to be taken as well, actions that represent some of the very acts that Farrakhan asks blacks to atone for: drive by shootings, carjackings, producing culturally degenerate films, drug use, and the like. Acting to uplift the black men listening to him, Farrakhan states: "We're not putting you down, brothers, we want to pick you up so with your wrap [rap], you can pick up the world. With your song, you can pick up the world. With your dance, with your music, you can pick up the world."[42]

In promoting black unity and asking for action, Farrakhan lists direct actions for black Americans to take. Specifically, he wants his listeners to join some organization that works to help black Americans. He lists many: the NAACP, Urban League, All African People's Revolutionary Party, Nation of Islam, PUSH, Congress of Racial Equality, Southern Christian Leadership Conference. The purpose is to "become a totally organized people and the only way we can do that is to become a part of some organization that is working for the uplift of our people."[43]

Farrakhan also asks the men in the audience to help register over 8 million blacks who remain unregistered to vote. Echoing Malcolm X, Farrakhan states that whatever one's party affiliation might be does not matter. The focus should be on obtaining local results for your community. He wants a "third force. Which means that we're going to collect Democrats, Republicans and independents around an agenda that is in the best interest of our people. We're no longer going to vote for somebody just because they're black."[44]

Action involves more than simply becoming socially and politically active in local communities, it involves the spiritual nature of mankind, and in his final calls for action Farrakhan stresses this point. He asks that each person listening to him return to their local community and join a church or temple so that they might better develop their spiritual nature. Perhaps most striking of his calls to action is the pledge that he asks the men at the march to take. In unison, each man repeated after Farrakhan their love for each other and that they would begin to foster their spiritual, social, economic, and moral growth. This would be done not solely for self-benefit, but for the benefit of their families and for black people nationwide. The men pledged to go home and build up the infrastructures of thier communities. They swore not to use violence of any kind against their families or anyone, except to defend themselves. They pledged to stop the use of illegal drugs. They pledge to support black owned and operated businesses.[45]

Racism and Hatred?

Farrakhan took time in his speech to address issues of racism and anti-Semitism: "God brought the idea through me and he didn't bring it through me because my heart was dark with hatred and anti-Semitism, he didn't bring it through me because my heart was dark and I'm filled with hatred for White people and for the human family of the planet."[46] To President Clinton, Farrakhan states, "you spoke ill indirectly of me, as a purveyor of malice and hatred. I must hasten to tell you, Mr. President, that I'm not a malicious person, and I'm not filled with malice."[47] The underlying importance of overcoming attacks on his character are made apparent when Farrakhan discusses how he is pointing out the wrong with the country: "But, let me say in truth, you can't point out wrong with malice . . . [or] with hatred. Because, if [you do] then the bitterness and the hatred becomes a barrier between you and the person whom you hope to get right. . . ."[48] Directly speaking to those members of the press who have said that he is anti-Semitic, Farrakhan states that he does not like arguing with Jewish leaders, and suggests that it is time to sit down and talk with those leaders about how relations can be improved.[49]

THE RESPONSE OF THE PRESS

There were 107 articles included for review in this chapter. Sixty were news articles, forty were opinion pieces, and seven were editorials. The coverage of the speech is intermingled with general coverage of the Million Man March. In almost all stories about the march, however, Farrakhan plays a prominent roll. The press framing of Farrakhan breaks down into four distinct areas. Overwhelmingly, the primary frame through which the march and Farrakhan's speech is viewed revolves around the press's depiction of Farrakhan's character. Less sweeping frames include Farrakhan's message, the verbal exchange between President Clinton and Minister Farrakhan, and finally, the comparisons between Martin Luther King Jr. and Minister Farrakhan.

Framing of Character: Farrakhan the Racist, Bigot, Etc.

The press asked whether the "message of uplift could be heard effectively beyond Mr. Farrakhan's own record as an aggressive black separatist leader."[50] This question of whether or not one could separate the message from the messenger played deeply on the mind of the press. The *Star Tribune* led with this line: "So, we have begun to field test the proposition that you can separate the message from the messenger."[51] Dan Schnur stated that "the best way to separate message and messenger would have been for those million men to have realized that . . . there was no need to go to Washington in the first place, not to just find something that they've had within themselves all along."[52] The *New York Times* stated that the "march presented difficult conflicts between message and messenger. . . . But few welcome Mr. Farrakhan as the chief messenger, and most fear that he will gain legitimacy from the march."[53] Perhaps the need to disassociate Farrakhan from the march was that the press had prejudged him; moreover, they carried this prior judgment with them while making assessments of his speech and contributions to the Million Man March.

The press portrayed Minister Farrakhan as a racist, sexist, bigoted, Jew-hating "homophobe." However, these allegations were based not on what he said at the Million Man March (the very event which occasioned the coverage), but rather upon the prior opinions of the reporters covering the March. Thus, the reporters were relaying their prior opinions as news. For example, The *Boston Herald* stated that "Farrakhan, whose inflammatory racial and religious views shrouded the march in controversy, was a flawed messenger for racial unity."[54] With similarly-worded sentiment, The *San Francisco Chronicle* stated that Farrakhan's "inflammatory remarks against Jews and whites have provoked considerable controversy. . . ."[55] The *Boston Globe* held a similar view: "the Black Muslim minister, who has often made remarks denounced as racist, sexist, and anti-Semitic. . . ."[56] The *New York Daily News* stated that "Farrakhan's past slurs against Jews recently expanded to add Arabs, Vietnamese, and Koreans to the list of 'bloodsuckers' of the black community. . . ."[57] The *St. Petersburg Times* stated that "members of the audience either supported him outright or supported the event and decided to ignore what he has said to alienate Jews, whites, women, and gays."[58]

The *Times-Picayune* stated that although the speech contained "racial blasts" it did "not repeat any anti-Semitic statements that have characterized some of his past speeches. Instead, Farrakhan, who in the past has called Jews 'bloodsuckers' said it may be time to meet with Jewish leaders."[59] The *Record* stated that critics regard Farrakhan as "anti-Semitic, anti-white, and homophobic. . . ."[60] The *Seattle Post-Intelligencer* stated that "Farrakhan has been accused of preaching a racially divisive, anti-Semitic, black separatist dogma. . . ."[61] The *Austin American-Statesman* stated that Farrakhan had been attacked "as an anti-Semite, an anti-Catholic and a foe of women. . . ."[62] The *St. Louis Post-Dispatch* reported that in his speech "he omitted the harsh references to Jews, to Christians, and to women that have earned him the reputation of a hate-monger."[63]

Whereas news stories tended strongly to suggest that Farrakhan is racist, sexist, and so on, editorials and opinion essays came right out and stated this was the case. For example, Tom Teepen boldly wrote: "All honor to the many black leaders who refused on principle to participate because Farrakhan is a career bigot—racist, anti-Semitic, homophobic and woman-baiting [sic]."[64] The *New York Daily News* editorially stated that Farrakhan's "hateful history" is everything, and that it was this "context" through which readers should view his speech. The editors later enlarged this context to include what they called Farrakhan's "vile anti-white, anti-Semitic bent."[65] The *Los Angeles Times* had a similar editorial bent: "Farrakhan, the Nation of Islam leader and *provocateur*—known for making bigoted assertions about whites and Jews. . . ."[66] The *Chattanooga Free Press* editorially asserted that although Farrakhan "toned down his racism" for his speech, he was a "vicious hater and power seeker. . . ." Moreover, he was making "an obvious effort . . . to assume the role of top national leader of the black segment of the American population" even though President Clinton was critical of his "frequently expressed . . . hatefulness and bitterness."[67] Jennifer Dokes wrote that the qualities of "respect, admiration and pride" for the marchers is "rendered moot . . . by raising the name of Louis Farrakhan." This is because "Farrakhan carries too much baggage for people . . . sensitive to bigotry and hate. . . . Although he didn't show himself to be a hate-monger when he [spoke], he did flash signs of a messianic complex."[68]

Jane Ely boldly stated that President Clinton's speech earlier that day left Farrakhan "a sore thumb in the drone of his particular reprehensible, bitter and shameful racism. Are Farrakhan and his many hateful contentions and rallying cries defensible? No."[69] According to Ely, Farrakhan showed "stern refusal to even soften his dangerous rhetoric of hate and dissension. . . ." And asserted that the Million Man March "may have been organized in hate, but it produced an ocean of love. . . ."[70] Dan Schnur wrote that "Like [Mark] Fuhrman and David Duke, Farrakhan is a racist. He is a bigot. His own demons, his own hatred, will drive him back into the shadows of public discourse."[71] Stuart Taylor began his essay with this line: "Only people tortured by a terrible thirst could have been assembled in such numbers at the behest of so detestable a demagogue as Louis Farrakhan, the white-bashing, Jew-hating, violence-threatening, sexist, homophobic leader of the Million Man March."[72] Thomas Eagleton called him the "bigoted messenger" who exhibits "bursts of hate."[73] Bill Kaplan wrote that "The best that can be said about Farrakhan is that he is clinically disturbed, obsessed with numerology. The worst is that he is an ecumenical purveyor of hate. Farrakhan is virulent toward Catholics, Jews, women, homosexuals and whites in general."[74] Lars-Erik Nelson wrote that "it's all too easy too denounce Farrakhan's bigotry. His remarks about Jews are vicious and uncivilized. And he surrounds himself with black-shirt, Gestapo wanna-be bodyguards and thugs. . . ."[75]

Little by way of evidence was provided for any of the above accusations. The standard press practice was to give assertions as evidence; these assertions were to be accepted as true. For example, Kimberly Crocket stated that it "is the Farrakhan of hate and intolerance that America must confront. The Farrakhan who just days before the march spoke in accusatory and inflammatory tones against Jews. The Farrakhan who chides Catholics and gays and regards women as second class citizens."[76] The *Washington Times* suggested that Farrakhan's "heated speeches in the past have attacked whites as devils and 'subhuman,' accused Jews of conspiring against blacks and ridiculed black leaders. . . ."[77] Stuart Taylor merely stated, "This is the man who just days before had bared his fangs by smearing Jews as 'bloodsuckers,' a man whose history is littered with the vilest kind of hate speech and visions of violence against Jews and other whites."[78]

Farrakhan's Message

The press prejudged the messenger, and this prejudgment affected the meaning given to Farrakhan's message. Two meanings were advanced by the press: one, that of the march itself, and two, that supposedly relayed by Farrakhan. The message the march sent was well expressed by The *Tampa Tribune*: "The message of self-reliance, family values and community uplift could have come from a Christian Coalition flier or a Pat Buchanan speech. But it didn't. It came from Monday's Million Man March for black men. . . ."[79] In short, the march was described in positive terms, whereas Farakhan was imputed to have given a negative message. For example, Kimberly Crockett stated, "They said you couldn't separate the message from the messenger, but several hundred thousand black men did. It is not what we saw at the Million Man March that was so revealing, but the response to what we heard. Throughout Louis Farrakhan's two-and-a-half-hour speech, there was no resounding roar from the crowd. There was no rousing crescendo of approval. There was no thunderous ovation. He was not christened, as he had hoped, with the crown of a black messiah or presented the staff of a national leader."[80] The *New York Daily News* editorially condemned Farrakhan's speech: it "was a mind-numbing screed filled with biblical references, arcane numerology and masonic mythology. [It was] psychobabble of an eight-step program for atonement. He spent what seemed an eternity dissecting the word semantically, historically, even musically."[81] The *New York Times* suggested that Farrakhan had sounded an "aggressive and divisive note, calling for African-American leadership in building 'a more perfect union' but also attacking Lincoln, the Founding Fathers, president Clinton and 'the power and arrogance' of white America."[82] Another *New York Times* story called the speech "a booming, rambling keynote speech that threatened to eclipse the occasion. [Farrakhan] extended his remarks with arcane references to the Bible, numerology and black renewal, laced with his sulfurous interpretations of history and denunciations of white supremacy."[83] The *Plain Dealer* called the speech "a fiery and disjointed key-note address . . . [that] lashed out at what he called a culture of white supremacy in the United States."[84]

A similar judgment was made by the *San Fransico Chronicle*: "In a fiery and disjointed speech that went on for almost two hours, Farrakhan lashed out at 'white supremacy,' calling it the 'real evil in America.'"[85] The *Washington Post* stated that Farrakhan's "climatic speech began with a sharp attack on Washington, Jefferson and Lincoln. . . . From there [he] went on for more than two hours, charging at one point that white supremacy was at the root of the nation's suffering and had produced a 'sick society and a sick world.' [And although he] called the Million Man March a day of atonement for black men, his address often focused on the historic sins of white America."[86] In a different article, the *Washington Post* described Farrakhan's speech as "a fiery and disjointed two-hour keynote address [in which he] lashed out at what he called a culture of white supremacy . . . enjoined back men to take more responsibility for their own lives, declared that the Rev. Martin Luther King Jr. was a greater patriot than either George Washington or Abraham Lincoln, and engaged in a long-distance colloquy with President Clinton. . . ."[87] Tom Teepen wrote that Farrakhan's "rambling, two-hour-plus speech had large chunks of the crowd breaking off and drifting away, like an iceberg breaking up. He offered, here and there, self-help homilies perhaps admirable but unexceptional. NO obvious harm was done, but, disturbingly, [he] repeatedly lapsed into baffling nonsense. He wandered off into weird numerological raps, muttered about Masonic ritual and mystic symbolism and tendered something incomprehensible about the first four letters of 'atonement'. . . . It was at times kind of nuts-o, in part just dream-book superstition. . . ."[88] Although these descriptions clearly indicate the negative characterization of the speech by the press, they do not describe fully the two main areas (white supremacy and Farrakhan's separatism) and two minor areas (atonement and the pledge/action) covered by the press.

White Supremacy. An exception to prove the rule, the *Times-Picayune* provided the fullest explanation of what Farrakhan said concerning white supremacy, stating:

he hammered away at a persistent theme: that the "real evil in America is the idea that undergirds the setup of the Western world, and that idea is called white supremacy." Farrakhan . . . said white supremacy is destructive to both black people and white people. The idea means white people think they should rule just because they are white, he said. Speaking to white people, Farrakhan said: "That makes you sick. And you produce the sick society and a sick world." For black people, white supremacy means that "every great invention we make, you put 'white' on it. . . ." He said the notion has poisoned religion, education, politics, law, economics, social ethics and morality. "White supremacy has to die in order for humanity to live," he said.[89]

According to the *Boston Globe*, Farrakhan said " 'white supremacy' is the enemy of both blacks and whites, and at the root of the racial problems plaguing the country. 'This old mind of white supremacy has to die in order that a new mind can come to birth,' he said. 'Any mind of white supremacy is repulsive to God, and any mind of black inferiority is repulsive to God.' "[90] The *Chicago Sun-Times* wrote that Farrakhan "urged blacks to unify while railing against what he said was an American society that is oppressive, dominated by whites and intolerant of anyone of color. '(The) idea of white supremacy is you should rule because you're white,' Farrakhan said. . . . 'That makes you sick, and you produce a sick society and a sick world.' "[91] The *Asheville Citizen-Times* provided an example of the most commonly used white supremacy quote. Implying that Farrakhan was addressing only white America, the paper stated: " 'White supremacy,' he said, is the root of America's suffering. 'That makes you sick,' Farrakhan said, 'and you produce a sick society and a sick world.' "[92] The *Washington Post* simply said that Farrakhan charged "at one point that white supremacy was at the root of the nation's suffering and had produced 'a sick society and a sick world.' "[93]

The majority of the examples of press framing in this area were even less detailed. The *Boston Herald*, for example, simply said, "Farrakhan denounced 'white supremacy' as 'the real evil in America.' "[94] The *Plain Dealer*, mirroring numerous articles, stated: "In a fiery and disjointed key-note address, Farrakhan lashed out at what he called a culture of white supremacy in the United States."[95] The majority of articles touching upon this area followed suit: "In a fiery and disjointed speech . . . Farrakhan lashed out at 'white supremacy,' calling it the 'real evil in America. Freedom cannot come from white folks, nor from standing in this place to make a statement to this great government. Freedom comes from no one except the God who can liberate the soul.' "[96] The *St. Petersburg Times* wrote that Farrakhan addressed these "remarks to whites in general and in particular to President Clinton. . . . 'There's still two America's—one black, one white, separate and unequal. There is a great divide, but the real evil in America is not white flesh, or black flesh. The real evil in America is the idea that undergirds the setup of the Western world. And that idea is called white supremacy. . . . ' "[97] The *Seattle Post-Intelligencer* stated: "Farrakhan maintained that the idea of 'white supremacy,' which he said is as much alive today as it was in the days of slavery, is at the heart of the country's troubles and must be eradicated because it had created 'a sick society and a sick world.' "[98]

Separatism. The press depicted Farrakhan as being a separatist and divisive, with many papers simply asserting that Farrakhan was a "divisive" leader. Black and white America, Farrakhan was said to be stating, are to simply "go and do their own thing." The *New York Times* provided a common example of this when it wrote that Farrakhan sounded an "aggressive and divisive note, calling for African-American leadership in building 'a more perfect union' but also attacking Lincoln, the Founding Fathers, President Clinton and 'the power and arrogance of white America.' [The] appeal was by blacks to blacks and, if not explicitly separatist, spelled out no clear role for white people."[99] Jane Ely wrote: "Minister Farrakhan and his appeal for racial separatism have contributed way too much to the chasm of bile and distrust that has widened understanding among races and, especially in recent days, threatened to heat to a boil that could ever scar the base that is America. Worse, through his stern refusal to even soften his dangerous rhetoric of hate and dissention, Farrakhan clearly has shown his intent to pursue his relentless way as far as he can in separating the races and fomenting their distrust of one another."[100]

The *Los Angeles Times* stated that despite "the many issues that divide him from most Americans—including his racist comments, advocacy of black separatism, and his nationalist hybrid of Islamic scripture—Farrakhan's message of self-reliance and independence from white America strikes a responsive chord that many find lacking in other black leaders."[101] The *Tampa Tribune* felt that the crowd would be "unlikely to accept the separatist, anti-Semitic philosophy of . . . Farrakhan. . . ."[102] Thomas Eagleton admitted to confusion when he wrote, "When he talks about black men taking responsibility for their own well-being, accepting responsibility and caring for their families, he's as conservative as Clarence Thomas. When he talks about God sending the idea of the march to and through him, he is off on a flight of egotistical fancy. When he attacks the Founding Fathers, Abraham Lincoln and the 'power and arrogance of white Americans,' he puts on his separatist, nationalist hat."[103]

Atonement. Atonement was also mentioned by the press in a rather specific manner, a manner that minimized the importance of Farrakhan's message. The *Boston Globe* suggested that Farrakhan "urged the men to 'atone' for past wrongs and take control of their own lives."[104] The *Chicago Sun-Times* simply stated that the event was organized "as a day of atonement and unification for blacks across the country."[105] Editorially speaking, the *Daily News* stated that the men came "for a day of atonement and reconciliation" but that they "and the millions who share their quest for a better life deserve better than Farrakhan's self-aggrandizement. With the nation watching, he smothered their hopes with the psychobabble of an eight-step program for atonement. He spent what seemed an eternity dissecting the word semantically, historically, even musically."[106] The *New York Times* stated that the black men who attended the rally heeded a "call for personal atonement and racial solidarity" but then reported that Farrakhan's speech compounded "the controversy that led up to the rally over whether the message of uplift could be heard effectively beyond Mr. Farrakhan's own record as an aggressive black separatist leader. [The] crowd . . . seemed more intent on its own camaraderie and personal renewal than on the abstruse, passionate manner of Mr. Farrakhan's messages in urging black men to take the initiative in their lives and communities."[107] Ignoring Farrakhan's stress on the eight steps to atonement, the *Washington Post* stated that although "Farrakhan called the Million Man March a day of atonement for black men, his address often focused on the historic sins of white America."[108]

Action. Farrakhan made specific calls for action to the black men in his audience, the most dramatic of which was a pledge. Notable as the exception to the rule, the *Kansas City Star* offered perhaps the most complete descriptions of the pledge given by the press: "At his direction [Farrakhan] . . . the thousands before him pledged in unison to stop the abuse and disrespect of black women, the sexual abuse of children . . . to forswear drugs and to support the black news media and black artists. And to underscore the toll that violence exacted in the black neighborhoods, they responded with fists raised high to Farrakhan's call 'that from this day forward, I will never raise my hand with a knife or gun to beat, cut, or shoot any member of my family or any human being, except in self-defense.'"[109] The remainder of coverage was considerably less detailed. For example, the *San Diego Union-Tribune* wrote that Farrakhan "urged the men to go home and join black organizations . . . to take hold of political power, unite against racism, and cleanse black communities of crime, drugs and violence. [He] led the crowd in a pledge that 'from this day forward I will never raise my hand with a knife or a gun to beat, cut, or shoot any member of my family or any human being except in self-defense.'"[110] The *Des Moines Register* wrote that "Hundreds of thousands of black men shouted promises to forswear violence and improve their lives Monday in a revival-style chant led by . . . Farrakhan. 'I pledge that from this day forward, I will never raise my hand with a knife or gun to beat, cut, or shoot any member of my family or any human being, except in self-defense. . . . '"[111]

The vast majority of press descriptions contained even fewer details. Editorially speaking, the *Daily News* stated that at "his best, Farrakhan led the assembled in a pledge to care for their families and their communities, to take responsibility for themselves."[112] The *Record*, in keeping with the lion's share of press reports, glossed over Farrakhan's administration of the pledge: the men "heeded the call of controversial Nation of Islam Leader Louis Farrakhan [for a march] to reaffirm their commitment to their community and to atone for the behavior that has adversely affected it. 'I pledge that from this day forward, I will never raise my hand with a knife or gun to beat, cut, or shoot any member of my family or any human being, except in self-defense,' they pledged at the climax of the gathering."[113] Kimberly Crockett provides yet another example of distancing Farrakhan from the pledge: "the most significant call of the day—which was nearly lost by the length of Farrakhan's speech—was the pledge at the end of the rally."[114]

Minister Louis Farrakhan versus President William J. Clinton

The press framed Farrakhan's speech, in part, as a reaction to comments made earlier in the day by President Clinton in Austin, Texas, and was quick to contrast the two speeches and speakers: "Clinton's goal of inclusion has little in common with Farrakhan's separatism. . . ."[115] The *Washington Post* wrote that Farrakhan had "engaged in a long distance colloquy with President Clinton, responding to a speech on race relations that Clinton gave in Texas earlier in the day."[116] The *New York Times* stated that "Mr. Clinton has the same split verdict as many of his political peers, praising the Washington marchers for 'standing up for personal responsibility' but adding: 'One million men do not make right one man's message of malice and division. No good house was ever built on a bad foundation.' In response, Mr. Farrakhan said of the march, 'Whether you like it or not, God brought the idea through me.' "[117] In a different *New York Times* article, Farrakhan was depicted as taking "issue with Mr. Clinton's own speech on racial unity earlier in the day in Texas. 'Socially, the fabric of American is being torn apart, and we can't gloss it over with nice speeches, Mr. President, sir. . . . ' Complimenting Mr. Clinton for a 'great speech,' Mr. Farrakhan added with some bitterness, 'You spoke ill indirectly of me as a purveyor of malice and hatred.' The president had appeared to refer to Mr. Farrakhan in praising the theme of the Washington rally while adding, 'One million men do not make right one man's message of malice and division."[118] Adding only that President Clinton urged the Nation to " 'clean our house of racism,' " The *Plain Dealer* used the exact same wording as the *New York Times*, above.[119]

The *San Francisco Chronicle* reported President Clinton saying that " 'white racism may be black people's burden, but it's white people's problem. We must all take responsibility for our ourselves [*sic*], our conduct and our attitudes. America, we must clean our house of racism.' Although he did not mention him by name, Clinton also took a swipe at Farrakhan. . . . 'One million men are right to be standing up for personal responsibility, but one million men do not make right one man's message of malice and division.' "[120] The *San Diego Union-Tribune* stated that Farrakhan had "challenged President Clinton over an indirect slap he believed the president had directed at him earlier in the day. Clinton had not mentioned Farrakhan by name during a speech he delivered . . . but few doubted he was directing his comments at Farrakhan when he said, 'One million men do not make right one man's message of malice and division.' Farrakhan, addressing himself directly to Clinton, said, 'You honored the marchers, and they are worthy of honor. But, of course, you spoke ill, indirectly, of me as a purveyor of malice and hatred.' Denying he was bigoted, anti-Semitic or racist, Farrakhan added: 'I must tell you that I come in the tradition of the doctor who has to point out, with truth, what's wrong.' "[121] The *Des Moines Register* wrote that the president had "expressed disapproval of Farrakhan [and] clearly criticized [his] explosive rhetoric that has brought charges of anti-Semitism, sexism and bigotry. 'One million men do not make right one man's message of malice and division,' Clinton said."[122] The *Chattanooga Free Press* wrote that the president "was critical of the hatefulness and racism frequently expressed by Farrakhan, while being careful not to name him. Mr. Clinton said: 'One million men are right to be standing up for personal responsibility. But one million men do not make right one man's message of malice and division.'"[123]

The *Times Picayune* highlighted well the press-generated conflict between President Clinton and Minister Farrakhan:

Farrakhan lashed out against Clinton, who had spoken earlier in the day on race . . . stressed the need for better communication and understanding between white people and black people, equal opportunities for all Americans, better education and community-based policing. [He] made frequent mention of the Million Man march, praising its stated goals: "One million men are right to be standing up for personal responsibility . . . but one million men do not make right one man's message of malice and division," a reference to Farrakhan. Farrakhan responded . . . "socially, the fabric of America is being torn apart . . . and we can't gloss it over with nice speeches, my dear Mr. President. . . ." Farrakhan said that even though Clinton had spoken ill of him indirectly, "I must hasten to tell you . . . that I'm not a malicious person, and I'm not filled with malice."[124]

Minister Louis Farrakhan versus Reverend Martin Luther King Jr.

In addition to framing Farrakhan's speech as a rejoinder to President Clinton's speech, the press also sought to compare Minster Farrakhan's speech with the speech given by Martin Luther King Jr. in 1963. Although the context and purposes for the two marches and speeches were vastly different, the press pointedly judged Farrakhan's effort against that of King. The *Chicago Sun-Times* wrote that the "event was the sixth-largest gathering in the capital's history and surpassed the 250,000 attendance at Martin Luther King's 1963 March on Washington."[125] The *San Francisco Chronicle* reported a similar view: "by almost any standard its organizers could claim success. The crowds easily exceeded the 250,000 people who assembled for the 1963 March on Washington, which many regard as the high point of the modern civil rights movement."[126]

Aside from raw numbers, the press forced comparisons between the press-implied purpose of King's speech and the press-implied purpose of Farrakhan's speech. Editorially speaking, the *Daily News* described well this comparison: "[Farrakhan's] goal seemed to be his own inauguration as the leader of black America. Contrast that with the greatest moment in civil rights history, the 1963 March on Washington. There the Rev. Martin Luther King Jr. spoke briefly but left the nation with an enduring dream. For it to be realized, there must be a healing of the races. Despite repeating his call for dialogue with Jews, Farrakhan's vile anti-white, anti-Semitic bent disqualifies him."[127]

The *New York Times* stated that the "throng of 400,000 . . . was an impressive measure of the occasion. This crowd, virtually all black men, exceeded by more than 100,000 the integrated turnout in the 1963 civil rights march on Washington led by Dr. Martin Luther King Jr. Mr. Farrakhan appeared to offer no oratorical competition to Dr. King, who delivered his historic 'I have a dream' speech in fifteen minutes."[128] The *Plain Dealer* expressed similar sentiments: "Farrakhan's long speech before his Million Man March . . . was almost anticlimactic. He spoke to a huge but thinning throng, as thousands streamed away. It was not the emotional equivalent of Dr. Martin Luther King Jr.'s 'I Have a Dream' speech thirty-two years ago."[129] The *Washington Post* stated: "Viewed from a cultural and sociological perspective, there was a certain momentum, if not inevitability, to the Million Man March that had little to do with Farrakhan. Just as the 1963 march was held at a critical early point in that era's civil rights movement, yesterday's rally came at a time when race relations had returned to the forefront of the national debate."[130]

The *Chicago Sun-Times* boldly summed up the Million Man March this way: "That many people . . . assembling in peace to pledge atonement for their shortcomings, was inspiring. Oh, that the message from Minister Louis Farrakhan, leader of the Nation of Islam, had risen to the occasion. Unfortunately, he failed. Would that he had taken a lead from the 'I Have Dream' speech of Dr. Martin Luther King Jr. and raised his voice in an uplifting tone. Farrakhan spoke 150 minutes . . . of divisiveness, contrasted with the 19 minutes of 'bring us together' oratory of Dr. King. By all measurements, less was better."[131] Greg Tucker wrote that the Nation of Islam had gained some respect through its programs which rid some neighborhoods of drugs and gangs, but "their leader's desire for racial separation runs counter to the dream of the Rev. Martin Luther King spoke of nearly thirty years ago—a dream that many, black and white, still hold."[132]

Bill Maxwell devoted an entire editorial to comparisons between Farrakhan and King. The key lines were drawn:

King . . . who spoke to a mass that included blacks and whites, boldly sought peace. He wanted to heal the nation's wounds, to bring the nation's races together. He wanted to give African-Americans, long denied full citizenship, legal rights and access to the American Dream that had been kept out of their reach by Jim Crow laws and racist sentiments everywhere. Farrakhan . . . too, seeks peace—a peace among black men. King's vision of America was conciliatory and inspired by forging alliances between blacks and whites and Jews and others. Farrakhan, while acknowledging the injuriousness of racism and white supremacy, asks for his followers to turn away from dependence on others and to build alliances among themselves.[133]

Laura Ingraham asked if we ought to worry about Farrakhan's brand of civil rights. She answered her own question, "Yes, because unlike cultural and political leaders who have attempted to close the racial divide (most notably Martin Luther King), Mr. Farrakhan . . . sees racial balkanization as a natural and desirable phenomenon."[134] The *St. Louis Post-Dispatch* summed well the framing of the press: "America has left behind the hallowed memory of Martin Luther King when blacks and whites assembled to share King's vision of all races walking hand in hand. King's 'I Have a Dream' speech would have sounded out of place at the Million Man March. Farrakhan is not the new Dr. King."[135]

SUMMARY

Let us now turn to answering the questions I posed in the introduction to this book. The frames within Louis Farrakhan's speech and those within the press coverage of the speech are noticably different.[136] Farrakhan focuses on the process blacks and whites must go through to reach racial unity. The press focuses upon Farrakhan's character.

How Did Minister Farrakhan Frame the Issue?

Farrakhan's speech presents his audience with a complex blending of religion and politics. Several times in his speech he reminds audience members that he gave the call to march on Washington. He had seen the divisions between blacks and whites in America, and sees black communities across the country as the place to begin healing the divisions between the races. His speech is framed in such a manner that the major problem is depicted as the racial division brought on by a lingering white supremacy. Both blacks and whites must work to eliminate this. This is a complex problem and calls for multiple solutions that must be enacted at the same time.

The division can be overcome in part by blacks and whites accepting responsibility for their part in black America's problems. At the personal level, blacks must follow God and stop hurting each other. Farrakhan likens many blacks to the Prodigal Son. They are eating husks of corn when all they have to do is repent, clean up, and rejoin the feast at God's table. However, following God involves a cultural renewal. Whites, too, must take responsibility, but at the level of government. White supremacy, notably represented by the Willie Lynch story, is responsible for dividing blacks.

A lingering white supremacy harms both whites and blacks. Whites have "whitened" history and religion; blacks have become fractured and "put down." Both races must evolve, as part of the movement toward the more perfect American Union, out of white supremacy. Farrakhan does not imply that the races cannot live together, rather he suggests that they each have their own work to do before coming together in the evolution of a more perfect union.

To reach this perfect union, blacks must face the government that has caused and is causing the division within black communities across the land. Before healing can occur, the government must atone for its past wrongs, namely, white supremacy. This is the unfinished business facing whites as well. Whites must look to the past of slavery and atone. Once this happens, however, blacks must accept this, forgive, and move on. While waiting for the government to atone, black Americans must also atone. This mutual process of growth involves eight stages: point out the fault, acknowledge the fault, confess the fault, repent, make amends, forgiveness, reconciliation, and perfect union. Blacks must look to themselves during this process, and should not look to whites or the government until this process is undertaken. They must look to themselves as a source of strength.

Farrakhan's understanding of action involves more than atonement, however. Blacks must accept blame for troubled communities, with whites and blacks accepting blame for the lingering white supremacy. Blacks must also join organizations that promote black unity. As a people, they must organize to help themselves. All these actions involve spiritual renewal: join a church, synagogue, temple, and take the pledge. The pledge is the cornerstone of Farrakhan's envisioned change. Black men are asked to resume leadership of their families and communities, acting as mentors and protectors.

How Did the Press, Responding to Minister Farrakhan, Frame the Issue?

Few papers described Farrakhan's speaking ability. One positive exception was the *Kansas City Star*, which stated that Farrakhan spoke in a voice that could "flow like a river of silk and then suddenly ignite as if fed by gasoline and a single match. . . ."[137] Usually, when Farrakhan's ability was mentioned, it was to call the speech "rambling" and "long." Overwelmingly, the press framed Farrakhan's speech as a critique of his character. However, the press had prejudged him, and used this judgment to define his character during the march. The press said Farrakhan was a racist, a bigot, a sexist, an anti-Semite, and a "homophobe." These judgments were based solely on the press's prior opinon on Minister Farrakhan, not on what he said in his speech. News articles were subtle in how they charged Farrakhan with racism, sexism, etc. They would often quote the words of others, offering no supporter to rebut the charges, or they would simply assert that others had said so: "often made remarks denounced as racist, sexist and anti-Semitic. . . ." Opinon essays and editorials simply stated he was racist, ect.: "A vicious hater and power seeker who toned down his racism" for this speech. Because Farrakhan was framed as so vile a man, the press had to ask if one could separate the message from the messenger, since Farrakhan was obviously a "flawed messenger for racial unity."

In this manner the press actually reported on two messeges. One was the message from the march and the other was what the press said Farrakhan's message to the marchers was. Farrakhan's message was racist. The message of the march, which the marchers were to have separated from the messenger, was of unity and brotherhood. If one focused on Farrakhan, then the "respect, admiration and pride" for the marchers would be "rendered moot." Farrakhan's message was depicted as being narrowly focused on white supremacy and separatism. Black and white America should simply go on and "do their own thing." However, according to the press, "very few" of the marchers failed to "discard most of . . . Farrakhan's divisive rhetoric."

Little was mentioned of Farrakhan's sophisticated explanation of atonement. Although atonement was very often given as the reason for the march, Farrakhan had been separated from the march, and thus separated from the message of atonement. Little was mentioned of Farrakhan's detailed call for action or the pledge he administered to the gathered men. If the pledge was mentioned, Farrakhan was separated from it.

The press also focused on a long distance exchange between President Clinton and Minister Farrakhan. The president was depicted as giving a message of inclusion in contrast to Minister Farrakhan's message of separatism. The president was shown to separate the marchers from Farrakhan, and Farrakhan was shown as defending himself as the organizer of the march. Articles framing the speech in this manner mainly cast Farrakhan as responding to President Clinton's speech, saying that the marchers are noble and should not be confused with "one man's message of malice and division."

Finally, the press forced comparisions between Minister Farrakhan and Reverend Martin Luther King Jr. King's speech was short and inclusive whereas Farrakhan's was long and advocated separatism. King focused on unity; Farrakhan focused on black nationalism. King was good; Farrakhan was bad.

Did the Frames Converge to Present a Unified Contextual Whole?

At no time did the frames of the press accurately match those presented by Farrakhan. Overall, the press took an extraordinary negative view of Farrakhan. Of forty opinion essays, two were positive concerning the event, eight took a more or less objective view of the event, and a full thirty were negative, focusing upon Farrakhan. Five of the seven editorials were distinctly negative toward Farrakhan, with two taking a more objective view of the event. Overall, Farrakhan garnered the attention from the march, but he was villainized.

Farrakhan would have blacks and whites in America walk separate paths on the road to forgiveness and unity. Blacks must look first to themselves, atone, and then forgive. Whites must do the same, with blacks accepting white atonement. Farrakhan spoke at length to the divisions between and within black communities acrosss the nation. He relayed the Willie Lynch story to highlight the importance of overcoming these divisions for black healing and unity. The press ignored this story, and instead cast Farrakhan as pushing for black separatism, even though he did not advocate this in his speech.

Farrakhan saw that the healing of black hurts must come from two main sources. First, blacks must atone for their own sins, and then walk away from the actions that have hurt black communities across the nation. They must also accept the second source of black healing: government and white atonement for white supremacy. Only when these actions are taken can healing occur. The press mentioned atonement, but separated it from its spiritual dimensions and from the notion of a white supremacy that hurts both blacks and whites. When white supremacy is mentioned, it is used to impugn Farrakhan's character, casting him as a name-calling demagogue trying to denigrate white Americans.

The press brought with it judgments made prior to Farrakhan's speech. It then relayed these judgments as news about the march. Whereas Farrakhan's march message was a complex blend of spirtual and secular action, the press only relayed Farrakhan's message through a narrow secular light that was tainted by the press's own prejudgment of Farrakhan.[138]

NOTES

1. Minister Louis Farrakhan is the national representative of the Honorable Elijah Muhammad and the Nation of Islam. The Nation of Islam was founded in 1930 by Fard Muhammad and developed into a national organization under the leadership of Elijah Muhammad between the years of 1934 and 1975. Farrakhan has been associated with the Nation of Islam since 1955. From 1956 to 1965

Farrakhan was the Minister of Muhammad Temple No. 11 in Boston, Massachusetts. In 1965 he was appointed as Minister to Temple No. 7 in New York City. He has helped to build mosques and formal study groups in over eighty cities in America. In 1979, he published *The Final Call*. For additional information on Minister Farrakhan and the Nation of Islam, see the Nation of Islam Web site <http://www.noi.org> and *The Final Call* (<http://www.finalcall.com/>).

2. Louis Farrakhan, "Million Man March Speech." Transcript from Minister Louis Farrakhan's remarks at the Million Man March <http://www.cgi.cnn.com/US/9510/megamarch/10–16/transcript/index.html>.

3. Ibid., 7.

4. Ibid., 6.

5. Ibid., 13.

6. Ibid., 9.

7. Ibid., 10–11.

8. The authenticity of the Willie Lynch speech is dubious at best. For information on the speech itself see the Web site provided by the University of Missouri–St. Louis Thomas Jefferson Library Reference Department: <http://www.umsl.edu/services/library/blackstudies/lynch.htm>. The library states that the provenance "of the following text is unclear. This speech was purportedly given by a slave owner, William Lynch, on the bank of the James River in 1712. Analysis now suggests that the document was written in the mid to late twentieth Century." See <http://www.umsl.edu/services/library/blackstudies/narrate.htm> for an analysis of the speech.

9. Farrakhan, 4. The Lynch speech may be found at numerous Web sites. No original version of the text seems to be in existence, although each site I have found the speech on asserts that it is authentic. However, no evidence is provided, nor are any sources listed for the speech. This copy, similar to the one used by Farrakhan and countless others on the web, was taken from a now defunct Web site. Sites where the speech may be found include <http://www.duboislc.com/html/WillieLynch.html>; <http://www.blackspeak.com/speeches/slavecontrol.htm>; <http://www.muhammadspeaks.com/WillieLynch.html>; <http://www.blackmind.com/MVSG/willie.html>; <http://www.uky.edu/StudentOrgs/AWARE/archives/lynch.html>.

10. Ibid.

11. Ibid., 11.

12. Ibid.

13. Ibid.

14. Ibid.

15. Ibid., 11–12.

16. Ibid., 12–13.

17. Ibid., 13.

18. Ibid.

19. Ibid.

20. Ibid., 5.

21. Ibid.

22. Ibid.

23. Ibid., 6–7.

24. Ibid., 3.

25. Ibid.

26. Ibid., 5.

27. Ibid., 7.

28. Ibid., 5.

29. Ibid.

30. Ibid., 6.

31. Ibid.

32. Ibid.

33. Ibid.

34. Ibid.

35. Ibid.

36. Ibid.

37. Ibid.

38. Ibid., 7.

39. Ibid., 14.

40. Ibid., 13.

41. Ibid.

42. Ibid.

43. Ibid., 14.

44. Ibid.

45. Ibid., 16.

46. Ibid., 3.

47. Ibid., 7.

48. Ibid., 8.

49. Ibid., 15.

50. Francis X. Clines, "The March on Washington: Overview," *New York Times* (17 October 1995): A1.

51. Tom Teepen, "Separating Message from Messenger at the Million Man March," *Star Tribune* (21 October 1995): A18.

52. Dan Schnur, "The March Wasn't Really Necessary," *San Francisco Chronicle* (18 October 1995): A23.

53. R.W. Apple Jr., "The March on Washington: News Analysis: Ardor and Ambiguity," *New York Times* (17 October 1995): A1. An assertion never proven.

54. Andrew Miga, "On the March! Black Unity Rally Draws Thousands to Nation's Capital," *Boston Herald* (17 October 1995): A1.

55. Louis Freedberg, Teresa Moore, and Aurelio Rojas, "Black Men Heed Unity Call," *San Francisco Chronicle* (17 October 1995): A1.

56. Zachary R. Dowdy, "Black Men Hear Appeal to Action," *Boston Globe* (17 October 1995): A1.

57. William Goldschlag, Dave Eisenstadt, and Raphael Sugarman, "Farrakhan Foes Quick to React Minister Should Atone, They Say," *Daily News* (17 October 1995): 23.

58. David Dahl and Jennifer Thomas, "The Million Man March," *St. Petersburg Times* (17 October 1995): A1.

59. Holly Yeager, "Leaders May Make Amends," *Times-Picayune* (17 October 1995): A4.

60. William Douglass and Monte R. Young, "Strength in Numbers: Largest Ever Rally of Blacks in the Capital," *The Record* (17 October 1995): A1.

61. Christopher Hanson, "Black Men Make a Stand: Hearts Are Joined in a Mass Pledge of Responsibility," *Seattle Post-Intelligencer* (17 October 1995): A1.

62. R.W. Apple Jr., "Men on Mall Push Race Issue to the Fore," *Austin American-Statesman* (17 October 1995): A1.

63. Bill Lambrecht, "The Minister, the March, and the Mission," *St. Louis Post-Dispatch* (22 October 1995): B1. These specific assertions contained within news accounts may also be found in an additional twenty news stories.

64. Teepen.

65. Editorial, "Minister Me Holds Court," *Daily News* (17 October 1995): 32.

66. Editorial, "Resonance Across an Entire Nation: March Sounds a Message to All Americans and Their Leaders," *Los Angeles Times* (17 October 1995): B8.

67. "The Washington March," *Chattanooga Free Press* (17 October 1995).

68. Jennifer Dokes, "Don't Let Farrakhan Overshadow Marchers' Earned Respect, Pride," *Arizona Republic* (18 October 1995): B4.

69. Jane Ely, "Clinton Had a Powerful Message, Too," *Houston Chronicle* (18 October 1995): 22.

70. Ibid.

71. Schnur.

72. Stuart Taylor Jr., "An Omen of Hate, Not Hope," *Connecticut Law Tribune* (23 October 1995): 11.

73. Thomas Eagleton, "The March Others Could Not Produce," *St. Louis Post-Dispatch* (22 October 1995): B3.

74. Bill Kaplan, "Return to '20s No Roaring Success for Society, Blacks," *Wisconsin State Journal* (25 October 1995): A11.

75. Lars-Erik Nelson, "Farrakhan Preached A Positive Message," *Daily News* (18 October 1995): 31.

76. Kimberly Crocket, "Black Men Took Positive Message without Anointing Farrakhan," *Phoenix Gazette* (18 October 1995): B5.

77. Brian Blomquist, "Farrakhan to Support Candidates Accepting 'Third Power' Agenda," *Washington Times* (19 October 1995): A1.

78. Taylor. Later in his essay Taylor does provide specific quotes from specific speeches given by Farrakhan. However, they fail to substantiate the claims made by Taylor in his article. Of note is that Taylor is *only one of two authors of the 107 read for this chapter that actually cites sources*. The best, although isolated, example of this was provided by Robert A. Maranto, "The Farrakhan-Duke Parallels," *Times-Picayune* (24 October 1995): B5.

79. William March, "March Meaning: Enormous Turnout Raises Questions About Political Direction of Blacks," *Tampa Tribune* (19 October 1995): Nation/World 1.

80. Crockett.

81. Editorial, "Minister Me Holds Court."

82. Apple, "The March on Washington."

83. Clines.

84. "Black Men Hear Call for Unity: Farrakhan Leads Throng in Exuberant March," *The Plain Dealer* (17 October 1995): A1.

85. Freedberg et al.

86. David Maraniss, "A Clear Day, A Cloud of Contradictions: At Event Des-

ignated for Reconciliation, Its Organizer Stresses White America's Sins," *Washington Post* (17 October 1995): A19.

87. Michael A. Fletcher and Hamil R. Harris, "Black Men Jam Mall for a 'Day of Atonement': Fiery Rhetoric, Alliances, Skepticism Mark March," *Washington Post* (17 October 1995): A1.

88. Teepen.

89. Yeager.

90. Dowdy.

91. Charles Pereira, Doug Mills, Mark Wilson, and Brian Jackson, " 'We Are One' 400,000 Black Men Join Show of Atonement, Unity," *Chicago Sun-Times* (17 October 1995): A1.

92. "Million Man March Largest Black American Gathering Since 1963," *Asheville Citizen-Times* (Asheville, NC) (17 October 1995): A1.

93. Maraniss.

94. Miga.

95. "Black Men Hear Call for Unity."

96. Freedberg et al.

97. Dahl and Thomas.

98. Hanson.

99. Apple, "The March on Washington."

100. Ely. Both sentences are the original text.

101. Sam Fulwood III, "Blacks Ponder Next Steps after Historic Rally," *Los Angeles Times* (18 October 1995): A1.

102. March.

103. Eagleton.

104. Dowdy.

105. Pereira et al.

106. Editorial, "Minister Me Holds Court."

107. Clines.

108. Maraniss.

109. David Goldstein, "March Heralds Racial Unity: Estimates of the Crowd in Washington Range from 400,000 to 2 Million," *Kansas City Star* (17 October 1995): A1.

110. Marcus Stern, "Black Men Answer Call for Atonement," *San Diego Union-Tribune* (17 October 1995): A1.

111. "Black Multitude Sends Message of Hope, Pride," *Des Moines Register* (17 October 1995): A1. The *Asheville Citizen-Times* used the exact same wording to begin its article: "Million Man March."

112. Editorial, "Minister Me Holds Court."

113. Douglass and Young.

114. Crockett.

115. "Thoughts on Race," *USA Today* (19 October 1995): A12. President Clinton's speech found in Office of the Press Secretary, "Remarks by the President in Address to the Liz Sutherland Carpenter Distinguished Lectureship in the Humanities and Sciences," *White House* (16 October 1995).

116. Fletcher and Harris.

117. Apple, "The March on Washington."

118. Clines.

119. "Black Men Hear Call for Unity."

120. Freedberg et al.

121. Stern.

122. "Black Multitude." The *Asheville Citizen-Times* used the exact same wording in its article: "Million Man March."

123. "The Washington March."

124. Yeager. Similar statements were made by the following papers: Christopher Hanson, "Black Men Make a Stand: Hearts Are Joined in a Mass Pledge of Responsibility," *Seattle Post-Intelligencer* (17 October 1995): A1; R.W. Apple Jr., "Men on Mall Push Race Issue to the Fore," *Austin American-Statesman* (17 October 1995): A1; John R. Starr, "Farrakhan Is One Sorry Leader," *Arkansas Democrat-Gazette* (19 October 1995): B9.

125. Pereira et al.

126. Freedberg et al.

127. Editorial, "Minister Me Holds Court."

128. Clines.

129. Jonathan Tilove, "March Seems a Holiday after Summer of Tension," *The Plain Dealer* (17 October 1995): A1.

130. Maraniss.

131. "Kup's Column," *Chicago Sun-Times* (18 October 1995): 64.

132. Greg Tucker, "An Inspiring March Leaves Crucial Questions Behind," *The Capital* (22 October 1995): A11.

133. Bill Maxwell, "Separated by Time and Ideology," *St. Petersburg Times* (18 October 1995): A12.

134. Laura Ingraham, "Mr. Farrakhan's Message . . . and the Message of the Men," *Washington Times* (18 October 1995): A21.

135. Eagleton.

136. For an analysis of the framing strategy used by ABC, CBS, and NBC see S. Craig Watkins, "Framing Protest: News Media Frames of the Million Man March," *Critical Studies of Media Communication* 18.1 (2001): 83–101. Watkins examines only the pre-march coverage and excludes Farrakhan's comments.

137. Goldstein.

138. Using Lexis-Nexis, a search was performed with the key word "Farrakhan." Additional search terms included "Million Man March." The range of articles ran from 17 October 1995 to 29 October 1995 inclusive.

Chapter Five

Reggie White: "Speech before the Wisconsin Legislature"

We're a very judgmental nation. We need to be a nation that's a caring nation, an understanding nation, a compassionate nation.
—Reggie White

Think about it: Arguably the most intelligent, respected, dignified man in professional sports just revealed himself to be a moron.
—Mike Fisher

To many Americans, Reggie White is a football hero. His athletic prowess on the gridiron has earned this ordained minister the nickname of "The Minister of Defense." In addition to his football heroics, White has been recognized for his humanitarian actions, being awarded the Byron "Whizzer" White Humanitarian Award for his service to the local community. He also has been awarded the Simon Wiesenthal Center's Tolerance Award "for his commitment to fostering tolerance and pursuing his vision for a better America" and was the recipient of the Jackie Robinson Humanitarian Award.[1] He is the founder of Urban Hope, a charitable organization specializing in helping inner-city residents start small businesses. It was, in part, to talk about this ministry that White was invited to speak before the Assembly.

White covered three main issues in his 25 March 1998 speech before the Wisconsin State Legislature. First, he describes a notion of personal success that incorporates compassion and community. Second, he advances an analogy of ancient Rome to the United States and asked if God is blind to the sin of our nation. Finally, he advances his notion of responsibility.

REGGIE WHITE'S SPEECH

Compassion and Community

White states that he is speaking in order to share, along with several Wisconsin legislators, "some of our dreams and our concerns for our nation."[2] He stresses that he is speaking as a private citizen, not as a "politician" or a "pastor"; even so, he believes strongly "that it takes a compassion to really deal with people."[3] White shares that years before he had come to the realization that he "cared about more of what Reggie White has and more of what Reggie White was than I did about my fellow man, and because of that challenge [he] started doing street ministry."[4] Formed from this early street ministry is the project Urban Hope, which creates economic opportunities for those mired in poverty. White felt that "people would come in to [Urban Hope] and our message would be able to get over to them the way we wanted to by helping to meet their needs."[5] All of this comes with the realization that "you cannot help people if you don't care about people, if you don't have a compassion for them."[6]

White shares the success of this faith-based program, stressing that it had "created a microcomputer program, an entrepreneur school and a housing initiative, and the community came together to do this, from the businessman to the government."[7] He stresses that "our goal for Urban Hope is to teach responsibility" and provide compassion, which is "making sure that people in their communities are taken care of."[8] Compassion involves helping others, and White firmly states that "until we as Americans learn to have extreme compassion for our people, this country will never move into the direction that we need it to."[9]

In addition to compassion, White spoke to the specific problems facing black communities in America today. "You have a majority, and particularly in the black community, a majority of young people's fathers are either in jail or dead, and that's a problem. It's a problem when in our corrective facilities in America, that 40 percent of the men in jail in the total population, including women, are black men. So we have a problem in our community, and the problem is we don't have enough fathers in our community. In the process of not having enough fathers in our community, we're not being able to train our children in the aspects that they're supposed to be trained in."[10]

White suggests additional problems which flow from his sense of compassion for those in need: "Today in our nation we're not protecting one another. We don't have compassion for one another. It seems as though we as Americans are doing more to get on top and stay on top than trying to help the man down at the bottom. . . ."[11] White also sees the correctional system in America as flawed. He sees it as a profit-making industry making "between 30 and 40 billion dollars a year. It's a business. The only way to keep that business going, we have to incarcerate."[12] Perhaps implying that many are incarcerated due to drugs, White asks where all of the drugs and guns in urban communities come from. In answer he states: "It's not coming from these inner cities. These kids and these people in these communities don't have enough money to be distributing these drugs, to be distributing the guns into these communities. When are we as people going to wake up and realize that crime is coming outside of the communities, and because the crime is coming outside the communities, we ask ourselves another question. Why would these young people deal drugs? Why would these young people distribute guns in their communities? They're doing it because they lack other opportunities."[13]

Denied Black Opportunities. According to White, some opportunities for advancement were kept from blacks because of economics: "When I look at the history of America, and particularly the history of slavery, one of the main reasons that Africans were enslaved was because of economics and skin color. Now, let me explain what I'm talking about. During the time that the New World was to be built, the Europeans had to make a decision whether they were going to enslave their own. They couldn't enslave their own because their own could assimilate. They couldn't enslave the Indians because the Indians knew the territory, and the Indians knew how to sneak up on people. But the only people they could enslave was the Africans because of their skin color. We couldn't assimilate, and because of our skin color if we escaped, we were sent back to our plantations pretty much."[14] White contends that since the time of slavery the government would periodically "do something to make sure that the black man was not able to compete economically."[15] Although the past thirty or so years has witnessed unparalleled progress and integration, White suggests that there is more to understand about integration and desegregation: "Without assimilation there's no desegregation, nor is there integration, because people of all ethnic backgrounds have to be able to compete economically in order to build their families."[16] Slavery, White argues, has left its mark upon the black communities, and is still leaving its mark: "The conditions of the inner cities has hurt our families and other people's families also. . . ."[17]

Admiration of the Races? White uses his explanation of slavery's development to highlight the different gifts possessed by the races, saying that when God made the different races, He gave them differing gifts. White speaks admiringly of Americans of Jewish descent: "One thing I really admire about the Jewish community is that when they give their sons [and daughters] bar [bat] mitzvah when they're at the age of thirteen . . . they're celebrating their man and womanhood."[18] Concerning black Americans, White states: "Black people are very gifted in what we call worship and celebration. A lot of us like to dance, and if you go to black churches, you see people jumping up and down, because they really get into it."[19] White Americans have gifts too, and are "blessed with the gift of structure and organization. You guys do a good job of building businesses and things of that nature and you know how to tap into money pretty much better than a lot of people do around the world."[20] Americans of Hispanic descent were included as well: "Hispanics are gifted in family structure. You can see a Hispanic person and they can put twenty or thirty people in one home. They were gifted in the family structure."[21] White calls attention to Asians, as well, and Indians: "the Asian is very gifted in creation, creativity and inventions. If you go to Japan or any Asian country, they can turn a television into a watch. They're very creative. And you look at the Indians, they have been very gifted in spirituality."[22]

The purpose in pointing out these gifts was to highlight the positive general characteristics of the different racial groups. White wants listeners to think in terms larger than individual racial characteristics, however: "When you put all of that together, guess what it makes. It forms a complete image of God. God made us different because he was trying to create himself."[23] White states that in the Bible we are compared to sheep. Invoking the image of God the Good Shepherd, White stresses that one of the problems facing all of us is that "we pushed the shepherd aside. . . ."[24] White's organization, Urban Hope, is a faith-based organization that stresses spiritual growth; returning to that theme, White lists the spiritual problem facing the nation: "America is far away from trusting God" even while we put "In God We Trust" on our money and even though "this country was built on aspects of who God is."[25] For White, "faith and obedience" are cornerstones of prosperity under God and "we must understand that if we want our nation to be a Godly nation, that we have to follow God and we have to seek his counsel."[26]

White next explains how Urban Hope helps the poor and downtrodden. From the resources it receives, it then invests in "businesses so we can give people jobs, so we can give people an opportunity to own businesses. We've got to give them an opportunity to build their families and educate their children."[27] White says churches have not done enough and he blames "the church more that any institution in America today for the problems that we're dealing with . . . because there's too much money running through the church."[28]

Homosexuality as a Sin. White blends the spiritual and the secular in his speech, and relies upon both his personal experience as leader of Urban Hope and as a minister to guide his assertions. After focusing on compassion and the problems facing many black urban communities, White details the problems facing America and the spiritual consequences of those problems. He asks, "Is God blind to the sin of our own nation? Will he continue to bless us as he looks on our idols of silver and gold, on our pride of our personal achievements, on our prevailing rebellion against him?"[29] Showing concern for America, White states: "The Bible repeatedly warns that without repentance judgment is inevitable. Righteousness exulted a nation, but sin is a reproach to many. America is not big enough to shake her fist in the face of a holy God and get away with it, and as I read this I want to explain something. As America has permitted homosexuality to establish itself as an alternate lifestyle, it is also reeling from the frightening spread of sexually transmitted disease. Sin begets its own consequence, both on individuals and nations."[30] White is not singling homosexuality out for special treatment as a sin, since he states that he is "talking about all sin."[31] However, he does see a specific problem with the practice of homosexuality in America, namely that it "has been talked about [and] has really become a debate in America."[32]

Specifically on the issue of homosexuality White states:

Now, I believe that one of the reasons that Jesus was accused of being a homosexual is because he spent time with homosexuals. I've often had people ask me, would you allow a homosexual to be your friend. Yes, I will. And the reason I will is because I know that that person has problems, and if I can minister to those problems, I will.

But the Bible strictly speaks against it, and because the Bible speaks against it, we allow rampant sin including homosexuality and lying, and to me lying is just as bad as homosexuality, we've allowed this sin to run rampant in our nation, and because it has run rampant in our nation, our nation is in the condition it is today.

Sometimes when people talk about this sin they've been accused of being racist. I'm offended that homosexuals will say that homosexuals deserve rights. Any man in America deserves rights, but homosexuals are trying to compare their plight with the plight of black men or black people.

In the process of history, homosexuals have never been castrated, millions of them never died. Homosexuality is a decision. It's not a race. And when you look at it, people from all different ethnic backgrounds are living this lifestyle, but people from all different ethnic backgrounds are also liars and cheaters and malicious and backstabbers.

We're in sin, and because this nation is in sin, God will judge it if we don't get it right.[33]

Analogy with Ancient Rome

White advances an argument about the current American condition that rests on an analogy with ancient Rome. Specifically, White suggests that the conditions in ancient Rome, which eventually caused its downfall, are "strongly similar to the events which are occurring in our own nation."[34] He enumerates six key similarities. First, Rome originally possessed a strong family structure in which discipline was maintained. This structure was gradually replaced with state controls and permissiveness. White believes that today we have "eliminated discipline," but need to reestablish it in an atmosphere of love: "[W]hen I discipline my children, I discipline them, [and then] I sit them down and have them explain to me why I did and then after that I hug them and kiss them. In America they say 70 percent of the fathers don't hug or kiss their sons after the age of six. Our sons need affection. And that's a discipline I'm talking about. I'm not talking about abuse."[35]

The second similarity White notes concerns the education of our children. Initially, Roman children were home educated; parents, not the state, took responsibility for the education of their children. The third similarity involves prosperity. White states that strong "Roman families produced a strong nation."[36] The fourth similarity involves "national achievement. Great building programs began in Rome. A vast network of roads united the empire. Magnificent palaces, public buildings and coliseums were constructed."[37] The fifth similarity involved the "infiltration of a lie. As Roman families prospered, it became fashionable to hire educated Greeks to care for the children. Greek philosophies, with its humanistic and garish base, was soon passed on to the Roman families."[38] Finally, Rome engaged in persecution of Christians.

White then lists the reasons we should see similarities. "We're giving our kids over to other people to teach when they need to be taught at home. We're actually giving them over to babysitters. They need to be taught by their mothers and their fathers, and if they're taught by their mothers and fathers, they will respect everyone around them."[39] He also brings up the growth of big government. As Rome went from Republic to Empire, government services and bureaucracy grew rapidly. Tracing this effect on the Roman family, White states: "by the . . . first century A.D. the father had lost his legal authority. It was delegated to the village then to the city then to the state and finally to the empire. Unemployment was a perennial problem. To solve it the government created a multitude of civil service jobs including building inspectors, health inspectors and tax collectors."[40]

The derivative results of these analogies lead White to list a roll call of social ills that plague modern urban areas, including fatherless children and abortion due to lack of responsibility between couples: "if a man and a woman are going to lay down and get pregnant, then they need to be faced with responsibility. We can't just keep killing off children because it's just a fashionable thing to get rid of them when we don't want them."[41]

Responsibility

Throughout White's speech runs a strong theme of responsibility. He states that "Children want fathers" and our "children are dying," but this would not be the case if more Americans took responsibility for their actions. White displays empathy with the plight of single mothers when he says that "mothers have been raising our children and been doing a good job in many respects, but it's hard for a mother to raise a child when they don't have the resources to do it and they're the only ones there."[42]

White touches upon the theme of responsibility when he sums up some of the problems he has brought up: we "can't continue to sit in our offices. We can't continue to sit back and watch. I believe that as people, as politicians and as leaders there has to be something that's done. We cannot just visit the communities when we want to be voted in. We have to get the feel of what the people need. We have to talk to them."[43] He suggests that men in particular "have lost touch with reality. We've lost touch with responsibility. We've lost touch with our own children, and we've lost touch with what's going on around us."[44]

White speaks to the plight of many poor and dispossessed in our nation, stating that "We're a very judgmental nation. We need to be a nation that's a caring nation, an understanding nation, a compassionate nation. And I promise you, if we give it over and seek God's purpose for what he wants to do in this state, I promise you if our leaders do that, then we'll see a change."[45] He also spoke to the leadership of our nation, saying that "wicked leaders are the cause of fallen nations. If we're constantly involved in wicked things and we're trying to tell people that they need to do right, our nation is in trouble and people will not listen. So we have a problem. We have to establish leadership, and people need to know that their leadership is seeking God and seeking his understanding and they will attack sin just as much as they will attack any other problems."[46]

In closing, White speaks to working within a team concept, with synergy: "working together . . . the interaction of two or more individuals or forces which enable their combined power to exceed the sum of their individual power."[47] Using his winning Super Bowl experience as an example, White discusses team dynamics, and also speaks to the totality of team experience: "When the team loses, everybody loses and everybody feels the same pain of the loss. That's why we encourage you and say to you, Republicans and Democrats in the State of Wisconsin, that there's a team aspect. There needs to be synergy. And I promise you, if there's synergy, there will be a change with the problems that are occurring in this state and around the country."[48]

RESPONSE OF THE PRESS

Of the 127 articles examined for this chapter, ninety-seven were news stories, twenty-six were opinion essays, and four were editorials. Taken together, these stories depicted a shocked Wisconsin State legislature unified in its negative reaction to White's speech. The *Buffalo News* stated that although White "received a hero's welcome," after he began to speak, legislators "sat silently, shocked and stony-faced.... [White] charged on undeterred for nearly an hour as lawmakers sank lower and lower into their chairs."[49] The *Chicago Sun-Times* wrote that White's comments "turned the Assembly's applause into stunned silence."[50] The *Denver Rocky Mountain News* stated that the lawmakers were "stunned" by White comments.[51] The *Detroit News* used similar wording: White "stunned" lawmakers with his "speech that turned ... applause to silence."[52] The *Houston Chronicle* also reported that White's remarks "turned the [lawmakers'] applause to stunned silence."[53] The *Milwaukee Journal Sentinel* wrote that "lawmakers were stunned" by White's speech.[54] The *Patriot Ledger* was even more descriptive, writing that "Lawmakers leaped from their seats to give Reggie White a hero's welcome of cheers and applause ... they smiled and clapped [when he began his speech]. But a few minutes later, White lost some of his fans. Legislators sat silently, shocked and stony-faced [as White continued]."[55]

Homosexuality and Stereotypes

What was it that made seasoned lawmakers sit stoney faced? The main points of White's speech, as presented by the press, provide us with the answer to that question. The press focused almost exclusively on those small portions of the speech that touched upon the topics of racial gifts and homosexuality. For example, the *Buffalo News* stated that "White espoused theories on homosexuality, race, and slavery. 'Homosexuality is a decision, it's not a race,' White said. 'People from all different ethnic backgrounds live in this lifestyle. But people from all different backgrounds also are liars and cheaters and malicious and back-stabbing.' " On race White said, " 'Each race has certain gifts ... blacks are gifted at worship and celebration, whites are good at organization.... Hispanics were gifted at family structure, and you can see a Hispanic person, and they can put twenty, thirty people in one home.' "[56] The *Chicago Sun-Times* similarly reported that White's remarks focused on "homosexuality, race, and slavery.... 'Homosexuality is a sin, and the plight of gays and lesbians should not be compared to that of blacks.... Homosexuality is a decision, it's not a race.... People from all different ethnic backgrounds live in this lifestyle. But people from all different backgrounds also are liars and cheaters and malicious and back-stabbing.' " On race

White was reported as saying, "Blacks are gifted at worship and cele-bration. . . . If you go into a black church, you see people jumping up and down because they really get into it. . . . whites are good at organi-zation. . . . You guys do a good job of building businesses . . . and you know how to tap into money. . . . Hispanics were gifted at family struc-ture. . . . ' The Japanese and other Asians are inventive and 'can turn a television into a watch. . . . ' Indians are gifted spiritually, he said."[57]

The press provided readers with a narrowly focused description of White's speech, and this narrow focus continued throughout the two weeks following the speech. For instance, the *Denver Rocky Mountain News* summed White's speech by saying that "he denounced homosex-uality and made what some considered offensive remarks about racial differences. White said blacks like to dance, Asians could 'turn a televi-sion into a watch,' Hispanics knew how to put twenty or thirty people under the same roof, and whites were good at making money."[58] The *Detroit News* simply stated that White gave "remarks on homosexuality and race" and also said in his speech that the "United States has gotten away from God, in part by allowing homosexuality to 'run rampant.' 'Homosexuality is a decision; it's not a race,' said White, an ordained minister. 'People from all different ethnic backgrounds live in this life-style. But people from all different backgrounds also are liars and cheat-ers and malicious and back-stabbing.' White also said he has thought about why God created different races. Each race has certain gifts, he said."[59] The *Houston Chronicle* essentially reported the same remarks as the other papers mentioned above: "White made remarks on homosex-uality, race and slavery. . . . He said the United States has gotten away from God, in part by allowing homosexuality to 'run rampant.' He said, 'Homosexuality is a decision; it's not a race.' He added that blacks are gifted at worship and celebration and whites are good at organization. Hispanics . . . are strong in family structure ('You can see a Hispanic per-son, and they can put twenty, thirty people in one home'). The Japanese and other Asians are inventive, and 'can turn a television into a watch,' and 'Indians are gifted spiritually.' "[60] The *Milwaukee Journal Sentinel* re-ported similarly, saying that White "denounced homosexuality and made what some considered offensive remarks about racial differences. In his speech, White said blacks like to dance, Asians could 'turn a tele-vision into a watch,' Hispanics knew how to put twenty or thirty people under the same roof, and whites were good at making money."[61] The *New York Times* provided the fullest description of White's speech:

[White] drew sharp criticism from some state legislators [for] his remarks con-cerning a range of racial and ethnic groups in an off-the-cuff talk. . . . [His] com-ments ranged from remarks on race relations to his interpretation of Scripture. White said that homosexuality is "one of the biggest sins" in the Bible and said that he was "offended" by gay and lesbian groups that compare their struggle for civil rights to the struggles of African-Americans. "In the process of history, homosexuals have never been castrated," as enslaved blacks were, he said. "Millions of them never died. Homosexuality is a decision. It's not a race." In his effort to promote racial harmony, the Packer player, who is black, said that each racial and ethnic group has its own "gifts," that, when taken together, form "a complete image of God." But in describing those gifts, white said that blacks "like to sing and dance," while whites "know how to tap into money."[62]

Few papers reported that White had been invited to speak about Urban Hope; however, those that did failed to relay comments White made about this project. For example, the *Tampa Tribune* wrote that White "was invited by Republican leaders to talk about his New Hope project [*sic*]. The project, which operates in Wisconsin and Tennessee, encourages urban redevelopment and promotes minority ownership of small businesses. But his comments ranged from remarks on race relations to his interpretation of Scripture. White said that homosexuality is 'one of the biggest sins' in the Bible. . . . In his effort to promote racial harmony, [White], who is black, said that each racial and ethnic group has its own 'gifts. . . . ' But in describing those gifts, White said that blacks 'like to sing and dance,' while whites 'know how to tap into money.' He said that Hispanic people 'are gifted at family structure. You can see a Hispanic person and he can put twenty or thirty people into one home.' "[63] *USA Today* wrote that "legislators expected to hear about [White's] community work. . . . They did, but White's . . . speech . . . also included remarks on homosexuality, race and slavery that turned the Assembly's applause to stunned silence. White said the USA has gotten away from God, in part by allowing homosexuality to 'run rampant.' Homosexuality is a sin, and the plight of gays and lesbians should not by compared to that of blacks, White [said]. White also said he has thought about why God created different races. Each race has certain gifts, he added, suggesting that African-Americans are gifted at worship and celebration; that whites are good at organization; and that Hispanics 'were gifted in family structure, and . . . they can put twenty, thirty people in one home.' "[64]

The *Washington Post* reported the same aspects of White's speech: White was "expected to talk about his community work. . . . But his . . . speech also included remarks on homosexuality, race, and slavery that turned the assembly's applause to stunned silence. White said the United States has gotten away from God, in part by allowing homosexuality to 'run rampant.' Homosexuality is a sin, and the plight of gays an lesbians should not be compared to that of blacks, White [said]. 'Homosexuality is a decision, it's not a race' [he said]. 'People from all different ethnic backgrounds live in this lifestyle. But people from all different ethnic backgrounds also are liars and cheaters and malicious and back-stabbing.' " The *Post* also made mention of the comments pertaining to race when it added, "White, who is black, said he has thought about why God created different races. Each race has certain gifts. . . ."[65] The *Capital Times* news story offered these interpretations: "White's comments . . . in which he assailed gays as 'sinners' used racial stereotypes to promote his view of racial harmony, and described President Clinton as lacking in common sense . . . have touched off a firestorm of debate. [His] inflammatory talk went national. . . . White said: Homosexuality is 'one of the biggest sins in the Bible,' and he was offended by efforts to compare discrimination against gays and lesbians to racism. Each race has different 'gifts,' but when they are combined, 'it forms a complete image of God,' he said. He used a variety of ethnic and racial stereotypes to illustrate his points."[66]

Other papers similarly focused on the comments White made concerning homosexuality and ethnicity. The *Dayton Daily News*, for example, stated that "White included remarks on homosexuality, race and slavery that turned the Assembly's applause to stunned silence."[67] The *Columbian* wrote that lawmakers "leaped from their seats to give Reggie White a hero's welcome of cheers and applause. . . . They smiled and clapped as [he] described . . . his early attempts to preach in the nation's central cities. . . . But legislators sat silently, shocked and stony-faced, as White [moved] into theories on homosexuality, race and slavery."[68] The *Fresno Bee* similarly reported White's comments, writing that "lawmakers were stunned by [White's] rambling, hour-long speech in which he denounced homosexuality and made what some considered offensive remarks about racial differences."[69] The *Milwaukee Journal Sentinel* stated that "White spoke against homosexuality and stereotyped various races and ethnic groups."[70] The *Sentinel* also called White's speech "preaching" and explained the press reactions by saying, "The furor was set off because in giving [his speech], White condemned homosexuality as a sin and used a set of descriptions of the 'gifts' of different races and ethnic groups—whites, blacks, Hispanics, Asians—in ways that many people took as offensive stereotypes."[71]

The *San Antonio-Express-News* wrote that "White, who usually preaches harmony, accomplished the opposite with a sermon to Wisconsin lawmakers that civil rights groups said Thursday amounted to gay- and race-bashing."[72] The *St. Petersburg Times* echoed the above: "The Packers' Reggie White, who usually preaches harmony, accomplished the opposite with a sermon to Wisconsin lawmakers that civil rights groups Thursday said amounted to gay- and race-bashing. White, a minister, called homosexuality a sin and spoke in racial stereotypes, contending blacks were gifted worshipers, whites were good at tapping into money and American Indians weren't enslaved because they knew the territory and 'how to sneak upon people.' "[73] The *Washington Post* wrote that White "condemned homosexuality and characterized segments of Americans in a stereotypical fashion that shocked many. . . . White, invited by the . . . legislature to speak about urban renewal efforts . . . used the opportunity . . . to share his views about homosexuality, which he considers a sin. He further opined that God created different races for a reason and endowed each with special gifts. White's descriptions, presented in rambling oratory, reinforced what to many are offensive racial stereotypes."[74]

The *Austin American-Statesman* summed White's comments by writing: White "said 'homosexuality is one of the biggest sins in the Bible.' An African American, White also said that blacks 'like to sing and dance' while whites 'know how to tap into money' and he also used stereotypes of Hispanics, Asians and Native Americans."[75] The *New York Post* wrote that "White told Wisconsin legislators that: homosexuality is a sin, whites are good at making money, Puerto Ricans can live twenty to thirty in a room, and the Japanese are talented at turning TVs into watches. Lawmakers sat in stunned silence as the 290-pound lineman, who is also an ordained minister, went on a tear about gays and different races."[76] The *Houston Chronicle* said White gave a "fiery speech in which he used racial stereotypes and condemned homosexuality."[77]

Opinion essays and editorials echoed well the sentiments expressed in regular new articles. For example, J.A. Adande wrote that "White sent the process of reasonable discussion back to the Stone Age. Any time a person's attempts to praise the diversity of society sound as bad as, if not worse than, his railing against homosexuality, then you know he isn't making sense."[78] Speaking for everyone exposed to White's speech, Jennifer Frey wrote that White defined his speech as being

about recognizing our differences and "coming together as a society" under the guidance of God. No one else heard it that way. This is what White did in the Wisconsin assembly on Wednesday: He preached against intolerance with words that were intolerant. He preached against prejudice with words that reflected prejudices. He preached against promoting hate while promoting attitudes that foster hate. In his long, rambling sermon, White offended almost every ethnic group imaginable . . . by buying into racial and ethnic stereotypes. He offended whites. He offended Hispanics. He offended Asians. He offended American Indians. He even made stereotypical comments about blacks. . . . White denounced homosexuals as 'sinners' and stated that he was offended that gays "compare their plight with the plight of black people. . . ."[79]

Tom Knott wrote that "you do not traffic in stereotypes. White, an ordained minister who plays for the Packers, apparently forgot the rule during a speech before the Wisconsin legislators. . . . White did his best not to leave anyone out. Blacks, whites, Asians, Hispanics and Indians. White tried to be an equal-opportunity offender."[80]

John McClain wrote that in "his speech, which lasted an hour and offended many who were present and should have offended many around the country, White blasted homosexuals, claiming they are a big reason for many of the nation's problems. He also made disparaging remarks about blacks, whites, Asians and Hispanics."[81] Bob Gilbert wrote that White's "diatribe before the Wisconsin Legislature . . . triggered sharp criticism. . . . White . . . seemed to be stereotyping races with his comments. He said that blacks are gifted at worship and 'like to dance,' American Indians 'sneak up on people,' Hispanics are good at family structure and crowd 'twenty or thirty people in one home. . . . ' He reserved his harshest comments for gays and lesbians, saying homosexuals are sinners."[82] James T. Campbell wrote that "In a rambling address before the Wisconsin Legislature last week, White managed to stereotype and offend gays, blacks, whites, Hispanics, Asians and native Americans."[83]

The *Wisconsin State Journal* editorially stated that "as a motivational speaker on race relations [White's] a chair-squirming rookie. There wasn't a stereotype left upturned Wednesday, when White . . . addressed the state Assembly. The 'Minister of Defense' had been invited to talk about his church-based New Hope [sic] project, which encourages urban redevelopment and minority ownership of business, but his speech quickly [turned] into a litany of opinions on gays, blacks, white, Asians . . . well, you name the group, Reggie sacked 'em."[84] The *Capital Times* editorially stated that White "chose to deliver a speech that was laced with ethnic, racial and sexual stereotypes. At the invitation of [a Republican], White explained that, to his view, blacks 'like to dance,' American Indians 'sneak up on people,' Hispanics crowd 'twenty or thirty people in one home,' Asians 'can turn a television into a watch,' and whites 'know how to tap into money.' White reserved his harshest characterizations for gays and lesbians, claiming that homosexuality is 'one of the biggest sins in the Bible.' White complained that 'homosexuals are trying to compare their plight with the plight of black men and black people.' "[85]

Criticisms of White

Noticeably absent in the coverage of White's speech were quotations from those who supported his position. Instead, the press reported widespread condemnation of White's remarks. For example, the *Chicago Sun-Times* reported Rep. Rosemary Potter (D-Milwaukee) as saying, " 'We're all diminished by racial stereotypes, and it's very inappropriate that he used this platform as a hero to make inappropriate, inaccurate and offensive statements that hurt people. . . . ' "[86] Assembly speaker Scott Jensen (R-Brookfield), the lawmaker who invited White, was often quoted as calling "White's comments about homosexuality 'disappointing.' "[87] The *New York Times* reported that White's "comments provoked an almost immediate outcry, particularly from Democrats in the Legislature. Representative Carpenter, a Milwaukee Democrat, said he was 'very saddened and hurt' by White's comments and called on him to disavow any racist intent. [A]nother Democrat from Milwaukee, who is black, said that in White's speech, 'Every group seems to have been attacked.' "[88] *USA Today* reported another Milwaukee Democrat lawmaker, Walter Kunicki, as saying, " 'This is the first time I've been at a loss for words. . . . You can still tell from the tension in the room that much of this was offensive.' "[89] The *Capital Times* introduced criticism of White's comments before providing its readers with portions of his speech to consider. Rep. Tim Carpenter, for example, was quoted as saying, " 'I was shocked. . . . After the speech, we [fellow Democrats] were walking around like something out of *Night of the Living Dead.*' He said he was personally offended by White's racist and stereotypical comments, and concluded, 'I think the honor of the Assembly has been stained.' "[90] The *Wisconsin State Journal* quoted "Rep. Tammy Baldwin, D-Madison, the Assembly's only openly lesbian member" as saying that "she's heard a lot of hurtful words. 'But what saddens me is that this comes from the state's most popular role model. I want to help create a world where young people can grow up without fear or hatred of gays and lesbians.' "[91]

The *St. Petersburg Times* quoted David Smith, "spokesman for the Human Rights Campaign, a gay and lesbian political action group" as saying that "White showed 'complete disrespect' for gay Americans. . . . ' " The paper also quoted Felmers Chaney, "president of the Milwaukee chapter of the [NAACP:] 'Reggie is not one of those who speaks for all of us, and he shouldn't attempt to do that.' "[92] The *Washington Post* quoted David Smith as well: " 'Clearly Mr. White showed a great deal of disrespect to a number of groups—not only gay Americans, but including gay Americans. These are certainly not remarks you would expect to hear from a role model and respected figure in the sports world.' "[93] The *Star Tribune* quoted Rev. Paul Gretz as saying that "White's comments smacked of intolerance and added, 'there are many people who are born-again Christians who don't side with Reggie White.' "[94] The *Commercial Appeal* quoted Chris Ahmuty, the executive director of the ACLU of Wisconsin, as saying that White may have wanted the races to work well together, " 'but obviously using racial stereotypes doesn't help. . . . People should not let it slide just because he is a sports hero or celebrity. . . . ' "[95]

The *Palm Beach Post* reported that White gave a speech that "civil rights groups . . . said amounted to gay and race-bashing. White did not back off . . . from his remarks . . . that left some legislators cringing and some activists criticizing him."[96] The *Milwaukee Journal Sentinel* quoted numerous critics of White's point of view. For example, the paper quoted a

leading national expert on black churches . . . [Dwight Hopkins] "people who condemn gays and lesbians usually also condemn blacks. Black churches were founded because of discrimination . . . so it's disheartening and a gross inconsistency to hear my fellow Christian brother condemn another group of Christians and exclude them from the faith." Bonnie Voss, associate director of the Wisconsin council of Churches . . . said White "expressed very traditional Biblical interpretations that reinforce stereotypes. Many denominations are struggling with issues of ordaining gays and lesbians, but most of those denominations have more compassionate or modified views [than Reggie White]." [Also included were the thoughts of Doug Nelson,] "executive director of the AIDS Resource Center of Wisconsin [who] was profoundly disappointed" in how Reggie communicated his message.[97]

The *Times Union* quoted HRC's (Human Rights Campaign) David Smith: " 'Respect for diversity is a fundamental American value and clearly Mr. White showed complete disrespect for a number of groups of Americans, most specifically gay Americans.' "[98] The *Knoxville News-Sentinel* summed the criticism this way, "Critics of White's speech say it sends a message of intolerance. He may not intend it to, but his thoughtless railing often smacks of the worst form of racism."[99]

The press also attacked White through opinion essays, and editorials. Whereas regular news stories tended to attack White through the selective use of quotations, opinion essays and editorials used both the words of others and direct assertions. For example, J.A. Adande wrote, "some people should know when to shut up. White sold his and every other race short when he relied strictly on stereotypes. In a way I'm glad White shared his thoughts on race and ethnicity with us, because it showed just how narrow a frame of mind he was operating within when he denounced homosexuals. It's bad enough to spew this ignorance before the media, but to do it on the floor of a legislative body makes it even worse."[100] Steve Kelly was particularly acidic:

Reggie White must have thought he was in some smokey nightclub . . . not the Wisconsin State Assembly. [He sounded] like some throwback comic from the 1950s borscht belt, insulting every ethnic and sexual persuasion. The only thing White was missing was a rim shot. Oh, yeah, and some common sense. The defensive end was positively offensive. The speech sounded like Jimmy the Greek talking to Al Campanis talking to David Duke. Who was White's speechwriter, Jesse Helms? This speech gave new meaning to the term "cheesehead." And the saddest thing of all is White was serious. White thought he was talking about harmony. Instead he was illustrating the dangers of ignorance. White was wrong, dangerously wrong. Before the speech, White was deciding whether to stay [with the Packers for another season]. After his performance in the [legislature], he had better hope he has another season left in his creaking body.[101]

Jennifer Frey wrote that "White sounded like a bigot, and he sounded like a hypocrite. Mostly, though, he sounded like a fool. He also is incredibly arrogant. And incredibly ignorant. And when ignorance meets arrogance, some pretty stupid things often end up being said. [Many of his] statements were a product of ignorance. But White did not stop there. Demonstrating . . . his intense religious intolerance, White denounced homosexuals as 'sinners' and stated that he was offended that gays 'compare their plight with the plight of black people.' "[102] Joe Hart opined, "For all these years that he's supposedly graced our presence, we didn't think Reggie White knew the first thing about an offensive attack. Then again, no one suspected that the Preacher Man majored in anthropology, history, human sexuality and sacking at the University of Tennessee. [White] took leave of his senses . . . when he spoke to the State Assembly. 'I have a dream' it was not. It was more like, 'We have a nightmare.' White revealed a mean-spirited side usually reserved for offensive tackles and quarterbacks. We all know Reggie has a bad back. We didn't know he's also afflicted with, at best, bad manners and worse judgement. Had a legislator gotten up in front of the Assembly and spewed the kind of lunacy White did, he or she would have been shouted down. . . . [White has been] rightfully flagged for illegal use of mouth."[103]

Tom Oates wrote, "White wreaked more havoc than he ever did in an opposing backfield. [And he] jammed his sizable football cleats into his mouth. . . ."[104] Mike Bruton wrote that White "is no Jesse Jackson" and was "using fundamentalist dogma. . . . It would serve White well to understand that one can't push simplistic, fundamentalist views if he hopes to step into the larger professional and social arena away from football. His stereotypes were bad enough, but the most inflammatory thing White said sounded like a homophobic rant."[105] Ron Borges wrote that White is "no genius" and that "point was in full evidence this week when he addressed the Wisconsin legislature. . . ."[106] Mike Lupica asked, "Do I think White is homophobic? It certainly sounded that way. A lot of rough, tough athletes, even ordained ones, are. Makes them feel even rougher and tougher."[107] Jonathan Rand suggested that "When celebrities get fawned over enough, they become intoxicated by their own opinions. It's as if whatever they say must be right just because they say it. It's that mind-set, not to mention a preacher's zeal, that allowed White to claim homosexuality is a 'sin,' blacks are gifted at celebration and worship, whites know how to tap into money [and so on]. He . . . said he won't change his mind, and he won't. White is too dogmatic to reconsider his remarks."[108] Mike Fisher asked readers to "Think about it: Arguably the most intelligent, respected, dignified man in professional sports just revealed himself to be a moron."[109]

This line of attack on White continued throughout the press coverage of his speech. For instance, Dave Hyde hoped that "White gets grilled like a cheap cheeseburger, just the way he deserves. American sports have been dotted in recent years with the white graduates of the Al Campanis Idiot School of Anthropology. This is the first time a black athlete of prominence went national in the same context."[110] The *Wisconsin State Journal* editorially stated that "White got just about everything wrong [with] his repetition of stereotypes and petty prejudices. . . ."[111] James T. Campbell wrote that "Reggie may have been better served by simply apologizing, rather than trying to defend his ignorance. That's what too many slaps to the helmet can do."[112] Earl Ofari Hutchinson suggested that "more African-Americans [need] to reexamine their defective definitions of manhood and confront their own homophobia. And that should start with Reggie White."[113] Rob Zaleski asserts that White is "a jock—meaning that his views in general are probably somewhat primitive. Reggie White is arrogant. Again, no real surprise since most celebrities tend to be arrogant. Reggie White represents a large segment of American society. Truth is, there are millions of macho-right-wing types who feel exactly as Reggie does. I continued to be mystified how anyone professing to be a religious leader could be filled with such rage and intolerance over the issue of homosexuality. NO, Reggie isn't evil. He's more like the oddball uncle who exists in most families. . . ."[114] Michael Paul Williams wrote: "Let's talk about stereotypes. Like 'holier-than-thou' preachers. And 'dumb jocks.' Reggie White did both stereotypes proud with his recent speech. . . . The speech—funny, sad and vicious—left one wondering whether White had absorbed too many blows to the head. . . . It wasn't the first time someone hid behind religion in justifying his or her bigotry."[115]

Press Notions of Tolerance

After mentioning White's comments about dancing blacks and money-making whites, the *Capital Times* editorially stated that "some will laugh off the absurd association of white skin with financial wizardry or black skin with dancing."[116] The title of this editorial, "White Fumbles on Tolerance," demonstrates a particular notion of tolerance constructed by the press, and foreshawdows that a particular defintion of tolerance will be used: "those who apologize for White's remarks ought to think long and hard about the message of intolerance that they send to Wisconsinites."[117] Jennifer Frey provided readers with a look at the press definition of tolerance and free speech. Speaking of Fuzzy Zoeller's comments about Tiger Woods, Frey stated: "his words offended some people, Woods among them. For that reason, Zoeller was wrong."[118] Thus if one offends, one is intolerant.

Theotis Robinson Jr. offered a most succinct statement on tolerance, as envisioned by the press. White's "views and beliefs are unacceptable."[119] The press also made it clear that if you did not agree with their position on White's speech, then you were wrong. For instance, Alan Borsuk wrote that the editorial writer for the *Houston Chronicle* "was concerned about White's suggestion that the media took some of his remarks out of context. 'I don't think he gets it, in the sense that what he said wasn't misinterpreted.' The problem was exactly with what White said, and the reporting of it can't be blamed on the media, [the editor said]. Addressing White [the *Chronicle*] said, 'Incredibly enough, it seems mainstream America agrees with you, which is the most disturbing fact of all. You have proven that general homophobia and racism continue to run rampant in our society.' "[120] Mike Bruton stated that with "the exception of the comments about gays, [he didn't] believe [White] said what he did in a mean-spirited fashion. Ignorance was what burned him."[121]

Homosexuality Genetically Determined

Through its reportorial practice, the press directly addressed its belief that homosexuality is genetically determined. For example, the *Houston Chronicle*, along with numerous other papers, quoted Wisconsin Assembly speaker Scott Jenson as saying White's comments "about homosexuality [were] 'disappointing. Homosexuality is a genetic predisposition, not a decision,' Jensen said."[122] The *Star Tribune* reported the comments of Rev. Paul Braetz, a homosexual pastor: " 'I never had a choice in the matter—it's who I am. It's like a white person telling a black person, 'If you want to, you can be white.' "[123] No opposing points of view were presented.

Although news stories tended to provide the assertions of non-press sources concerning their opinion that homosexuality is genetic, editorials and opinion essays simply stated homosexuality was genetically determined. In addition, these opinion essays and editorials often asserted that science had settled this question. For example, J.A. Adande wrote, "I wonder if White has read any of the medical studies that indicate there are genetic predispositions toward homosexuality."[124] William Wineke wrote, "White He assumes [sic] homosexuality is a choice and that homosexuals shouldn't be covered by civil rights laws because they have the ability to choose to be heterosexual. I've yet to see any serious scientific evidence that White is correct."[125] Ron Borges wrote: "the man who invited [White to speak] said he was disappointed in White and that he believes homosexuality is a genetic predisposition, not a choice. Scientifically that is believed to be the case. . . ."[126] Theotis Robinson Jr. wrote: " 'In the process of history, homosexuals have never been castrated,' declared White, who obviously has done little research to support that view. Then he borrowed from Dan Quayle's informed view that 'homosexuality is a decision' and not the way some people are born. This despite ever-increasing evidence to the contrary."[127] John Carrol implies the same when he wrote: White said, " 'Homosexuality is a decision. . . . People from all different ethnic backgrounds live in this lifestyle.' Utterly charming. I'd like to say that sort of ignorance was rare, but my e-mail suggests otherwise."[128]

White's Apology

Following his speech, White said that his comments were made in a spirit of bringing members of our society together and that they were not intended to stereotype. One would assume that such a statement would have modified press discussion of the issue—it did not do so. Eight days after his speech, however, White issued a *clarification* that the press labeled an *apology*. The *Buffalo News* led with the following sentence: "Reggie White said Thursday he may have used inappropriate examples of racial differences in remarks to Wisconsin lawmakers during a speech that also criticized homosexuality. 'I must stress that I in no way intended for my comments to personally hurt anyone, and for that, I apologize. But I do not apologize for standing on God's word when it comes to sin in my life and others. My attitude is to hate the sin and love the sinner.' "[129] There were a total of twenty-one stories carrying essentially the same version of White's clarification. White was reported as saying that he had "made a point that our society is fortunate to be comprised of different races and cultures. I must admit that my examples may have been somewhat clumsy and inappropriate on how the races differ, but my intent was not to demean anyone. If I did, I humbly ask for your forgiveness."[130] This effectively ended discussion about White.

SUMMARY

Let us now turn to answering the questions I posed in the introduction to this book. Based on the coverage White's speech received, I'm inclined to believe that the overwhelming majority of journalists writing about White did not actually read his speech. For example, reading the entire speech, or even simple fact checking, would have alerted numerous papers, including the *New York Times*, and the *Wisconsin State Journal*, that White's project is Urban Hope, not New Hope as they and numerous other papers reported.[131] In addition, White spoke on several different issues. He described compassion, responsibility, and community in ways that highlighted a notion of personal success. During this time he shared examples of how his ministry, Urban Hope, operates. He did mention the "gifts" of the various races, doing so to point out that America was blessed to have so many different racial talents. He also advanced an analogy of ancient Rome to the United States and asked if God is blind to the sin of our nation. He referenced several sins, including homosexuality, stressing that one must have compassion for those that sin, including homosexuals.

In constrast, the press focused exclusively on the comments White made concerning race and homosexuality. Specifically, the stories were framed in such a manner that the emphasis White placed on compassion and right action was ignored.

How Did Reggie White Frame the Issue?

White spoke to the Legislature as a private citizen. He spoke about his organization Urban Hope, and also about the need to have compassion for those in need. White detailed problems in urban communities across the country, but mainly focused on those problems facing black urban communities. In particular he focused on fatherless black youths, stating unequivocally that there were not enough fathers in black communities. White also attacked the correctional system. For White, that 40% of inmates across the country are black men is a distinct problem that contributes to trouble in black communities. White spoke to the problems of guns and drugs in inner cites, and stated that they came from outside those areas. Youths deal in drugs and commit other crimes because there are no other opportunities for them within black inner-city areas.

White believes that blacks have been denied opportunities. He traces this back to the age of slavery, stating that blacks were enslaved due to their skin color. Being black, they could be easily detected, since they would be unable to assimilate within white society. Slavery and the legacy of segregation have kept black Americans from progressing as well as whites economically: "Without assimilation there's no desegregation, nor is there integration, because people of all ethnic backgrounds have to be able to compete economically in order to build their families."

White accepts the differences among the races, and wished to draw attention to these differences in a positive manner. He asked why God made different races in the first place. Each race, according to White, were given different gifts by God. Jews, blacks, whites, Indians, and those of Asian and Hispanic descent were all listed as being gifted in particular areas. White intended to highlight particular positive general characteristics. He asked his audience to add all of these different gifts together and define the sum as the "complete image of God. God made us different because he was trying to create himself." White compares humans to sheep, with God as the Good Shepherd. Yet we have pushed aside the Shepherd, says White, but we need to return to trusting God. White speaks to Urban Hope fulfilling this need since it seeks to help the poor and downtrodden.

White speaks directly to the problems facing America, drawing an analogy with ancient Rome, but also speaks directly to the spiritual problems facing the country. He cites homosexuality as an example of sin, yet it is not the only sin he discusses. He does, however, use it as an extended example. Specifically, White states that he was "talking about all sin," although he does see a real problem with homosexuality, and believes it to be a sin. White wants to minister to homosexuals, just as he would to liars and cheaters and others whose activities are acts of sin. Aside from homosexuality being a sin, White also sees homosexuals who demand special rights as denigrating the effort for black civil rights. White specifically speaks out against homosexuals who equate their plight with the historic plight of black Americans. White ultimately states that "Homosexuality is a decision. It's not a race. And when you look at it, people from all different ethnic backgrounds are living this lifestyle. . . ." Thus homosexuality is a lifestyle and not to be equated with immutable racial characteristics.

How Did the Press, Responding to Reggie White, Frame the Issue?

The press relayed White's speech as shocking all those who heard it. It was depicted as so offensive that the Wisconsin State Legislature was unified in its shocked reception of the speech. According to the press, White "turned applause into stoney silence" with his speech, spoke almost exclusively on the topics of race and homosexuality, and was mean-spirited and demeaning. The standard press line on this speech stated that White's remarks included comments on "homosexuality, race and slavery. . . . 'Homosexuality is a sin, and the plight of gays and lesbians should not be compared to that of blacks. . . . Homosexuality is a decision, it's not a race. . . . People from all different ethnic backgrounds live in this lifestyle. But people from all different backgrounds also are liars and cheaters and malicious and back-stabbing.' " On race White was reported as saying, "'Blacks are gifted at worship and celebration. . . . If you go into a black church, you see people jumping up and down because they really get into it . . . whites are good at organization. . . . You guys do a good job of building businesses . . . and you know how to tap into money. . . . Hispanics were gifted at family structure. . . . ' The Japanese and other Asians are inventive and 'can turn a television into a watch. . . . ' Indians are gifted spiritually, he said." The press focused almost exclusively on this small portion of White's speech. Few papers mentioned White speaking to the need for compassion or his Urban Hope project. Those that did do so, including the *New York Times*, referred to White's project incorrectly as New Hope. White's comments were generally framed as derisive, and presented devoid of their context:

"The Packers' Reggie White, who usually preaches harmony, accomplished the opposite with a sermon to Wisconsin lawmakers that civil rights groups Thursday said amounted to gay- and race-bashing. White, a minister, called homosexuality a sin and spoke in racial stereotypes, contending blacks were gifted worshipers, whites were good at tapping into money and American Indians weren't enslaved because they knew the territory and 'how to sneak upon people.' "

Regular news articles *suggested* White was a racist or "homophobic": This was accomplished by quoting only those who denounced. Rep. Tim Carpenter, for example, was quoted as saying, " 'I was shocked. . . . After the speech, we [fellow Democrats] were walking around like something out of *Night of the Living Dead*.' He said he was personally offended by White's racist and stereotypical comments, and concluded, 'I think the honor of the Assembly has been stained.' " The press overwhelmingly castigated White for his comments.

Whereas regular news articles *suggested* White was a racist or "homophobic," editorials and opinion essays simply *stated* this as true. Overwhelmingly, the press considered White's comments, if not White himself, racist and "homophobic." "Some people should know when to shut up. White sold his and every other race short when he relied strictly on stereotypes. In a way I'm glad White shared his thoughts on race and ethnicity with us, because it showed just how narrow a frame of mind he was operating within when he denounced homosexuals." And, "White sounded like a bigot, and he sounded like a hypocrite. Mostly, though, he sounded like a fool. He also is incredibly arrogant. And incredibly ignorant. And when ignorance meets arrogance, some pretty stupid things often end up being said. Demonstrating . . . his intense religious intolerance, White denounced homosexuals as 'sinners' and stated that he was offended that gays 'compare their plight with the plight of black people.' " Yet another asked, "Do I think White is homophobic? It certainly sounded that way. A lot of rough, tough athletes, even ordained ones, are. Makes them feel even rougher and tougher." Although White did not express hatred for any group, and even offered clarification after the speech, many papers expressed that he was motivated by hatred: "For a defensive player, he's incredibly offensive. . . . Comments like these, that express hatred for gays and lesbians and hatred and stereotypes for other racial groups, have a negative impact on our society."

The press also provided readers with a look at what it believes tolerance to mean. Speaking of Fuzzy Zoeller's comments about Tiger Woods, one columnist stated: "his words offended some people, Woods among them. For that reason, Zoeller was wrong." Implying that any point of view offensive to the press is incorrect, another columnist simply stated that White's "views and beliefs are unacceptable." In addition, the press relayed its belief that homosexuality is genetic by offering assertions in regular news stories, opinion essays, and editorials: "White He assumes [*sic*] homosexuality is a choice and that homosexuals shouldn't be covered by civil rights laws because they have the ability to choose to be heterosexual. I've yet to see any serious scientific evidence that White is correct."

Finally, What Time, If at All, Did the Frames Converge to Present a Unified Contextual Whole?

At no time did the frames of the press match those of White. The press presented the public with the thinest of slices concerning the content of White's speech. Moreover, the press failed to accurately relay the context surrounding even this small portion of the speech. Of the 128 articles used for this chapter, ninety-eight were news articles, twenty-six opinion, and four were editorials. Of the twenty-six opinion essays, twenty were negative toward White.[132] Of the four editorials, three were negative, the other neutral. The press found twenty different pro-homosexual supporters to quote for information, whereas only six sources for pro-White were found. However, four of those sources are found in the same article which appeared only once. Thus, in effect, the press managed to find a 10 to 1 ratio against White's position.

The press pushed its interpretation of the speech and refused to listen to any contradictory voices: Jennifer Frey wrote that White defined his speech as being "about recognizing our differences and 'coming together as a society' under the guidance of God. No one else heard it that way."[133]

NOTES

1. <http://sports.nfl.com/2000/playerhighlights?id 532>.

2. All quotations ascribed to Reggie White, unless otherwise noted, are from Reggie White, "Remarks by Reggie White," Wisconsin State Legislature (25 March 1998) <http://www.legis.state.wi.us>.

3. White, 1.

4. Ibid.

5. Ibid.

6. Ibid.

7. Ibid., 2.

8. Ibid.

9. Ibid., 3.

10. Ibid., 2.

11. Ibid., 3.

12. Ibid.

13. Ibid.

14. Ibid.
15. Ibid.
16. Ibid.
17. Ibid.
18. Ibid., 4.
19. Ibid.
20. Ibid.
21. Ibid.
22. Ibid.
23. Ibid.
24. Ibid.
25. Ibid.
26. Ibid.
27. Ibid., 5.
28. Ibid.
29. Ibid., 6.
30. Ibid.
31. Ibid.
32. Ibid.
33. Ibid.
34. Ibid., 7.
35. Ibid.
36. Ibid.
37. Ibid.
38. Ibid.
39. Ibid., 8.
40. Ibid., 7.
41. Ibid.
42. Ibid., 8.
43. Ibid.
44. Ibid.
45. Ibid., 9.
46. Ibid.
47. Ibid., 10.
48. Ibid.
49. "Reggie White Speech Stirs Controversy," *Buffalo News* (26 March 1998): C2.
50. "Speech by Packers' White Turns into Sermon on Race," *Chicago Sun-Times* (26 March 1998): 95. I found this particular phrase used often by the press.
51. "White 'Sacks' Lawmakers," *Denver Rocky Mountain News* (26 March 1998): C2.
52. "Packers' White Stuns Wisconsin Legislature with Speech," *Detroit News* (26 March 1998): D2.
53. Ed Spaulding, "Sports Notebook," *Houston Chronicle* (26 March 1998): 10.
54. Amy Rinard, "Speech by White Upsets Assembly with Views on Race, Homosexuality," *Milwaukee Journal Sentinel* (26 March 1998): 1.
55. "Football Hero's Speech Shocks Lawmakers," *Patriot Ledger* (26 March 1998): 36. This is a common theme that runs through the first week of coverage.

White was met with applause and cheers due to his football celebrity status, but then lawmakers were shocked into a stone-faced silence once White actually began his speech. No reporter ever questions how veteran politicians could be so shocked. For additional examples, see, "White's Speech Shocks Wisconsin Lawmakers," *Columbian* (Vancouver, WA) (26 March 1998): C2; "White's Remarks Shock, Offend," *Fresno Bee* (26 March 1998): D5; Alan J. Borsuk and Meg Kissinger, "White Stands by His Remarks," *Milwaukee Journal Sentinel* (27 March 1998): 1; "Sports Brief," *Austin American-Statesman* (27 March 1998): D2; Bill Hoffmann, "Fury Over Greenbay Yakker," *New York Post* (27 March 1998): 5; Theotis Robinson Jr., "Reggie White's Speech Deserves Criticism," *Knoxville News-Sentinel* (30 March 1998): A10.

56. "Reggie White Speech Stirs Controversy."

57. "Speech by Packers' White Turns into Sermon on Race."

58. "White 'Sacks' Lawmakers."

59. "Packers' White Stuns Wisconsin Legislature with Speech."

60. Spaulding.

61. Rinard.

62. "Remarks by Packers' White Draw Criticism in Wisconsin," *New York Times* (26 March 1998): C3. The remainder of the descriptions follow the same quotes used by the other papers cited thus far. The only additional information the *Times* reported was that White "also said that early Americans chose to enslave blacks, rather than Indians, 'because Indians knew the territory, and knew how to sneak up on people.' "

63. "White's Comments Draw Fire," *Tampa Tribune* (26 March 1998): 3.

64. Gary Graves, "White's Views on Race, Gays Stun Legislators," *USA Today* (26 March 1998): C3.

65. "Packers' White Gives Views to Wisconsin Legislature," *Washington Post* (26 March 1998): E2.

66. David Calendar, "Reggie Speech Stirs Up Storm," *Capital Times* (26 March 1998): A1. The examples of the "stereotypes" were the very same provided by the other papers in this study. Note, however, that the reporter judges White's comments as stereotypical and does not allow readers to come to their own conclusions. White's actual comments regarding President Clinton are rather circumspect: "Throughout history wicked leaders are the cause of fallen nations. People often ask me, well, what do you think about the president's situation. Well, if I see what's exactly going on, then I can give my opinion. If it's what everybody is saying what's going on, I put it this way. Our nation is saying the economy is good, we don't care about what he does. I do. I care about what he does and what you do. And the reason I do is because this, the Bible says that the man that falls into the ways of the adulterer, he lacks common sense. If our leaders don't have any common sense, we're in trouble. This nation is in trouble."

67. "Reggie White Speaks on Race, Homosexuality," *Dayton Daily News* (26 March 1998): C5.

68. "White's Speech Shocks Wisconsin Lawmakers."

69. "White's Remarks Shock, Offend."

70. Bob Wolfley, "Remarks May Cost White Job in TV," *Milwaukee Journal Sentinel* (27 March 1998): Sports 1.

71. Borsuk and Kissinger.

72. "Packers' White Blasted for Stereotyping Races," *San Antonio Express-News* (27 March 1998): C1.

73. "Reggie White's Speech Met by Sharp Replies," *St. Petersburg Times* (27 March 1998): C11.

74. Liz Clarke, "Packers' White Stands by Remarks," *Washington Post* (27 March 1998): D1.

75. "Sports Briefs: White Keeps Stance on Sensitive Remarks." Incomplete quotation marks are in the original.

76. Hoffmann.

77. "NFL," *Houston Chronicle* (3 April 1998): Sports 9.

78. J.A. Adande, "White Crosses the Line and Is Ruled Offside," *Los Angeles Times* (27 March 1998): C1.

79. Jennifer Frey, "White's Opinions Laced with Ignorance, Arrogance," *Washington Post* (27 March 1998): D1.

80. Tom Knott, "White Drops Ball on Subject of Race," *Washington Times* (27 March 1998): B1.

81. John McClain, "Speech Illustrates Double Standards on Racial Issues," *Houston Chronicle* (29 March 1998): 22.

82. Bob Gilbert, "White's Comments Divisive, Lack Facts," *Knoxville News-Sentinel* (29 March 1998): BC7.

83. James T. Campbell, "When a Good Guy Puts His Foot in His Mouth," *Houston Chronicle* (30 March 1998): A16.

84. Editorial, "White's Strengths Lie Elsewhere," *Wisconsin State Journal* (27 March 1998): A9.

85. Editorial, "White Fumbles on Tolerance," *Capital Times* (26 March 1998): A12.

86. "Speech By Packers' White Turns into Sermon on Race."

87. Spaulding.

88. "Remarks by Packers' White Draw Criticism in Wisconsin." Same quotes found in "White's Comments Draw Fire," *Tampa Tribune* (26 March 1998): Sports 3.

89. Graves. This same quote was reported in "Packers' White Gives Views to Wisconsin Legislature," *Washington Post* (26 March 1998): E2.

90. Calendar.

91. Mike Flaherty, "Packers' White Tackles Politics," *Wisconsin State Journal* (26 March 1998): A1. These criticisms of White from Rosemary Potter, Tim Carpenter, Walter Kunicki, Tammy Baldwin, and Robert Turner, were continually quoted in the majority of papers during the days following the speech.

92. "Reggie White's Speech Met by Sharp Replies."

93. Clarke.

94. "White Doesn't Back Off from His Remarks," *Star Tribune* (27 March 1998): C3.

95. Robert Imrie, "White's 'Sermon' Provokes a Blitz," *Commercial Appeal* (27 March 1998): D1.

96. "Pack's White Apologizes for His Stinging Sermon," *Palm Beach Post* (27 March 1998): C2.

97. Margo Huston and Tom Heinen, "Religious Leaders Divided over White's Comments," *Milwaukee Journal Sentinel* (28 March 1998): News 4.

98. "Criticized White Stands by Comments," *Times Union* (Albany, NY) (28 March 1998): C2. This quote was carried by numerous papers. For example, see "White Pays the Price for Controversial Talk," *San Diego Union-Tribune* (28 March 1998): D3.

99. Gilbert.

100. Adande.

101. Steve Kelley, "Insensitive Speech Made White Serious Laughingstock," *Seattle Times* (27 March 1998): E4.

102. Frey.

103. Joe Hart, "Reggie Flagged for Illegal Use of Mouth," *Capital Times* (Madison, WI) (27 March 1998): B1.

104. Tom Oates, "Will White Pay for Comments?" *Wisconsin State Journal* (27 March 1998): B1.

105. Mike Bruton, "Reggie Manages to Insult All," *Ventura County Star* (Ventura County, CA) (29 March 1998): B6.

106. Ron Borges, "White's Point Shouldn't Be Missed," *Boston Globe* (29 March 1998): D8.

107. Mike Lupica, "White and Wrong," *Daily News* (New York) (29 March 1998): 90.

108. Jonathan Rand, "White's Controversial Remarks Aren't Surprising," *Kansas City Star* (29 March 1998): C8.

109. Mike Fisher, "White Shows Why Athletes Shouldn't Be Role Models," *Fort Worth Star-Telegram* (30 March 1998): Sports 2.

110. Dave Hyde, "Reggie White Deserves to Be Grilled for Comments," *Sunday Gazette Mail* (29 March 1998): D9.

111. "On Race: Replace Stereotypes with a Must Do Agenda," *Wisconsin State Journal* (29 March 1998): B2.

112. Campbell.

113. Earl Ofari Hutchinson, "A Diminished View of Manhood Underlies Black Fears of Gays," *Pacific News Service* (31 March 1998): np.

114. Rob Zaleski, "Reggie Teaches Us Some Lessons," *Capital Times* (Madison, WI) (6 April 1998): D1.

115. Michael Paul Williams, "There's No Monopoly on Ignorance," *Richmond Times Dispatch* (6 April 1998): B1.

116. Editorial, "White Fumbles on Tolerance." A12.

117. Ibid.

118. Frey.

119. Robinson.

120. Alan J. Borsuk, "Response to White Still Mixed," *Milwaukee Journal Sentinel* (4 April 1998): 1.

121. Bruton.

122. Spaulding. The Jensen quote was used numerous times by various news organizations around the country. See, for example, "Remarks by Packers' White Stun Wisconsin Legislators," *Star Tribune* (26 March 1998): C1; "Football Hero's Speech Shocks Lawmakers," *Patriot Ledger* (Quincy, MA) (26 March 1998): 36; Sharon Theimer, "White Speech Makes Him 'Minister of Offense,' " *Chattanooga Free Press* (26 March 19980: F4; Sharon Theiner, "White's Remarks on Homosexuality, Race Shock Lawmakers," *Austin American-Statesman* (26 March 1998): C1.

123. Nolan Zavoral and Susan Hogan-Albach, "Anti-Gay Remarks Draw Some Boos, Support," *Star Tribune* (27 March 1998): B2.

124. Adande. Also in "Reggie Spells Out Misguided Notions in Black and White," *Buffalo News* (28 March 1998): B2.

125. William Wineke, "He Doesn't Have It All, and That's OK," *Wisconsin State Journal* (28 March 1998): C1.

126. Borges.

127. Robinson.

128. Jon Carroll, "The Poison and the Antidote," *San Francisco Chronicle* (31 March 1998): F8.

129. "White Apologizes for 'Inappropriate, Clumsy' Remarks," *Buffalo News* (3 April 1998): B2.

130. Dwight Adams, "Briefly Sports," *Indianapolis Star* (3 April 1998): C5.

131. "Arena: Sports Briefing," *Denver Rocky Mountain News* (26 March 1998): C2; "Remarks by Packers' White Draws Criticism in Wisconsin," *New York Times* (26 March 1998): C3; "White's Talk Targets Racial, Ethnic Groups," *Sacramento Bee* (26 March 1998): D2; "White's Comments Draw Fire," *Tampa Tribune* (26 March 1998): Sports 3; "White's Remarks on Homosexuality, Race Stun Lawmakers," *Austin American-Statesman* (26 March 1998): C1; "Packers' White Blasted for Stereotyping Races," *San Antonio Express-News* (27 March 1998): C1; Editorial, "White's Strengths Lie Elsewhere," *Wisconsin State Journal* (27 March 1998): A9.

132. Of note is that there were twenty-three different columnists and that seventy-nine of the total articles appeared in the Sports sections of the newspapers. Using Lexis-Nexis, a search was performed with the key word of "White." Additional search terms included "Reggie," "Wisconsin," "race," and "homosexual." The range of articles ran from 26 March 1998 to 10 April 1998 inclusive.

133. Frey.

Chapter Six

Trent Lott: "Armstrong Williams Show Interview Remarks"

And you should not try to mistreat them or treat them as outcasts.

—Trent Lott

Lott's views spawn hate.

—*Seattle Post-Intelligencer*

On 15 June 1998, syndicated columnist and conservative radio talk-show host Armstrong Williams interviewed Senator Trent Lott (R-MS) for approximately two hours. According to Mr. Williams, the interview was conducted in Senator Lott's Washington offices, with mainstream press reporters present to observe the interview.[1] The interview was conducted for a planned Father's Day special on the Armstrong Williams Show, and thus the theme of the interview was family values. Midway through the interview, Williams asked Senator Lott about Reggie White and the subject of homosexuality. After replying, Senator Lott left the room to cast a vote on the Senate floor, and returned approximately thirty minutes later to continue the interview. Prior to resuming the interview, Williams introduced Senator Lott to every reporter in the room, including reporters representing the Associated Press, the *Washington Post*, and the *New York Times*. The day after the interview, major media outlets reported only on the topic of homosexuality. Following the initial press reports, America's Voice network released the following statement to the media:

Text of a soundbite from an Interview with Senator Trent Lott for the America's Voice television network by Armstrong Williams, recorded on June 15th.

WILLIAMS: Reggie White got into serious problems with certain people in this country because he said the act of homosexuality, in and of itself, was a sin. As a Southern Baptist, certainly, which you are, and as a Pentecostal, certainly, what my faith has taught me, do you agree with Reggie White?

LOTT: Yes.

WILLIAMS: Is it a sin?

LOTT: It is.

WILLIAMS: So why was there such an outrage for him saying that?

LOTT: In America now, there's an element that wants to make that alternative lifestyle acceptable or normal in every respect.

Now, I want to emphasize very importantly—and I think Reggie White would do the same thing—you should still love that person! And you should not try to mistreat them or treat them as outcasts. You should try to show them, you know, a way to deal with that problem, just like my father had problems, as I said, with alcoholism. Other people have sex addiction. Other people are kleptomaniacs. There's all kinds of problems and addictions, and difficulties, and experiences of things that are wrong! But, you should try to work with that person to learn to control that problem and to build a life that, I think, is called for by the Bible.[2]

Armstrong Williams described Lott's comments as given in a "tone of love and warmth," and with a "caring" attitude. Never in the interview did Senator Lott equate homosexuals with kleptomaniacs, alcoholics, or sex addicts; rather, he used these as examples of persons with problems that still need love and help as they overcome their challenges. Following the initial news stories in the press, America's Voice, the network sponsoring Williams's show, sent copies of the entire interview to multiple news organizations. According to Williams, these tapes clearly showed that during the interview Senator Lott also spoke about the alcoholism of his father and the devastating impact that it had upon his family. In addition, the Senator had stressed the love he bore his father, which was an important part of the interview that was to be aired in time for Father's Day. Thus, the press knew the purpose of the interview, were present during the entire interview, and had access to the full tapes of the interview. However, only the seventy-five second exchange concerning homosexuality made the headlines. According to America's Voice, because of the initial reaction of the press, the interview was never aired.

THE RESPONSE OF THE PRESS

The press immediately condemned Senator Lott for his comments, and linked them to the stalled ambassadorial nomination of James Hormel.

However, there was confusion over how the comments came into being since most press reports failed to mention the context in which the Senator's comments were made. Some press outlets reported, for example, that the remarks were made while "taping an interview for the 'Armstrong Williams Show' on the America's Voice television network."[3] The *New York Times* wrote only that Senator Lott "made his remarks in a forty-minute taped interview conducted by Armstrong Williams for the America's Voice network, a cable television network."[4] The *Record*, as did most papers reporting any context, merely stated that Senator Lott gave his remarks to " 'The Armstrong Williams Show' on the America's Voice television network."[5] The *Los Angeles Times* reduced this further to, "remarks in a television interview" in which he "told conservative activist Armstrong Williams. . . ."[6] The *Sacramento Bee*'s William Endicott stated, "In a radio interview [Lott] told a conservative talk show host. . . ."[7] The *San Diego Union-Tribune* embellished and wrote, "Sen. Trent Lott . . . yesterday agreed with a conservative talk show host. . . ."[8] A few days after the event, the context of the remarks, if mentioned at all, merited only this: "Lott . . . in a television interview. . . ."[9]

Essentially, the press framed Lott as intolerant at best, hateful and bigoted at worst. It accomplished this by limiting reporting on the content of Lott's remarks, openly denouncing Lott, accusing him of bigotry against James Hormel, stating that homosexuality is genetic, and equating Lott's comments with discrimination.

Content of the Remarks

The fullest description of the comments made by Senator Lott are found in the *Buffalo News*, which led with this sentence: "An official of the nations's largest gay political group says Senate Majority Leader Trent Lott is showing the right wing's influence by saying homosexuals should be helped with a problem that he describes as 'just like alcohol . . . or sex addition . . . or kleptomaniacs.' " Later in the article the paper stated, "Armstrong Williams asked Lott whether he considers homosexuality a sin, and Lott replied, 'Yeah, it is.' Lott added: 'You should still love that person. You should not try to mistreat them or treat them as outcasts. You should try to show them a way to deal with that problem, just like alcohol . . . or sex addiction or kleptomaniacs. There are all kinds of problems, addiction, difficulties, experiences of things that are wrong, but you should try to work with that person to learn to control that problem. . . . ' "[10] Of special note is that on the first day of coverage only a handful of papers relayed the comments pertaining to love; thereafter, those comments were all but excised from the official reporting of the event: "The White House and gay organizations blasted Senate Majority Leader Trent Lott yesterday for suggesting that homosexuality was a problem, 'just like alcohol . . . or sex addiction or kleptomaniacs.' "[11] *United Press International*, misquoting, stated that "Lott said homosexuality is a sin but homosexuals should be helped. He said, 'You should try to show them a way to deal with that problem, just like alcohol, or sex addiction, or kleptomaniacs.' "[12] Later the comments were downgraded to simple summary: "Lott compared homosexuals to alcoholics, sex addicts, and kleptomaniacs."[13] The *Buffalo News* simply stated that "Lott . . . described homosexuality as an addiction that can be treated like alcoholism or kleptomania."[14]

Denunciation of Lott and His Followers

The press was unable to relay Senator Lott's comments without interpretive commentary. This held true whether the articles were of the news, opinion, or editorial variety. For example, the *Albuquerque Journal* editorially stated that Senator Lott "reached new lows in calling homosexuality an addiction of the same type as alcoholism, kleptomania, and 'sex addiction.' "[15] The *Dayton Daily News* editorially wrote that "Senate Majority Leader Trent Lott has opened himself to dumbfounded ridicule by making ludicrous statements about homosexuality."[16] Debra Saunders stated that Senator Lott "made a big boo-boo. He said something dumb about homosexuals, when he compared homosexuality to alcoholism, sex addiction and kleptomania."[17] The *San Francisco Chronicle*, speaking editorially on the tobacco bill in the Senate, inserted that Lott "publicly disgraced himself by describing homosexuality as a 'sin' comparable to 'alcohol or sex addiction.' "[18] The *St. Louis Post-Dispatch* editorially stated that "Mr. Lott is using the cutting edge rhetoric of homophobia, a rhetoric more sophisticated but just as malicious as the fire-and-brimstone language that Pat Robertson used recently when warning of God's meteorological revenge on Orlando. The new homophobia is dangerous. . . ."[19]

Early in its coverage the press linked House Majority Leader Dick Armey (R-TX) to Lott's views. The *San Francisco Examiner* wrote without ascription to sources that the Republican party was 'embarrassed by stupid comments from the likes of Trent Lott [and] Dick Armey . . . about the nature of sexuality and sin. Lott . . . said homosexuality is a sin, but a treatable one, like kleptomania. . . ."[20] Carl T. Rowan stated that Senator Lott "has not only declared that homosexuals are sinners, he says they manifest a sickness 'like alcohol and sex addiction' and need help. Dick Armey was quick to defend Lott. . . ."[21] William Endicott wrote that "the Senate Republican leader told a conservative talk show host that homosexuality is a sin and then likened it to alcoholism, kleptomania and sex addiction. His pal, Dick Armey, the House Republican leader, quickly came to Lott's defense, declaring that 'the Bible is very clear on this,' and adding that 'both myself and Senator Lott believe very strongly in the Bible.' "[22]

As a rejoinder to the press-constructed views of Lott and Army, the press reported the comments of White House Press Secretary Mike McCurry.[23] The *Patriot Ledger* constructed this story: "the White House and Senate Majority Leader Trent Lott traded barbs yesterday as Lott's comments on homosexuality continued to stir strong words. Lott's statement on Monday that homosexuality was like an addiction shows 'how difficult it is to do rational work in Washington' . . . Mike McCurry said."[24] *USA Today* provided a fuller statement: "White House spokesman Mike McCurry accused Lott of 'backward' thinking out of step with modern science. 'The fact that the majority leader has such views, apparently consistent with some who are fairly extreme in his party, is an indicator of how difficult it is to do rational work in Washington. . . . ' "[25] The *Commercial Appeal* added that the White House "blasted Senate Majority Leader Trent Lott for describing homosexuality as a sin comparable to alcoholism, saying his 'backward views' showed the Republican Party at its most extreme. President Clinton's spokesman Mike McCurry told reporters that Lott's statement showed how difficult it was to do business in Washington in a variety of areas, 'when you are dealing with people who are so backward in their thinking.' "[26] The *San Antonio Express-News*, along with numerous other papers, reported McCurry's comments concerning the alleged difficulty in working with Republicans and Senator Lott " 'because they have views that are, to put it charitably, quite out of date.' "[27]

Senator Lott's office did offer a rejoinder to the well-reported White House attack.[28] Although the press did report these comments, they were watered down to a partial sentence carried by only a few papers: "Lott's communications director, Susan Irby, fired back, saying that working in Clinton's White House hardly qualified someone 'to tell the American people what is right and what is wrong.' "[29] The *Buffalo News* added that Irby said what McCurry " 'considers to be backward are the views and values of a great majority of Americans. . . . ' "[30]

Senator Lott's views were quickly linked to mainstream religious views and, more specifically, to conservative views. The constituencies represented by these views were depicted as "extremists." For instance, the *Buffalo News*'s lead sentence, using an oft-cited quotation, made the connection clearly: "An official of the nation's largest gay political group says Senate Majority Leader Trent Lott is showing the right wing's influence by saying [what he did]. 'It's an indication of how the extreme right wing has a strangle hold on the leadership' of Congress. . . . 'It's comments like that that show he is much more in step with extreme elements than any other.' "[31] The *Milwaukee Journal Sentinel* wrote that Lott was "immediately criticized by an official of [a] lesbian and gay political organization [Human Rights Campaign], who accused him of being captive to conservative groups."[32] The *Courier-Journal* editorially stated: "Let it not be said that . . . Lott is out of touch. By all accounts, in fact, he's been very frequently in touch with conservative Christian dynamo James Dobson and other leaders of the religious right. . . ."[33]

The press coverage immediately reported what "critics" of Lott said about his comments. For example, the *San Francisco Chronicle* wrote that "Critics said Lott's comments reflect the growing influence within the Congress and the Republican Party of socially conservative groups such as Gary Bauer's Family Research Council and James Dobson's Focus on the Family."[34] This paper also quoted Elizabeth Birch, executive director for the Human Rights Campaign (HRC), which James Hormel was instrumental in funding: "Republican leadership has gone through contortions to appease James Dobson, and the extremist rhetoric will backfire . . ."[35] Richard L. Tafel, executive director of the Log Cabin Republicans, a gay rights group, was repeatedly quoted as saying that whether it was ignorance or "blatant pandering to James Dobson and the radical right, it's wrong. . . ."[36] The *San Francisco Examiner* summed up well the sentiments expressed numerous times, saying Lott's "professed outlook on gay people is not surprising in light of his conservative constituency and the desire of the Republican leadership to keep the Christian right in its lopsided tent."[37] The *Austin America-Statesman* summed this line of thinking well when it wrote that White House spokesman Mike McCurry "attributed Lott's comments to the growing influence of social conservatives and the religious right in the Republican Party. . . . He said they were drawing Republican leaders toward 'the extreme point of view in American political life.' "[38]

Bigotry Against Hormel

Leading with the quotation of another critic, "Lott's comments show 'how the extreme right wing has a stranglehold on the leadership' of Congress," the *Star Tribune* added that "Conservative leaders such as Dr. James Dobson, president of Focus on the Family, have met with Lott and other congressional leaders, urging them to push to reduce taxes for many married couples and pursue other conservative priorities. 'It may also explain why he hasn't scheduled time for the nomination of James Hormel,' Stachelberg said."[39] As this quotation suggests, the press intentionally linked Lott's comments to the stalled nomination of James Hormel. For instance, the *Houston Chronicle* wrote, "A handful of conservatives have blocked a confirmation vote, charging that the heir to a meat-packing fortune is a gay activist that has offended religious people."[40] Less than a week after Senator Lott's comments were made, the press wrote in such a way to make it seem as if Senator Lott had been addressing Hormel's nomination when he made his comments regarding homosexuality. The *Dayton Daily News* exemplifies this intentional misreporting: Lott "was discussing the nomination of a gay man to be ambassador to Luxembourg."[41] The linking of Lott's views and Hormel's Senate confirmation were pursued with ferocity. The *Austin American-Statesman* wrote that the "White House and Sen. Paul Wellstone, D-MN seized upon Lott's remarks to call for ... nomination of James Hormel ... to be brought to the Senate floor. Lott, at the behest of a number of conservative senators, has refused to move the nomination to the floor."[42]

Few papers reported the reason given by Lott for not scheduling the Hormel vote. Exceptions to this rule were terse. The *San Antonio Express News*, for example, wrote that "Lott has refused to bring Hormel's nomination up for a vote, saying it would take too much time."[43] The *Des Moines Register* wrote that "Earlier this month on CNN's 'Late Edition' show, Lott said for the first time that he opposes Hormel's nomination, viewing him as an aggressive advocate of the gay lifestyle."[44] These few instances of the press reporting Lott's alledged reasons for delaying the vote on Hormel show that the press was aware of them, but, generally speaking, chose not to publish them. Although a handful papers reported the reasons given by those opposing Hormel—the *Chattanooga Free Press* stated that "his confirmation has been delayed by a small group of conservatives [who] say the problem is not his homosexuality but his active support of gay causes"—*the majority simply made the case that Lott and others were opposing Hormel simply because he is a homosexual.*[45] The *San Francisco Chronicle* quoted Mike McCurry, who used a press conference to "voice the administration's strongest protest to date over the stalled nomination of ... Hormel. 'Why would they oppose someone who is otherwise well-qualified to be a U.S. ambassador, other than the prejudice that exists in their minds against people who are gay and lesbian?' McCurry asked. 'They're refusing to move forward on that nomination because he's gay."[46] The *Daily News* echoed McCurry's comments with a quote from a Senator: "Sen. Alfonse D'Amato (R-NY) ... said ... Lott ... is blocking a vote on James Hormel's nomination ... simply because Hormel is gay. 'I fear that Mr. Hormel's nomination is being obstructed ... for one reason only: the fact that he is gay....' "[47] The *New York Times* wrote that supporters "of Mr. Hormel have charged that his selection is being opposed mainly because he is openly gay."[48]

D'Amato's sentiments were echoed in news stories and editorials. The *Hill* actually went so far as to put words into the mouths of those objecting to the Hormel nomination: "all cited Hormel's homosexuality as the reason his nomination should not be approved."[49] The *St. Petersburg Times* editorially stated that "Lott is holding up the Senate vote on James Hormel ... because Hormel is openly gay."[50] The *San Francisco Chronicle* editorially followed suit when it asked, "Does anyone doubt that Hormel's homosexuality, not the bogus argument that he 'promotes' it, is the reason for the opposition?"[51] The *Boston Globe* stated that "The White House is making a concerted push for the philanthropist James Hormel to become ambassador to Luxembourg, setting the stage for a battle with conservatives who oppose the nominee because he is gay."[52] The *Los Angeles Times* editorially asserted that it "has been nine months since [the] nomination of James Hormel.... The holdup has nothing to do with Hormel's qualifications. No, Hormel's nomination is instead being obstructed by a handful of conservative senators solely because he is a homosexual."[53] The editors of the *Fort Worth Star-Telegram* were just as bold: "Whatever the reasons they may give, the Republican senators preventing consideration of the Hormel nomination do so because Hormel is gay and has supported gay causes...."[54] The *Plain Dealer*, speaking editorially of Senator Lott and Dick Armey, stated that "Hormel's homosexuality alone is, according to their reading of their religion, reason enough to oppose his nomination."[55]

Homosexuality Is Genetic, Thus No Sin

The press was preoccupied with depicting Senator Lott as wrong in his views on homosexuality, and they aggressively asserted that homosexuality is a genetic predisposition. Although Senator Lott was clear in saying that homosexuality was a sin, and that it was a psychological disease similar to alcoholism and kleptomania, he never stated whether he believed homosexuality to be genetic or not. However, the press went to great lengths to say that homosexuality was not a sin and that it is genetic.

According to the press, homosexuality could not be a sin because it is genetically acquired and several priests said it is not a sin. For example, the *Chattanooga Free Press*, along with other papers, reported HRC spokesman David Smith: "theologians may interpret the Bible differently but 'religious disagreement should never justify discriminatory public policy.' "[56] The *Washington Times* wrote that the HRC had "called the remarks by the Republican leaders a ploy to shore up their base of support among religious conservatives."[57] The *Austin American-Statesman* asserted that the "political dispute set off by Lott comes at a time of intense debate in religious circles, especially within Protestant churches, over whether certain verses of the Bible should still be read as condemning homosexuality."[58] The *Star Tribune* editorially wrote that Senator Lott "holds the belief that homosexuality is a sin, thus discounting the character and worth of a great many fellow human beings."[59] Many papers relayed the statement given by Senator Paul Wellstone (D-MN), who "told the Senate he thought Lott is mistaken. 'I am concerned about calling homosexuality a sin, comparing it to problems of alcoholism or other diseases. I am concerned because of the medical evidence. I am concerned because this statement takes us back from where we are.' "[60] Bud Kennedy wrote that Dick Armey "was at it again this week, citing verses . . . and saying piously, 'I abide by the Bible.' This is the new mantra for Armey and . . . Lott . . . particularly since Christian radio psychologist James Dobson flew into town a few weeks ago and administered a severe paddling for their failure to promote a moralist agenda backed by Republican social conservatives." This columnist went on to accuse Lott and Armey of "holier-than-thou-arrogance."[61] Editorially speaking, the *San Francisco Examiner* stated that "Lott's condescension toward a sizable segment of Americans, whom he considers sinful" is in part due to the "desire of the Republican leadership to keep the Christian right in its lopsided tent."[62] Openly gay member of congress, Rep. Barney Frank, was quoted by numerous papers as saying that the labeling of gays as sinners was " 'an appeal to the haters, the right-wing minority. . . . ' "[63]

This assertion that homosexuality is not a sin and is genetic continued throughout the coverage of Senator Lott's comments. For instance, the *Chattanooga Times* stated well the theme presented by many in the press, that Lott's comments "thrust [him] into the debate of whether homosexuals have chosen their sexual orientation or whether it is biologically predetermined."[64] For the press, however, the answer is clear and pushed hard: Homosexuality is genetically predetermined. William Endicott wrote that "Lott apparently believes in a literal interpretation of the Bible, [so] I suppose we can assume he is a rarity among us—a man without sin. It's kind of amazing, really, that in the face of scientific and medical evidence to the contrary, Lott and Armey still cling to the fundamentalist belief that people are not born gay or lesbian but choose that lifestyle."[65] James O. Goldsborough pushes this type of thinking to the extreme: "Morality, from which the notion of sin is derived, is a function of choice. To the degree that homosexuality is not a matter of choice, it cannot be sinful."[66] The *Chicago Sun-Times* summed well the sentiments of almost every paper analyzed for this chapter: "Lott said homosexuality is an affliction. . . . this view runs contrary to the American Psychiatric Association, which twenty-five years ago concluded that its not a disorder of any kind. The Log Cabin Republicans, whose members are gay, said of Lott's remarks: 'Its's wrong and it will cost the party.' "[67]

The press used two major sources for their pronouncements on homosexuality: their own opinions and the opinions of gay activists. For example, the *Buffalo News* stated that Lott's remarks have thrust him "into a controversy that has engulfed the scientific, gay and conservative communities: whether homosexuals have chosen their sexual orientation or whether it is biologically predetermined. Many in the gay community say homosexuality is predetermined by biology. Some conservatives and other groups believe homosexuality is a chosen lifestyle and have searched for a 'cure' for being gay."[68] Note the use of quotation marks around "cure." Now imagine them around the words "biologically predetermined." Clearly the the *Buffalo News* intended to cast suspicion on the conservative point of view. The *Star Tribune* wrote that "Following the lead of the American Psychiatric Association, the American Psychological Association declared in 1975 that it no longer considered homosexuality a mental disorder. Some scientific studies have found differences between the genes and brain structures of homosexual and heterosexual people."[69]

The *Palm Beach Post* wrote that the comments by Lott and Armey "prompted Sen. Paul Wellstone . . . to fire back on the Senate floor . . . saying being gay or lesbian is genetically predetermined."[70] The *Washington Times* stressed the comments by the White House, in which Mike McCurry said that " 'this is a case in which, contrary to fact, contrary to statements of the medical community and those who are expert, the majority leader [Lott] has taken an incorrect view that homosexuality is a disease.' "[71] McCurry, speaking for the president, stated that it is difficult to get business done with "people who are so backwards in their thinking. For over twenty-five years, it's been quite clear that sexual orientation is not an affliction, it is not a disease, it is something that is a part of defining one's identity.' Mr. McCurry apparently referred to a vote of its members by the American Psychiatric Association, taken more than two decades ago, to rescind its earlier definition of homosexuality as a disease.[72] The *Austin American-Statesman* quoted the HRC as saying that the comments of Lott and Armey " 'are out of step with the American people and prevailing medical and mental health opinion and in step with James Dobson and his extreme right-wing rhetoric.' "[73]

This line of reasoning continued throughout press coverage of the interview, with the press relying heavily upon the comments of homosexual activists to prove that homosexuality is genetically determined. For example, the *Buffalo News* quoted the executive director of the HRC, who "offered to explain to Lott the modern scientific views of the biological basis of homosexuality. [She] noted that the American Psychiatric Association removed sexual orientation from its list of mental disorders in 1973."[74] The *Des Moines Register* reported Winnie Stachelberg (HRC), who was imputed to say that "Lott is 'out of step' with scientific studies of the causes of homosexuality. Following the lead of the American Psychiatric Association, the American Psychological Association declared in 1975 that it no longer considered homosexuality a mental disorder. Some scientific studies have found differences between the genes and brain structures of homosexual and heterosexual people."[75] *USA Today* reported the comments of the HRC, saying that group "called Lott's comments outrageous and ignorant. Elizabeth Birch, executive director of the group, told Lott and Armey in polite letters that the American Psychiatric Association removed sexual orientation from its list of disorders twenty-five years ago."[76] The *St. Louis Post-Dispatch* editorially stated that "Gay groups countered Mr. Lott's remarks by citing the views of the American Psychiatric establishment and a growing body of evidence that homosexuality is primarily biologically determined."[77] The *St. Petersburg Times* editorially charged that "Lott's views run counter to prevailing medical understanding of homosexuality—it is a component of sexual identity and not a disease."[78] Homosexual activist Richard Tafel wrote that "There is simply no excuse for an educated person to believe that homosexuality is a disease that can be 'cured.' The American Psychological Association put this issue behind them a quarter-century ago."[79]

When not relying on assertions from homosexual activists, the press asserted its own opinion and stated continually that the APA does not consider homosexuality a mental disorder. For example, the *Courier-Journal* editorially wrote, "Never mind that it's been over twenty years since the American Psychological Association stopped considering homosexuality a mental disorder. Never mind that centuries of effort have failed to yield an effective 'treatment'—and no competent medical professional would recommend one today. And never mind that researchers in the past ten years have reported that the curable 'sin' is passed from parents to children. . . . For Mr. Lott, it appears in this case that religion is a substitute for research and reason. Is that true for his party, too?"[80] The *San Francisco Chronicle* reported Senator Dianne Feinstein (D-CA) as saying "she was 'shocked' by Lott's comments and flatly disagrees with his conclusions."[81] Editorially speaking, the *Times-Picayune* wrote that "If . . . Lott cared about facts, he might notice that the American Psychiatric Association doesn't view gay people as mentally ill. Most reputable scientific research suggests that sexual orientation is set at birth or not long thereafter, and common sense suggests that gay people have no more 'choice' about being homosexual that straight people do about being heterosexual. Unfortunately, common sense fades in the face of prejudice."[82] The *Albuquerque Journal* editorially stated that the "prevailing medical opinion today is that homosexuality is in most instances an inherited characteristic and not a learned behavior. Individuals are born with their sexual orientation in place—much as they are born with their hair color and ultimate height determined by genetic variables beyond their individual control."[83] The *San Francisco Examiner* editorially agreed with the remarks of Mike McCurry, who was "on target labeling Lott's brand of thinking as 'backward.' The American Psychiatric Association decided twenty-five years ago to scrap the classification of homosexuality as a mental disorder."[84] In addition to saying that "Lott's views spawn hate," the *Seattle Post-Intelligencer* editorially stated that "Sad and contrary to the preponderance of medical and scientific evidence, Lott's statement is informed by the myth that homosexuality is an addiction. . . ."[85] The *San Francisco Chronicle* editorially asserted that "Lott showed his ignorance . . . when he compared gays to kleptomaniacs, alcoholics and sex addicts. The American Psychiatric Association long ago removed homosexuality from its list of disorders."[86] Editorially speaking, the *Plain Dealer* stated "With all due respect to Senate Majority Leader Trent Lott, sexual orientation is as akin to kleptomania as keyboards are to eclairs. That is, not at all."[87]

Opinion writers revealed the same tactic of asserting their opinion as truth and of quoting homosexual activists. For example, Donn Esmode wrote, "Granted, there are gay alcoholics. And gay kleptomaniacs. And maybe even a few gay alcoholic kleptomaniacs. And someday, they may stop drinking and thieving. But they won't ever stop turning their heads when a cute guy walks by."[88] William Endicott stated that "It's kind of amazing, really, that in the face of scientific and medical evidence to the contrary, Lott and Armey still cling to the fundamentalist belief that people are not born gay or lesbian but choose that lifestyle. Lott and Armey also ignore evidence of a biological basis for homosexuality and the fact that the American Psychiatric Association removed sexual orientation from its list of mental disorders twenty-five years ago. 'A pure display of ignorance,' the Rev. Jerry Sloan, a Sacramento gay activist, said. "[89] James O. Goldsborough asserted that "By comparing homosexuality to alcoholism, kleptomania, and 'sexual addiction,' Lott shows his ignorance. Alcoholism, like all drug addictions, is a disease, treatable in hospitals, clinics and groups like Alcoholics Anonymous. Kleptomania is described by Webster's as 'a persistent neurotic impulse to steal, especially without economic motive.' Scientifically speaking, Lott doesn't know what he's talking about. Instead of trying to make us all into monogamous, heterosexual belt-lashers like him, we should pay more attention to the science on the subject. The latest science . . . points to homosexuality as a genetic condition. I leave this debate to the scientific and moral experts, certain only of this: Lott and Armey are not among them."[90] Theotis Robinson Jr. wrote that "Lott, in one fell swoop and with no training in the fields of psychiatry or psychology, negated the work in psychiatric research began in [sic] 1956 by Evelyn Hooker which culminated in 1973 with the American Psychiatric Association officially removing homosexuality from its categorization as a disease."[91] Rob Morse wrote that the Republicans were being "embarrassed by stupid comment from the likes of Trent Lott, Dick Armey and Don Nickles about the nature of sin and sexuality."[92]

Discriminatory Thoughts

The press labeled Lott's comments as discrimination. The *Daily News*, for example, opined that the "demonization of gays is un-American.

[The] Grand Old Party is having a grand old time demeaning gays and lesbians. Trent Lott is so vexed by homosexuality that he equated it with sex addiction, alcoholism and kleptomania."[93] The *Buffalo News* reported the Log Cabin Republicans as saying that "Lott had insulted all gay members of his party, and the National Gay and Lesbian Task Force accused him [Lott] of feeding the intolerance that can fuel hate crimes."[94] The *San Francisco Chronicle* reported comments by Mike McCurry, saying that in "blunt language . . . McCurry said Lott's comparison of gays to kleptomaniacs, sex addicts and alcoholics reveals a prejudice that is, 'to put it charitably, quite out of date.' "[95] The paper went on to write that the " 'Republican leadership has gone through contortions to appease James Dobson, and this extremist rhetoric will backfire because the majority of Americans oppose discrimination,' said David Smith [HRC]."[96] The *Buffalo News* reported Barney Frank's comments to a largely gay church, "It's an appeal to the haters, the right-wing minority."[97]

Editorials echoed regular news content. For example, the *Times Picayune* stated editorially that Lott's call to love homosexuals was "a show of faux tolerance. . . .[W]e can't figure out why he thinks gay people are such a threat, but trashing them is becoming something of a habit for Sen. Lott."[98] The *San Francisco Examiner* editorially wrote of "Lott's condescension" and "open prejudice toward gays."[99] The *New York Times* editorially followed suit and wrote: "Discrimination against people on the basis of their sexual orientation is outlawed in Luxembourg. . . . It is illegal in San Francisco, where Mr. Hormel lives, and in Washington— except in such places as Congress, where Republican leadership has made a fetish of it lately."[100] Editorially speaking, the *Star Tribune* wrote that Senator Lott "should not . . . use his prejudice as justification for discriminatory action against gays and lesbians."[101] The *Dayton Daily News* editorially stated that Senator Lott had made "ludicrous statements about homosexuality" that sounded "like hatred cast as love."[102] The *San Francisco Chronicle* editorially asserted that "some Republicans are so intent on pandering to the Religious Right that they are willing to use discrimination and intolerance as political tools."[103] The *Los Angeles Times* editorially asserted that "It's time to end this embarrassing display of bigotry and let a vote [on Hormel] take place."[104] The *Charleston Gazette* editorially asserted that "hostility to gays lingers among conservatives. Is America an intolerant nation that shares the harsh Republican view?"[105] The *St. Petersburg Times*, in a strongly-worded editorial, denounced Senator Lott, saying he "has a right to believe homosexuality is a sin, but he commits one when he uses his power to discriminate against gays. [Lott] has a duty to Americans not to let his ugly personal prejudices drive the management of Senate business. [He should] put his homophobia aside."[106]

There was no difference between the content of editorials and the opinion essays writing on this topic. Carl T. Rowan, speaking of Trent Lott and Dick Armey, stated that it "is interesting that the bashers of homosexuals" will take "the Bible literally."[107] Editorially speaking, the *Seattle Post-Intelligencer* wrote that by "blocking the Hormel vote, Lott is responding to the political pressures of some hard-line senators and anti-gay figures such as [James] Dobson. [S]uch a practice is itself morally bankrupt, especially when it spawns ill will and hate against American citizens."[108] Cokie Roberts and Steven V. Roberts wrote that the Republicans "intend to make gay-bashing a central part of their election campaign." [Moreover, Republicans are embracing] the holy trinity of issues dear to the religious right: assailing abortion, promoting prayer and harassing homosexuals." They called the comments of Lott and Armey "hate-mongering" and that it "threatens to stain the whole party with its brand of self-righteous intolerance. But what these Republicans are doing is much worse. Their cynical decision to demonize gays is mean-spirited and un-American. They deserve to be repudiated."[109] Steve Dunleavy wrote that "Thankfully, gay-bashing is an aberration of the past, Trent Lott notwithstanding."[110] Deb Price wrote that the Republicans have a "narrow-minded" ideology. She called Trent Lott an "extremist," who along with other Republican leaders is "pandering to the right-wing radicals." The "far-right groups" are at "the Republican Party's rotten core" and that is "why we now hear Trent Lott ignorantly condemning homosexuality. . . ." But not "every Republican in Congress shamelessly kowtows to prejudice. Unfortunately, the despicable Republican scapegoating of those of us who're gay extends far beyond our nation's capital."[111]

SUMMARY

Let us now turn to answering the questions I posed in the introduction to this book. This case study allows us to see clearly how the press sets an agenda and also sets a frame. Out of two hours of interview time, the press intentionally chose to focus on seventy-five seconds of comment. Even those press outlets that were not present at the interview had the opportunity to read the transcript of the entire interview; they chose instead to relay Senator Lott's comments out of context. Moreover, they did not report all of the comments. Instead, the press used the interview as an opportunity to impugn the character of a prominent conservative and to promulgate its own views on homosexuality and the Hormel nomination.

How Did Senator Lott Frame the Issue?

During the interview, Senator Lott discussed numerous issues, including his relationship with his father. Senator Lott had especially mentioned the alcoholism of his father. He stressed the difficulty of dealing with that illness and also of how one must deal with it: in a manner reflecting love and understanding. When asked about homosexuality, the Senator made reference to this previously established context. He did say that the act of homosexuality is a sin, one sin among many. In addition, he linked homosexuality as a condition similar in scope to alcoholism and kleptomania. He also stressed that "you should still love that person" and help them to "control that problem and to build a life that . . . is called for by the Bible."

How Did the Press, Responding to Senator Lott, Frame the Issue?

The press *chose* to focus on seventy-five seconds worth of two hours of conversation between Mr. Williams and Senator Lott. Some reporters were actually in the room while the interview occurred, and following initial press reports, a transcript of the entire interview was made available to the press. The press, however, continued to focus only upon the comments Senator Lott made concerning homosexuality, and then purposefully linked these comments to the stalled ambassadorial nomination of openly gay businessman James Hormel.

In general, the context of Senator Lott's remarks were not reported. Those few papers that did report some context usually left out the Senator's remarks concerning treating homosexuals with love and compassion. The press, almost to a paper, derided Senator Lott for his comments, calling them "new lows" and "ludicrous statements." The press went so far as to speak for the Republican party when it stated that Republicans were "embarrassed by [the] stupid comments" of Lott.

While editorials and opinion essays openly denounced Senator Lott, news stories piled on the denunciations of others. For example, White House press Secretary Mike McCurry was most frequently quoted as having "accused Lott of 'backward' thinking out of step with modern science. 'The fact that the majority leader has such views . . . is an indicator of how difficult it is to do rational work in Washington.' " Lott's views were linked to mainstream religious and conservative views. The constituencies representative of those views, however, were depicted as extremists, out of touch with mainstream America. The press then quoted homosexual activists as representing mainstream American thought.

Although Senator Lott made no mention of James Hormel, the press used the Senator's comments to explain why the Hormel nomination had not been approved. At its simplistic best, the reason given by the press for the delay was Lott's alleged bigotry against homosexuals. Some papers went so far as to write that Lott was discussing Hormel's nomination when he made his remarks concerning homosexuality. Although the assertions of bigotry were widely reported, only a handful of papers relayed Lott's previously stated reasons for refusing to advance the nomination: Hormel's homosexual activism and alleged anti-Catholic bigotry. Thus the press was aware of the reasons, but decided not to publish them in favor of relaying their own opinions as truth. The majority of papers simply made the case that Lott and other Republicans were opposing Hormel simply because he is gay: "Lott is holding up the Senate vote on James Hormel . . . because Hormel is openly gay."

The press also used Senator Lott's comments as an opportunity to advance its opinion that homosexuality is genetic, and that homosexual behavior is not a sin. Lott did state that homosexuality was a sin, and that it is a condition similar to alcoholism, but he never mentioned genetics. However, the press was firm in advancing its conviction that homosexuality could not be a sin because it is genetic. The press advanced no evidence for this belief of the genetic origins of homosexuality; rather they simply asserted this as truth, often through the words of politicians or homosexual activists: " 'I am concerned about calling homosexuality a sin, comparing it to problems of alcoholism or other diseases. I am concerned because of the medical evidence.' " Some papers even mocked Senator Lott's beliefs: "Lott apparently believes in a literal interpretation of the Bible, [so] I suppose we can assume he is a rarity among us—a man without sin. It's kind of amazing . . . that in the face of scientific and medical evidence to the contrary, Lott . . . still cling[s] to the fundamentalist belief that people are not born gay. . . ." Still others pushed this logic to the point of incredulity: "Morality, from which the notion of sin is derived, is a function of choice. To the degree that homosexuality is not a matter of choice, it cannot be sinful." Most papers simply asserted their opinion as accepted truth: "Lott's views run counter to prevailing medical understanding of homosexuality—it is a component of sexual identity and not a disease."

The only sources for these views of genetics and sin were the words of homosexual activists, a handful of liberal or homosexual priests, and the press's own opinion. The press often stated that the American Psychiatric Association had removed homosexuality from its lists of mental disorders approximately twenty-five years ago, yet not one paper explained the political circumstances of that decision: "Lott showed his ignorance . . . when he compared gays to kleptomaniacs, alcoholics and sex addicts. The American Psychiatric Association long ago removed homosexuality from its list of disorders."

Based on its own opinions, the press called Lott's comments and alleged actions "discrimination," "condescension," and "open prejudice." As one editorial put it, Senator Lott "has a right to believe homosexuality is a sin, but he commits one when he uses his power to discriminate against gays. [Lott] has a duty to Americans not to let his ugly personal prejudices drive the management of Senate business. [He should] put his homophobia aside."

Finally, What Time, If at All, Did the Frames Converge to Present a Unified Contextual Whole?

At no time did the frames of the press match those of Lott. The press intentionally presented the public with a seventy-five second slice of the Senator's comments. In addition, the press failed to accurately relay the context surrounding even this small portion of his comments. Of the 111 articles used for this chapter, fifty-seven were news articles, thirty-one opinion, and twenty-three were editorials. Of the thirty-one opinion essays, twenty were negative toward Lott, seven (six by the same author) were neutral in presentation, and three could be considered supporting Lott in some way.[112] Of the twenty-three editorials, twenty were negative, two neutral, and one supported Lott. The press found twenty-two different pro-gay supporters—including the White House—to quote for information, whereas only eight sources pro-Lott were found. However, four of those sources appeared only once. Thus, in effect, the press managed to find an 11 to 2 ratio against Lott's position.

A common strategy used by the press was to state that Lott has a right to believe whatever he wants, but believing what he does about homosexuals makes him a bigot and behind the times. The press provides reasons to oppose his point of view, but brings in no experts to justify its own opinion. Ultimately, the press pushed its interpretation of the speech and refused to listen to any contradictory voices.

NOTES

1. The information concerning the interview was provided to me by Bob Sutton, president and CEO of America's Voice, and Paul Lyons, support staff, through numerous phone interviews and e-mail exchanges. Armstrong Williams also provided contextual information during a phone interview on 24 August 2000. America's Voice declined to provide me with a complete transcript of the interview, although they were most generous with their time during the phone interviews. For information on Armstrong Williams see <http://www.armstrongwilliams.com> and <http://www.talkamerica.com/rightside/>.

2. Text provided by America's Voice Network. <http://www.americas voice.com>.

3. Alan Fram, "Stance on Homosexuality Draws Criticism of Lott," *Buffalo News* (16 June 1998): A9.

4. Alison Mitchell, "Lott Says Homosexuality Is a Sin and Compares It to Alcoholism," *New York Times* (16 June 1998): A24.

5. Jim Abrams, "Lott Sets Off War of Words about Gays," *The Record* (17 June 1998): A7.

6. Marc Lacey, "GOP Wins, Loses Votes with Its Comments on Gays," *Los Angeles Times* (17 June 1998): A19.

7. William Endicott, "Lott Throws a Big Stone," *Sacramento Bee* (20 June 1998): A3.

8. Alison Mitchell, "Homosexuality a Sin, Senate GOP Chief Tells Talk Show," *San Diego Union-Tribune* (16 June 1998): A2.

9. Editorial, "Senator, Put Prejudice Aside," *St. Petersburg Times* (22 June 1998): A8.

10. Fram.

11. Larry Sutton, "Homosexuals Are Afflicted, Senate Big Sez," *Daily News* (17 June 1998): 26.

12. "Gay Church Invites Armey, Lott," *United Press International* (19 June 1998).

13. Carolyn Lochhead, "Lott Interviewer Faces Sex Harass Suit," *San Francisco Chronicle* (18 June 1998): A2.

14. "Speaking to Homosexual Congregation, Frank Assails Remarks by Lott, Armey," *Buffalo News* (22 June 1998): A4.

15. Editorial, "Lott's Views on Gays Poison Confirmation," *Albuquerque Journal* (18 June 1998): A18.

16. Editorial, "The Issue Now: Can Lott Learn?" *Dayton Daily News* (22 June 1998): A6.

17. Debra Saunders, "City of Tolerance Intolerant Toward Salvation Army," *St. Louis Post-Dispatch* (19 June 1998): C19.

18. Editorial, "Nebulous Future for Tobacco Bill," *San Francisco Chronicle* (17 June 1998): A22.

19. Editorial, "Lott in Sodom," *St. Louis Post-Dispatch* (20 June 1998): 34.

20. Rob Morse, "A Case of Agenda Confusion," *San Francisco Examiner* (23 June 1998): A2.

21. Carl T. Rowan, "The Devil and Dick Armey," *New York Post* (22 June 1998): 23.

22. Endicott.

23. White House, Office of the Press Secretary. "Press Briefing by Mike McCurry" (16 June 1998).

24. "Officials Trade Barbs Over Gays," *Patriot Ledger* (17 June 1998): 4.

25. Jill Lawrence, "Lott's Comments on Homosexuals Touch Off Furor," *USA Today* (17 June 1998): A7.

26. "In Washington," *Commercial Appeal* (17 June 1998): A6.

27. Judy Holland, "Debate Over Homosexuality Follows Armey's Comments," *San Antonio Express-News* (17 June 1998): A13.

28. Repeated requests for the transcript of the press release were ignored by Senator Lott's office.

29. "Officials Trade Barbs Over Gays."

30. Jackie Frank, "White House Rips Lott for 'Backward' Views on Homosexuality," *Buffalo News* (17 June 1998): A11.

31. Fram.

32. "Lott Says Homosexuals Sin, Need Treatment," *Milwaukee Journal Sentinel* (16 June 1998): 8.

33. Editorial, "Oblivious to the Facts," *Courier-Journal* (17 June 1998): A12.

34. Marc Sandalow, "Firestorm Over Lott Remarks on Gays," *San Francisco Chronicle* (17 June 1998): A1.

35. Ibid.

36. Ibid.

37. Editorial, "Trent Lott's Gay Theory," *San Francisco Examiner* (18 June 1998): A18.

38. Alison Mitchell, "Debate Erupts Over Homosexuality, Armey Defends Lott Remarks," *Austin American-Statesman* (17 June 1998): A6.

39. "Lott Enters Fray, Says Homosexuality Is a Sin," *Star Tribune* (16 June 1998): A6.

40. Bennett Roth, "Senate Debate on Gay Nominee Turns Increasingly Nasty," *Houston Chronicle* (27 June 1998): A2.

41. Editorial, "The Issue Now: Can Lott Learn?"

42. Mitchell, "Debate Erupts Over Homosexuality."

43. Holland.

44. "Lott: Homosexuals Need Assistance, 'Like Kleptomaniacs,' " *Des Moines Register* (16 June 1998): 5.

45. Jim Abrams, "Vote Pushed on Gay Nominee," *Chattanooga Free Press* (17 June 1998): A9. One of the only other full and accurate descriptions of what opponents of Hormel said was contained in the *San Diego Union-Tribune*: "The four conservative Republicans [Trent Lott, Majority Whip Don Nickles (R-OK), Dick Armey, and James Inhofe (R-OK)] argue that Hormel, 64, a San Fransico philanthropist, Democratic Party donor and homosexual rights activist, would try to promote a 'gay agenda' in Luxembourg, a predominately Roman Catholic nation." In Judy Holland, "D'Amato Decries GOP Effort to Block Gay's Bid for Ambassadorship," *San Diego Union-Tribune* (19 June 1998): A15. The *Buffalo News* was the only paper that reported Senator Tim Hutchinson's (R-AR) comments: " 'I talked with Jim Hormel myself and asked him to disavow some of the groups that ridicule and disdain organized religion, the Catholic Church in particular, and he refused to do that. . . . The question is one of suitability and whether he's sensitive to organized religion. Luxembourg is a country that is 97 percent Catholic.' " "Speaking to Homosexual Congregation, Frank Assails Remarks," *Buffalo News* (22 June 1998): A4.

46. Sandalow.

47. Thomas M. DeFrank, "AL: Anti-Gay View Stalls Envoy Bid," *Daily News* (19 June 1998): 48.

48. James Dao, "Chiding G.O.P., D'Amato Pushes for Vote on Gay Nominee for Envoy," *New York Times* (19 June 1998): B4.

49. Philippe Shepnick, "Helms Says D'Amato Woos Gay Vote," *Hill* (24 June 1998): 6.

50. Editorial, "Senator, Put Prejudice Aside."

51. Editorial, "Hormel-Bashing," *San Francisco Chronicle* (23 June 1998): A18.

52. Ann Scales, "GOP Resists Gay Nominee," *Boston Globe* (24 June 1998): A11.

53. Editorial, "The Sin's in The Senate," *Los Angeles Times* (24 June 1998): B6.

54. Editorial, "Policy and Morals," *Fort Worth Star-Telegram* (24 June 1998): 14.

55. Editorial, "Let Him Go," *The Plain Dealer* (27 June 1998): B10.

56. Abrams, "Vote Pushed on Gay Nominee."

57. Nancy E. Roman, "McCurry vs. Lott on a Point of Theology: Is Homosexuality a Sin, Sickness, or Choice?" *Washington Times* (17 June 1998): A1.

58. Mitchell, "Debate Erupts Over Homosexuality."

59. Editorial, "Civic Sin: Lott Seems to Favor Blind Prejudice," *Star Tribune* (17 June 1998): A20.

60. Tom Hamburger, "Wellstone Tries Again to Force Vote on Hormel Nomination," *Star Tribune* (17 June 1998): A10.

61. Bud Kennedy, "Armey Adds Moral Smugness to His Ego Trip," *Fort Worth Star-Telegram* (18 June 1998): Metro, 1.

62. Editorial, "Trent Lott's Gay Theory."

63. "Speaking to Homosexual Congregation."

64. "Senator Opposes Ambassador Pick," *Chattanooga Times* (22 June 1998): A6.

65. Endicott.

66. James O. Goldsborough, "Lott, Armey, and Politics of Ignorance," *San Diego Union-Tribune* (22 June 1998): B7.

67. "Sunday News: The Week That Was," *Chicago Sun-Times* (21 June 1998): 22.

68. Fram.

69. "Lott Enters Fray."

70. "GOP'S Armey Renews Homosexuality Debate," *Palm Beach Post* (17 June 1998): A14.

71. Roman.

72. Ibid.

73. Mitchell, "Debate Erupts Over Homosexuality."

74. Frank.

75. "Lott: Homosexuals Need Assistance."

76. Lawrence.

77. Editorial, "Lott in Sodom."

78. Editorial, "Senator, Put Prejudice Aside."

79. Richard L. Tafel, "Does GOP's Tent Have Room for Gays?" *The Record* (23 June 1998): L09

80. Editorial, "Oblivious to the Facts."

81. Sandalow.

82. Editorial, "Sen. Lott's Tolerance Issues," *Times Picayune* (18 June 1998): B6.

83. Editorial, "Lott's Views on Gays Poison Confirmation."

84. Editorial, "Trent Lott's Gay Theory."

85. Editorial, "Lott's Views Spawn Hate," *Seattle Post-Intelligencer* (19 June 1998): A12.

86. Editorial, "Hormel-Bashing."

87. Editorial, "Let Him Go."

88. Donn Esmode, "Lott's Ignorance Apparent in Remarks about Homosexuals," *Buffalo News* (18 June 1998): B1.

89. Endicott.

90. Goldsborough. Goldsborough does cite two researchers, from the Salk Institute and the American Psychological Association, who "suggest" that genetics is the cause.

91. Theotis Robinson Jr., "Cynics Cite Scripture for Own Purposes," *Knoxville News-Sentinel* (22 June 1998): A10.

92. Morse.

93. Editorial, "Some Straight Talk about the GOP," *Daily News* (27 June 1998): 16.

94. Frank.

95. Sandalow.

96. Ibid.

97. "Speaking to Homosexual Congregation."

98. Editorial, "Sen. Lott's Tolerance Issues."

99. Editorial, "Trent Lott's Gay Theory."

100. "Let Them Vote on Mr. Hormel," *New York Times* (22 June 1998): A18.

101. Editorial, "Civic Sin."

102. Editorial, "The Issue Now: Can Lott Learn?"

103. Editorial, "Hormel-Bashing."

104. Editorial, "The Sin's in the Senate."

105. Editorial, "Hating Gays GOP Intolerance," *Charleston Gazette* (26 June 1998): A4.

106. Editorial, "Senator, Put Prejudice Aside."

107. Rowan.

108. Editorial, "Lott's Views Spawn Hate."

109. Cokie Roberts and Steven V. Roberts, "Gay Bashing Divides GOP and the Nation," *Daily News* (24 June 1998): 31.

110. Steve Dunleavy, "Rights, Schmights . . . Mayor Is Wrong on This," *New York Post* (25 June 1998): 5.

111. Deb Price, "Republican Leadership Has Forgotten Inclusiveness," *Detroit News* (27 June 1998): C5.

112. Of note is that there were twenty-one different columnists. Using Lexis-Nexis, a search was performed with the key word "Lott." Additional search terms included "Trent," "Armstrong Williams," and "homosexual." The range of articles ran from 16 June 1998 to 29 June 1998 inclusive.

Chapter Seven

William J. Clinton: "Remarks by the President at Human Rights Campaign Dinner"

[W]e have to broaden the imagination of America. We are redefining, in practical terms, the immutable ideals that have guided us from the beginning.

—William J. Clinton

There was nothing radical or even exceptional about what Clinton had to say Saturday night.

—*Atlanta Journal and Constitution*

On 8 November 1997, President Clinton became the first American president to attend and speak at a fund raiser sponsored by a homosexual rights organization: the Human Rights Campaign (HRC).[1] In his short speech, less than twenty-five minutes, the president touched upon numerous issues, including redefining American ideals, the inclusion of homosexuals as a federally-protected minority, and his nomination for the head of the Federal Government's Office of Civil Rights.

PRESIDENT CLINTON'S SPEECH

A "problem" had compelled the president to run for office: the "country seemed to be drifting and divided" as it moved toward the next century.[2] The president said that he "sat down alone" before running for office and asked himself, "what is it that you want America to look like when you're done if you win?" His answer was that he wished for this to "be a country where every child and every person who is responsible enough to work for it can live the American dream. I want this country to embrace the wider world and continue to be the strongest force for peace and freedom and prosperity, and I want us to come together across all our lines of difference into one America."

Coming together involves a particular understanding of what "one America" would look like and how citizens would act. It also involves reconstructing what Americans believe about themselves and the values they hold dear. The president states that as a country we "have had to continue to lift ourselves beyond what we thought America meant. Our ideals were never meant to be frozen in stone or time." For the president, the evolution of thought involves a particular vision of equality: "Keep in mind, when we started out with Thomas Jefferson's credo that all of us are created equal by God, what that really meant in civic political terms was that you had to be white, you had to be male, and that wasn't enough—you had to own property, which would have left my crowd out when I was a boy." The idea of intentionally changing values and ideals is introduced as natural, with the president implying that those who would not embrace his idea of change are simply unimaginative: "Over time, we have had to redefine the words that we started with, not because there was anything wrong with them and their universal power and strength of liberty and justice, but because we were limited in our imaginations about how we could live and what we were capable of and how we should live." The president highlights and embraces this change: "the story of how we kept going higher and higher and higher to new and higher definitions—and more meaningful definitions—of equality and dignity and freedom is in its essence the fundamental story of our country."

A portion of the change the president envisions involves his introduction of a new definition of equality that equates homosexuality with immutable characteristics such as race and ethnicity. In this sense, the president advances a different definition of equality than that used by the majority of Americans. In a sense, he is redefining equality and the idea of civil rights to include homosexual behavior, and makes this clear in his speech:

Fifty years ago, President Truman stood at a new frontier in our defining struggle on civil rights. Slavery had ended a long time before, but segregation remained. Harry Truman stood before the Lincoln Memorial and said, "It is more important today than ever to ensure that all Americans enjoy the rights [of freedom and equality]. When I say all Americans, I mean all Americans."

Well, my friends, all Americans still means all Americans. We all know that it is an ideal and not perfectly real now. We all know that some of the old kinds of discrimination we have sought to rid ourselves of by law and purge our spirits of still exist in America today. We all know that there is continuing discrimination against gays and lesbians. But we also know that if we're ever going to build one America, then all Americans—including you and those whom you represent—have got to be a part of it.

After redefining the notion of equality, asserting it as a right, and linking homosexuality with race and ethnicity, the president moves into a general discussion of civil rights. Although he omits God from the reference and instead begins with *inalienable*, the president does use America's contemporary understanding of "God given rights": "no president can grant rights. Our ideals and our history hold that they are inalienable, embedded in our Constitution, amplified over time by our courts and legislature." The president also casts his understanding of rights at the level of the individual alone: "All America loses if we let prejudice and discrimination stifle the hopes or deny the potential of a single American. All America loses when any person is denied or forced out of a job because of sexual orientation."

Through this line of thought, the president focuses on the individual, presents a new construction of civil rights classes, and calls for passage of legislation that would codify his views: "So when we deny opportunity because of ancestry or religion, race or gender, disability or sexual orientation, we break the compact. It is wrong. And it should be illegal. Once again I call upon Congress to honor our most cherished principles and make the Employment Non-Discrimination Act the law of the land."

At one point in his speech the president is interrupted by a member of the audience yelling "People with AIDS are dying." The president responds with what appears to be a spontaneous addition to his planned remarks: "People with AIDS are dying. But since I've become president we're spending ten times as much per fatality on people with AIDS as people with breast cancer or prostate cancer. And the drugs are being approved more quickly. And a lot of people are living normal lives. We just have to keep working on it."

The president's speech culminates with his asking support for the passing of the Non-Employment Discrimination Act and his nomination for the position of head of the Federal Government's Office of Civil Rights: Bill Lee.[3] "Now, I want to ask you for a favor. You want us to pass the Employment Non-Discrimination Act. You know when we do—and I believe it will pass—you know when we do it will have to be enforced. The law on the books only works if it is also a law in the life of America." The president links Bill Lee with the audience he is addressing: "But he, too, comes from a family that has known discrimination and now he is being discriminated against, not because there is anything wrong with his qualifications, not because anybody believes he is not even-tempered, but because some members of the Senate disagree with his views on affirmative action."

The president also speaks to those who have reservations about homosexual behavior:

There are some people who aren't in this room tonight who aren't comfortable yet with you and won't be comfortable with me for being here. On issue after

issue involving gays and lesbians, survey after survey shows that the most important determinant of people's attitudes is whether they are aware—whether
they knowingly have had a family or a friendship or a work relation with a gay
person. Now, I hope that we will embrace good people who are trying to overcome their fears. After all, all of us can look back in history and see what the
right thing to do was. It is quite another thing to look ahead and light the way.
Most of us, as we grow older, become—whether we like it or not—somewhat
more limited in our imaginations. So I think one of the greatest things we have
to do still is just to increase the ability of Americans who do not yet know that
gays and lesbians are their fellow Americans in every sense of the word to feel
that way. [W]e have to broaden the imagination of America. We are redefining,
in practical terms, the immutable ideals that have guided us from the beginning.
Again I say, we have to make sure that for every single person in our country,
all Americans means all Americans.

THE PRE-SPEECH PRESS COVERAGE

The president received two days of press coverage prior to delivering
his speech. Because of this, we can examine how the press framed the
president's speech *before* he delivered it, and then look for changes made
to that frame caused by the president's speech. Overall, the press stressed
the historical nature of the speech and asserted that there was nothing
out of the ordinary about the president speaking at a homosexual activist
organization's fundraiser. In addition, the press framed the speech in
oppositional terms—civil rights activists versus conservative critics—
positively framed comments from homosexual critics, and equated the
concept of homosexual rights with civil rights in general.

Nothing Unusual

The *Arizona Republic* led with this line: "[S]ignifying a surge in the
visibility of the gay and lesbian community, President Clinton will become the first sitting president to address a gay-rights event. [The] president has decided with one conspicuous stroke to give voice to the
community's calls for equality. No matter what he says at the annual
gala of the country's largest gay and lesbian political organization . . .
Clinton's mere presence in the hotel ballroom will make a statement. . . ."[4] The *Christian Science Monitor* stated that the president's "attendance, a historic first, will showcase what the administration says is
an increased level of national tolerance, if not acceptance, of homosexuals
in this country due in part to its policies."[5] The *Times-Picayune* stated
that "He [Clinton] knows exactly what it means for him to be appearing
at the [HRC] dinner, and I think he is doing so specifically for the purpose of sending a message that lesbian and gay Americans are as much
a part of the American family as every other American citizen. . . . Gay
and lesbian leaders . . . view his speech as a historic sign of their coming

of age as a civil rights movement. 'We have a long way to go, but the country has been transformed,' said Elizabeth Birch [HRC Executive Director]."[6]

The *Buffalo News* spoke in unison with a majority of papers when it said that "No matter what he says in his speech, Clinton's mere presence at the [HRC's] first annual national dinner will make history and to many activists signals the maturation of a movement once relegated to the fringes of American society."[7] The *Houston Chronicle* phrased this same message differently: "President Clinton will break a barrier in American politics tonight when he publicly addresses the nation's largest gay and lesbian rights organization with a message of inclusion and a promise of support."[8] The *Los Angeles Times* reported the White House as saying that the president would " 'try to take this whole conversation up a notch,' focusing on the themes of uprooting discrimination—particularly in the workplace—and more effectively enforcing civil rights laws."[9] The *News and Observer* quoted unnamed "White House officials" allegedly stating that "Clinton is not trying to make history, but to build on his theme of celebrating diversity and smoothing relations among disparate groups of people. 'The struggle for gays and lesbians to gain equal status and recognition in this country has never been recognized in such a public, formal and serious way by any president of the United States. And this president has, more than any other . . . seemed to understand these issues and has done more to advance them.' "[10]

Civil Rights Activists versus Conservative Critics

While highlighting the unprecedented aspect of the president's speech, the press cast the meaning behind the president's appearance in oppositional terms. As this headline suggests, *civil rights activists* were depicted as fighting it out with *conservative critics* over the meaning of the appearance: "Clinton to Address Gay Activists; Saturday Speech Called 'Historic Step' by Some, 'Disgraceful' by Critics."[11] The *Washington Post*, as did most papers, used the terms "gay rights leaders," and "conservative activists."[12] The *News and Observer* also painted the image clearly, and labeled the groups: "White House officials, gay-rights advocates and their conservative opponents."[13] "Civil rights activists," represented almost exclusively by homosexual activists, were portrayed as highlighting the historic nature and anticipated ramifications of President Clinton's appearance. Elizabeth Birch, Executive Director of HRC, was repeatedly reported as saying the president was " 'taking a bold, historic step.' "[14] The *Atlanta Journal and Constitution* wrote that the "Human Rights Campaign . . . has high hopes that the appearance could trigger new gains for legal protections for homosexuals. 'Different presidents . . . have been handed different civil rights challenges,' said [Elizabeth] Birch.... 'President Clinton has been handed...a gay civil rights movement, and history will judge him ... on whether he did or did not rise to the occasion for this group of Americans.' "[15] This paper went on to say that "Activists have long sought to link gay and lesbian rights with the broader issue of civil rights. The [HRC] will emphasize that at the dinner by presenting their national civil rights award to the Leadership Conference on Civil Rights...[which] is being given the award 'to honor their outstanding work to end discrimination based on sexual orientation.' "[16]

The *Christian Science Monitor* also quoted Elizabeth Birch: " 'There is a transformation going on,' she says, crediting the White House's ENDA effort. By pushing for equality for all Americans, including homosexuals, 'the president has absolutely altered the air we breathe....' "[17] The *Atlanta Journal and Constitution* quoted an anonymous White House source as saying, " 'I think the president will speak broadly about civil rights for all Americans, including gay and lesbian Americans, and our continuing struggle as a nation to breathe life in and give full meaning to the Bill of Rights and the Constitution....' "[18] The *Denver Rocky Mountain News* added that the "White House said Clinton wanted to speak at the [HRC] dinner to condemn job discrimination against homosexuals and to promote the force of law behind that effort."[19]

Opinion essays and editorials shared this same frame. For example, Deb Price speculated that ever since the president "was so badly burned by the gays-in-the-military fiasco, [he] has kept gay people at arm's length, making sure that his most supportive actions were off-camera or behind closed doors. Agreeing to a speech so public, so high-profile as tonight's marks a tremendous change in his willingness to be publicly associated with gay rights. And it may well signal his determination to use his office as a bully pulpit on behalf of gay rights in a way he hasn't before."[20] The *San Francisco Chronicle* stated that the "president will use his bully pulpit to call for an end to discrimination based on sexual orientation, a move that gay leaders are calling 'historic....' Clinton will use the opportunity to say that the 'guarantee of civil rights in this country includes gays and lesbians.' "[21]

Set in opposition to homosexuals simply trying to have civil rights were depictions of conservative organizations trying to prevent them from obtaining those rights: "Clinton's address...is expected to draw condemnation from social conservatives," wrote the *Houston Chronicle*.[22] The *Los Angeles Times* exemplified this frame well when it led with this statement:

President Clinton will rekindle a divisive debate tonight when he becomes the first sitting president to make a public address to a gay and lesbian organization. To many in the gay and lesbian community, Clinton's keynote speech at a fundraising event sponsored by the [HRC] is a symbolic milestone reflecting their continued assimilation into American society. "The president of the United States—the leader of the most powerful and prestigious nation in the world—has taken that prestige and power and said to the gay and lesbian community that you're part of the country as a whole. . . ." Conservative critics argued that Clinton's speech is an unprecedented endorsement of a fringe community that threatens to corrupt American children. "It is a tragedy that he is using his bully pulpit to endorse homosexuality, which is destructive and unhealthy to families and communities."[23]

Although those supporting the homosexual agenda were called *gay rights* groups and *civil rights* groups, they were never labeled *liberal*, whereas all critics of the president's plan or appearance were labled *conservative* or *anti-gay*. For example, the *Star Tribune* reported that "Conservative groups criticized the planned appearance."[24] The *Atlanta Journal and Constitution* wrote, the "planned appearance drew criticism from conservative groups."[25] Limited quotations from pro-family groups were provided. For example, Robert Knight, of the Family Research Council (FRC), was quoted as saying " 'The president has no business lending the prestige of his office to this type of behavior. . . . It's disgraceful for the president who says he cares about young people's health enough to oppose smoking to openly embrace a group that promotes a far deadlier lifestyle.' "[26] Knight was also quoted by The *San Francisco Chronicle*, which wrote: "Clinton's appearance has provoked a torrent of protests by religious conservatives. . . . 'It sends a message that homosexuality is not only morally OK, but even something that the president will use the bully pulpit to validate,' said Robert Knight. . . ."[27] Gary Bauer (FRC) was quoted as saying that " 'There's a consistent pattern here that the administration wants the rest of America to put aside their moral-based objections to the gay-rights agenda. . . . ' "[28] Also quoted was Brent Bozell of the Media Research Council, " 'Mainstream America doesn't believe that the gay lifestyle ought to be glorified by the president.' "[29] These examples are exceptions, for the statements by critics of the HRC dinner were rarely presented.

Homosexual Critics

There exists another group of critics, however, that received much more press than those arguing against the president's appearance: homosexual activists. The press framed the president's association with homosexuals in controversial terms. The president had given them "some rights," but had denied them others to which they were entitled. For example, the *Arizona Republic* stated that "Gay and lesbian leaders . . . say Clinton has both delighted and disappointed them more than any other president. . . . '[T]his president has, more than any of his predecessors, seemed to understand these issues and has done more to advance them. . . . That's not to say that many of us have not been disappointed by any specific actions or inactions by this administration.' "[30] The *Christian Science Monitor* reported that "despite his broad support in the gay community, Mr. Clinton is also facing fire from pro-gay rights interests. Act-Up, the international AIDS awareness organization, will also reportedly be on hand to protest. . . . And then there are those who still chafe at what they believe is the president's biggest single misstep, 'Don't Ask, Don't Tell.' Moreover, some describe the president's actions, such as the appointment of homosexuals within his administration, as lacking substance. 'Most of what the administration has done has been symbolic' " one homosexual activist was quoted as saying.[31]

Continuing this frame, *USA Today* wrote that the president's appearance "highlights an often uneasy relationship between the administration and gays, who had enormous expectations for Clinton after he courted them in 1992. Many in the gay community felt betrayed by Clinton's policies on AIDS, gays in the military and same-sex marriage. Gay activists applaud Clinton for coming to speak . . . but also say he has made them more cynical about the political process. . . . Clinton drew heavy fire from gays and lesbians during last year's campaign when he supported, though grudgingly, legislation forbidding federal recognition of same-sex marriages. And while he has increased AIDS funding, some critics say it should be higher."[32] Along these same lines, the *Austin American-Statesman* wrote that "Clinton has disappointed his gay supporters by failing to fulfill his promise to end the bar on gays in the military and by signing a bill that recognizes only heterosexual marriages. But outside of those, [Elizabeth] Birch said that Clinton has delivered for her group. . . ."[33] Deb Price wrote, "In accepting HRC's invitation, Clinton probably had his eye on his legacy. While he, without a doubt, has done more for gay Americans than any other president, Clinton ironically also signed into law the two most anti-gay bills in our nation's history—'Don't Ask, Don't Tell' and the Defense of Marriage Act."[34]

Often the criticism of homosexual activists was provided after the president's numerous advancements to homosexual causes were provided for readers to ponder. For example, the *Houston Chronicle* wrote that "Clinton appointed 100 openly gay officials his first term and twenty-five to thirty-five more in his second. . . . He created the first White House liaison to the gay community. . . . He provided more money for AIDS research and endorsed the Employment Non-Discrimination Act (ENDA) [which sole purpose was to add "sexual orientation" to protected classes.] Yet Clinton backtracked on his [promise] to allow openly gay people to serve in the military. Also, he signed the

Defense of Marriage Act, which allowed states to refuse recognition of same-sex marriages."[35] The *Los Angeles Times*, too, mentioned these items: Clinton "won praise from gay and lesbian groups for staging a large fund-raiser event with a gay audience and promising to lift the ban on homosexuals in the military. . . . He then came under intense criticism from many of these same groups by backtracking on that pledge. . . . His standing further dropped among many gays and lesbians when he signed a measure that defined marriage as a heterosexual union only. [However,] the homosexual community has applauded Clinton for appointing more than 100 open gays and lesbians to position in his administration. 'Some great progress has been made—more than any other administration in history.' "[36] The *Washington Post* stated "That does not mean gay rights activists do not want more. Although Clinton has named more than 100 openly gay appointees to his administration, the [HRC] has been pressing the White House to include more in positions that must be confirmed by the Senate, on the theory that those tend to be the most coveted jobs."[37]

Homosexual Rights Equals Civil Rights

Evident from the pre-speech press coverage is the effort to equate homosexual rights with civil rights. For example, the *Atlanta Journal and Constitution* stated that "Activists have long sought to link gay and lesbian rights with the broader issue of civil rights. The [HRC] will emphasize that at the dinner by presenting their national civil rights award" to an organization that works to secure rights for homosexuals.[38] The *Houston Chronicle* reported that an "openly gay Texas state representative" had "said the gay community must remember that quest for civil rights 'is a process, it is not an event.' "[39] The *Los Angeles Times* wrote that the president's attendance and speech "could have great symbolic importance" and compared it "to President Truman's decision to speak to the National Association for the Advancement of Colored People."[40] Comparing homosexuals to "Italian-Americans," the *New York Times* pointed out that the president's "advocacy on behalf of Italian-Americans never threatened to swamp his presidency . . . as did his unsuccessful push to integrate gay men and lesbians fully in the armed services. Nor has Mr. Clinton provoked gales of Italian-American fury in the way he outraged many homosexuals during his campaign last year by signing legislation intended to prevent single-sex marriages."[41]

THE POST-SPEECH RESPONSE OF THE PRESS

After the president gave his speech, the press framing continued the same as before the speech, with one notable exception: pro-family critics were no longer reported, rather they were paraphrased by the press and simply called, "conservative critics." The general meaning of the president's speech, as established by the press before he gave it, essentially remained the same, and the press generally ignored the president's statements on the issue made while on *Meet the Press*.[42] For example, the *Boston Globe* stated that the president's speech was "a historic and symbolic gesture" and that "America must abandon its old prejudices and become tolerant of sexual differences if it is truly to become one nation."[43] The speech, the *Boston Globe* continued, "was considered a turning point not only in his temperamental relationship with America's gay and lesbian community, but also in his own efforts to make the cause of gay equality part of his presidential legacy."[44] The *Daily News* stated that the president "broke a historic barrier . . . lending his voice and presidential seal to a glitzy gay rights fund-raiser. Clinton, who acknowledged 'there are some people who won't be comfortable with me for being here,' promised he would fight for legislation to protect gays and lesbians from being fired for their sexual orientation. 'Being gay, the last time I thought about it, seemed to have nothing to do with the ability to read a balance sheet, set a bone or change a sparkplug.' "[45]

The *Los Angeles Times* wrote that the president had made a "precedent-setting appearance [and had] urged the nation to accept gays and lesbians as full-fledged members of the American community. 'If we're ever going to build one America, then all Americans, including you and those you represent, have got to be part of it.' "[46] The *New York Times* insisted that the president "deftly turned aside occasional hecklers [and] was also thunderously applauded upon restating his support for a law to protect homosexuals from discrimination in the workplace, and upon issuing a peppery defense of Bill Lann Lee, his contested nominee to be Assistant Attorney General for Civil Rights. Mr. Clinton said that Mr. Lee 'is being discriminated against,' not because of his qualifications but 'because some members of the Senate disagree with his views on affirmative action.' Mr. Clinton did not make a routine speech tonight, instead calling for a redefinition 'of the immutable ideals that have guided us from the beginning' to include acceptance of gays and lesbians. But, in his speech, the president was cautious."[47]

The *Times-Picayune* wrote that the president "did what no sitting president had ever done: He addressed a gay and lesbian organization, saying, "All Americans means All Americans. All America losses if we let prejudice and discrimination stifle the hopes or deny the potential of a single American. All America loses when any person is denied or forced out of a job because of sexual orientation.' "[48] The *Washington Post* stated that a "half-century after President Harry S. Truman declared his commitment to civil rights before a largely black crowd . . . President Clinton last night pledged similar solidarity in the battle for equal rights for gay and lesbian Americans. The president used the opportunity to make a pitch for his embattled nominee for chief civil rights enforcer, Bill Lann Lee. . . . [He] vowed to continue lobbying for passage of [ENDA], which would bar workplace bias based on sexual orientation. The president's speech avoided stronger language that some aides and activists hoped he would use."[49]

The *Washington Times* commented that the president, "with strong words and a symbolic wink at lesbian TV personality Ellen DeGeneres, last night embraced the agenda of the activist homosexual movement and pledged to bring them employment equal rights that many voters have rejected. 'We all know that there is continuing discrimination against gays and lesbians but we also know that if we're ever going to build one America, then all Americans including you . . . have got to be a part of it.' With many of his top aides in the audience, Mr. Clinton focused his speech on [ENDA], which would bar job discrimination based on sexual orientation. 'It should be illegal,' he said of discrimination against homosexuals."[50] The *San Francisco Examiner* merely stated that the president's "unprecedented address to the nation's largest gay political organization . . . marked a milestone for him and for efforts by homosexuals to gain political office and protection against discrimination. Clinton's willingness to attend the $250-a-ticket fund-raiser by the 200,000-member [HRC] capped gains that gay men and lesbians have made during the Clinton administration. White House Press Secretary Mike McCurry said Clinton in his address to the HRC's 1,500 guests wanted to encourage Americans to 'recognize that diversity is part of America's strength.' "[51]

No Reason for Controversy

Numerous papers, while echoing the framing of the speech shown above, stated that the president advocated nothing controversial in his speech. For example, the *Buffalo News* wrote that the president kept to "relatively non-controversial territory. . . . Instead he urged congress to pass legislation protecting homosexuals from job discrimination and confirm Bill Lann Lee, his nomination as assistant attorney general for civil rights."[52] In a similar manner the *St. Petersburg Times* wrote that the president had "burst a political taboo" by addressing the HRC's gala, and that he kept to "relatively non-controversial territory. . . . Instead he urged congress to pass legislation protecting homosexuals from job discrimination and confirm Bill Lann Lee, his nomination as assistant attorney general for civil rights."[53] Following suit, the *Chattanooga Free Press* merely stated that the president spoke "Saturday night at a fundraiser for the nation's largest lesbian and male homosexual group. . . . White House officials billed Clinton's dinner address to the [HRC] as a 'community outreach' gesture not unlike his recent participation in the National Italian American Foundation dinner. The president planned nothing more provocative than reiteration of his endorsement of legislation protecting homosexuals from job discrimination and a plug for Senate confirmation of Bill Lann Lee. . . . Elizabeth Birch, executive director of [HRC], characterized Clinton's appearance as historic and his record 'completely in sync' with her organization's nondiscrimination agenda."[54] The *Austin American-Statesman* also interpreted the president's address in this way: the president kept "to relatively noncontroversial territory, steering clear of TV's Ellen. . . . Instead, he urged Congress to pass legislation protecting homosexuals from job discrimination and confirm Bill Lann Lee. . . . He told the audience . . . that people 'who aren't comfortable yet with you need to learn to see lesbians and gays as fellow Americans committed to freedom and equality. Should we change the law? You bet. Should we keep fighting discrimination? Absolutely. . . . But we have to broaden the imagination of America. We are defining in practical terms the immutable ideals that have guided us from the beginning.' White House officials billed the event as a community outreach gesture not unlike his recent participation in the National Italian American Foundation dinner."[55]

Columnists and editorials offered the same point of view that regular news articles advanced. For instance, Tom Teepen wrote that the president "did more than just give the [HRC's] anti-discrimination cause a small and passing boost. He also put future presidents in a bit of a box on the issue. . . . It will be notable in the future if a president refuses similar invitations. Balking presidents will be cornered into explaining why they are begging off, at least making political gay-bashing additionally awkward for pols who like to play to the anti-homosexual bleachers. . . . The immediate and formal purpose of Clinton's speech was to push for enactment of federal legislation that would outlaw job discrimination against gays and lesbians. Clinton was on fairly safe turf for his gesture. If the president's appearance can't as a result be called exactly brave, it was still bold."[56] The *Atlanta Journal and Constitution* editorially wrote that "the impact of the bully pulpit can come from not only what the president says, but also where he says it. That's why President Clinton's speech last weekend to the [HRC] had historic significance. While it still has far to go, American society in recent years has made strides in accepting homosexuals as people who deserve the same rights as other citizens. In one night, Bill Clinton moved the office of the president a huge step forward on this issue. There was nothing radical or even exceptional about what Clinton had to say Saturday night."[57]

Columnist Christopher Matthews wrote that "Merely by walking through the doors of the Grand Hyatt Hotel, he spoke dramatically of where he stands politically. Just as Harry Truman fifty years ago was the first president to address a black civil rights group, Clinton holds a similar place of respect for breaking this latter-day barrier."[58] Deb Price wrote that "Clinton aligned himself with the gay quest for equality, saying, 'We have to broaden the imagination of America. We are redefining, in practical terms, the immutable ideals that have guided us from the beginning.' Working toward a society that fully embraces gay Americans is both a 'good obligation' and a 'grand opportunity,' he proclaimed."[59] The *Providence Journal-Bulletin* editorially stated that the president's address was the first by a sitting president, and that "previous one's feared that subject of gay rights was too hot to handle. Our view is that the president, being leader of all Americans, should feel free to address virtually any group in the country."[60]

Equality for Homosexuals

Treating homosexuals "equally" was a major frame employed by the press. However, this term was never clearly defined. Many assertions were implied by this frame, however. For example, the press relayed well the White House assertion that President Clinton is doing for homosexuals what President Truman did for black Americans. In so doing, the assertion that homosexuals ought to be in the same protected class as racial and ethnic minorities is advanced. The *Boston Globe* wrote that the president "compared himself to President Harry S. Truman taking a stand against segregation fifty years ago. 'Harry Truman stood before the Lincoln Memorial and said, "It is more important today than ever to ensure that all Americans enjoy the rights of freedom and equality." When I say all Americans, I mean all Americans,' he said. [Thus he] linked the fight by gays and lesbians against discrimination with the more overarching struggle for equality. . . ."[61] The *Daily News* quoted Elizabeth Birch thanking president Clinton for " 'being the first President of the United States in history to stand up for our [homosexuals] civil rights.' "[62]

The *Los Angeles Times* stated that President Clinton had made "efforts to advocate equal rights for gays and lesbians" and was the "first incumbent president to participate in an event of this kind. . . . [He] repeated the words of President Truman, who stood in front of the Lincoln Memorial fifty years ago to endorse equal rights for African Americans. The president quoted Truman . . . 'When I say all Americans, I mean all Americans.' Clinton added his own postscript: 'Well my friends, all Americans still means all Americans.' "[63] The *Times-Picayune* was more forceful in making the assertion: "Clinton built his speech around the 'when I say all Americans, I mean all Americans' theme Harry Truman used fifty years ago during a time when slavery had ended, but segregation remained. 'Well, my friends,' Clinton told the crowd of 1,500, 'all

Americans still means all Americans.' 'We are a very young movement, and every once in a while in American history, critical civil rights challenges get delivered up to certain presidents,' [HRC's] Elizabeth Birch said."[64] The *Washington Post* led with this statement: "A half-century after President Harry S. Truman declared his commitment to civil rights before a largely black crowd gathered at the Lincoln memorial, President Clinton last night pledged similar solidarity in the battle for equal rights for gay and lesbian Americans. Clinton echoed Truman's historic remarks to the NAACP. . . . Truman that day vowed his support for equality for all Americans, 'And when I say all Americans,' Truman said, 'I mean all Americans.' 'Well my friends,' Clinton said last night, 'all Americans still means all Americans.' By equating the gay rights movement with the struggle for racial equality, Clinton risked igniting a backlash among conservatives and among some African American leaders who resent such comparisons."[65]

The *Commercial Appeal* also led with an echo of the president's remarks: "A half-century after President Truman declared his commitment to civil rights before a largely black crowd gathered at the Lincoln Memorial, President Clinton Saturday night promised a similar crusade on behalf of equal rights for gay and lesbian Americans. Clinton consciously echoed Truman's historic remarks to the NAACP. . . . Truman that day vowed his support for equality for all Americans, 'And when I say all Americans,' Truman said, 'I mean all Americans.' 'Well my friends,' Clinton said Saturday night, 'all Americans still means all Americans.' By equating the gay rights movement with the struggle for racial equality, Clinton risked igniting a backlash among conservatives and among some African American leaders who resent such comparisons."[66] The *Sunday Gazette Mail* added the president's words: " 'When we deny opportunity because of ancestry or religion, race or gender, disability or sexual orientation, we break the compact. It is wrong and it should be illegal.' "[67]

Opinion essays and editorials reported this same linking of homosexual rights and civil rights. Christopher Matthews wrote that "Just as Harry Truman fifty years ago was the first president to address a black civil rights group, Clinton holds a similar place of respect for breaking this latter-day barrier."[68] Chuck Colbert wrote that "In careful and intelligent words, the president provided a heartfelt rationale for extending civil rights protection to gay men and lesbians in the workforce. . . . Until all Americans really means all Americans, shouldn't every one of us become a gay civil rights activist, too?"[69] Deb Price wrote that if the president "had made only perfunctory remarks, the evening still would have been historic. But he elevated it to a noble occasion by staking out the moral high ground on behalf of the gay civil rights movement, describing it to the nation as part of the never-ending struggle to make the American ideal of equality a reality for all."[70]

This theme of equating homosexuality with race as a civil rights class was not lost on Ben Wattenberg. He wrote that the HRC "sees itself as the moral and historical heir to the black civil-rights movement.... The archetype of the black civil-rights struggle pervaded the rhetoric and symbolism of the gala. Clinton eloquently expressed the argument for gay equality, reflecting that sexuality has nothing to do with 'the ability to read a balance book, fix a broken bone or change a spark plug.' "[71]

Clinton Is Good for Gays, But Not Good Enough

Positive comments attributed to homosexual activists about President Clinton were found throughout the coverage of the speech. For example, Elizabeth Birch was given a great deal of space by the *Boston Globe* for her comments about the president's contributions to the homosexual agenda: " 'the fact is that if you compare President Clinton to any other leader in the history of this country, his record is extraordinary.' She ticked off a list, which including his nomination of [openly gay] philanthropist James Hormel.... Birch also credited Clinton with appointing more than 100 openly gay people to administrative jobs; ordering Federal agencies to implement nondiscrimination policies; issuing an executive order mandating that gays and lesbians no longer be considered a security risk ... and increasing funding for the treatment and research of AIDS and HIV."[72] The *Times-Picayune* reported her as saying " 'President Clinton gets high marks for putting gay issues on the radar screen of America. No president has ever brought gay [issues] into the public discourse the way this president has.' "[73] The reporter then listed the same accomplishments given by the *Boston Globe* above.

Although some critics of the homosexual agenda were given press space prior to the president's speech, they were all but absent following the speech. Much criticism was presented, but it was now framed to assert that the president had not gone far enough in meeting the demands of homosexual activists. Thus the president was framed as having done so much (deserving of praise), *but falling short and needing to do more* (deserving of criticism). For example, Tom Teepen wrote, "If the president's appearance can't as a result be called exactly brave, it was still bold. Clinton has tried to do right by gay and lesbians rights, but the record is mixed. His attempt to end discrimination in the military fizzled into the equivocating don't-ask, don't-tell policy that has done little more than redecorate the same old closet. Cornered on the topic during his re-election campaign, the president disavowed homosexual marriage as a legal option."[74] The *New York Times* reflected that the president "has had deep differences with gays and lesbians, disappointing many at the beginning of his first term by backing down in efforts to fully integrate homosexuals into the military, and disappointing them again at the end of that term by signing legislation intended to prevent single-sex marriage."[75] The *Times-Picayune* wrote that "many leaders of gay and lesbian organizations were unhappy with the compromise Clinton made with Congress that produced the 'don't ask, don't tell' policy on gay men and lesbians in the military. In 1992, he had pledged to end the ban on gay people in the military. Several also have said they were disappointed when he signed legislation that allows the states not to recognize same-gender marriages, and with his unwillingness to lift the ban on using federal money for needle exchange programs."[76] The *San Francisco Examiner* wrote that despite the spending boosts and his appointments, Clinton has angered many in the gay rights community. In 1993, he abandoned a 1992 campaign pledge to allow gays to openly declare their homosexuality and remain in the armed forces. Clinton instead ordered a compromise 'don't ask, don't tell, don't pursue' policy, which gays say allows the military to continue to discriminate against them. He opposes needle exchange programs. . . . And during last year's presidential campaign, he signed into law a GOP-sponsored ban on extending federal benefits to partners in homosexual-couple relationships. 'There is no question that the Clinton presidency has been marked by some disappointments.' "[77]

Editorials displayed this line of thought as well. For example, the *Des Moines Register* editorially stated that the president's speech was "applaudable for its intent, [but] fell short in the arena of full disclosure." The editorial continued, stating that the president's "call to 'broaden the imagination of America' deserves praise. . . . [However, after] his infamous 'don't ask, don't tell' debacle on gays and lesbians in the military, Clinton's stature among gays and lesbians took a nose dive. His standing in conservative circles, already weakened by his half-hearted effort to reach out to the gay and lesbian community, plummeted even further."[78] M. Charles Bakst, while issuing some praise, took the president to task for not doing enough: "Forget for a moment that it took Mr. Clinton years to do this [speak to HRC]. Or that his don't ask–don't tell policy on gays in the military is a national embarrassment. Or that his embrace of an anti-same-sex marriage bill was a disgrace. I give him credit for backing a bill to ban job discrimination and for appointing a record number of gays. When the day comes that everyone recognizes that [we are all Americans] gays will presumably be treated equally, even in the military and even when it comes to marriage."[79]

Criticism from pro-homosexual groups was well-covered by the press. Conspicuous in its absense, however, was criticism from pro-family groups. When such criticim was presented, these critics were not characterized as *pro-family*, but rather as *anti-gay* or *conservative*. For example, the *Boston Globe* stated that for "antigay groups . . . Clinton's appearance is tantamount to an endorsement of a lifestyle with which they disagree. 'It's a disgrace to the bully pulpit to promote this behavior,' said Kristin Hansen, a spokeswoman for the conservative Family Research Council. '[This] is very clearly an effort to raise money for the Democratic Party.' " However, such criticism was blunted by this assertion ascribed to gay representative Barney Frank: "it hardly matters what conservative Christians think about Clinton's speaking to the [HRC]. 'People who are significantly motivated by their opposition to gays and lesbians being treated fairly never voted for Bill Clinton and are not going to vote for Al Gore,' Frank said."[80] The *Daily News* lumped ACT UP and the Family Research Council together: "The nation's most rabidly pro- and anti-homosexual activists were outraged by Clinton's appearance. . . . [ACT UP stated:] 'Gays should be furious with Clinton's failure to do more to promote AIDS research and treatment.' Robert Knight of the [FRC] was equally incensed. 'It's disgraceful he's using the bully pulpit to validate behavior which is immoral.' "[81] The *Sacramento Bee* divided the groups protesting into two: "anti-gay demonstrators and AIDS protestors. . . . Christian conservatives voiced disgust at what Andrea Sheldon, executive director of the Traditional Values Coalition, called 'an American President kissing up to the wealthiest extremists of the amoral left.' "[82]

The *Washington Times* called the protestors, "anti-gay and AIDS activists. . . ."[83] The *Record* also called those who disagree with the radical homosexual agenda, anti-gay: "anti-gay demonstrators and AIDS protesters. . . . Conservatives gleefully suggest that the increased visibility of gay issues, particularly legal homosexual marriage, will lead to a backlash against the Democrats."[84] The *Chattanooga Free Press* reported the HRC's assertion that it " 'should be in the normal course of business that the president would address this constituency [of homosexual activists].' " Then it stated, "Still, Christian conservatives voiced disgust. . . . [A]nti-gay demonstrators and AIDS protestors . . . planned to picket. . . ."[85] The *San Francisco Chronicle* quoted a director "at the conservative Family Research Council" as saying that the president's address was " 'an unfortunate misuse of the highest office in the land.' "[86]

Those Heckling Gay Rights Activists

Of particular note is the manner in which the press reported the president's comments on HIV/AIDS funding. Only eight of ninety papers reported the comments, and all did so in the same manner; that is, leaving out the full presidential quote. For instance, the *Los Angeles Times* wrote that as he "spoke, Clinton was interrupted twice by AIDS activists who screamed out about people needlessly dying because of the lack of needle exchange programs for drug users, who are at high risk of becoming infected with the AIDS virus. Clinton said, 'I'd have been disappointed if you hadn't been here tonight. People with AIDS are dying. But since I became president, we're spending ten times as much on AIDS research and treatment programs.' "[87] The *New York Times* wrote that the president faced one man who "cried out, 'People with AIDS are dying!' The crowd hushed him, but Mr. Clinton chuckled. 'I'd have been disappointed if you hadn't been here tonight,' he said. He added, 'People with AIDS are dying, but since I became president we're spending ten times as much' combatting the disease. Mr. Clinton's words were drowned by applause that quickly turned into yet another standing ovation."[88]

Those in the audience stood and cheered for what the President said, but the press did not report the entire sentence. Of this portion of the president's speech, the *St. Petersburg Times* reported that "several members of the militant ACT-UP homosexual group also disrupted the speech. One shouted, 'People are dying of AIDS' to boos and hisses. Clinton laughed off the disruption. 'This, too, is part of what makes America great,' he said. 'Nobody has to be afraid when he or she screams at the president.' "[89] The *Times-Picayune* asserted only that the president's appearance caused some protests "from some who believe he has not done enough on gay and lesbian issues. Three members of ACT UP, an AIDS activist organization, interrupted his speech. One shouted, 'People are dying.' "[90] The *Washington Post* wrote that "three AIDS activists interrupted Clinton's speech with shouting. 'People with AIDS are dying,' one screamed. The audience immediately cheered Clinton, who responded, 'Wait, wait, wait. I'd have been disappointed if you hadn't been here tonight. People with AIDS are dying. But since I became president, we're spending ten times as much' on research."[91]

The *Washington Times* wrote that the president had "bragged about his record funding programs to fight AIDS, although the group ACT UP— the AIDS Coalition to Unleash Power—protested outside and charged that the White House hasn't done enough to cure the disease. One ACT UP protester inside the Hyatt interrupted Mr. Clinton's address, but the president said he has fought AIDS and 'we just have to keep working on it.' "[92] The *Commercial Appeal* wrote only that the president had "brushed off brief disruptions by AIDS activists complaining he had not done enough to fight the disease."[93] *USA Today* wrote that "Several protesters heckled Clinton during his speech. Their complaint: that Clinton has not been aggressive enough in increasing AIDS research funding or in making federal funds available to promote needle exchanges for drug users."[94]

SUMMARY

Let us now turn to answering the questions I posed in the introduction to this book. Essentially, the president framed his speech as being unexceptional: there is nothing unusual about homosexuals, so there ought to be nothing unusual about speaking to one of their activist groups. Within this broad context the president framed three issues: his nomination for the head of the federal government's Office of Civil Rights, redefining American ideals, and the inclusion of homosexuality as a federally protected minority. The press concurred with the president and began its coverage two days before the president actually spoke. The press echoed many of the president's points. It framed the speech as noncontroversial but important since this was the first time a president had spoken before a homosexual group. The press also equated homosexual rights with civil rights in general, and stated that the president had done much, but not enough for homosexuals.

How Did President Clinton Frame the Issue?

President Clinton, prior to running for president, stated that the main problem with America was that it was "drifting and divided." He wished to unite Americans into "one America." This would be accomplished through reconstructing what Americans believed about themselves and their values. The president implied that those not seeing this path were simply "unimaginative."

The president focused on his understanding of equality, linking homosexuality with immutable characteristics such as race and ethnicity. The president thus redefined the general American understanding of equality by linking homosexuality with race. This he placed in the context of a continued, positive progression of the "immutable ideals that have guided [Americans] from the beginning." The president links this understanding of equality with ENDA, which would add homosexuality as a federally protected class co-equal with race and ethnicity: "All America loses when any person is denied or forced out of a job because of sexual orientation." The president does not offer evidence of job discrimination or explain specifics about ENDA. The president does mention that under his administration, per patient spending for those with AIDS had risen to ten times that of patients with prostate cancer or breast cancer.

The president's assertions about equality grounded his request to those present to support ENDA and his nomination for the head of the Office of Civil Rights: Bill Lee. The president asserts that those who are not supporting Bill Lee's confirmation are discriminating against him because Lee supports affirmative action. Thus, the president redefines discrimination to include disagreement on policy: "some members of the Senate disagree with his views on affirmative action." The president implies that those who "aren't comfortable" with homosexuals and their agenda simply do not know any homosexuals. So, if you disagree with him, you simply do not understand.

How Did the Press, Responding to President Clinton, Frame the Issue?

The press began discussion on the president's speech two days before the president actually delivered it. These articles stressed that the president would be the first American president to address a homosexual rights group, therefore homosexuals have politically come of age. According to the press, simply by appearing the president would send a message: "Gay and lesbian activists say Clinton's speech marks a coming of age for a political movement that has become a national force only in the past decade." Thus the press maintained that "No matter what he says in his speech, Clinton's mere presence at the [HRC's] first annual national dinner will make history and to many activists signals the maturation of a movement once relegated to the fringes of American society."

This interpretation was set between homosexual activists' statements about the historic nature of the occasion and critics of the movement. Consistently homosexual activists were depicted as "civil rights" activists and those who disagreed with them were depicted as "conservative critics" or "anti-gay," never "pro-family." Conservatives were cast in a light of trying to prevent homosexuals from obtaining equal rights with heterosexuals. Although the statements of homosexual activists were consistently presented, pro-family activists were infrequently quoted. Homosexual activists, while reported as giving praise to Clinton, were also depicted as his critics since they asserted that the president had not gone far enough with the changes they desired: "Gay and lesbian leaders . . . say Clinton has both delighted and disappointed them more than any other president." In addition, President "Clinton appointed 100 openly gay officials his first term. . . . He created the first White House liaison to the gay community. . . . He provided more money for AIDS research and endorse [ENDA]. Yet Clinton backtracked on his [promise] to allow openly gay people to serve in the military. Also, he signed the Defense of Marriage Act. . . ."

Post-speech coverage essentially continued the same framing. Basically, instead of writing that the president's appearance *will break* "historic barriers," the press wrote that his appearance *broke* "historic barriers." The press did focus on ENDA and the contested confirmation of Bill Lee. They maintained that ENDA would only "protect homosexuals from discrimination in the workplace," and that Lee would only enforce civil rights law. However, the press asserted along with the president that Lee had been discriminated against: "Mr. Clinton said that Mr. Lee 'is being discriminated against,' not because of his qualifications but 'because some members of he Senate disagree with his views on affirmative action." The press implied that there is widespread job discrimination against gays and that ENDA and Lee were not controversial: the president kept to "relatively non-controversial territory.... Instead he urged congress to pass legislation protecting homosexuals from job discrimination and confirm Bill Lann Lee, his nomination as assistant attorney general for civil rights."

The press advanced well the president's new notion of equality. This was accomplished in part by the wide reporting of the Clinton–Truman analogy described above. Ultimately, the press placed homosexuality in the same class as race and ethnicity. They also, in addition to the president's own efforts, equated *homosexual rights* to *civil rights. Homosexual* activists were often called *civil rights* activists. This was frequently accomplished through linking President Clinton's speech with President Truman's speech to the NAACP: the appearance and speech "could have great symbolic importance.... [It is similar] "to President Truman's decision to speak to the national Association for the Advancement of Colored People...." This also included linking homosexuality to race and ethnicity: "the president's advocacy on behalf of Italian-Americans never threatened to swamp his presidency ... as did his unsuccessful push to integrate gay men and lesbians fully into the armed services." The press also had difficulty even admitting that homosexual activists had an agenda: "Clinton, however, was careful to not endorse what many consider the more radical 'agenda' of the gay community."[95]

The president continued to receive praise and condemnation from the press in much the same manner as was given prior to his speech: he had done much, but not enough for homosexuals. Little criticism was presented from pro-family groups, and when it was included, it was as a foil to the most radical elements of the homosexual rights movement who were criticising the president for not doing enough for homosexuals: "The nation's most rabidly pro- and anti-homosexual activists were outraged by Clinton's' appearance...." No paper mentioned the president's brow-raising statement about his increasing spending ten times as much per AIDS patient as for those with breast and prostate cancer.

Did the Frames Converge to Present a Unified Contextual Whole?

The frames of the president and press blended well. Overall, the press took a positive view of the president's action and of his speech. Of the ninety different articles used for this chapter, sixty were news stories, twenty-six were opinion essays, and four were editorials. Of the opinion essays, sixteen were positive toward the president's speech, eight were negative, and two took a neutral stance toward the speech. Of note is that seven of the eight negative essays were the same essay reprinted. Of the editorials, three were positive and one negative. Of thirty-two different sources that the press cited, twenty-two were either homosexual or open supporters of the homosexual agenda. Only ten different pro-family supporters were included.

The press generally supported the statements made by the president. With regard to Bill Lee, the president linked him to the audience he was addressing by saying that Lee had suffered discrimination like they had, but for his views on affirmative action. Thus the president turns differences of opinion into discrimination, something the papers failed to mention. The press supported the president's position on Bill Lee. The president was reported as "issuing a peppery defense of Bill Lann Lee." However, no defense was given; it was only asserted one was presented. The press also supported the president in his efforts to pass ENDA, calling this "relatively non-controversial territory," and stating that this bill would only act to protect homosexuals from job discrimination.

The press also provided support by intentionally overlooking weak elements in the president's speech. For instance, the press stated that "In careful and intelligent words, the president provided a heartfelt rationale for extending civil rights protection to gay men and lesbians in the workforce." The president provided no rationale, however, he only *insisted* that this should be the case. Although the president and the press aggressively asserted that homosexuals were being denied basic rights, neither presented evidence to support this claim. Finally, with the Non-Employment Discrimination Act, the president sought to provide his new conception of equality the force of law. Not one paper mentioned this. Instead, the press actively framed the president's appearance as unexceptional and the speech as noncontroversial, thus consigning the redefinition of America's immutable ideals to the ordinary. In another act of actively supporting the president, the press failed to mention the extremely controversial statement made by the president regarding spending ten times as much per AIDS patients as is spent on patients with prostate or breast cancer.

The press also presented a slanted image of Americans who speak out against the homosexual agenda. Almost always these citizens were characterized as "conservative activists" or as "anti-gay." They were never characterized as pro-family. Contrary to this, supporters of the homosexual agenda were not called liberal, instead they were described sometimes as "gay activists," but usually as "civil rights activists."

The press did criticize the president. However, this was done in such a manner that his controversial acts and comments were made less controversial since the criticism was for the president not fully enacting the homosexual agenda. Thus the press would praise the president for pro-homosexual acts taken during his administration, and then criticize the president for not doing more that the homosexuals wanted; this made the steps thus far taken by the president, regardless of how radical, seem noncontroversial. The press cited pro-homosexual activists at a rate of 2 to 1 over those opposed to the president's speech, which helped to cast in the light of the minority those who disagreed with the president.

NOTES

1. The Human Rights Campaign Web site describes the HRC as "the largest national lesbian and gay political organization [which] has more than 360,000 members, both gay and non-gay. With a national staff, volunteers and members throughout the country, HRC: lobbies the federal government on gay, lesbian and AIDS issues; educates the public; participates in election campaigns; organizes volunteers; and provides expertise and training at the state and local level. Founded in 1980, HRC maintains the largest full-time lobbying team in the nation devoted to issues of fairness for lesbian and gay Americans." <http://hrc.org/mainset_about_us.asp>

2. All quotes ascribed to President Clinton are from the following text unless otherwise noted: The White House, Office of the Press Secretary, "Remarks by the President at Human Rights Campaign Dinner" (8 November 1997). Press reports were obtained using Lexis-Nexis. A search was performed with the key word "Clinton." Additional search terms included "Human Rights Campaign," "HRC," and "homosexual." The range of articles ran from 7 November 1997 to 20 November inclusive.

3. For an analysis of the Non-Employment Discrimination Act, see Robert H. Knight, "The Employment Non-Discrimination Act: An Unwarranted Expansion Of Federal Power," at <http://www.frc.org/insight/is96g4hs.html>. Some excerpts of Kennedy's article suggest this act will set

the stage for an enormous expansion of federal power over employers. This violates the principle of federalism embodied in the 10th Amendment. Guarantees an onslaught of costly litigation, which would hurt small businesses most of all. Paves the way for quotas based on sexual preference, regardless of a provision that stipulates that no quotas are allowed. (Proponents of the 1964 Civil Rights Act promised that it would never lead to racial quotas.) Prohibits employers from disciplining employees for sexual activity on or off the job and from taking such activity into account in any way. Defines "sexual orientation" so broadly that all sexual proclivities, from pedophilia to bisexuality, are given special protection and thus moral status on par with sex within marriage. Creates a broad cultural force that rewards and protects sexual perversion at the expense of traditional marriage and family. Poses a serious threat to employers' and employees' freedoms of religion, speech and association. The law would ensure that employers could no longer take their most deeply held beliefs into account when making hiring, management and promotion decisions. This would pose an unprecedented intrusion by the federal government into people's lives.

4. Jodi Enda, "Clinton to Address Gay-Rights Event, 1st Sitting Chief to Do So," *Arizona Republic* (7 November 1997): A16.

5. Skip Thurman, "Clinton to Openly Advocate Gay Rights," *Christian Science Monitor* (7 November 1997): US 4.

6. Jodi Enda, "Clinton to Speak at Gay-Rights Gala," *Times-Picayune* (7 November 1997): A10. Quote ascribed to Kate Kendall.

7. Peter Baker, "Attention by Clinton Has Brought Gay Rights into the Political Open," *Buffalo News* (8 November 1997): A3.

8. Nancy Mathis, "President to Address Gay Rights Group; Speech Shows Human Rights Campaign Clout," *Houston Chronicle* (8 November 1997): A1.

9. Elizabeth Shogren, "Clinton's Speech to Gays, Lesbian Will Be a First," *Los Angeles Times* (8 November 1997): A1.

10. "Clinton to Deliver Address at Gay-Rights Event," *News and Observer* (8 November 1997): A8. Quotation ascribed to Jeffrey Montgomery, Associate Director of the Triangle Foundation.

11. Julia Malone, "Clinton to Address Gay Activists: Saturday Speech Called 'Historic Step' by Some, 'Disgraceful' by Critics," *Atlanta Journal and Constitution* (7 November 1997): A1.

12. Peter Baker, "Clinton at Gay Rights Gala Will Be a Presidential First," *Washington Post* (8 November 1997): A1.

13. "Clinton to Deliver Address at Gay-Rights Event."

14. Malone, "Clinton to Address Gay Activists: Saturday Speech Called 'Historic Step' by Some, 'Disgraceful' by Critics."

15. Julia Malone, "Clinton to Address Gay Activists, Outraging Some Conservatives," *Atlanta Journal and Constitution* (7 November 1997): A9.

16. Delia M. Rios, "Clinton to Address Gay Rights Activists," *Atlanta Journal and Constitution* (8 November 1997): A10. Quote ascribed to no source.

17. Thurman.

18. Malone, "Clinton to Address Gay Activists, Outraging Some Conservatives."

19. Ann McFeatters, "Clinton Is Asked to Omit Anti Gays as Hate Topic," *Denver Rocky Mountain News* (8 November 1997): A57.

20. Deb Price, "President's Speech Means He's Finally Delivering on Promise to Reach Out to Gays," *Detroit News* (8 November 1997): C1.

21. Marc Sandalow, "Tonight's Speech to Gays a Presidential Precedent," *San Francisco Chronicle* (8 November 1997): A1.

22. Mathis.

23. Shogren. "Clinton's Speech to Gays, Lesbian Will Be a First."

24. "National Digest," *Star Tribune* (7 November 1997): A4.

25. Malone, "Clinton to Address Gay Activists: Saturday Speech Called 'Historic Step' by Some, 'Disgraceful' by Critics."

26. Ibid.

27. Sandalow.

28. Jodi Enda, "Clinton Reaches Out to Gays," *Cincinnati Enquirer* (7 November 1997): A7.

29. "Clinton to Deliver Address at Gay-Rights Event." The Media Research Center's Web site can be found at <http://www.mrc.org/>

30. Enda, "Clinton to Address Gay-Rights Event."

31. Thurman.

32. Bill Nichols, "Gay Gathering Takes Gauge of a President, Clinton Lauded, Warily, as Would-Be Heirs Are Warned," *USA Today* (7 November 1997): A11.

33. Julia Malone, "Clinton to Go Address Gay Rights Group," *Austin American-Statesman* (7 November 1997): A18.

34. Price, "President's Speech."

35. Mathis.

36. Quote ascribed to David Mixner, a "gay activist" and "old friend" of the president. Shogren, "Clinton's Speech to Gays, Lesbians Will Be a First."

37. Baker, "Clinton at Gay Rights Gala."

38. Rios.

39. Mathis.

40. James Bennet, "In Milestone, President Will Address a Gay Group," *New York Times* (8 November 1997): A11. These sentiments were ascribed to an unnamed "aide."

41. Ibid.

42. See White House, Office of the Press Secretary. "Interview of the President by NBC'S 'Meet The Press'" (9 November 1997). Available from the White House: <http://www.whitehouse.gov/> for the president's interview on *Meet the Press*.

Q: Let me turn to a cultural issue. Tonight you will be attending a gay rights dinner, the first sitting President in the history of the country to do so. What statement are you trying to make?

THE PRESIDENT: Well, Tim, you know, I grew up in the segregated south in the '40s and '50s. And all my life, from the time I was a child, I was taught and I have believed that every person in this country—no matter what their differences are, in their lifestyle or their race or their religion, if they obey the law, show up for work every day or show up for school, if they're good citizens, they ought to be treated with respect and dignity and equality. And they should be subject to no discrimination in the things that we all have to have access to, like education and a job and health care. What I'm trying to do is to continue to move that forward.

I know this is a difficult issue for a lot of Americans. I know that particularly for Americans who've never known anyone who was gay or lesbian personally, it's an issue that often arouses discomfort. But I think it's the right thing to do. I think we have to keep working until we say for everybody, the only test should be: are you a law-abiding, hard working citizen; do you do the things we require of all citizens. If you do, you should be subject to no discrimination and you ought to be part of the family of America. That's what I believe. And if my presence there tonight advances that goal, then that's a good thing.

Q: Do you believe that homosexuality should be taught in schools as an acceptable alternative lifestyle?

THE PRESIDENT: No, I don't think it should be advocated. I don't think it should be part of the public school curriculum.

But, on the other hand, I don't believe that anyone should teach school children that they should hate or discriminate against or be afraid of people who are homosexuals. That is the real issue. The real issue is the one that we're going to take up next week at the White House with the Hate Crimes Conference. We're going to have the first Hate Crimes Conference ever at the White House next week. And we're going to deal with that, not only against homosexuals, but against other groups of Americans.

I don't believe that we should be in the business of ratifying or validating or politicizing the issue. I think the real problem in America is still continuing discrimination and fear and downright misunderstanding.

Q: Now, Vice President Gore caused a stir when he said that Ellen—the TV star who will be honored tonight at the dinner—he said, "millions of Americans were forced to look at sexual orientation in an open light." Was Vice President Gore correct?

THE PRESIDENT: Well, I think when she did that on television, and you got to see the interplay with her family and her friends who were not homosexual, you got to see all that—I think for many Americans who themselves had never had a personal experience, never had a friend or a family member who's a homosexual—it did give them a chance to see it in a new light. So I think he was accurate about that.

My experience in life—all I can tell you is what my experience is—and I'm not talking about as president, I'm talking about as a citizen, as a person—is that most people's attitudes about how homosexuals should be treated really are determined more than anything else based on whether they have ever known someone who is homosexual. Now, whether most people's attitudes about whether the lifestyle should be condoned or condemned is a function, perhaps, of their religious training. But we're not talking about people's religious convictions here. We're talking about how people in the public arena, as citizens, should be treated in terms of their right to education, to jobs, to housing, and to be treated free of discrimination.

And that is the agenda that I want to further for all Americans. And that is what I think we ought to be focusing on.

43. Ann Scales, "President Takes Stand on Gay Rights," *Boston Globe* (9 November 1997): A1.

44. Ibid.

45. Kathy Kiely, "Prez Gets a Big Welcome at Gay Rights Fund-Raiser," *Daily News* (9 November 1997): 4.

46. Elizabeth Shogren, "Clinton, in Historic Speech, Urges Acceptance of Gays," *Los Angeles Times* (9 November 1997): A20.

47. James Bennet, "Clinton Is Greeted Warmly as He Speaks to Gay Group," *New York Times* (9 November 1997): A30.

48. Kathy Lewis, "Speech to Gay Group a First," *Times-Picayune* (9 November 1997): A1.

49. Peter Baker, "Clinton Equates Gay Rights, Civil Rights," *Washington Post* (9 November 1997): A18.

50. Paul Bedard, "Clinton Promises Gay Rights in Workplace," *Washington Times* (9 November 1997): A1.

51. Stewart M. Powell, "Clinton Talk at Gay Event a Milestone," *San Francisco Examiner* (9 November 1997): A1.

52. Sandra Sobieraj, "Clinton's Address to Gay and Lesbian Rights Group Is a First," *Buffalo News* (9 November 1997): A12.

53. "Clinton Addresses Gays but Meets 'Ellen' in Private," *St. Petersburg Times* (9 November 1997): A3.

54. Sandra Sobieraj, "Clinton 1st President to Address Gay Group," *Chattanooga Free Press* (9 November 1997): A1.

55. Sandra Sobieraj, "Clinton Speaks to Gays, but Meets 'Ellen' Backstage," *Austin American-Statesman* (9 November 1997): A2.

56. Tom Teepen, "Clinton's Boost for Gay Civil Rights," *Cox News Service* (10 November 1997).

57. Editorial, "Clinton Simply Endorses Equal Rights," *Atlanta Journal and Constitution* (11 November 1997): A14.

58. Christopher Matthews, "Clinton's Historic Gay Rights Speech," *San Francisco Examiner* (13 November 1997): A23.

59. Deb Price, "Clinton Addresses [*sic*] a Grand Day for Gays and Lesbians, a Great Day for America," *Detroit News* (14 November 1997): E2.

60. Editorial, "He's President of Everyone," *Providence Journal-Bulletin* (17 November 1997): B4.

61. Scales.

62. Kiely.

63. Shogren, "Clinton, in Historic Speech, Urges Acceptance of Gays."

64. Lewis.

65. Baker, "Clinton Equates Gay Rights, Civil Rights."

66. Baker, "Clinton Addresses Gay Rights Gala."

67. Sandra Sobieraj, "Clinton Addresses Gays, Avoids 'Ellen' Controversy," *Sunday Gazette Mail* (9 November 1997): A1.

68. Matthews.

69. Chuck Colbert, "All Americans Means Gay Americans, Too," *New American News Service* (13 November 1997). Parenthetical material in original.

70. Price, "Clinton Addresses."

71. Ben Wattenberg, "Clinton Courts Gay Lobby," *Chattanooga Free Press* (15 November 1997): A5.

72. Scales.

73. Lewis.

74. Teepen.

75. Bennet, "Clinton Is Greeted Warmly as He Speaks to Gay Group."

76. Lewis.

77. Powell. Quote by David Smith, HRC's communications director.

78. Editorial, "No Risk, but Something Gained," *Des Moines Register* (14 November 1997): 14.

79. M. Charles Bakst, "Clinton and Gays: His Tardy Message Can Still Be Helpful," *Providence Journal-Bulletin* (20 November 1997): B1.

80. Scales.

81. Kiely.

82. Sandra Sobieraj, "U.S. Must Broaden Idea of Equality, Clinton Tells Gays," *Sacramento Bee* (9 November 1997): A10.

83. Bedard.

84. Sandra Sobieraj, "Clinton Addresses Gay Group's Fund-Raiser," *The Record* (9 November 1997): A13.

85. Sobieraj, "Clinton 1st President to Address Gay Group."

86. Powell.

87. Shogren, "Clinton, in Historic Speech, Urges Acceptance of Gays."

88. Bennet, "Clinton Is Greeted Warmly."

89. "Clinton Addresses Gays but Meets 'Ellen' in Private." Story of woman arrested by SS for not shaking the president's hand.

90. Lewis.

91. Baker, "Clinton Equates Gay Rights, Civil Rights."

92. Bedard.

93. Baker, "Clinton Addresses Gay Rights Gala."

94. Bill Nichols, "Clinton Criticized for Gay Group Talk," USA Today (10 November 1997): A7.

95. Ibid.

Chapter Eight

Press Bias, Politics, and the Media Manipulation of Controversial Issues

The power of the press is very great, but not so great as the power of suppress.

—Lord Northcliffe

Americans look to the press to provide the information they need to make informed political choices. How well the press lives up to its responsibility to provide this information has a direct impact upon Americans: how they think about and act upon the issues that confront them. The practices of the press are easily discerned when one looks for the frames used by the press when it tells a story. I did that in this book by looking at how political actors framed their speeches and comparing this with the press framing of that speech. Having read this far you know how different the frames have been in the case studies presented. There were 683 articles from 116 different newspapers examined for this study, and the conclusion to be drawn is clear: the mainstream press in America is an anti-Democratic institution. How this is so will be explained in this chapter.

OVERVIEW OF PRESS PRACTICES

In its raw form, agenda-setting theory states that the press tells us what to think about but not what to think, and that we learn about an issue in direct proportion to press coverage of that issue. The notion of agenda-extension moves beyond agenda-setting theory because it identifies an evaluative component to media coverage of issues and events. Looking at press coverage of issues from this perspective highlights a dangerous consideration: the press not only tells us what to think about (agenda-setting), but it also tells us *how* to think about it (agenda-extension). This evaluative component has been called *priming* and *framing* by various communication and political science researchers. Priming refers specifically to the contextual cues embedded within a news story that would be used by the public to evaluate the subject matter at hand. For public political speeches this would imply that the public would be primed to evaluate politicians by how well they handled certain issues in relation to the evaluative cues provided by the media.

My concern in this book has been to highlight the frames used by the press. Frames are central organizing ideas within a narrative account of an issue or event. Frames provide the interpretive cues used by readers to make sense of neutral facts. The case studies in this book have demonstrated that the press, intentionally or not, constructs frames in opposition to those who do not agree with their political agenda. Specifically, this framing took the form of direct opposition to the points of view expressed by Senator Davidson, Minister Farrakhan, Senator Lott, Minister White, and certain portions of President Clinton's statements that did not comport with press ideals. This direct opposition irreparably harmed these speakers' ability to explain their point of view to the American public. Unless the reader had firsthand access to transcripts of these speeches, all information was filtered through the frame of the press. As Robert E. Denton said, "It is virtually impossible to distinguish between our political system and the media as separate entities."[1] Thus, the context, through which the statements made by these political leaders were understood, changed; a new context was provided by the press which also framed the statements in such a way that the original meaning of the messages were changed. In this manner the above-listed political actors were not treated fairly as news sources, but rather they were forced into an oppositional role to that of the press. The notable exception to this was the favorable response of the press to certain elements of President Clinton's speeches. In those instances in which his policy statements agreed with the political ideology of the press, the president received positive coverage. In general, however, those political actors who articulated political points of view outside of the acceptable band of press politics were presented as being on the wrong side, articulating one definition of the situation, while the press, on the right side, advanced another. For Davidson, Farrakhan, Lott, and White, the oppositional framing was so extreme that the press introduced so-called critics who took an oppositional view that always duplicated the view of the press, as expressed in opinion essays and editorials.

Frames are composed of certain keywords, metaphors, concepts, and symbols; they work by highlighting some features of reality over others. In short, they make some facts rather than others more salient or relevant to the person exposed to the frame. As communication researcher David Weaver stated, "salience is key to any attempt to put a certain spin or interpretation on an issue, event, product or person. By highlighting or emphasizing certain aspects, or attributes, the media can influence not only what we think about, but how we think about it."[2] In his coverage of Farrakhan's speech, *New York Times* reporter R.W. Apple demonstrated well that reporters often know that the way they cover an event will influence how readers perceive that event: "If the message delivered by coverage of the march is one of racial polarization, white anger against blacks could intensify. But if the emphasis is kept on today's repeated appeals for the regeneration of the black family and the need for strong African-American male role models, the march could have a more emollient effect."[3] As we saw in the Farrakhan chapter, Apple's colleagues *chose* to frame the event as divisive; they focused on contention and hate, rather than upon the countless positive messages that were conveyed by speakers, including Farrakhan.

In framing, it is not the frequency of a word, metaphor, or concept that accounts for it strength, but rather how it is consistently framed across time. As these case studies have demonstrated, the press consistently and cohesively advanced specific frames that existed throughout coverage of a speech. Moreover, similar frames were found to exist on specific issues, even though the speakers, speeches, and events were different. For example, the mainstream press frames concerning homosexuality are well set, and thus the same frame—homosexualtiy as genetic— was imposed on both Senator Lott and Reggie White, *even though Lott did not raise that issue.*

Recall the work of Brigitte Lebens Nacos mentioned in the Introduction. Nacos found a strong relationship between editorial positions and the content of "objective" political news coverage.[4] I found this relationship to be extremely strong as well. In all six case studies the general framing of news stories duplicated the frames used by both editorial and opinion pages. Although news stories tended to be more subtle in their denunciations and endorsements, they did echo editorial positions. Editorials and opinion essays would assert their opinions forcefully. News stories would echo these same opinions by relying on the quotations of like-minded sources. What was readily apparent in news articles, opinion essays, and editorials was a willingness of the press to advance its own ideals concerning appropriate political and social behavior. There was no difference between the frames used by regional papers and national papers. Regional papers were, however, more likely to report the thoughts of local residents; yet these thoughts usually matched the predominant frame used by the press. In addition, regional papers were more likely to report what the local congressional leaders had said on a particular issue.

What is of concern here is the press advancement of its own agenda and beliefs. Concerning public affairs, Thomas Patterson has written that the "news media cannot provide the guidance that citizens need. The function of news . . . is to signalize events. In carrying out this function properly, the press contributes to informed public opinion. However, politics is more a question of values than of information. To act on their interests, citizens must arrive at an understanding of the relationship of their values and those at stake in public policy. Political institutions are designed to help citizens make this connection. The press is not."[5] Although dangerous enough concerning everyday issues, when concerning controversial issues, this practice of advancing its own partisan interpretation of events over a neutral presentation of facts is especially dangerous, for the public needs an account of facts that is as objective as possible. The general level of speculation, analysis, and judgment—aggressively underpinned with political ideology—in news articles, opinion essays, and editorials, makes it exceedingly difficult for political leaders—elected or not, Democrat, Republican, or any other—to impart their conception of the issues accurately.

Journalistic Codes of Ethics

Shortly after World War II, the Commission on Freedom of the Press, often called the Hutchins Commission, took up the issue of press ownership and responsibility. The report of the commission, entitled *A Free and Responsible Press*, represented the growing trend in American media toward advocating social responsibility. The basic premise of the commission was that "the power and near monopoly position of the media impose on them an obligation to be socially responsible."[6] This idea of social responsibility is summed up by Theodore Peterson: "Freedom carries concomitant obligations; and the press, which enjoys a privileged position under our government, is obliged to be responsible to society for carrying out certain essential functions of mass communication in contemporary society."[7]

The Hutchins Commission, anticipating this need, listed these standards for press performance.

1. The press must provide "a truthful, comprehensive, and intelligent account of the day's events in a context which gives them meaning."[8]
2. The press must serve as a "forum for the exchange of comment and criticism."[9]
3. The press must project "a representative picture of the constituent groups in society."[10]

4. The press must assume responsibility for "the presentation and clarification of the goals and values of the society" in which it operates.[11]

5. The press must provide "full access to the day's intelligence."[12]

The overwelming majority of mainstream papers in America subcribe to the sentiments expressed by the Hutchins Commission, and this is seen in their own statements of principle and codes of ethical conduct. For example, the *Washington Post* asserts it still adheres to the 1935 principles penned by then publisher Eugene Meyer. Four of Meyer's principles have special relevance to this study: "The first mission of a newspaper is to tell the truth as nearly as the truth can be ascertained. The newspaper shall tell ALL the truth so far as it can learn it, concerning the important affairs of America and the World. The newspaper's duty is to its readers and to the public at large, and not to the private interests of its owners. The newspaper shall not be the ally of any special interest, but shall be fair and free and wholesome in its outlook on public affairs and public men."[13]

The American Society of Newspaper Editors' (ASNE) statement of principles has been in existence since 1922. Articles 1 and 4 are particularly relevent to this study:

ARTICLE I: The primary purpose of gathering and distributing news and opinion is to serve the general welfare by informing the people and enabling them to make judgments on the issues of the time.

ARTICLE IV: Every effort must be made to assure that the news content is accurate, free from bias and in context, and that all sides are presented fairly. Editorials, analytical articles and commentary should be held to the same standards of accuracy with respect to facts as news reports. Significant errors of fact, as well as errors of omission, should be corrected promptly and prominently.[14]

The Society of Professional Journalists holds similar views:

Members of the Society of Professional Journalists believe that public enlightenment is the forerunner of justice and the foundation of democracy. The duty of the journalist is to further those ends by seeking truth and providing a fair and comprehensive account of events and issues. Conscientious journalists from all media and specialties strive to serve the public with thoroughness and honesty. Journalists should be honest, fair and courageous in gathering, reporting and interpreting information. Journalists should: Test the accuracy of information from all sources and exercise care to avoid inadvertent error. Deliberate distortion is never permissible. Tell the story of the diversity and magnitude of the human experience boldly, even when it is unpopular to do so. Examine their own cultural values and avoid imposing those values on others.[15]

The Associated Press Managing Editors Code of Ethics states in part that:

1. The good newspaper is fair, accurate, honest, responsible, independent and decent.
2. Truth is its guiding principle.
3. It avoids practices that would conflict with the ability to report and present news in a fair, accurate and unbiased manner.
4. The newspaper should serve as a constructive critic of all segments of society. It should reasonably reflect, in staffing and coverage, its diverse constituencies.
5. The newspaper should guard against inaccuracies, carelessness, bias or distortion through emphasis, omission or technological manipulation.
6. The newspaper should strive for impartial treatment of issues and dispassionate handling of controversial subjects.[16]

The general themes of these codes of conduct are clear. The press *voluntarily* commits to providing the American public with the *full details* of important issues within an *unbiased context*. In short, the press says it acts to serve *all Americans* regardless of political position. One should differentiate between news sources that do not purport to be objective and those that do, however. Talk radio, for example, is overwelmingly right-leaning in America. Yet talk radio hosts provide *commentary*, and do not purport to being objective in how they present the news. Maintream media, represented by the papers included in this study, and those ascribing to the codes of conduct cited above, do purport to being unbiased and objective in their reportorial practice. This is why biased news coverage is so pernicious coming from these papers. They hide behind the mantel of objectivity while injecting their own political ideology into the very information they give to the public as objective news. As Gary C. Woodward has written, "political journalism is—against its own high standards—a flawed enterprise," because it cannot live up to its stated goal of objectivity.[17]

Clearly the press has broken numerous aspects of the above codes in the case studies presented in this book. In the sections that follow, we will see that by its political composition and its biased reportorial practices, the press not only breaks its own code of ethics, it functions as an anti-democratic institution since it undermines the very democratic ideals it professes to uphold.

POLITICS OF THE PRESS

Based on the six case studies presented in this book, I believe the press exhibits an easy willingness to advance its own ideals concerning appropriate pubic policy. Furthermore, what is advanced are typically idealized norms of left-wing ideology. In short, there is a demonstrable liberal bias to the mainstream press in America. What is of concern here is not that the bias is liberal, *but that such a bias is so extensively present throughout the institution.* Whether liberal or not, that the press advances its own agenda and beliefs instead of providing information necessary for citizens to make informed political decisions is simply devastating to the free functioning of American democracy. Although pernicious enough in everyday reporting, when dealing with controversial issues it is especially dangerous, for the public needs an account of facts that is as objective as possible. Underpinned with an idealized left-wing ideology, the general level of speculation, analysis, judgments, and unsupported assertions makes it exceedingly difficult for a political leader— particularly Republicans, Independents, Moderates, or Conservatives— to impart their ideas accurately to the American people.

That the press exhibits a narrow brand of liberal thought is demonstrated well by this study. Moreover, the policy stances of the press echo their political self-descriptions, which are far removed from the political demographics of the American public at large. One of the earliest full descriptions of the political map of the press was conducted by Robert Lichter who in 1981 published survey data generated from media self-descriptions. What Lichter found is sobering: at "least 81% of the news media had voted for the liberal Democrat for President in every election going back to 1964. He found that 90% favored abortion; 83% found nothing wrong with homosexuality; only 47% believed adultery to be wrong; 50% had no religious affiliation; and 85% seldom or never attended church or synagogue."[18]

Elaine S. Povich, in 1996, published similar results, although limited to Washington journalists. Povich found the following: When asked about the Contract with America, 59% of journalists thought it an election year ploy, only 3% thought it a serious reform proposal. Sixty-two percent agreed or somewhat agreed that their job was to suggest potential solutions to social problems. Perhaps most striking was the self-description of political orientation. Twenty-two percent said they were liberal, 39% liberal to moderate, 30% moderate, 7% moderate to conservative, and 2% conservative. Party affiliation was 50% Democrat, 37% independent, 4% Republican, and 9% other parties.[19] Eighty-nine percent voted for Bill Clinton in 1992.[20] Contrast this with the rest of America: 18% said they were liberal, 40% moderate, and 39% conservative.[21] Party affiliation was 31% Democrat, 39% independent, and 30% Republican.[22] Forty-five percent voted for Bill Clinton in 1992. On the issues mentioned above, 42% of Americans would favor a law that would restrict all abortion except to save the life of the mother.[23] When asked about how they feel, 74% of Americans consider homosexual behavior unacceptable.[24] Seventy-nine percent felt adultery was always wrong (up to 90% if "almost always wrong").[25] Eighty-three percent consider themselves Protestant or Catholic (2% Jewish), and 61% attend church or synagogue at least once a month.[26]

There have been other polls of journalists in America. They all show the same politically homogenized press. Following the Lichter study, a Times Mirror survey found that 56% of the press considered themselves to be very to somewhat liberal, with only 18% very to somewhat conservative.[27] In 1995, after charges of liberal bias were widespread, the dynamics of press self-reporting changed: now only 22% of the national press considered themselves liberal, 5% conservative, and almost two-thirds, 64%, considered themselves moderate.[28] Some rather startling data has emerged which strongly suggests a mighty liberal leaning among members of our national press. For example, whereas 89% of Washington reporters voted for Bill Clinton in 1992, only 7% voted for George Bush. Only 4% were registered Republicans, whereas 50% said they were Democrats.[29] Tim Graham asked, "Did this preference for Clinton seep into media coverage? Reporters thought so. A substantial majority (55 percent) . . . believe that George Bush's [1992] candidacy was damaged by the way the press covered him. Only 11 percent feel that Gov. Clinton's campaign was harmed. . . . Interestingly, that didn't mean reporters believed coverage was unfair. 80 percent graded election coverage as good or excellent. . . . Damaging Bush and aiding Clinton weren't just politically satisfying, but journalistically virtuous."[30] As Howard Kurtz of the *Washington Post* stated: "There is a diversity problem in the news business, and it's not just the kind of diversity we usually talk about, which is not getting enough minorities in the news business, but political diversity, as well, anybody who doesn't see that is just in denial."[31]

These self-descriptions of journalists reveal a stunning difference between the composition of Americans and the press that purports to provide them with news they can use. *U.S. News & World Report* stated: "There is reason to worry that the cultural chasm between the majority of Americans and the Washington media is widening. A survey taken for *U.S. News* in the spring of 1995 found that 50% of voters thought the news media are strongly or somewhat in conflict with their goals, while only 40% thought the media are strongly or somewhat friendly to their goals. This was the worst approval rating of any group measured—even lower than the ratings for elected officials and lawyers."[32] Along these same lines, Michael Barone, writing in the *American Enterprise* stated: "Mainline journalism is by no means reliably pro-Democratic, as Clinton White House staffers will attest, but it is reliably anti-Republican. The Center for Media and Public Affairs documented that in the fall 1994 campaigns the three major networks gave Newt Gingrich 100% negative coverage. If journalism's reputation for liberalism, combined with the industry's drive for 'multicultural' hiring, keeps driving away conservatives and attracting liberals, there will soon be problems. Problems with the quality and accuracy of news coverage, and problems with audience rebellion."[33]

Although the information above may seem conclusive to many, saying one is liberal, or one is a Democrat, or that one votes almost exclusively for Democrats, or endorses social positions of which a majority of Americans disagree, does not mean that one cannot engage in neutral reportorial practices. However, based on the results of this study, the overwelming majority of journalists do allow their political ideology to taint their reporting. This willingess to inject partisan bias into news reports is in part explained by the move toward more interpretive as opposed to descriptive news writing. On this point Thomas Patterson wrote that today, "facts and interpretation are freely intermixed in news reporting. Interpretation provide the theme, and the facts illuminate it. The theme is primary; the facts illustrative. As a result, events are compressed and joined together within a common theme. Reporters question politicians' motives and give them less of a chance to speak for themselves."[34] In addition, admissions coming from the press corps itself show a remarkable degreee of candor about willingness to engage in partisan politics as standard reportorial practice.

Take, for example, former CBS News correspondent Bernard Goldberg writing in the *Wall Street Journal*: "There are lots of reasons fewer people are watching network news, and one of them, I'm more convinced than ever, is that our viewers simply don't trust us. And for good reason. The old argument that the networks and other 'media elites' have a liberal bias is so blatantly true that it's hardly worth discussing anymore. No, we don't sit around in dark corners and plan strategies on how we're going to slant the news. We don't have to. It comes naturally to most reporters."[35] Robert Novak, writing for *USA Today* stated that "members of the national media tend to share a uniformly liberal ideology. This does not mean they are meeting secretly every other week in someone's basement to get their marching orders. Rather, their ideology originates from a number of left-of-center experiences in their univeristy education, tightly knit peer groups, and the mileu of popular culture since the 1960s."[36] Evan Thomas, former *Newsweek* Washington Bureau Chief, plainly stated, "There is a liberal bias. It's demonstrable. You look at some statistics. About 85% of the reporters who cover the White House vote Democratic, they have for a long time. There is a, particularly at the networks, at the lower levels, among the editors and the so-called infrastructure, there is a liberal bias. There is a liberal bias at *Newsweek*, the magazine I work for."[37] Even legendary anchor Walter Cronkite stated, "Everybody knows that there's a liberal, that there's a heavy liberal persuasion among correspondents."[38]

I do not wish to belabor the point, but I do wish to highlight these words penned by Lynne Cheney who illustrates well the potential of biased reporting and its potential effects upon consumers of news:

A study of the New York Times shows a . . . trend in newspapers. From 1960 to 1992, the average continuous quotation or phrase from a candidate in a front page story fell from 14 to six lines. Reporters thus have increased power to turn the words and deeds of candidates into illustrative material for stories they want to tell.

When the Washington Post's ombudsman examined the pictures, headlines, and news stories that ran in her newspaper during the concluding 73 days of the 1992 campaign, she calculated that nearly five times as many were negative for Bush as for Clinton.

Unfortunately, content analyses done by the Center for Media and Public Affairs show that this activist journalism failed to offer voters a more substantive campaign. In fact, systematic comparisons of campaign reporting with the candidates' actual speeches show that the candidates discussed concrete policy issues far more frequently and in greater detail than did either print or broadcast reports. News coverage not only remained negative, it became less balanced and more laden with commentary than it had been during the 1988 campaign.[39]

Journalists are increasingly injecting themselves into the political realm at the expense of those they cover. A good example of this, as mentioned by Cheney above, is the "shrinking soundbite." On this point Thomas Patterson wrote:

[In] 1968, when presidential candidates appeared in a television news story they were usually pictured speaking; 84 percent of the time, candidates' images on the television screen were accompanied by their words. The average "sound bite"—a block of uninterrupted speech by a candidate on television news—was 42 seconds. By 1988, the 42 second sound bite had shrunk to less than 10 seconds and has remained at this level ever since. The voiceless candidate has become commonplace: for every minute that presidential candidates speak on the television newscasts, the journalists who are covering them talk five minutes. . . . Newspaper coverage has followed the same pattern. In 1960, the average continuous quote or paraphrase of a presidential candidate's words in a front-page New York Times story was 14 lines. By 1992, the average had fallen to six lines. On television and in the newpaper, the politician's views are now often subsumed in a narrative devoted primarily to expounding the reporter's view of politics.[40]

That the press leans heavily to the left on social issues is abundantly clear.[41] In the present study numerous references were made by the press on a range of issues beyond race and homosexuality. For example, not allowing congressional leaders to bring their faith into public debate: "We face calamity as a nation if our Congress is ever dominated by the passions of members who push their special interpretations of what the

Bible says. We have some clear constitutional prohibitions against this. . . ."[42] Southern Baptists are "backward thinking."[43] Rob Morse shows unbridled contempt for the Republicans when he wrote: "You have to wonder how a party can win elections by promising a gay pushed back in every closet, a Clinton in every clink, and an abortion in every back alley, but that's what conservative Republicans are trying to do."[44] Arianna Huffington wrote: "Into the vacuum of a GOP agenda so devoid of substance that it makes 'Spice World' look like 'Citizen Kane,' various abhorrent fungal growths have blossomed. In the beginning, there was Pat Robertson, and it was not good. And on the second day, we had Trent Lott. And it was also not good."[45] The *Charleston Gazette* showed where it stood on the issues of abortion and parental notification laws: "This week, the House voted to block the Food and Drug Administrion from approving any 'missed-period' drugs that end preganacy. (Disgustingly, West Virginia Democrats Nick Rahall and Alan Mollohan joined this assualt on women's rights.) And this week, a House committee voted to jail any grandmother, aunt or other person who takes a pregnant [under-age] girl out-of-state for an abortion, to evade a state's parental-notification law."[46]

The *New York Times* declared editorially that "President Clinton put the nation's most important social problem where it belongs, at the top to the national agenda. He went beyond the obvious need for racial justice to the practical and even economic reasons why the United States must nurture its increasingly diverse society." In another *New York Times* example: "Foes of affirmative action were disappointed that he did not reject what they consider to be the failed path of quotas and racial preferences. Advocates of more aggressive action on race and poverty were disappointed that he did not commit more resources for job-training and education. They express lingering bitterness over the welfare law enacted last year that is likely to deepen poverty and racial despair." Although making references to others, this section of the editoral demonstrates support for affirmative action, shows bias against welfare reform, and also demostrantes a form of racial profiling: the belief that more blacks are in poverty than whites.[47] The *San Francisco Examiner*, editorially speaking, provides a good insight into the liberal policy stances embraced by the press. Speaking on President Clinton's initiative on race speech, the paper stated: "His 1992 electoral promise to advance equal rights for gays fizzled in his agreement to the humiliating 'don't ask, don't tell' policy on homosexuals in military service. In his 1996 signing of Republican pushed welfare 'reform' legislation, he deserted liberal principles in moving to dismantle the federally supported safety net for America's poor, who include disproportionate numbers of the racial minorities about whom he is voicing new concern."[48] Lovell Beaulieu, speaking of Proposition 209, stated "As parts of the country strive to turn back the clock on race-related programs and race-specific initiatives, the president of the world's greatest superpower leads her into battle. He may pull it off; then again, he may not. But even if he doesn't, the greatest defeat would have come if he did not try."[49] As did almost every single paper in this study, Beaulieu shows definite affirmative action support. This, even though 83% of Americans are against giving preferences in job hiring and school admission on the basis of race.[50]

How the press defines tolerance is also a clue to their ideological leanings. Tolerance is a much bandied word today, and its true meaning is often lost. Tolerance is "the action or practice of tolerating; toleration; the disposition to be patient with or indulgent to the opinions or practices of others; freedom from bigotry or undue severity in judging the conduct of others; forbearance; catholicity of spirit."[51] Steven Greenhut wrote, "It used to be OK to . . . stand up for tolerance in its original sense: Putting up with—though not endorsing—behavior you find offensive or immoral. But not anymore."[52] The "not anymore" refers in part to the practices of the press that turns this original meaning of tolerance on its head. Today, tolerance goes beyond its more traditional meaning of recognizing and respecting the right of others to think and believe differently from you. Simply put, it used to embrace the idea that everyone is entitled to their own opinions. The new tolerance goes beyond this in that all opinions (unless they are different from those held by the press) are of equal worth; one must endorse, affirm, and praise what others are and do.

Take the Lott case, for example. When Senator Lott said that James Hormel's open advocacy of homosexuality, and his fellowship with gay groups that advocated anti-Catholicism was wrong for a man nominated to be ambassador to a country that was over 90% Catholic, the press claimed Lott to be intolerant. As the press put it, "Senate Majority Leader Trent Lott holds the belief that homosexuality is a sin, thus discounting the character and worth of a great many fellow human beings. Well, that's his right. The majority leader should not, however, use his prejudice."[53] This clearly shows that not affirming homosexuality is considered prejudice, and by extension, intolerance. The *San Francisco Examiner* demonstrates this same type of thinking: Lott's "condescension" and his "open prejudice toward gays."[54]

The press conflates tolerance with acceptance and approval. With the old notion of tolerance we could "realize, and respect, the identity of something, without respecting the thing itself."[55] Tolerance now means for the press that one cannot even disagree with a particular position (e.g., saying that homosexuality is a sin), and allows the press to say that simply disagreeing with their position leads to discrimination. Although the press speaks of discrimination often, what form it takes or how it is practiced is rarely explained. However, by looking at what the press says, discrimination can (in the case of homosexuality, for example) take the form of not actively affirming the lifestyle or by believing religiously that homosexuals are sinners, or by believing psychologically that homosexuals are suffering from a mental disturbance.

Showing its political agenda, the *Capital Times* suggested strongly that if you disagree with them (or agree with Reggie White) that you are intolerant: "When . . . White chose to deliver a speech . . . that was laced with ethnic, racial and sexual stereotypes, he was wrong. And those who would appologize for [or agree with] White's remarks ought to think long and hard about the message of intolerance that they send."[56] The *Capital Times* continued, stating that such "talk has rarely been heard in public life since George Wallace left the school house door."[57] Jennifer Frey wrote that White "preached against intolerance with words that were intolerant. He preached against prejudice with words that reflected prejudices. He preached against hate while promoting attitudes that foster hate." Because White offered a point of view different from that embraced by the press, he was labled intolerant: as presented by the press he "sounded like a bigot, and he sounded like a hypocrit." Frey's brand of tolerance has no tolerance for what she considers intolerant: White "should not . . . be allowed to spew those opinions on the floor of the Wisconsin Assembly."[58] Thus in the name of tolerance, the press would deny freedom of speech and freedom of religious thought to those with whom they disagree.

Simply put, if you do not agree with the point of view of the press, your point of view does not count. Rob Zaleski demonstrates this through the use of a stereotype: White is "a jock—meaning that his views in general are probably somewhat primitive."[59] Paul Williams shows this same intolerance in the name of tolerance: "Let's talk about stereotypes. Like 'holier-than-thou' preachers. And 'dumb jocks.' Reggie White did both sterotypes proud."[60] Tolerance, to the press, means that one cannot believe homosexualtiy to be a sin or that sexual behavior is different from race. It means that one cannot believe that different cultures have different strengths. It means that one cannot believe that affirmative action is wrong or that other solutions to the problems facing black communities might be more effective. In its most basic sense, tolerance means that you agree with the press on all issues, otherwise, you are intolerant.

BIASED PRESS PRACTICES

There are numerous ways in which the press injects its political bias into its reports. Thomas Patterson, speaking generally of the mainstream press in Western countries, including the United States, wrote: "partisanship can and does intrude on news decisions, even among journalists who are conscientiously committed to a code of strict neutrality. [And

this] partisan bias occurs at measurable levels throughout the news systems of Western Democracies. As we have seen . . . journalists' opinions
affect the interpretation of facts, and fairness leans to the left."[61] Although not readily apparent when reading one story, or even one paper
consistently, when looking comparatively at numerous papers and articles on different issues, several distinct practices come to light: sandwiching, lopsided use of sources, labeling, anti-conservative slants, and
ommission of alternate facts (which will be presented in a separate section).

Sandwiching

This practice refers to the placement of something between two other
things of very different character. The press maintains that it is fair since
it reports "both sides" of an issue. Although it is true that the "other
side" is often presented (although not always as the Davidson case study
demonstrated), the manner in which it is presented can detract from its
potential impact. Generally speaking, the press places whatever side of
the issue it does not support in between complimentary points of view,
which invariably agree with the position espoused by the press. For example, the Daily News ran this story on Lott: (Layer 1) "Sen. Alfonse
D'Amato . . . said Trent Lott . . . is blocking a vote on James Hormel's
nomination as ambassador to Luxembourg simply because Hormel is
gay. 'I fear Mr. Hormel's nomination is being obsructed . . . for one reason only: the fact that he is gay'. . . ." Three more paragraphs supported
this point of view. Then Lott's side (Layer 2) is presented: "Lott spokesman Susan Irby said Lott had received D'Amato's letter, but 'we have
also heard from a number of people who don't share those views.' " The
reporters then write (Layer 3): "His [Hormel's] nomination was overwhelmingly approved by the Senate Foreign Relations Committee in the
fall, but it has languished since then amid fierce opposition by social
conservatives." The article ends with the reporters quoting D'amato
again: "D'Amato described Hormel as 'a highly qualified nominee'
whose credentials 'are easily equal to or greater than those of most ambassadorial nominees."[62] Thus the story begins with a position opposed
to Lott (Layer 1), then a brief insertion from Lott's side is put in place
(Layer 2), and then the story ends with an insertion opposing Lott's point
of view again (Layer 3). Although Lott's side is grudgingly and tersely
presented, by being sandwiched between two opposing points of view
its salience is minimized.

During the coverage of President Clinton's One America speech criticisms by opponents of the president—Conservatives and Republicans—
were very often found at the end of articles. The Houston Chronicle shows
this strategy of sandwiching. For example, after twenty-one paragraphs

(Layer 1), in which all but one were Clinton quotes or supportive explanations, The *Houston Chronicle* stated (Layer 2): "Ward Connerly, a member of the University California Board of Regents and the chief proponent of Proposition 209, bristled at Clinton's defense of affirmative action. 'He's not about to convince me that discrimination is right,' said Connerly, who is black. Connerly . . . said it was not the opponents' responsibility to find an alternative. Connerly said he was alarmed at the decline in minority enrollment at some University of California law schools because it indicated that racial preferences had been heavily used." The president is allowed to have the last word, however (Layer 3): "But Clinton said those who maintain the sole measurement for admission should be test scores set aside that standard when it comes to the children of alumni or students with athletic ability. The president said a diverse student body has its own educational value. 'If you close the door on them, we will weaken our greatest universities, and it will be more difficult to build the society we need in the 21st century,' he said."[63]

Although highlighting the president's appeal (Layer 1)—"To those of you who oppose affirmative action . . . I ask you to come up with an alternative"—The *Los Angeles Times* offered only a brief paragraph for the detractors—"Ward Connerly, the anti-affirmative-action crusader and champion of Proposition 209"—to speak (Layer 2): "All week, Connerly and his allies have sought to pressure the White House, noting polls that show most Americans prefer race-neutral policies for college admissions and government programs." Again, this small criticism is offset by the president's own words, for this very next paragraph reads (Layer 3): "Connerly watched impassively as the president defended the concept of affirmative action, citing the military as a shining example: 'so much for the argument that excellence and diversity don't go hand in hand,' Clinton said."[64]

The *Milwaukee Journal Sentinel* provides another example (Layer 1): President Clinton will become the first sitting president to address a homosexual rights gathering . . . where he will share top billings with . . . Ellen DeGeneres. 'He is taking a bold, historic step,' said Elizabeth Birch, executive Director of the Human Rights Campaign. . . ." (Layer 2): "The planned appearance drew criticism from conservative groups." (Layer 3): "But outside of these 'painful moments' [where the president did not support all homosexual agenda items], Birch said that Clinton had delivered for her group by ordering federal agencies not to discriminate by sexual orientation, vastly increasing AIDS funding and appointing more than 100 openly gay people to government posts."[65]

These layers are not always in such neat order. For example, the press may well present its own point of view, then present supporting quotes for that point of view, and finally present the opposing point of view.

For example, the *Milwaukee Journal Sentinel* wrote this of Reggie White's speech (Press view): "State lawmakers were stunned . . . by comments made by . . . Reggie White. In a rambling, hour-long speech on the floor of the Assembly in which he denounced homosexuality and made what some considered offensive remarks about racial differences." Next came the supportive quotes (Supportive views): " 'We're all diminished by racial stereotypes, and it's very inappropriate that he used his platform as a hero to make inappropriate, inaccurate and offensive statements that hurt people,' said Rep. Rosemary Potter (D-Milwaukee)." After selectively providing White's quotations without context, the paper again presents detractors to White, finally ending with White's point of view (Oppositional view): " 'My whole point was to let people know why it's important that we as races work together.' "[66]

Unbalanced Use of Sources

Another way in which the press supported one position over another was in the unbalanced use of sources for quotations. Many of the positions expressed by the press are developed using quotes from other than press sources. However, look at the number of pro-press individuals being quoted versus the number of anti-press individuals being quoted. The press finds those who agree with its position much more readily than those who do not.

Race	*Homosexuality*
Davidson (14:1)	Lott (22:8)
Clinton (3.2:1)[67]	White (20:6)
Farrakhan (all negative)	Clinton (23:10)

The ratios above suggest that the press has a definite ability to find numerous sources that agree with its own position on the issues (Democrats and liberal political activists in particular). Whereas there are usually a wide variety of liberal sources, conservative sources are more often than not limited to a few national-level spokesmen. The press also was able to find *local* liberal sources for inclusion, but extremely few local conservative sources. If one only considers using those sources that appear in more than one news article, the ratio is even higher in favor of the press. For example, four of the six sources supportive of White were to be found in the same article and appeared only once. Thus the ratio changes to as high as 10:1 in the case of White.

The use of sources is a strong example of how the press claims to show "both sides" of an issue, while actually making the conservative view look like the minority view. Simply put, whatever position the press agrees with will find a 2:1 or higher ratio of different sources quoted that support that same position. So although both sides are presented, one side, the press-supported side, will look stronger in terms of overall support.

Labeling

The press decried stereotypes, but used them extensively against those with whom they disagreed. Of particular note is the way the press uses the term "civil rights activists." Only those who support affirmative action, the homosexual agenda, and other *left-leaning* causes are considered "civil rights activists." For example, in the chapter on Reggie White we saw that the press used the term "civil rights groups" or "civil rights activists" for groups that spoke against White (thus supporting the position of the press), but called all others "conservative groups" or "conservative activists." Thus we have the *"conservative* Family Research Council" but the "Human Rights Campaign," not the *liberal* Human Rights Campaign.[68] You would also find the "Human Rights Campaign," but a "number of conservative leaders and groups"[69] Not one paper called the HRC or even ACT UP "liberal." Yet almost all called the Family Research Council and Focus on the Family "conservative." Simply put, anyone who opposed the point of view adopted by the press was labled as "conservative."

The press also linked homosexual activists with civil rights activits; in race issues, the press labled all supporters of affirmative action as civil rights activists and anyone opposed as "conservative." Invariably, through news articles, opinion essays, and editorials, the press revealed that it supports the opposite position of those individuals and groups it labels conservative. This strategy in and of itself identifies the left-leaning nature of the press. When listing the groups it quotes, the press rarely explains who these groups are. Moreover, group constituencies are not mentioned. So, while the Human Rights Campaign is listed as the largest homosexual rights group, no membership numbers are given. When Focus on the Family is mentioned, it is listed as a conservative or extremist group, but never is it mentioned that it has a constituency of over 2.6 million.

Another way that the press labeled was through the use of abusive ad hominem attacks—simple name calling. Words used to describe Senator Davidson included "racist" and "bigot." White was refered to as a "homophobe," as "stupid," a "jock," and as a "dumb jock." Senator Lott was refered to as a "hater," a "homophobe," "narrow-minded," "extremist," "prejudiced," and "right-wing radical." Farrakhan was called "racist," "sexist," "bigoted," "anti-semitic," "Jew hating," and "homophobe." Labels such as these were not given for President Clinton, however. The press routinely resorts to name calling in its attempt to villify those with which it disagrees. For example, James Dobson, a psychologist and president of Focus on the Family, has been called by our mainstream professional press the following: "dingbat," "zealot," "crazy," "intolerant," "ayatollah," and the " 'Godzilla of the Right,' who is similar to David Duke of the Ku Klux Klan."[70] Constrast this with supporters of affirmative action and the homosexual agenda being called "civil rights activists." An example of how this labeling acts to hurt conservatives can be seen when examining how the press responded to President Clinton and Reggie White's comments on Americans of Hispanic descent. In his speech on Race Relations, President Clinton said: "I have come to love the intensity and selflessness of my Hispanic fellow Americans toward la familia."[71] The president's stereotype received no negative comments from the press. Reggie White stated essentially the same idea, albeit less eloquently: "Hispanics are gifted in family structure. You can see a Hispanic person and they can put twenty or thirty people in one home. They were gifted in the family structure."[72] White was metaphorically crucified. The difference between the two comments is that the president was embracing a liberal policy stance avidly supported by the press, and White was embracing conservative ideals opposed by the press.[73]

Reliably Anti-Conservative

The six case studies have demonstrated that the mainstream press shows a distinct bias against conservative ideas. Although the press does not embrace all liberal ideas, it is realiably anti-conservative. Given that the majority of Republicans are conservative, it is safe to say that the press will also show a distinct bias against Republicans, although Republicans that embrace liberal ideals will receive good press. As mentioned earlier "Mainline journalism is by no means reliably pro-Democratic. . . ."[74] It is, however, reliably anti-conservative, and thus generally anti-Republican.

Many in the press could not disguise their anti-Republican sentiments. Some of this is subtle. For example, the *Ventura County Star*, after quoting several objecting Wisconsin Assembly Democrats, stated that "Republicans were more forgiving. After White's comments, many stayed in the Assembly chambers to have their picture taken with him."[75] Joe Hart was less subtle and wrote, "Just wondering: did any of those conservative-leaning politicos genuflect and then kiss Reggie's Super Bowl ring?"[76] Cokie Roberts and Steven Roberts wrote: "The Strategy of some Republican leaders is now clear. They intend to make gay-bashing a central part of their election campaign this fall. [W]hat these Republicans are doing is much worse [than President Clinton not truly pushing for homosexuals in the military]. Their cynical decision to demonize gays is meanspirited and un-American. They deserve to be repudiated."[77] The

Daily News likened the Republican concerns of the nomination of James Hormel as "far more than a GOP frat-boy fight."[78] The *Capital Times* editorially asserted that "Some will argue that Jensen [and other conservatives in the Wisconsin State Assembly] were pleased with White's remarks because they will foster divisions in society—divisions that are necessary for conservatives to advance their agenda."[79] Deb Price, echoing the words of many journalists, wrote: "Practicing a pup tent ideology, they've staked out an ideology far too narrow-minded to fit most Americans. [H]igh ranking Republican extremists such as Senate Majority Leader Trent Lott and House Speaker Newt Gingrich mouth off. . . . [Republicans are] pandering to the right-wing radicals. . . . [The] far right groups at the Republican Party's rotten core. . . . Not every Republican in Congress shamelessly kowtows to prejudice. Yet, come November, a vote for any Republican . . . is a vote to keep Gingrich, Lott and their ilk in charge. [The] despicable Republican scapegoating."[80]

BIASED PRACTICES: EXCLUSION OF OPPOSITIONAL INFORMATION

The press, who are supposed to protect and advance the *public interest*, ignore large portions of the public when they advance certain *personal* and *political interests* over the public's right to know all pertinent information about a given subject. In the section above we have seen numerous ways that the press introduces its bias into the reportorial process. One part of framing that is commonly ignored is how a frame is supported by information that is left out. Not only do frames lower the salience of some information, but those who do the writing leave out contradictory information since it does not fit in with the established frame. This failure to report information that would contradict the press's own point of view or that would harm the standing of those with whom the press sympathizes is yet another way in which the press introduces its bias.[81] As communication researcher Robert Entman has written, the "media's inadvertent reinforcement of existing attitudes through omission is far from the trivial effect that many scholars imply. Holding support under adverse new conditions is a crucial goal in politics, not just winning over new supporters. So one way the media wield influence is by omitting or de-emphasizing information, by excluding data about an altered reality that might otherwise disrupt existing support."[82] A small-scale example of this occurred during the HRC fundraising dinner. Elizabeth Birch made rather extreme comments about TV icons, yet hardly any press outlets reported upon them. For example, Birch stated, " 'I dreamed of an America where even Buffy and Jody [of 'A Family Affair'] could grow up to be gay. We all knew that Mr. French was, and . . . I just want to tell you we've come a long way since Miss

Jane on 'The Beverly Hillbillies.' "[83] Such an odd statement coming from the head of an extremely powerful homosexual lobbying organization seems to deserve attention. It received hardly a passing glance.

Another example of the exclusion of harmful or oppositional information is seen when examining President Clinton's comments at the HRC dinner. The president, in response to homosexual activist hecklers in the crowd, stated that, "People with AIDS are dying. But since I've become president we're spending 10 times as much per fatality on people with AIDS as people with breast cancer or prostate cancer. And the drugs are being approved more quickly. And a lot of people are living normal lives. We just have to keep working on it." This is a strikingly controversial statement concerning public policy and where public funds should go for the public health. This comment received little press attention, except to say the president responded well to hecklers. As these examples show, the press selectively quoted the president: " 'People with AIDS are dying. But since I became president, we're spending 10 times as much' *on research.*"[84] Also, " 'People with AIDS are dying, but since I became president we're spending ten times as much' *combatting the disease.* Mr. Clinton's words were drowned by applause that quickly turned into yet another standing ovation."[85] What the press omits is that the standing applause was after the president had said he was spending 10 times as much on AIDS research per patient as he was for breast and prostate cancer. Yet the press kept this information from the American public—not one paper in this study provided the president's complete sentence.

The above examples are small in that they reveal almost incidental exclusions of material. One can easily say that the press does not have time to report everything, and must make decisions about what to include in the coverage. Although this is true, it is also true that the press strategically excludes information that would run contrary to its established political frames for understanding American politics, culture, and society. We can see this well when looking specifically at the issues of race and homosexuality covered in Chapters 2 through 7.

Press Views on Race

The press advanced very definite points of view regarding race relations in America. Some of these were directly stated and others were implied by the collective weight of the comments contained in news stories, editorials, and opinion essays. Essentially put, according to the press, almost all minority ills are a result of lingering white racism or prejudice. Blacks, according to the press, cannot be racists, affirmative action is good for blacks, and anything that would interfere or change affirmative action (such as Proposition 209) is wrong. The *Des Moines*

Register demonstrates how racism is a white problem: "Yet something is missing. Maybe it's jobs. Despite the robust economy, unemployment among African-Americans, especially those in low-income urban areas, often doubles, sometimes triples that of whites. For many African-Americans, and other minorities, race relations often boil down to myths and stereotypes whites have toward them."[86] Clearly, this implies white prejudice being at the roots of black problems, yet it also demonstrates another aspect of reportorial practice. This striking assertion is not followed by evidence. Its exits on its own and was presented as true based soley upon the press's acceptance of it as the truth.

The implication that only whites can be racists skews press reporting in that suspect comments by some black leaders go unreported. For example, Jesse Jackson is not labeled a racist or bigot for his remarks at the Million Man March. Although few papers reported the remarks, they are incindiary: " 'Clarence Thomas and Gingrich organized the march—just like Bull Conner organized the march in 1963.' "[87] Certainly one of the foremost leaders in black America comparing a supreme court justice and then Speaker of the House to the Alabama police chief who ordered police dogs and fire hoses turned on non-violent black protesters is a comment worthy of press notice. Former Illinois Representative Gus Savage was given this same kid-glove treatment. His comments were particulary damning to whites: " 'White dreams have crippled many black children and white values have maimed many black families because of selfishness and greed. . . . ' "[88] Such comments coming from black leaders were explained away as "anger," not racism or hate.[89]

That the press regularly accepts such comments coming from black leaders is indicative of its mindset that the majority of minority ills result from white prejudice. Columnist Louis Freedberg represents well the underlying premise of the press: "Many blacks are tired of pleas from whites for more dialogue. After all, it is not blacks, but whites, who must come to terms with their racism. Show us what you are going to do, they say, instead of just talking."[90] Editorially speaking, the *St. Louis Post-Dispatch* stated that President Clinton "can at least put forth programs that offer hope to those blacks affected by lingering racism. The problems run deep: Both business disinvestment and middle-class flight have devastated cities and left behind poor people with few means of escape. Addressing these social conditions would amount to an attack on racism. It would deprive outsiders of an excuse for making the most stereotypical judgment about the behavior of minorities and the poor living in impoverished cities."[91] These types of press statements ignore other reasons for businesses leaving cities—heavy tax burdens, for example—they also ignore middle-class blacks leaving the urban areas for the suburbs in order to escape crime. The answer, however, falls back on the press's premise that white racism and prejudice are the problem: "a much better and lasting response to both the legacy of slavery and racism is a genuine commitment to diversifying America's educational and economic opportunities."[92]

The chapter on President Clinton's "Initiative on Race" clearly demonstrated the press belief that racism, bigotry, and general prejudice remain the root causes of all minority ills. Affirmative action is seen as the only viable way to end these problems. The press takes for granted the sorry state of white-black relations in America, and says that ending affirmative action will have devastating effects on minorities since the country will be unable to resolve these problems. Affirmative action will cause whites, who flee from contact with blacks, to interact with minorities. Once whites interact more with blacks and other minorities they will appreciate their differences.

Diversity is a positive quality in almost every press report in which it is mentioned. The press has a single-minded definition of diversity, however, and it uses this understanding for support in any discussion about race. It is a reductionistic and simplistic definition: diversity was implicitly defined to be based on skin color. Ruben Navarrette Jr. exemplifies this thinking when he writes, "Facing an audience of college students as multicolored as a coastal rainbow, he [the President] extolled the virtue of diversity and reiterated his support for [affirmative action]."[93] The terms diversity and multiculturalism are often used interchangeably by the press. The press spoke for all Americans when it stated that "we believe in a multicultural society. . . ." This multiculturalism, though, was based only on skin color, as evidence when one paper, speaking of the president's advisory board said that it was right for the president to choose "one of these and three of those. . . ." Multiculturalism, as practiced by the press, places Americans into cultural and intellectual positions based soley upon the color of their skin. This focus on skin color reduced the range of ideas brought forth by those of different skin colors. That is to say, the press implies that all blacks think one way; all Americans of Hispanic descent think another, and so on. One columnist wrote that cities without different ethnic groups are "white-bread" and thus boring; cities with ethnic groups that provide "food" and "sound" make a city interesting, however.

The American Society of Newspaper Editors' (ASNE) Mission Statement on Newsroom Diversity exemplifies this narrow-minded view of diversity: "While American newsrooms have become more *diverse* in recent years, newspapers will fall short of achieving *racial parity* in newsrooms with the population by 2000. ASNE reaffirms its commitment to *racial parity* in newsrooms and to full and accurate news coverage of our nation's *diverse* communities."[94] The *Denver Rocky Mountain News* stated that "California, where [the President] decided to give his race-relations speech because of its ethnic mixture, just voted to abolish affirmative

action—meaning, for example, that minorities will no longer get preference in public universities. Already, the number of blacks going to
medical, law and graduate schools in California is declining, Clinton
noted. At the same time, the number of Asian Americans in those schools
is *rising out of proportion*. 'We must not try to stop equalizing economic
opportunity,' Clinton warned."[95] But what about Americans of Asian
descent denied admission under affirmative action? This also shows a
conception of diversity based on national percentages, not opportunity.
Yet even with single-minded focus on diversity, the American Society of
Newpaper Editors stated, "The typical newspaper journalist is still a liberal, college-educated, white-male baby boomer."[96]

The press also focused on the notion of equal opportunity. Like the
press's understanding of diversity, its understanding of equal opportunity was simplistic and reductionistic also. Simply put, equal opportunity meant proportional representation as an end goal; thus, not an
equality of opportunity, but rather an equality of outcome based on proportional racial representation. The *Denver Rocky Mountain News* reported
that "California, where [the president] decided to give his race-relations
speech because of its ethnic mixture, just voted to abolish affirmative
action—meaning, for example, that minorities will no longer get
preference in public universities. Already, the number of blacks going to
medical, law and graduate schools in California is declining, Clinton
noted. At the same time, the number of Asian Americans in those schools
is rising out of proportion. 'We must not try to stop equalizing economic
opportunity,' Clinton warned."[97] Numerous papers reported this, yet almost all failed to suggest that anything other than lingering racism and
ongoing discrimination could be the cause of the dropping enrollments.
Few papers noted that enrollments of Americans of Asian ancestry had
been climbing, suggesting that affirmative action had been keeping these
otherwise qualified Americans out of school simply because of the color
of their skin. Carl Rowen offers another example of the press focus on
equality of outcome, not opportunity: "The president also is deeply disturbed that Hispanic Americans are not sharing in the nation's economic
progress to the same extent as other ethnic groups, and he wants to know
what he and the federal government can do to right that injustice. . . ."[98]
Thus demonstrating how the press looks for equality of outcome and
not equality of opportunity.

Affirmative action is a favored press program, and in support of it the
press would bolster an assertion of the president with an assertion of its
own. For example, the *Tampa Tribune* wrote that "Clinton said the results
[of Proposition 209] has been minority enrollments in graduate programs
are 'plummeting.' Indeed, the enrollment of minority students has
dropped significantly since the University of California regents voted to
end affirmative action for admissions in 1995. 'We must not resegregate

higher education or leave it to the private universities to do the public's work,' he said. 'To those who oppose affirmative action, I ask you to come up with an alternative. I would embrace it if I could find a better way.' "[99] The press failed to mention any of the alternatives that have been put forth, and reporters failed to provide numbers in support of their assertions.

Also showing the press support for affirmative action was its focus on elite schools impacted by California's Proposition 209. Rarely was a question asked about how long the drop may continue, or why it was happening, or where the rejected students were going; only that there was a drop and it was bad. The drop was blamed on lingering racism and prejudice. Norman Lockman stated that the "president seems to believe that many people simply don't know about the effects of racism. Now faced with evidence that killing affirmative action has reduced law school admission in California by 80%, Clinton says he believes there a chance the new law based on Proposition 209 may be changed." This example, similar to others, suggests racism to be at the root of all black problems; and also suggests that those who opposes affirmative action are ignorant about racism.[100] What the press left out was that while elite schools, such as UCLA and the Boalt school of law, may have seen enrollment drops, schools not in the top tiers actually saw enrollment *increases*. On the surface this information suggests that many minorities were being admited into top schools without proper qualifications. Moreover, the dropout rates for minorites at these elite schools was higher than that for whites and Asians, suggesting also that many underqualified minority students were being admitted under the guise of affirmative action programs. As Karl Zinmeister states: "under preferential race admission at the University of California at Berkeley, black undergrads were dropping out at the rate of 42% (compared to only 16% of whites). That not only blasts the self-confidence of many black youngsters, but also feeds to impressions of black inferiority among other students."[101] This is important information for those considering the effect of affirmative action and Proposition 209. Yet the press suppressed this information, thus squelching true democratic debate on the issue.

The press suggests that Americans are simmering with both overt and deeply held prejudices and stereotypes, yet no evidence is provided. Contrast this with recent poll data showing that 95% of Americans would vote for a black president.[102] Add to that the observation that "Americans are actually quite tolerant compared to residents of other developed nations."[103] To support this assertion, Karl Zinmeister points out that 13% of the population views blacks "unfavorably." Compare that with 21% of those in Great Britain viewing the Irish "unfavorably," or the 42% of French who view North Africans "unfavorably," or the 45% of West Germans who view Turks "unfavorably."[104]

Simply put, the press leaves out alternative information that would contradict its ideological posturing. This is seen clearly in two practices that define the press preoccupation with race. One, the press holds its point of view to be the correct one, so it does not provide evidence to support its claims. Two, because it so willingly embraces its own point of view, the press fails to provide alternate points of view or contradictory information (even when that information is clearly correct).

Several examples will demonstrate how the press ignores essential information. The press continually asserts that race relations in America are horrible, then asserts that the country needs affirmative action. Yet poll data contradicts this press assumption. Although it is true that only 38% of adults think that race relations are generally good, that number rockets to 72% when considering one's own community. When one considers 10th graders of the class of 2000, more blacks than whites think that race relations in America are generally good, 63% to 61%.[105] These numbers belie the stark assertions of the press. Although the press continually hammered home that black problems are caused by white racism, most blacks feel decidely different. For instance, a *Time*/CNN poll found stark contrasts between the thinking of black Americans and the thinking of the press. When asked if the problems that most blacks face are caused primarily by whites, only 18% of black teens agreed and 29% of black adults agreed. More black adults (51%) felt that failure to take advantage of available opportunities was more of a problem than discrimination by whites (26%). This is information not made available by the mainstream press, and certainly not included in any of the news articles covered in this book.[106]

As the press continues to stress prejudice and discrimination, thereby driving a wedge between blacks and whites, black parents (89%) and white parents (92%) say that too much is made of the differences between blacks and whites and not enough of what they have in common. Whereas the press focuses almost exclusivly on diveristy, multiculturalism, and integration, both black and white parents overwelmingly reject this focus. When asked what should be a bigger priority for schools across America, only 8% of black parents and 5% of white parents said diversity and integration. Instead, a focus on raising academic standards and achievements was listed by 80% of black parents and 88% of white parents. This enormous disinterest in diversity continues when looking at hiring practices. Whereas the press wishes for every school and workplace to be racially balanced, black parents (77%) and white parents (64%) want the best teachers hired, regardless of their race.[107] The media also wants its readers to believe that all but bigoted Americans want racial preferences. The American Civil Rights Institute found, however, that "an overwelming majority of Americans oppose racial preferences in government programs. . . . About four in five . . . voters (82.5%)—in-

cluding nearly the same percentage of African-American voters (78.7%)—
favor federal legislation that prohibits government discrimination and
preferential treatment on the basis of race, color. . . . Nearly nine in ten
(87.2%) Americans say that race should not be a factor in admission to
a public university or college, including eight in ten (82.2%) African-
American voters. American voters overwhelmingly support (83.2%) colorblind affirmative action programs, and with even greater support
among African-American voters (89.6%)."[108]

In addition, the press pointedly revealed its view of what the politics
of black Americans should be. This was reflected in the sources consulted
for quotations. Although the press was able to field an impressive array
of liberal black leaders, it was unable to provide readers with the same
numbers of conservative black leaders. Aside from Representative J.C.
Watts and Ward Connerly, no other prominent black conservatives were
mentioned. Thus, well-known and respected black conservatives were
pointedly ignored by the press: Kay Coles James, Star Parker, Glenn
Loury, Racine Williams, Robert Woodson, Donna Warner, Tony Evans,
Roxanne Petteway, Raleigh Washington, Allan Keyes, Walter Williams,
Ken Hamblin, Thomas Sowell, Larry Elder. There are so many more, but
the press will not make the effort to seek them out.[109]

Moreover, the press pointedly omits points of view from black leaders
who have alternate visions for the problems facing black communities.
Although the press continually states that racism and bigotry are the
reasons for black problems, the Joint Center for Political and Economic
Studies found that "education, health care and crime were top concerns.
Fighting racism and tax reform were at the bottom of the list."[110] The
Independent Black Majority has stated that other factors beside racism
carry more weight when discussing black problems: "the destruction of
the black family, a culture steeped in 'violence, profanity and promiscuity,' ignorance about the proven power of capitalism and lack of spirituality were the primary obstacles to black success."[111] By continually
asserting that black ills are a result of white prejudice and lingering racism, and that affirmative action will help solve this problem, the press
ignore evidence suggesting that black culture itself may have a large part
to play in low black educational achievement. For example, Berkeley
linguistics professor John H. McWhorter has written that a "self-
destructive anti-intellectualism pervades black America and exerts a
downward pull on every aspect of life."[112] The thesis put forth by the
press, that all black ills result from white racism, is clearly challenged
when one considers

the superior performance of black immigrants from Africa and the West Indies.
Presumably, they face identical problems with white racism. As for the quality
of schools where many black children live, there are two confounding statistics.

The first is that Asian and other immigrants have done very well academically in some of the same inner-city schools, and the second is that the majority of black children are not attending crumbling inner-city schools. In fact, only about 20% of black children attend such schools. But even in suburbs and the better neighborhoods of cities, black children lag well behind whites. [B]lack children of parents who earn $70,000 per year do worse on the SAT than white students whose parents make $6,000 a year [sic]. And black children whose parents both have advanced degrees fail to score as well as white children whose parents have completed only high school.[113]

The press also fails to provide its readers with other types of information due to its particular framing of black Americans as victims. For example, as the press decried the income gap between whites and blacks, it failed to mention that "among blacks and whites of the same family status, age, and educational level, we are nearing parity in earnings today."[114] Even better news for black Americans: Black couples outstripped white couples in income gains between the years 1967 and 1997.[115]

Another, more striking example, concerns racial crimes. Although the media wants its readers to believe that blacks are singled out for criminal punishment due to racism, U.S. government statistics paint a different picture. Blacks make up roughly 12% of the population, yet they "commit more than a third of all serious crimes . . . [and a] majority of violent crimes committed by blacks involve a white victim."[116] In 1991, the U.S. Bureau of Justice Statistics (BJS) painted a sobering picture: considering all violent crimes, there were 55,301 instances of white on black crime and 572,458 instances of black on white crime.[117] More recent BJS figures show the same ratio. Although the media does point out the high homicide rate in black communities, it pointedly ignores that blacks "were 7 times more likely than whites to commit homicide in 1998."[118] The majority of homicides are intraracial, with white on black homicide rates approaching 3%; however, black on white homicide rates are approaching 20%.[119]

The press depiction of blacks as victims leads to the omission of information the public needs. For example, I am certain those of you reading this have heard of the heinous murder of James Byrd Jr., the black Texan dragged to his death in June 1998 by two white men. What about the equally heinous murder of Patricia Stansfield in August 1998? Just two months after James Byrd Jr., was murdered, Stansfield was abducted by a black man, Christopher Coleman, in Streator, Illinois. Coleman had stolen a car, tied Stansfield to the back bumper, and then dragged her for two miles to her death. A Lexis-Nexis search produced 934 articles on the Byrd murder, whereas the Stansfield murder yielded no articles. Another gruesome dragging death occured in February 2000: six-year-old Jake Robel, white, was dragged to his death when Kim Davis, black, hijacked Robel's mother's car. Fifty-seven articles appear in Lexis-Nexis about this murder, with all but twelve in the local *Kansas City Star*. No mention of race was contained in fifty-five of the fifty-seven articles. The two that did mention race did so to say, "do not bring race into this."[120]

The hate crime murder of Michael Westerman provides another example of the inablility of the press to report fairly on matters involving race. Westerman was a nineteen-year-old white man who was shot to death in front of his wife. Four black youths were involved with the shooting, for no other reason than Westerman had displayed a Confederate battleflag on his truck. This was clearly a brutal hate crime. Since his murder, Westerman found his way into only nineteen stories according to Lexis-Nexis. For the press, Byrd's murder was motivated by the hatred and prejudice of the killers; Westerman's murder was motivated because he displayed the battleflag, not because of the hatred and racism of the killers: his murder was made out to be his own fault. As *USA Today* wrote, "Westerman was shot in the heart as he drove with his wife, Hannah, on a rural highway just past the Kentucky-Tennessee border. Officials say the Confederate flag that flapped from the back of his pick-up led to Westerman's death."[121] No mention was made of a possible hate crime.

A similar case involves Ronald Taylor, black, who shot five white males, murdering three. Eyewitnesses reported Taylor yelling racial epithets at whites he passed, but telling black bystanders they were in no danger. The press was quick to downplay any possiblility of a hate crime: "Increasingly, state hate-crimes statutes are being brought to bear against minorities—raising questions about whether those who commit such violations against whites are acting out of racism—the classic motivation for a hate crime—or reacting in anger to a history of oppression and injustice."[122] Of course, the press was able to find someone to downplay any racial aspect: "Wilkinsburg Police Chief Gerald Brewer cautioned that it might be premature to classify the case as a hate crime. 'There's a lot of anger and hostility in this individual, so I think it's a little premature to simply define this as a racist event,' Brewer said."[123] By the time Taylor is brought up on charges of murder, the press has obliterated any thought of a hate crime: "Prosecutors said Monday that they will seek the death penalty against a man charged with killing three people during an attack that allegedly targeted whites. The victims were white; Taylor is black."[124] There were 160 articles mentioning Taylor, with over half, eighty-two, being in the local *Pittsburgh Post-Gazette*. Moreover, the stories framed this as a triple homicide, and not a hate crime. According to the press, if whites act out of anger it is a hate crime; if blacks act out of anger is is due to racial oppression and thus not a hate crime.

The press's ability to suppress gruesome examples of black on white crime is stunning. I am fairly certain those reading this have not heard of the murder of Todd and Stacy Bagley, either. While driving to church, the Bagleys were stopped, forced into the trunk of their car, driven to a remote area, shot in the head and then set on fire by four black youths. Only two articles appear in the Lexis-Nexis database, and neither report the race of the assailants or victims. Have you heard of Reginald and Jonathan Carr? In December of 2000, after a week-long crime spree (including one murder) that targeted only whites, the brothers (black) broke into an apartment, kidnapped at gunpoint three white males and two white women. After forcing the victims to drive to ATM machines and withdraw money, the Carr brothers had them drive to a remote area where they repeatedly raped the women and then had all five whites kneel on the ground. The Carr brothers then shot them all in the head. There was only one survivor. Local authorities claimed race was not a factor. The national news media did not report these brutal murders. Only one article appears in the Lexis-Nexis database, and it noticeably omits the race of the assailants or victims.[125] The list of heinous black on white crimes receiving little or no mainstream media coverage is amazingly long.[126]

The enormity of what the American mainstream press refuses to print is well demonstrated by information printed in the *Sydney Morning Herald*, an Australian newspaper:

most victims of race crime—about 90%—are white, according to the survey "Highlights from 20 years of Surveying Crime Victims," published in 1993. Almost 1 million white Americans were murdered, robbed, assaulted, or raped by black Americans in 1992, compared with about 132,000 blacks who were murdered, robbed, assaulted, or raped by whites, according to the same survey. Blacks thus committed 7.5 times more violent inter-racial crimes than whites even though the black population is only one-seventh the size of the white population. When these figures are adjusted on a per capita basis, they reveal an extraordinary disparity: blacks are committing more than 50 times the number of violent racial crimes of whites. According to the latest annual report on murder by the Federal Bureau of Investigation, most inter-racial murders involve black assailants and white victims, with blacks murdering whites at 18 times the rate whites murder blacks. The Bureau of Justice Statistics says 27 million non-violent crimes were committed in the United States in 1992, and the survey found that 31 per cent of the robberies involved black offenders and white victims (while only 2 per cent in the reverse).[127]

The reporter, Paul Sheehan, ends with a cautionary note toward the American media: "When all the crime figures are calculated, it appears that black Americans have committed at least 170 million crimes against white Americans in the past thirty years. It is the great defining disaster of American life and American ideals since World War II. All these are facts, yet by simply writing this story, by assembling the facts in this way, I would be deemed a racist by the American news media. It prefers to maintain a paternalistic double-standard in its coverage of black America, a lower standard."[128]

Press Views on Homosexuality

The press vehemently asserted that homosexuals are in need of additional civil rights legislation, and that they routinely suffer job discrimination. Furthermore, the press asserted that homosexuality is simply an alternative to heterosexuality, and that homosexual relationships should be thought of as equivalent to heterosexual ones. Homosexuality is genetic, according to the press; it cannot be changed. Biblical views which condemn homosexual behavior are anachronistic, extremely conservative, and simply wrong. Those that disagree with the press view are at best misinformed and misguided; at worst, they are hateful, intolerant, and bigoted. The press advanced a theme that the majority of American were bigoted against homosexuals. Poll data reveals, however, that Americans are quite tolerant, but choose not to affirm homosexual behavior. For example, Gallup polls reveal that 83% of Americans believe homosexuals should have equal rights when it comes to job opportunities (the main exceptions being jobs as clergy or elementary school teachers).[129] Fifty-two percent of Americans feel that homosexuality is an acceptable alternative lifestyle, that figure rising from 38% in 1992.[130] However tolerant Americans might be of homosexuals, they still do not affirm homosexual behavior: when asked about how they feel, 74% of Americans thought homosexual behavior unacceptable.[131] Oppositional information to each of the major press assertions exists. To each of these—that homosexuals are victims, suffer job discrimination, are just like heterosexuals in terms of demographics and sexuality, and that homosexuality is genetically caused—we now turn.

Homosexuals as victims. The press portrayed homosexuals as victims of rampant discrimination, and thus in need of hate crime laws and anti-job discrimination laws such as ENDA. No evidence for these assertions was ever presented, nor was any counter-evidence to the press assertions presented. As proof of continual discrimination and victimization, the press often referred to Matthew Shepard, a gay man murdered during a robbery. However, in its focus on homosexuals as victims, the press fails to present alternate information about homosexuals, especially when homosexuals are the ones doing the victimizing. Take for example, the murder of 10-year-old Jeffrey Curley. On 1 October 1997 he was kidnapped by homosexual lovers Charles Jaynes, twenty-two, and Salvatore Sicari, twenty-one. Jeffrey fought off Jaynes's sexual advances, and while Sicari drove Jaynes's car, Jaynes, approximately 300 pounds, sat on Jeffrey and smothered his face with a gasoline soaked rag. After Jeffrey died, the men took him to Jaynes's apartment where Jaynes sodomized the boy's corpse. Ultimately, the two men stuffed Jeffrey's body into a large plastic tub and dumped the boy's body into the Great Works River in Maine.[132] Jaynes was a member of the North American Man Boy Love Association (NAMBLA), a "pedophile group"[133] that seeks to assert a "benevolent nature of man/boy love, and to raise the consciousness of boy-lovers. . . . [M]embership is open to all individuals sympathetic to man/boy love in particular and sexual freedom in general."[134] A Lexis-Nexis search revealed over 1000 articles about Matthew Shepard since 9 October 1998, yet only 172 articles since 1 October 1997 about Curley's murder, all but eleven in one of the two *local* papers, the *Boston Herald* and the *Boston Globe*.[135]

This type of exclusionary coverage is typical. The brutal rape and murder of Jesse Dirkhising is another example. On 26 September 1999 in Rogers, Arkansas, two homosexuals, Davis Carpenter Jr., thirty-eight, and Joshua Brown, twenty-two, kidnapped Jesse, a 13-year-old boy. Jesse was drugged, strapped face-down to a bed with duct tape and belts, gagged with his own underwear, sexually tortured, smeared with feces, and repeatedly raped. At one point, Brown went to the kitchen for a sandwich, and Jesse suffocated to death. Police found in the apartment handwritten instructions and a diagram of how to position the boy, as well as other notes of fantasies of molesting children. A Lexis-Nexis search revealed only twenty-seven articles about Jesse Dirkhising since 26 September 1999. And those only appeared after the *Washington Times* ran a story on the lack of coverage on 22 October 1999—almost a full month after Jesse Dirkhising's murder.[136]

Although the Associated Press ran the Matthew Shepard story on the national wires, calling it a hate crime before Shepard died, the Dirkhising story was put out only on local wires. In fact, Lexis-Nexis reveals that no national level coverage occurred until after the previously mentioned *Washington Times* article emerged. Those articles were written *to justify the lack of coverage*, usually to state the murder did not merit national attention. Initial reports failed to even mention that the two assailants were homosexual. From the first day of coverage Matthew Shepard was identified as homosexual, and the robbery/murder was classified as a hate crime. The *Washington Post*'s ombudsman, E.R. Shipp, stated: "The Shepard story was news . . . because it 'prompted debate on hate crimes and the degree to which there is still intolerance of gay people in this country. It was much more than a murder story for us.' More 'routine' crimes may be ignored or limited to news briefs culled from wire services. The story of the Sept. 26 death of Jesse Dirkhising in Rogers, Ark., and the arrest of two male suspects, wasn't transmitted on the Associated Press's national news wires until Oct. 29. The *Post*, considering this a 'routine' story, carried a news brief on Oct. 30."[137]

However, as Mark Linder pointed out: "Concluding her Nov. 14 ombudsman column discussing coverage of the homosexual rape and murder of a 13-year-old boy in Arkansas, E.R. Shipp writes: 'That Jesse Dirkhising's death has not done so [sparked public expressions of outrage that themselves became news] to date is hardly the fault of the *Washington Post*.' Yet the same piece begins with this sentence: 'By the time Matthew Shepard died on Oct. 12, 1998, . . . his story had spread around the world.' It is disingenuous for the ombudsman of one of the premier newspapers in the United States to disclaim the influence of its own reporting on which stories 'spread around the world' and spark 'public outrage.'[138] Robert Knight provides us with a similar point of view: "On Nov. 9, *Time* magazine's Jonathan Gregg defended the media: 'The reason the Dirkhising story received so little play is because it offered no lessons. . . . Jesse Dirkhising's death gives us nothing except the depravity of two sick men. There is no lesson here, no moral of tolerance, no hope to be gleaned in the punishment of the perpetrators.' Gregg reflects the widely-held media belief that the only moral lesson worth teaching is tolerance. Doesn't every instance of punishing criminals—including and especially pedophiles and murderers—offer the rest of us hope? Because of Jesse's age, Gregg blames his murder solely on those who practice pedophilia. Likewise, David Smith of the Human Rights Campaign said, 'This has nothing to do with gay people.' Both ignored the increasing promotion of sadistic sex and pedophilia in mainstream homosexual publications, events and advertisements."[139]

Revealing an interesting aspect of the press, Jeff Jacoby wrote:

The *Post*'s ombudsman, E.R. Shipp . . . acknowledged that her paper had run some 80 items referring to Shepard, but only a single news brief mentioning Dirkhising. "Here at the *Post*, however, the two are seen as quite different," Shipp wrote. A hate crime homicide such as Shepard's . . . is "a special kind of killing," the *Post* has editorialized. . . . Arkansas authorities have not characterized the Dirkhising death as a hate crime." Could anything make clearer the perniciousness of treating some kinds of violence as "hate crimes?" Here lies Matthew Shepard, beaten to death by a pair of savages. Here lies Jesse Dirkhising, tortured to death by a different pair of savages. Each was an innocent. Each died in agony. Each left behind grieving family and friends. Each was the victim of a crime so vicious as to shock the conscience. But because Shepard's savages detested homosexuals, his death matters. Because Dirkhising's savages were driven by [homosexual] lust, his death is a nullity.[140]

Job Discrimination and Homosexual Demographics. Repeatedly, the press portrays homosexuals as a powerless minority. However, the press fails to provide Americans with detailed information about this segment of the population. Male homosexuals make up between 1% and 2.8% of the general male population, with lesbian numbers commonly half that of males.[141] Gordon J. Muir reports that data from the National Center for Health Statistics of the Centers for Disease Control "strongly suggest that the prevalence of even incidental homosexual behavior is less than 2% for men. Most studies report that women have about half of the male prevalence rate, so a general population estimate for homosexuality would fall below 1.5%."[142]

Records compiled by the *Wall Street Journal* in 1991 suggest homosexuals are actually a privileged group: the average *household income* of homosexuals was $55,430 compared to the national average of $32,144. This same article reported that 60% of homosexuals were college graduates compared to the national average of just 18%; 49% were in professional and management positions compared to the national average of 16%; and 66% of homosexuals took overseas vacations compared with the national average of just 14%.[143] Corroborating these figures, the *Advocate*, a national magazine for homosexuals, published in 1994 the first national survey of gay and bisexual men's sexuality and relationships. It found that on "average, respondents are highly educated. Two-thirds have at least a college degree, and nearly one-third have a graduate degree. Respondents are more affluent than the average American. Half have an annual [individual] salary [in 1994] of more than $36,000," compared with the $25,491 the *average individual* earner made in 1998.[144] Market advertising confirms the *Wall Street Journal's* picture. For example, a 1997 survey commissioned by Mulryan/Nash advertising agency paints "a portrait of a well-educated, affluent group. Household income exceeded $100,000 for 21% of the [homosexual] market . . . while 22% have graduate degrees. Some 55% hold management positions."[145]

Domestic violence also differentiates homosexuals from heterosexuals. The National Coalition of Anti-Violence Programs, a coalition of twenty-five lesbian, gay, bisexual, and transgender victim and documentation programs, released in 1998 its Annual Report on Lesbian, Gay, Bisexual, Transgender Domestic Violence. They found that studies indicate that "between 25% and 33% of lesbian, gay, bisexual and transgendered persons are abused by their partners. . . . [Moreover, this] would appear to be a tiny proportion of the number of actual cases."[146] Rates for heterosexual marriages average about 3 per 1000 households, or less than 1%.[147]

Pedophilia. The Dirkhising and Curley cases could have been used to explore the relationship between homosexuality and pedophilia. This connection was ignored, as were the two murders in general. Those few times that pedophilia is mentioned, it is to suggest that heterosexuals molest more children than do homosexuals: "Some gays are pederasts. Many more straight men are. Little boys are potential sex objects for some gay men, just as little girls are for some straight men."[148] It is well documented, however, that homosexuality has strong ties with pedophilia. For instance, Kurt Freund and R.J. Watson found that "the proportion of true pedophiles among persons with a homosexual erotic development is greater than that in persons who develop heterosexually."[149] Paul Cameron and W. Coburn, analyzing the correlation between homosexuality and child molestation, concluded that, "Homosexual acts were involved in 25% to 40% of the cases of child molestation."[150] Cameron sums it this way: "If 2% of the population [homosexual males] is responsible for 20% to 40% of something as socially and personally troubling as child molestation, something must be desperately wrong with that 2%. Not every homosexual is a child molester. But enough gays do molest children so that the risk of a homosexual molesting a child is ten to twenty times greater than that of a heterosexual."[151]

The ratio of heterosexual males to homosexual males is approximately 36:1, with gay males accounting for approximately 2.8% of the male population.[152] Yet Freund and Watson found that the instance of heterosexual to homosexual pedophilia is not 36:1, but rather a ratio of 11:1.[153] Put another way, "pedophilia is far more common among homosexuals than heterosexuals. The greater absolute number of heterosexual cases reflect the fact that heterosexual males outnumber homosexual males by approximately thirty-six to one. Heterosexual child molestation cases outnumber homosexual cases by only eleven to one, implying that pedophilia is more . . . common among homosexuals."[154] According to Larry Burtoft, "Regarding the prevalence of pedophilia amongst homosexuals, literature discussing the history of homosexuality . . . quasischolarly journals . . . as well as current materials published by the North American Man-Boy Association (NAMBLA) reveal that erotic relationships with children are a significant element in the homosexual community."[155]

The conclusions drawn by many scientists is clearly expressed by Burtoft: "Although by no means supported by the majority of homosexuals, and not even by all involved in pro-homosexual activism, nonetheless it must by recognized that homosexuals make up a disproportionate amount of child sexual offenders. Studies indicate that around 35% of pedophiles are homosexuals. While it is true that this represents a minority in comparison with heterosexual offenders, the significance lies in the fact that male homosexuals make up only 2% of the general population. Therefore, the 35% figure reveals that a child molester is seventeen times more likely to be a homosexual than heterosexual."[156] Corroborating this, researchers Freund, Heasman, Racansky, and Glancy reported on two studies that found 34% and 32% respectively, while in their own studies these researchers found a rate of 36%.[157]

Sexual practices. The press asserts that homosexuals are like heterosexuals in terms of their sexual activities. For example, in an interview concerning President Clinton's HRC dinner appearance, Elizabeth Birch, executive director of HRC, was quoted as saying, " 'Gay Americans are no more promiscuous than heterosexual Americans.' "[158] The press offered no comment on this statement, nor do they offer any oppositional information on this area. It is taken for granted that it is true. In comparing heterosexual practices to homosexual practices, however, one can look at the National Health and Social Life Survey, which provides a quick snapshot of American heterosexual sexual practices: "contrary to prurient expectations, the survey, based on interviews with a random sample of 3,432 people [*sic*] between the ages of 18 and 59, was a picture of sexual squareness: low rates of homosexuality and promiscuity, high rates of marital fidelity and connubial bliss. It showed that in a given year most Americans have only one sex partner; that the median lifetime number of partners for women is two and for men is six; that most people [*sic*] have sex less than twice a week. . . ."[159] The same study found that "More than four in five Americans had only one sexual partner, or no partner, in the past year. 26% report[ed] only one lifetime partner. . . ."[160]

Had the press looked into the validity of Birch's comment, it would have found more than a few differences between heterosexual and homosexual sexual activites. For instance, a 1978 study found that 43% of male homosexuals estimated having sex with 500 or more different partners. 79% said that more than half of these partners were strangers.[161] This level of activity shows little sign of change even after the AIDS epidemic. As mentioned earlier, the *Advocate* in 1994 published the results of its national homosexual sex survey: 57% of the homosexuals responding had more than thirty sexual partners over their lifetime, and 35% reported having more than 100 sexual partners.[162] These figures are in keeping with previously reported statistics: "A 1981 study revealed that only 2% of homosexuals were monogamous or semi-monogamous. . . ."[163]

Concerning sexual activity, homosexuals as a group are very different from heterosexuals. The average number of lifetime partners a homosexual has is fifty; heterosexuals have only four on average. Monogamous relationships (defined as 100% faithful to one's spouse or partner) are virtually nonexistent in homosexual relationships. Whereas with heterosexuals we find 83% having monogamous relationships, with homosexuals we find the percentage drops to less than 2%.[164] Even homosexual activists report this difference. For instance, Marshall Kirk and Hunter Madsen wrote that "the cheating ratio of 'married' gay males, given enough time, approaches 100%."[165] D. McWhirter and A. Mattison, "found that of the 156 [homosexual] couples studied, only seven had maintained sexual fidelity; of the hundred couples that had been together for more than five years, none had been able to maintain sexual fidelity. Kirk and Madsen noted that 'The expectation for outside sexual activity was the rule for male couples and the exception for heterosexuals.' "[166]

In addition to the above differences, homosexuals account for a disproportionate number of hepatitis A and B cases, and also of sexually transmitted diseases, especially gonorrhea,[167] with homosexual youths being twenty-three times more likely than their heterosexual counterparts to contract an STD.[168] As Janet Lever stated, "Gay men are one of the top risk groups for being exposed to hepatitis B. . . ."[169] Since tracking began in 1981, homosexuals have accounted for 65% of all reported AIDS cases in the United States, and today over one in ten urban gays have HIV.[170]

Genetic or Not? Poll data on American attitudes toward homosexuals has fluctuated over the years. One aspect of these changing polls is clear, however: Americans are more tolerant of homosexuality when they believe the behavior to be unchangeable than when they believe homosexuality can be changed.[171] Thus, the manner in which the press frames this particular aspect of homosexuality is crucial considering how it impacts the thinking of Americans on these issues.

The press overwhelmingly asserted that homosexuality is genetically determined. No other explanation was countenanced. Homosexuality is genetic—period. For example, James O. Goldsborough asserted that "Scientifically speaking, Lott doesn't know what he's talking about. Instead of trying to make us all into monogamous, heterosexual belt-lashers like him, we should pay more attention to the science on the subject. The latest science . . . points to homosexuality as a genetic condition. I leave this debate to the scientific and moral experts, certain only of this: Lott and Armey are not among them."[172] The *Courier-Journal* sums well the arguments used by the press: "Never mind that it's been over twenty years since the American Psychological Association stopped considering homosexuality a mental disorder. Never mind that centuries of effort have failed to yield an effective 'treatment'—and no competent medical professional would recommend one today. And never mind that researchers in the past ten years have reported that the curable 'sin' is passed from parents to children. . . ."[173] Oft-quoted homosexual activist Richard Tafel wrote, "There is simply no excuse for an educated person to believe that homosexuality is a disease that can be 'cured.' The American Psychological Association put this issue behind them a quarter-century ago."[174]

Press statements of this type were numerous: "It's kind of amazing, really, that in the face of scientific and medical evidence to the contrary, Lott and Armey still cling to the fundamentalist belief that people are not born gay or lesbian but choose that lifestyle."[175] "Lott is 'out of step' with scientific studies of the causes of homosexuality."[176] "Most reputable scientific research suggests that sexual orientation is set at birth or not long thereafter.... Unfortunately, common sense fades in the face of prejudice."[177] "Sad and contrary to the preponderance of medical and scientific evidence, Lott's statement is [mis]informed...."[178] The press often cited the APA's 1973 decision as definitive proof of the unchangeable nature of homosexuality, yet it never explained how that decision was made. The press never explained that only a third of voting members voted on the resolution, or that four years later 69% of psychiatrists "disagreed with the vote and still considered homosexuality a disorder."[179] There are numerous eyewitness testimonies that state "the APA vote to normalize homosexuality was driven by politics, not science."[180] Even homosexual researcher Simon LeVay in his book, *Queer Science*, stated: "Gay activism was clearly the force that propelled the APA to declassify homosexuality."[181]

The press was adamant that homosexuality is genetic and unchangeable. Moreover, they even went so far as to say the majority of Americans agree with them: "Today, the gay community uses the term "homosexual" to define the whole person. The central assumption of this view is that homosexuality is inborn, like race and gender. Gay advocates have successfully made this the prevailing view in our society. Who gay people are and what they do are widely considered one and the same thing."[182] Yet poll data clearly reveals a split American public: Although at its highest level ever, only 40% of Americans believe homosexuality to be genetically caused.[183] However, in making these claims, the press intentionally ignore scientific evidence that repudiates press opinion.

There is a large body of scientific literature on the subject of genes in homosexual behavior. A succinct summation of this literature comes from Byne and Parsons:

Recent studies postulate biologic factors [genetic, hormonal] as the primary basis for sexual orientation. *However, there is no evidence at present to substantiate a biologic theory, just as there is no evidence to support any singular psychosocial explanation.* While all behavior must have an ultimate biologic substrate, the appeal of current biologic explanations for sexual orientation may derive more from dissatisfaction with the current status of psychosocial explanations than from a substantiating body of experimental data. *Critical review shows the evidence favoring a biologic theory to be lacking.* In an alternative model, temperamental and personality traits interact with the familial and social milieu as the individual's sexuality emerges. Because such traits may be heritable or developmentally influenced by hormones, the model predicts an apparent non-zero heritability for homosexuality without requiring that either genes or hormones directly influence sexual orientation per se.[184]

There are associational sources ignored by the press as well. For example, the National Association for Research and Therapy of Homosexuality

(NARTH) is "a non-profit, educational organization dedicated to the research, therapy and prevention of homosexuality. NARTH, founded in 1992, is composed of psychiatrists, psychoanalytically-informed psychologists, certified social workers, and other behavioral scientists, as well as laymen in fields such as law, religion, and education."[185] The very existence of NARTH demonstrates that there is a sizable number of scientists and other professionals who believe homosexuality is not purely genetic. Yet the press never cited NARTH. A Lexis-Nexis search found only one article citing NARTH since its inception in 1992.[186]

On the issue of the genetic determinism of homosexuality, researchers A. Dean Byrd, Shirley E. Cox, and Jeffrey W. Robinson stated: "What is clear . . . is that the scientific attempts to demonstrate that homosexual attraction is biologically determined have failed. The major researchers now prominent in the scientific arena—themselves gay activists—have in fact arrived at such conclusions. Is homosexuality immutable? Hardly. There is ample evidence that homosexual attraction can be diminished and that changes can be made."[187] NARTH stated that "The best overall summary of most respected researchers is that homosexuality (like most other psychological conditions) is due to a combination of social, biological, and psychological factors."[188] NARTH provides numerous examples of these respected researchers.[189]

Columnist Donn Esmode illustrates well the unwillingness of the press to look beyond their own opinions: "Granted, there are gay alcoholics. And gay kleptomaniacs. And maybe even a few gay alcoholic kleptomaniacs. And someday, they may stop drinking and thieving. But they won't ever stop turning their heads when a cute guy walks by."[190] Esmond ignores, intentionally or not, the hundreds of organizations and their constituents that disagree with him. There are numerous organizations—religious and secular—that specialize in reparative therapy for homosexuals, none of which were mentioned by the press, or Esmond. For example, Exudus International is one of the largest ministries geared toward helping homosexuals out of the homosexual lifestyle.[191] Numerous other ministries exist, including Transformation Ministries, Desert Stream, Love in Action, Spatula Ministries, Cross-Over Ministries, Inc., Where Grace Abounds, New Creation Ministries, Ministerio Isaias 35, Inc., Ministerio Jehova Rapha-Nissi, and Peoplecanchange.com. A lengthy list of Christian ministries can easily be obtained by going to the Christianity and homosexuality homepage.[192] On the secular side, psychologists Stanton Jones and Mark Yarhouse wrote, "every study ever performed on conversion from homosexual to heterosexual orientation has produced some successes. The psychological methods have ranged [considerably]. Reported success rates have never been . . . suggestive of an easy path to change . . . those success rates have ranged between 33% and 50–60%."[193]

Also demonstrating the unwillingness of the press to countenance any other explanation save genetic for homosexual preference, is the dearth of articles reporting Leo Spitzer's 2001 study on homosexuality. Spitzer was the lead psychiatrist in obtaining removal of homosexuality from the American Psychiatric Association's list of mental disorders in 1973. In his 2001 study, however, Spitzer reported that "some people can change from gay to straight, and we ought to acknowledge that."[194] Of those interviewed for his study, "Spitzer concluded that 66% of the men and 44% of the women had arrived at what he called good heterosexual functioning."[195] A Lexis-Nexis search found only seven articles mentioning Spitzer's new study. Three specifically set out to discredit the results, and three failed to mention that Spitzer was the lead psychiatrist in obtaining removal of homosexuality from the American Psychiatric Associations's list of mental disorders. Burtoft states, "The fact that change *is* possible is the fundamentally important issue. Since it is, there is both hope for the individuals who desire change and irrefutable proof that homosexuality is not an immutable, unchangeable fact rooted in the physical constitution. Public policy enactments must face this fact, and recognize the difference between politically correct rhetoric and empirically verifiable reality."[196]

When the *Courier-Journal* editorially denounced Senator Lott, writing that "it appears in this case that religion is a substitute for research and reason," it spoke for the mainstream press.[197] Based on the wealth of existing oppositional scientific views, I believe we can rephrase that to read, "The mainstream press substitutes its opinions for research and reason." As Burtoft wrote: "There is no scientific proof, or anything approximating proof, that persons are 'born homosexual.' Whatever the exact causal factors may be, there is no justification for the claim that homosexuality is analogous to race or eye color or any other genetically determined trait. Any discussion of the causes of homosexual orientation must take into account a basic problem: *there presently exists no scientific consensus on the subject.*"[198]

ANTI-DEMOCRATIC NATURE OF THE MAINSTREAM PRESS

Contrary to its own assertions and in conflict with its self-adopted code of ethics, the press is decidedly biased in its presentation of information to the American polity. Simply put, the practices of the mainstream press are anti-democratic in numerous ways:

1. The press presents a consistent left-wing point of view among news stories, editorials, and opinion essays.

2. The press assumes a correct political and social point of view and acts to make Americans agree with them.

3. The press shuts out information that contradicts its point of view, thus acting to limit information that citizens need to make informed policy decisions.

4. The press, ignoring its own call for diversity, is overwelmingly liberal and Democratic in its composition.

5. The press actively harms conservatives while acting to help a narrow brand of liberals.

6. The press, although seeming to present both sides of an issue, makes oppositional comments seem the minority position by sandwiching them in between press-supported positions.

7. The press, by a rate of 2:1 and higher, consistently presents pro-press point of view sources, thereby making oppositional points of view seem the minority point of view.

In all of these actions, the press violates its own norms for fair reporting. Looking specifically at the standards outlined in the Hutchins Commission, we find each being violated by the mainstream press. The press fails to provide a truthful, comprehensive, or intellegent account of the day's events in a fair context. Instead, the press routinely omits information that contradicts its ideological commitments. The press fails to provide a forum for the exchange of comment and criticism. News stories and opinion essays represented well the political opinions expressed in editorials, thus demonstrating a narow range of acceptable ideas receiving publication. Although there are occasional letters from readers who disagree with the press point of view, and a handful of conservative commentary, *overwhelmingly* what is printed fits well within the left-wing point of view of the press. This was consistent across the country, with papers on the East Coast enacting the same political ideology as papers on the West Coast. Thus, there was almost no variety of thought within a particular paper, nor among papers nationwide.

The press fails to provide a representative picture of the constituent groups in society. Instead, the press depicts liberals as champions of civil rights, and conservatives as attacking those rights. Specific to this study, blacks and homosexuals were depicted as victims, and all contrary information to this point of view was suppressed or mocked. In this specific case, as in general, the press failed to assume reponsibility for the presentation and clarification of the goals and values of the society in which it operates. The political composition of the press is decidedly different from that of America. That itself is a disservice to Americans. In addition, the press acts to *impose* its values and goals on Americans instead of helping Americans to better understand the values and goals of those whom the press reports upon. Finally, the press fails utterly to provide full access to the day's intelligence. Although the press does cover breaking events, it presents that information in such a way that portions of that information is withheld if it would hinder the political goals of the press. Moreover, there is little difference of information presented from news article to news article, suggesting that the mainstream press over-rely on news wires and other press sources for information.

Just because the overwhelming majority of mainstream press outlets engage in biased reporting does not make them anti-democratic. What makes them function to undermine democracy is that they deny Americans information they need to make informed decisions on the policies that affect their lives. The role of the press is to provide this information, and when they continually fail to do so, intentionally or not, they engage in anti-democratic behavior. As Robert Entman stated, "Scholars have usually attempted to find evidence that the media are persuaders, deliberate causers of public thinking. It may be more realistic to think of the media as contributing to—but not controlling—the structure of publicly available information that shapes the way people can and do think politically."[199] I am inclined to believe that Entman underestimates the case since, by its reportorial practices, the press acts to persuade large numbers of Americans that they should think a particular way and if they do not so think, that they are lacking in some way. This is to say that the press acts to make them feel stupid, uninformed, or in possession of a point of view that large numbers of Americans do not agree with. Moreover, given the vociferous nature of attack editorials and opinion essays, many Americans might feel that they will have visited upon them the same type of conversation-stopping attacks if they voice disagreement with the press point of view.

The Spiral of Silence

By advancing a correct political point of view the press does extreme harm to American democracy. By believing its own point of view and political beliefs as the only correct view, the press seems to expect all Americans eventually to adopt them. This assumption, coupled with the virtually unfettered freedom of speech given to the press, allows the press to advance its views confidently and openly—even when its political beliefs are clearly the minority point of view. Minority view or not, those who reject or disagree with the views of the press will feel left out, eventually choosing to remain silent rather than express points of views that they feel, based on what the press reports, that the majority around them do not hold.

The work of social psychologist Soloman Asche highlights the ease with which many agree with what they perceive to be the majority point of view. In a series of experiments, Asche and colleagues asked a subject to determine which of three lines matched a fourth line in length. The answer was made obvious. Eight to ten persons took part in each multi-round test, with all but one collaborating with Asche. The collaborators would all agree on the obviously correct line during the first two rounds, but thereafter would agree that a wrong line was the correct match. When it came time for the true subject of the experiment to say which line was the correct match, Asche found that *only two of ten would stick to their original impressions*. Two of ten would agree with the majority two or three times and then revert back to their original thoughts. However, six in ten would continue to agree with the majority, even though the majority was clearly giving the wrong answer.[200]

The Asche experiments demonstrate well the great pressure to conform. The work of Elisabeth Noelle-Neumann sheds more light on this abstract process of self-silencing that occurs even in a democracy. Noelle-Neumann calls this process the spiral of silence. Essentially put,

The theory of the spiral of silence is based on the assumption that society—and not just groups in which the members are known to each other—threatens with isolation and exclusion those individuals who deviate from the consensus. Individuals, in turn, have a largely subconscious fear of isolation, which probably is genetically determined. This fear of isolation causes people constantly to check which opinions and modes of behavior are approved or disapproved of in their environment, and which opinions and forms of behavior are gaining or losing strength. The theory postulates the existence of a quasistatistical sense for making such assessments. The results of these assessments affect people's willingness to speak out, as well as their behavior in general. If people believe that their opinion is part of a consensus, they have the confidence to speak out in both private and public discussions, displaying their convictions with buttons and car stickers, for example. . . . Conversely, when people feel that they are in the minority, they become cautious and silent, thus reinforcing the impression of weakness, until the apparently weaker side disappears completely except for a hard core that holds on to its previous values, or until the opinion becomes taboo.[201]

Journalists seem to present the American polity with a snapshot of the world, of the attitudes and values that comprise public opinion. Yet instead of presenting a representative picture of the public's opinion, the press presents its own partisan views as the prevailing point of view. No one has first-hand experience in all areas of our collective life, thus our exposure to public opinion is mediated by necessity—we receive a substantial portion of it through the mediating efforts of the mainstream press. The selective reporting of the press, favoring a point of view that supports its own political leanings, is particularly pernicious. As Noelle-Neumann stated, "What does not get reported does not exist, or, stated somewhat more cautiously, its chances of becoming part of ongoing, perceived reality are minimal."[202]

The press, guided by its frames, selects news, and interprets the news, leaving out a vast array of information and points of view. These frames let readers know in an unambiguous manner when they can speak out and when they must remain silent. As Noelle-Neumann stated, "not in a single instance has the process of the spiral of silence run counter to the line taken by the media. The fact that an individual is aware that his or her opinion is supported by the media is an important factor in determining that person's willingness to speak out."[203] Communication researchers Carolyn A. Lin and Michael B. Salwen found similar results in their study of the national media coverage of the English as the National Language Referendum. They found that "perceived media coverage climate alone seemed to have an impact on one's willingness publicly to discuss a controversial issue, in the absence of a clear understanding of perceived national and local public opinion. It appears that respondants [to the study] were quite capable of identifying the perceived tone of media coverage on the issue. They became more willing to discuss this issue in public with the understanding that perceived media coverage on this issue was generally positive or 'supportive' in nature."[204]

As William P. Eveland Jr., and colleagues found in their study of actual and perceived public opinion about the Gulf War, the use of "news media influences perceptions of public opinion, and these perceptions in turn influence individual opinions."[205] Specifically, these researchers "demonstrated that exposure to U.S. news media . . . had a significant influence on perceptions of public opinion about the Gulf War. These perceptions, in turn, were strongly related to actual support for the war, with media use having a more limited direct influence. In the case of the Persian Gulf War, it seems that instead of just telling us what to think about, the news media told us what others thought, which influenced how we thought."[206] In short, when individuals perceive the climate of public opinion—as expressed through the media—to match their own beliefs, they are more willing to speak out in public than those who find the climate of public opinion—as expressed by the media—does not match their own point of view.

We can easily see from the case studies presented in Chapters 2 through 7 that the press let its readers know what the correct point of views were. As Noelle-Neumann stated, "the mass media have to be seen as creating public opinion: they provide the environmental pressure to which people respond with alacrity, or with aquiescense, or with silence."[207] With this in mind, let us now turn to the case studies contained in this book to see how the press urges readers to respond. Looking back at the summaries of the case studies we can see distinct points of views put forth by the mainstream press; these points of view are monolithic, *representing what the press wishes to be public opinion.* Aside from the nature of these press assertions, the press put forth statements that describe what one should think if one is exposed to someone who disagrees with the point of view embraced by the press. Examples of this type of behavior are commonplace.

The Davidson case study presents a tidy example of how the press acts to silence the public. One way that the press works is to categorize a person's speech as unacceptable, and then to present a non-press source echoing press thoughts; all this without rejoinder or alternate point of view, even if majorities of Americans disagree with the press point of view. As already shown in the Davidson chapter, a substantial majority of Americans view the Confederate battleflag as a symbol of Southern pride, not white supremacy or hate. Yet the press gave the negative meaning of the flag: pro-slavery, bigotry, and racism. After presenting this point of view, the press presented others who agreed with it: " 'His remarks [Sen. Davidson's] are not representative of the vast majority of Alabamians,' said Sen. Heflin."[208] Yet a 1995 poll of Alabama residents found that only a minority (27.1%) opposed flying the Confederate battleflag on top of the capitol—the very point of Davidson's speech; whereas a majority (52.2%) supported flying the flag.[209] A 1987 poll, giving only the options of favor or opposition found a vast majority (74.6%) in favor of flying the flag.[210] This is not, however, the impression given by the press coverage on this issue at all. The majority reading the paper would be made to feel as if their *super-majority position* were actually that of an *outcast minority*. Add to this the more assertive press statements and rhetorical questions such as this by the *Montgomery Advertiser*: "why would anyone write such divisive trash today?"[211] Presented with the press's erroneous, yet cohesive snapshot of public opinion, would the 74.6% of Alabamians wish to respond with alacrity, aquiescense, or with silence?

Looking at the Lott chapter, a case can be made that the press pushed those agreeing with Senator Lott into the realm of silence, and would embolden those who side with the press. The *Courier-Journal*, in an editorial titled "Oblivious to the Facts" stated, "For Mr. Lott, it appears in this case that religion is a substitute for research and reason. Is that true for his party, too?"[212] Editorially speaking, the *Times-Picayune* wrote that "If . . . Lott cared about facts, he might notice that the American Psychiatric Association doesn't view gay people as mentally ill. Most reputable scientific research suggests that sexual orientation is set at birth or not long thereafter, and common sense suggests that gay people have no more 'choice' about being homosexual that straight people do about being heterosexual. Unfortunately, common sense fades in the face of prejudice."[213] The *St. Petersburg Times*, in a strongly worded editorial, denounced Senator Lott, saying he "has a right to believe homosexuality is a sin, but he commits one when he uses his power to discriminate against gays. [Lott] has a duty to Americans not to let his ugly personal prejudices drive the management of Senate business. [He should] put his homophobia aside. . . ."[214]

Without conducting research of its own, the *Albuquerque Journal* editorially asserted that its beliefs about homosexuality are the prevalent scientific beliefs as well: "The prevailing medical opinion today is that homosexuality is in most instances an inherited characteristic and not a learned behavior. Individuals are born with their sexual orientation in place—much as they are born with their hair color and ultimate height determined by genetic variables beyond their individual control."[215] As the title to this editorial suggests—"Lott's Views on Gays Poison Confirmation"—if you disagree with the paper, you have poisonous views. The *Tennessean* was more direct in its condemnation of those who disagree with its point of view: "Despite believing that the statements [by Lott] are wrong, I nonetheless and without hesitation respect the right of the speakers to express their opinion, however misinformed."[216]

Carl T. Rowan implies that all who disagree with his point of view (thus agreeing with Senator Lott) are "the bashers of homosexuals."[217] The *St. Petersburg Times* stated that "Lott is entitled to his opinion. But as leader of our upper house, he has a duty to Americans not to let his ugly prejudices drive the management of Senate business."[218] Richard L. Tafel, calls all who agree with Lott uneducated: "There is simply no excuse for an educated person to believe that homosexuality is a disease that can be 'cured.' "[219] The *San Francisco Chronicle* implies that all who disagree with their point of view are bigoted and ignorant: those who agree with Lott "are willing to use discrimination and intolerance as political tools. Lott showed his ignorance last week. . . ."[220] In keeping with the press assertion that one has a right to express one's opinion, the *Los Angeles Times* made it clear that if you express opinions with which they disagree then you are bigoted: "Lott and his fellow anti-Hormel crusaders are entitled to their beliefs. . . . It's time to end this embarassing display of bigotry. . . ."[221] The *Charleston Gazette* called Senator Lott's comments a "tirade against gays" and then asked "[is] America an intolerant nation that shares the harsh Republican view?"[222] Deb Price wrote that Lott was "demeaning gays," and was an "extremist" "spouting anti-gay rhetoric" but that not "every Republican in Congress shamelessly kowtows to prejudice."[223] And the *Daily News* editorial suggests that if you agree with Lott you are "demonizing" homosexuals and are "un-American."[224]

In each of the above instances the press presents an image of public opinion, yet it is an image warped to reflect what the press believes is true. Those who disagree with the press are encouraged to keep quiet or face being labeled uneducated, homophobic, extremist, and so on. Those agreeing with Senator Lott are made to feel that the tide of public and scientific opinion have turned against them—and only the most dedicated citizens would persist with their opinions under such circumstances.

Unfortunately, the case study with Reggie White provides an eerily similar press attempt to silence those that do not agree with their point of view. Columnist J.A. Adande called White's comments about homosexuality "railing," and said it showed just "how narrow a frame of mind he was operating within when he denounced homosexuals. It's bad enough to spew this ignorance before the media, but to do it on the floor of a legislative body makes it even worse."[225] The *Milwaukee Journal Sentinel* asserted that White's remarks were "intemperate."[226] Mike Bruton accused White of "using fundamentalist dogma" during his "homophobic rant." Bruton stated that "It would serve White well to understand that one can't push simplistic, fundamentalist views. . . ."[227] John McClain wrote that "many couldn't believe what came out of [White's] mouth. It was his size-16 shoe. Actually, it was both shoes. He's just ignorant. . . ."[228] Jonathan Rand called White's comments "crass" and opined that "White's insensitivity shouldn't have come as a shock. [He's] a loose cannon as a guest speaker. . . . [Furthermore,] White is too dogmatic to reconsider his remarks."[229] The *Wisconsin State Journal* editorially stated that "White's litany of stereotyes was long and painful to . . . those . . . who have always prided themselves on seeing one another as human beings, rather than cliches. White got just about everything wrong. . . . In his repetition of stereotypes and petty prejudices. . . ."[230] Editorial writer James T. Campbell accused White of trying to "defend his ignorance. [But] that's what too many slaps to the helmet can do." He also stated, "Now, I'm no sociologist, but I know a few, and Reggie is not among them. Reggie is an ordained fundamentalist Christian minister, who obviously is a true believer in his unenlightened suppositions, judging from his unrepenting willingness to voice them."[231]

The press acts also to silence others even while touting the right of free speech. Jennifer Frey provides an example of how this works After saying White "sounded like a bigot . . . a hypocrite [and] a fool," Frey called White "arrogant" and "ignorant." She wrote that everything White said was a "product of ignorance" and "his intense religious intolerance"; moreover, Frey wrote that White "used religion to justify his own prejudices." However, Frey also wrote, "As a believer in free speech, I do not deny White the right to his opinions, nor the right to express them, no matter how horrible I—*and others*—may find them to be. He should not, however, be allowed to spew those opinions on the floor of the Wisconsin assembly simply because he was once able to throw a good sack."[232] Columnist Tom Oates highlights the press's peculiar understanding of free speech in America: "Freedom of speech is guaranteed in this country, and nowhere in the Constitution does it say that it must be intelligent, factually correct or even politically correct. White should be happy about that because his discourse on homosexuality and race was none of the above."[233] Dave Hyde speaks of freedom of speech as well: White "had every right to say what he did. In America's playbook, that's called the First Amendment. But with the pulpit White has built for his name comes a responsibility and so there is a price to be extracted now for each syllable. American sports have been dotted in recent years with the white graduates of the Al Campanis Idiot School of anthropology. This is the first time a black athlete of prominence went national in the same context."[234] In other words, those who think like White are idiots.

In each of the instances above, the press presents an image of public opinion, yet it is an image warped to reflect what the press believes is true. If you disagree with the press the message is clear: keep quiet or face being labeled uneducated, homophobic, narrowminded, and so on. What is particularly disquieting about the examples of both Lott and White is that they represent a national press consensus on the issue. This is to say, in the very forum designed for the free exchange of ideas we find a monolithic enterprise that silences Americans. Mike Fisher demonstrates well how the press can make the most intelligent and well-meaning individuals feel ignorant and out of touch with the public: "Think about it: Arguably the most intelligent, respected, dignified man in professional sports [Reggie White] just revealed himself to be a moron."[235] The implications are clear: if you speak up like White, you too will be seen as a moron. Steven Greenhut, the only columnist in the White case study to speak in opposition to the general press opinion, sums this Spiral of Silence section well: "What's happening here is a no-holds-barred attempt at thought control. It apparently no longer is acceptable to hold differing views on the rightness of homosexuality, let alone express them even in the most obsequious and well-intentioned manner. The overheated media response was indicative of the totalitarian way liberal elites intimidate into silence those who disagree with them. I'm sure most Americans got the message: Criticize homosexuality at your own peril. You may be turned into an outcast, called a religious fanatic or face a harassment lawsuit if you express your views to the wrong person."[236]

Identifying the press efforts at silencing Americans is not difficult once you know what to look for. Although looking at nationwide press coverage on a specific issue or speech will yield the aggregate press point of view, you can easily examine individual articles and essays for these attempts at silencing. For example, Rhonda Chriss Lokeman stated that "Even before his California speech Clinton was showing impressive momentum that should be appreciated by those who value racial harmony and equal opportunity as well as those who believe in the responsibility of government to insist on remedies to discrimination of the past."[237]

This assertion makes anyone who disagrees with Clinton (and by extension, Lokeman) out to be against racial harmony and equal opportunity. The *Baltimore Sun* stated that "Today, the gay community uses the term 'homosexual' to define the whole person. The central assumption of this view is that homosexuality is inborn, like race and gender. Gay advocates have successfully made this the prevailing view in our society. Who gay people are and what they do are widely considered one and the same thing."[238] This statement suggests that if you disagree you are out of touch with the "prevailing view." Poll data clearly reveals a split American public: although at its highest level ever, only 40% of Americans believe homosexuality to be genetically caused.[239] Yet Lokeman has the other 60% of Americans placed in the minority position. Deb Price wrote that if the president "had made only perfunctory remarks, the evening [at the HRC dinner] still would have been historic. But he elevated it to a noble occasion *by staking out the moral high ground* on behalf of the gay civil rights movement, describing it to the nation as part of the neverending struggle to make the American ideal of equality a reality for all."[240] Clearly this implies that if you disagree with the homosexual agenda that you are on the moral low ground.

So, although the press may not actually say the majority of Americans think a particular way, the very strength of press coverage suggests this. This is seen in the way the press asserts its own point of view, and then states that those who do not hold this view are misinformed, extremists, ignorant, and so on. It is also seen when looking at the number of different sources used by the press. At minimum, the press presents a 2:1 ratio of sources that favor the press point of view as reflected in editorials and opinion essays. This acts to imply that more Americans are in favor of the press point of view than not. Ultimately, by so strongly suggesting that its political point of view is that of the overwhelming majority of Americans, the press acts to silence the political voices of tens of millions of Americans.

Band of Correct Politics

When looked at from a national perspective, the press presents its readers with a narrow band of correct political thought. This was well demonstrated in the six case studies presented in this book. Essentially put, the politics represents liberal, upper-middle class, white baby-boomer activist politics. This narrow band of press-acceptable politics is clearly to the left of the political center and substantially to the left of the majority of Americans. The practical implications of this are clear. Those to the right of this band of liberal politics will be ostracized, ignored, or demonized. However, just as perniciously, those to the left of this narrow band will suffer the same fate. Thus an enormous range of political thought is delegitimized by our national press simply because those thoughts do not fit within what the press views as the correct type of thinking on any given issue. The result is that tens of millions of Americans are made to feel as if their political voices do not count; or, if they were inclined to speak out, they are made to feel as if they would be met with ridicule. This is simply shameful in a free democracy.

Based on the results of the six case studies in this book, and also upon observations of the news media in general, I am inclined to believe that the mainstream press in America today is a hypocritical institution, greviously flawed in its reportorial practices. The press voluntarily adheres to noble and high ethical standards. Its codes of conduct are thoughtful and well articulated. While insisting it is fair and objective, however, the press violates with abandon these ethical codes. All five items listed above in the Hutchins Commission's report are routinely violated on a national scale by the press. Recall that 116 mainstream papers were included in this study, and these from all areas of the country. The outright violation of its own codes of conduct is widespread and great. Intentional or not, the press acts to impart a narrow band of political thought as public opinion. By presenting Americans with this flawed image of public opinion, the press severly hinders the democratic process by misleading the public to accept a particular point of view as the norm. Clearly the role of the press is to represent fairly the constituent elements in American society. However, as each of the case studies in this book has shown, the press instead advances a heavily biased picture of the political landscape; one that highlights in a positive way the preferred political beliefs of the press.

Yet how does an entire institution become so overwelmingly homogenized politically? The notion of the Spiral of Silence can be used to explain this, in part. According to journalists' own descriptions, newsrooms are bastions of liberal thought. If a fresh-minded reporter is hired into this environment, what is he exposed to? All of his colleagues are liberal; and it is the rare exception to find a colleague who writes without a liberal slant. Because journalists hold similar values, they see events in a similar manner, and thus report similarly as well. In short, the "public opinion" of the newsroom encourages politically liberal thought. Those who wish to fit in and not suffer ridicule will keep silent or begin to adopt the political positions of those around them. Adopting the ideology of those they perceive as able to help their careers seems likely; the political opinions of the senior journalists and editors will take on special importance. Those few who do hold dissimilar views will keep quiet for fear of alienation, or worse, termination. The only alternative to acquiescence is to leave. Thus, one finds a monolithic, homogenized presentation of a correct political point of view. Given such an environment, many moderates and, certainly, conservatives do leave.

Too, the notion of "groupthink" helps explain how individual newsrooms maintain such a consitent political point of view. Groupthink describes a situation in which groups, in our case, news organizations, exhibit a high level of cohesiveness with members reluctant to deviate from the preferred group consensus. Because of this consensus, there is little, if any, argumentation or conflict of ideas among group members. Members tend to be isolated, possess biased leaders, and be exposed to stress. In our case, journalists are isolated socially and politically from the public they purport to represent; they possess politically biased leaders; and they are under constant deadline stress. The decision-making process is made inside the organization, and journalists listen to fellow journalists and editors over and above those outside the organization. According to Dominic A. Infante and colleagues, "the pressure of cohesiveness results in faulty, inadequate analysis. . . . Not enough possible solutions are examined because there is an early preference for a particular solution. Groupthink fosters an inadequate approach to information. When groupthink operates, there is typically inadequate research and thus a shortage of necessary information. Since there is an early preference for a particular solution, the information is processed in a biased fashion."[241]

The general reportorial practices of the press today are abhorent. The level of speculation, hearsay, arrogant assertion, and outright political advocacy make a mockery of the press's professed role of objective disseminator of news. News stories clearly reflect the political point of views expressed by editorials and opinion essays. Although dangerous enough in an individual paper, this study clearly demonstrated that news stories, editorials, and opinion essays presented the same political views nationwide. Thus, the press advances a consistent and cohesive image of political thought on a massive scale. As Allan Rachlin stated, "a press free from legal constraints imposed by an oppressive government can still undermine the possibility of pluralism and the requirements of democracy, if it is constrained instead by a narrow vision of the world that reproduces existing social relationships by inhibiting the possibility of realizing or even imagining alternative realities."[242] As an institution the mainstream press possesses negligible variety of thought. The few non-left political sources given voice have their voices made insignificant by the collective weight of mainstream press thought. In its role as provider of objective, balanced information for the American polity, the press fails miserably. As it now exists, the mainstream press is clearly an anti-Democratic institution.

NOTES

1. Robert E. Denton, "Rhetorical Challenges to the Presidency," paper presented at the annual convention of the Southern States Communication Association, New Orleans, 1 April 2000, p. 5.

2. David Weaver, "Reply to Kosicki's Column: Framing Should not Supplant Agenda-Setting," *Communication Theory & Methodology Newsletter* (Communication Theory & Methodology Divison of the Association for Education in Journalism & Mass Communication). <http://communication.sbs.ohio-state.edu/ctm/current/weaver.htm>

3. R.W. Apple Jr., "The March on Washington: News Analysis," *New York Times* (17 October 1995): A1.

4. Brigitte Lebens Nacos, *The Press, Presidents, and Crises* (New York: Columbia University Press, 1990).

5. Thomas Patterson, "The News Media: An Effective Political Actor?" *Political Communication* 14 (1997): 445.

6. See Fred S. Siebert, Theodore Peterson, and Wilbur Schramm, *Four Theories of the Press* (Urbana: University of Illinois Press, 1956), 5.

7. Ibid., 74.

8. Ibid., 87.

9. Ibid., 89.

10. Ibid., 91.

11. Ibid.

12. Ibid.

13. "Eugene Meyer's Principles for the *Washington Post*," *Washington Post* <http://www.washpost.com/gen_info/principles/>.

14. American Society of Newspaper Editors Statement of Principles. "ASNE's Statement of Principles was originally adopted in 1922 as the 'Canons of Journalism.' The document was revised and renamed 'Statement of Principles' in 1975." The full document can be obtained at <http://www.asne.org/kiosk/archive/principl.htm>.

15. Code of Ethics, Society for Professional Journalists <http://spj.org/ethics/code.htm>.

16. Numbers are mine. For the complete listing of the Associated Press's code of ethics, see <http://www.asne.org/ideas/codes/apme.htm>.

17. Gary C. Woodward, "Narrative Form and the Deceptions of Modern Journalism," *Political Communication Ethics: An Oxymoron?* ed. Robert E. Denton, Jr. (Westport, CT: Praeger, 2000), 127.

18. Reported by Brent Bozell III, "Media and Politics: Overcoming the Bias," Remarks given to The Union League Club (8 June 2000). Figure on acceptance of homosexuality from The People, The Press & Their Leaders (Pew Research Center for the People & the Press, May 1995).

19. This lop-sided party affiliation continues when one moves beyond Washington: 44% of reporters polled nationwide considered themselves Democrats; 34% as independents; only 16% identified themselves as Republicans. Freedom Forum-sponsored poll of 1,400 journalists across the country, 1992. <http://www.freedomforum.org/>.

20. Elaine S. Povich, *Partners & Adversaries: The Contentious Connection Between Congress & the Media* (Arlington, VA: The Freedom Forum, Inc., 1996), 170–180. A national sample of newspaper editors yielded similar results; 9% said they were liberal, 23% liberal to moderate, 35% moderate, 19% moderate to conservative, and 6% conservative. Party affiliation corresponded to this: 31% Democrat, 39% independent, 14% Republican, and 7% other parties; 60% voted for Bill Clinton in 1992.

21. These figures are rounded to the nearest percentage. Harris Poll, survey collection 911009, (June 1999), obtained from the Howard W. Odum Institute for Research in Social Science. <http://www.irrss.unc.edu/>. A September 1990 Harris Poll (901106) obtained from the same source shows little change in these divisions: 36.9% conservative, 41.4% moderate, and 17.8% liberal. An October 1988 *USA Today* poll (study number 3108) found a smaller number of liberals and conservatives: 32.7% conservative, 48.1% middle of the road, and 13.7% liberal.

22. Lydia Saad, "Independents Rank as Largest U.S. Political Group," Gallup News Service (9 April 1999). Figures for 1999 show 28% Republicans, 34% Democrats, and 38% independents. <http://www.gallup.com/pool/releases/pr990409.asp>.

23. Surveys by the Gallup Organization (April 1996). Reported in "Opinion Pulse: Issues," *American Enterprise* (September/October 1996): 93.

24. Data provided by The Roper Center for Public Opinion Research, University of Connecticut. Survey was conducted by the Gallup Organization, May 2001. <http://roperweb.ropercenter.uconn.edu/>.

25. Lydia Saad, "Most Americans Would Soften U.S. Military's Rules Against Adultery," Gallup News Service (13 June 1998) <http://www.gallup.com/poll/releses/pr970613.asp>.

26. Gallup Poll Topic: Religion <http://www.gallup.com/poll/indicators/indreligion.asp>.

27. The People, Press and Politics (Pew Research Center for the People & the Press, July 1985).

28. The People, The Press & Their Leaders.

29. Center poll for the Freedom Forum. Survey of 139 Washington bureau chiefs and congressional correspondents, released April 1996. <http://www.ropercenter.uconn.edu/>.

30. Tim Graham and Jim Naureckas, "Q: Does Media Coverage of President Clinton Reveal a Liberal Bias?" *Insight* (22 July 1996): 24.

31. "Our Delicately Balanced Media," The *American Enterprise* (July/August 1996): 13.

32. *U.S. News & World Report* (13 May 1996): 40. The Times Mirror Center for the People and the Press recently changed its name to the Pew Center.

33. Michael Barone, *American Enterprise* 7.2 (March/April 1996): 30.

34. Patterson.

35. Bernard Goldberg, "Networks Need a Reality Check," *Wall Street Journal* (13 February 1996): A14.

36. Robert Novak, "Political Correctness Has No Place in the Newsroom," *USA Today* 123.2598 (March 1995). Obtained from Proquest, no day given <http://proquest.umi.com/>.

37. *Inside Washington*, 12 May 1996.

38. Walter Cronkite, Radio and TV Correspondents Association Dinner (21 March 1996).

39. Lynne Cheney, *The American Enterprise* 7.2 (April/May 1996): 37.

40. Patterson, 451–452 Emphasis mine. For more on the interpretive turn in press reporting see, Thomas Patterson, "Bad News, Bad Governance," *Annals of the American Academy of Political and Social Scientists* 546 (July 1996): 97–108. Patterson also writes: "There is no justification for election coverage that allots six minutes to the journalist for every minute that a candidate speaks. The trend toward interpretive reporting has diminished the voices of those who are involved in the representation of values. Theirs must be the larger voice if the news is to provide the type of marketplace of ideas that serves democracy's needs." Patterson, "Bad News, Bad Governance," 108.

41. For additional examples of this see the Media Research Center's Media Bias Basics page: <http://www.mediaresearch.org/news/MediaBiasBasics .html>.

42. Carl T. Rowan, "The Devil and Dick Armey," *New York Post* (22 June 1998): 23.

43. Theotis Robinson, Jr., "Cynics Cite Scripture for Own Purposes," *Knoxville News-Sentinel* (22 June 1998): A10.

44. Rob Morse, "A Case of Agenda Confusion," *San Francisco Examiner* (23 June 1998): A2.

45. Arianna Huffington, "That Giant Sucking Sound Is the GOP Vaccum," *Chicago Sun-Times* (24 June 1998): 45.

46. Editorial, "Hating Gays GOP Intolerance," *Charleston Gazette* (26 June 1998): A4.

47. Editorial, "Opening a Conversation on Race," *New York Times* (16 June 1997): A14.

48. Editorial, "Talk and Action on Race: Clinton's Jawboning on Racial Matters Is Welcome—if a Trifle Late," *San Francisco Examiner* (18 June 1997): A16.

49. Lovell Beaulieu, "What Bill Clinton Could Do about Race Relations in America," *Des Moines Register* (15 June 1997): Opinion 1.

50. Gallup Organization Survey. Reported by *The American Enterprise* (September/October 1996): 93.

51. "Tolerance," *Oxford English Dictionary*. Online version <http:// dictionary.oed.com/>.

52. Steven Greenhut, "Criticism of the Gay Agenda Is Not a Hate Crime," *Las Vegas Review-Journal* (26 June 1998): B15.

53. Editorial, "Civic Sin: Lott Seems to Favor Prejudice," *Star Tribune* (17 June 1998): A20.

54. Editorial, "Trent Lott's Gay Theory," *San Francisco Examiner* (18 June 1998): A18.

55. Hoyt Hopewell Hudson, *Educating Liberally* (Stanford, CA: Stanford University Press, 1945) 12.

56. Editorial, "White Fumbles on Tolerance," *Capital Times* (Madison, WI) (26 March 1998): A12.

57. Ibid.

58. Jennifer Frey, "White's Opinions Laced with Ignorance, Arrogance," *Washington Post* (27 March 1998): D1.

59. Rob Zaleski, "Reggie Teaches Us Some Lessons," *Capital Times* (Madison, WI) (6 April 1998): D1.

60. Michael Paul Williams, "There's No Monoply on Ignorance," *Richmond Times Dispatch* (6 April 1998): B1.

61. Thomas Patterson and Wolfgang Donsbach, "News Decisions: Journalists as Partisan Actors," *Political Communication* 13 (1996): 466.

62. Quotation omitted in original. Thomas M. DeFrank and Timothy J. Burger, "Al: Anti-Gay View Stalls Envoy Bid," *Daily News* (New York) (19 June 1998): 48.

63. Nancy Mathis, "Clinton Calls for Dialogue on Race: Despite Raw Emotions, President Insists, 'We Must Begin,' " *Houston Chronicle* (15 June 1997): A1.

64. Jonathan Peterson, "Clinton Call for 'National Effort' to End Racism," *Los Angeles Times* (15 June 1997): A1. Nowhere did the press mention that the military is a monoculture, and that diversity is literally only skin deep.

65. Cox News Service, "Clinton to Address Gay Rights Group: Plan Draws Fire from Conservative Groups, Praise from Human Rights Campaign," *Milwaukee Journal Sentinel* (7 November 1997): 6.

66. Amy Rinard, "Speech by White Upsets Assembly with Views on Race, Homosexuality," *Milwaukee Journal Sentinel* (26 March 1998): 1.

67. Due to the large sample size, this is based on a random sample of forty articles.

68. Stewart M. Powell, "Clinton Talk at Gay Event a Milestone," *San Francisco Examiner* (9 November 1997): A1. Emphasis mine.

69. Bill Nichols, "Clinton Criticized for Gay Group Talk," *USA Today* (10 November 1997): A7.

70. "Dingbat," Judy Mann, "Clinton Surrounded in Dirt, but Where's the GOP?" *Washington Post* (26 April 1998): C23; "Ayatollah" and "Zealot," Editorial, "GOP Trap: Squeezed by Zealots," *Charleston (WV) Gazette* (6 May 1998): A4; "Crazy," Cokie Roberts and Steve Roberts, "Ideological Purity: Republicans Could be Headed for Trouble with Moderates and Economic Conservatives," *Dallas Morning News* (24 May 1998): J5; "Intolerant," Howard Park, "The Chief Character Defect of the Religious Right Is Intolerance," *Paradise (California) Post* (21 May 1998). "Godzilla of the Right," Frank Rich, "Godzilla of the Right," *New York Times* (20 May 1998): A23, found in Dobson, letter to Focus on the Family constituents, July 1998.

71. Clinton, 9.

72. White, 4.

73. Labeling, ironically, also works by lack of labels. Take, for example, the 2001 scandal involving Democratic Congressman Gary Condit. Standard reportorial practice is to identify members of Congress with their party affiliation. Condit, under scrutiny because of his numerous affairs, including one with Chandra Levy, his intern who disappeared, should be no different. However, research conducted by the Media Research Center between May and July 2001 shows that the major networks (ABC, CBS, and NBC) reported 179 stories on Condit, but his party affiliation was mentioned only fourteen times. Thus in only 8% of the stories was Condit identified as a Democrat. In many of those stories, however,

Condit was identified as a "conservative" Democrat linked to the "right-wing" in the Democratic party. This even though Condit's voting record has him, after "twelve years in Congress [with] a 48% rating from the American Conservative Union and a 52% score from the liberal Americans for Democratic Action." Found in Media Research Center, "Avoiding Gary Condit's Democratic ID," (12 July 2001). <http://www.mrc.org/news/reality/2001/Fax20010712.html>. This report focuses exclusively on broadcast, not print reporting.

74. Michael Barone, "The Return of Partisan Journalism," *The American Enterprise* 7.2 (March–April 1996): 30. David Gergen, writing in *U.S. News & World Report* (22 April 1996), reported on a recent Center for Media and Public Affairs study that found that the ABC, CBS, and NBC evening news programs evaluated Republican candidates negatively 61% of the time during the first two months of the presidential campaign.

75. "Whites [*sic*] Remarks Criticized," *Ventura County Star* (Ventura County, CA) (26 March 1998): B2.

76. Joe Hart, "Reggie Flagged for Illegal Use of Mouth," *Capital Times* (Madison, WI) (27 March 1998): B1.

77. Cokie Roberts and Steven V. Roberts, "Gay-Bashing Divides GOP and the Nation," *Daily News* (24 June 1998): 31.

78. Editorial, "Some Straght Talk about the GOP," *Daily News* (27 June 1998): 16.

79. Editorial, "White Fumbles on Tolerance."

80. Deb Price, "Republican Leadership Has Forgotten Inclusiveness," *Detroit News* (27 June 1998): C5.

81. This type of press bias is called "bias by omission" by Brent H. Baker. Baker documents well and thoroughly the practices of the major network news organizations in his book: *How to Identify, Expose & Correct Liberal Media Bias* (Alexandria, VA: Media Research Center, 1994).

82. Robert M. Entman, "How the Media Affect What People Think: An Information Processing Approach," *The Journal of Politics* 51.2 (May 1989): 367.

83. Paul Bedard, "Clinton Promises Gay Rights in Workplace," *Washington Times* (9 November 1997): A1.

84. Peter Baker, "Clinton Equates Gay Rights, Civil Rights," *Washington Post* (9 November 1997): A18. Emphasis mine.

85. James Bennet, "Clinton Is Greeted Warmly as He Speaks to Gay Group," *New York Times* (9 November 1997): A30. Emphasis mine.

86. Beaulieu.

87. Michael A. Fletcher and Hamil R. Harris, "Black Men Jam Mall for a 'Day of Atonement,' " *Washington Post* (17 October 1995): A1.

88. Associated Press, "Million Man March Largest Black American Gathering Since 1963," *Asheville Citizen-Times* (Asheville, NC) (17 October 1995): A1. Some of Savage's comments were printed in Michael Shear, "Messages of Anger, Atonement," *Washington Post* (17 October 1995): A21.

89. Fletcher and Harris, Associated Press, "Million Man March."

90. Louis Freedberg, "President Clinton's Ultimate Challenge," *San Francisco Chronicle* (15 June 1997): 9.

91. Editorial, "A President Confronts Race," *St. Louis Post-Dispatch* (18 June 1997): B6.

92. Ibid.

93. Ruben Navarrette Jr., "Clinton Must Extend Talk on Race Relations Past Affirmative Action," *Arizona Republic* (20 June 1997): B5. It is of interest to me that the actual graduating class was hardly diverse at all: *USA Today* reported that the "4,100 graduates listening to Clinton's address were 45% white, 34% Asian, 11% Latino, 2% black, 1% Native American and 7% 'other.' " "Inclusion, Not Rejection, Will Spur Racial Harmony," *USA Today* (16 June 1997): A18.

94. American Society of Newspaper Editors Mission Statement on Newsroom Diversity (20 October 1998) <http://www.asne.org/kiosk/diversity/DIVERSI TYf.html>. Emphasis mine.

95. Ann McFeatters, "Clinton Calls for Racial Unity; Who Will Listen?" *Denver Rocky Mountain News* (15 June 1997): A57. Emphasis mine.

96. "The Newspaper Journalists of the '90s," A Survey Report of the American Society of Newspaper Editors, April 1997, p. 5.

97. McFeatters.

98. Carl T. Rowen, "Clinton's Race Stance Is a Huge Gamble," *Buffalo News* (17 June 1997): B3.

99. "Clinton Focuses on Racial Divide," *Tampa Tribune* (15 June 1997): Nation/World1.

100. Norman Lockman, "Pollyanna Approach Better Than Hiding from Problem," *Montgomery Advertiser* (15 June 1997): F3.

101. Karl Zinmeister, "When Black and White Turn Gray," *The American Enterprise* (November/December 1998): 6.

102. Frank Newport "Americans Today Much More Accepting of a Woman, Black, Catholic, or Jew as President," Gallup News Service (29 March 1999) <http://www.gallup.com/poll/releases/pr990329.asp>.

103. Karl Zinmeister, "American Tolerance," *The American Enterprise* (November/December 1998):18.

104. Ibid.

105. CBS News, June 1997 (adults) and September 1997 (10th graders). In "Opinion Pulse," *The American Enterprise* (November/December 1998): 90.

106. Survey by Yankelovich Partners for Time and CNN, August 1997. In "Opinion Pulse," *The American Enterprise* (November/December 1998): 91.

107. Survey by Public Agenda, March–April, 1998. In "Opinion Pulse," *The American Enterprise* (November/December 1998): 92.

108. American Civil Rights Institute, "News Release: New Poll Shows Americans Overwelminlgy Oppose Racial Preferences," (10 June 1997). <http://www.acri.org/news/061097.html>. Poll conducted by Zogby International from a survey of 1,212 likely voters nationwide.

109. Stan Faryna, Brad Stetson, and Joseph G. Conti, eds., *Black and Right: The Bold New Voice of Black Conservatives in America* (Westport, CT: Praeger, 1997).

110. <http://www.jointcenter.org/>.

111. <http://www.ncne.com/blackhistoryfuture/intro.html>.

112. Mona Charen, "Will Anyone Listen?" *Washington Times* (22 January 2001) <http://www.washtimes.com>. Dr. McWhorter happens to be black too, and does not describe himself as a black conservative.

113. Ibid. Charen cites the work of Stephen Thernstrom and Abigail Thernstrom, *America in Black and White* (New York: Simon and Schuster, 1997).

114. Karl Zinsmeister, "Indicators: The Shrinking Income Gap," *The American Enterprise* (November/December 1998): 18.

115. Ibid.

116. Ibid.

117. Ibid.

118. U.S. Department of Justice, Bureau of Justice Statistics, "Homicide Trends in the U.S.," (1998) <http://www.ojp.usdoj.gov/bjs/homocide/race.htm>.

119. Ibid.

120. Greg Clark, "Don't Inject Race Into Boy's Tragic Death," *Kansas City Star* [Johnson County Edition] (15 March 2000): A2; and Greg Clark, "Boy Knew Love, Not Hate," *Kansas City Star* [Metropolitan Edition] (15 March 2000):A1.

121. Carol Castenada, "In Kentucky, Confederate Flag Is Fatal / Black Teens Accused of Killing Whites," *USA Today* (30 January 1995): A4.

122. Kim Murphy, "Hate Crime Charge Weighed in Pa. Shooting Rampage; Slayings: Witnesses Say Gunman Yelled Racist Epithets at Victims. Suspect, a Black Man, Is Accused of Ethnic Intimidation And Murder," *Los Angeles Times* (3 March 2000): A14.

123. Ibid.

124. "DA Seeks Death for Man Charged with 3 Murders," *Milwaukee Journal Sentinel* (26 September 2000): A5.

125. "Mid-America Digest," *Kansas City Star* (18 April 2001): B4. A story appearing in the *Dodge City Globe* omited all references to the race of the Carrs and their victims. <http://www.dodgeglobe.com/stories/041801/new__carr__bro.shtml>.

126. I cannot list all of them here, but each of these recieved little or no mainstream press coverage. Each would, I believe, be classified as a hate crime if the assailants were white and the victms black: in 1998 ten-year-old Tiffany Nicole Long, of Burlington, NC, was kidnapped, repeatedly raped, tortured, and murdered by three black teens; Richard Skelton, of Wood River, IL was beaten to death by ten black men in August of 1998; Susan Raye Moore and Tracy Rose Lambert, while leaving a night club in Cumberland County, NC, were abducted by members of a black street gang. They were found the next day in a field, executed. Gregory Griffith, who was attacked and beaten to death by a group of black men in August 1999; and Missy McLughlin, who in December of 1992 was kidnapped by a carload of black males. She was tortured and gang-raped, and then shot six times. One of the murderers later confessed that they had done it because of 400 years of oppression. Yet, like all of the incidents mentioned above, the media chose not to mention the race of the murders, or to call these hate crimes.

127. Paul Sheehan, "The Race War of Black Against White," *Sydney Morning Herald* (20 May 1995). Sheehan also noted that "Justice Department and FBI statistics indicate that between 1964 and 1994 more than 25 millon violent interracial crimes were commited, overwhelmingly involving black offenders and white victims, and more than 45,000 people were killed in inter-racial murders. By comparisons, 58,000 Americans died in Vietnam, and 34,000 were killed in the Korean war."

128. Ibid.

129. Darren K. Carlson, "Americans Divided on Cause of Homosexuality,"

Gallup News Service (9 May 2001). <http://www.gallup.com/pool/releases/pr010509c.asp/>.

130. Frank Newport, "American Attitudes Toward Homosexuality Continue to Become More Tolerant," Gallup News Service (4 June 2001). <http://www.gallup.com/pool/releases/pr010604.asp/>.

131. Data provided by The Roper Center for Public Opinion Research, University of Connecticut. Survey was conducted by the Gallup Organization, May 2001. <http://roperweb.ropercenter.uconn.edu/>.

132. Letter to author from Barbara Curley, 5 July 2001. Supplemented with press accounts from the *Boston Globe* and the *Boston Herald*.

133. Andrea Estes, "Boy's Death Blamed on Web," *Boston Herald* (17 May 2000): 03.

134. <http://www.nambla.de/join.htm>.

135. This is not to say that newspapers do not report cases of child molestation where homosexual acts occur. However, the identity of the perpetrator as homosexual or heterosexual is quite often left out, and the acts are not declared hates crimes as are heterosexual assaults on homosexuals. For an investigation into news coverage of homosexuality, see Paul Cameron and Kirk Cameron, "What Proportion of Newspaper Stories about Child Molestation Involves Homosexuality?" *Psychological Reports* 82.1 (1998): 863–871.

136. Joyce Howard Price, "Media Tune Out Torture Death of Arkansas Boy; Homosexuals Charged with Rape, Murder," *Washington Times* (22 October 1999): A1.

137. E.R. Shipp, "Reporting Two Killings," *Washington Post* (14 November, 1999): B6.

138. Mark W. Linder, [Letter to the Editor] "Selective Outrage," *Washington Post* (20 November 1999): A21.

139. Robert H. Knight, "A Tale of Two Killings: Was One of Them Underplayed?" *San Diego Union-Tribune* (3 December 1999): B7. See too, Joyce Howard Price, "Media Tune Out Torture Death of Arkansas Boy."

140. Jeff Jacoby, "Why This Death Didn't Count," *Boston Globe* (9 December 1999): A23.

141. The longstanding Kinsey-based figure of 10% is discredited. Researchers now report a small number of homosexuals. Because it is rare to find this information in a large daily, and the *New York Times* provided one of these rare exceptions, I use the figure reported in Tamar Lewin, "Sex in America: Faithfulness in Marriage Thrives After All," *New York Times* (7 October 1994): A1. The numbers include those who consider themselves bisexual as well. For scientific studies supporting the figures contained in the *New York Times* see, Edward O. Laumann, Stuart Michaels, John H. Gagnon, and Robert T. Michael, *The Social Organization of Sexuality: Sexual Practices in the United States* (Chicago: University of Chicago Press, 1994). Laumann et al. reported that 2.8% of males and 1.4% of females identified themselves as homosexual (p. 305). Paul Cameron and Kirk Cameron, reanalyzing the "definitive" 1994 University of Chicago study that listed male homosexuals at 2.8% of the American male population, found that that study had omitted Americans over the age of fifty-nine. Refactoring with those over fifty-nine years of age, Cameron and Cameron found the number of homosexuals was lowered to 2.3% for males and 1.2% for females. Paul Cameron

and Kirk Cameron, " 'Definitive' University of Chicago Sex Survey Over-estimated Prevalence of Homosexual Identity," *Psychological Reports* 82.1 (1998): 861–862.

Burtoft reports that "The Alan Guttmacher Institute reported in the March/April 1993 issue of *Family Planning Perspectives*, that 2.3% of 'sexually active men aged 20–39 have had any same-gender sexual activity during the last ten years,' with only 1.1% reporting exclusive homosexual contact during this period. These results essentially echo the findings in the May/June 1991 issue of the same journal, where it was reported that only 1.6% of those surveyed reported any homosexual contact the previous years, and .7% identified themselves as exclusively homosexual." Larry Burtoft, *Behind the Headlines: Setting the Record Straight, What Research Really Says about the Social Consequences of Homosexuality* (Public Policy Division: Focus on the Family, 1994), 106. Burtoft was quoting, respectively, John O.G. Billy et al., "The Sexual Behavior of Men in the United States," *Family Planning Perspectives* 25.2 (March/April 1993), 52–60, (Table 4, p. 59) and Tom W. Smith, "Adult Sexual Behavior in 1989: Number of Partners, Frequency of Intercourse and Risk of AIDS," *Family Planning Perspectives* 23.3 (May/June 1991) 102–107, (Table 2, p. 104).

Burtoft also reports on other studies concerning the homosexual population: "using 'the largest figures available' we find the numbers to be '5–6% for males and 2–3% for females.' This represents all individuals who have *ever* engaged in *any kind* of same-sex behavior. In other words, it includes those who tried it once and decided never again. For those individuals who engage in exclusive homosexual activity the *most generous* conclusion would seem to be no more than 3% of the population. The more realistic number for those who regularly and exclusively participate in same-sex behavior is probably much lower, somewhere between. 6% and 2% for males, and less than 1% for females" (p. 24). Emphasis in original. Quoted items from Milton Diamond, "Homosexuality and Bisexuality in Different Populations," *Archives of Sexual Behavior* 22.4 (1993): 303.

142. Gordon J. Muir, "Homosexuals and the 10% Fallacy," *Wall Street Journal* (31 March 1993): A14. Muir also provides numerous other examples of studies from around the globe, and examines the criticisms concerning the Kinsey studies from which the discredited 10% figure was obtained. See too, Felicity Barringer, "Sex Survey of American Men Finds 1% are Gay," *New York Times* (16 April 1993): A1.

143. Joan E. Rigdon, "Overcoming A Deep-Rooted Reluctance, More Firms Advertise to Gay Community," *Wall Street Journal* (18 July 1991): B1.

144. Janet Lever, "The 1994 Advocate Survey of Sexuality and Relationships: the Men. Sexual Revelations," *The Advocate* (23 August 1994): 18. The $25,491 is a 1998 IRS figure. Thus, one is comparing the *1994* $36,000 Advocate figure with a 1998 IRS figure. Emphasis mine.

145. David Armstrong, "Gay Consumers an Affluent Group: First Marketing Survey Corroborates Anecdotal Evidence," *Denver Rocky Mountain News* (10 February 1997): F9B. These figures come not without contention. Ronald Alsop stated that "the debate [over homosexual affluence] has created rifts within the gay community. Marketers say gay Americans should be recognized as a vibrant segment of the consumer market. But civil rights advocates maintain that an exaggerated image of comfort and success hurts their battles for protection from

workplace discrimination, the right to marry and other causes." ("Are Gay People More Affluent than Others?" *Wall Street Journal* [30 December 1999]: B1.) Thus, when homosexual activists found out that income figures demonstrated that homosexuals were well off financially, and thus might have a deleterious effect upon their agenda, they attacked the figures and set out to portray themselves as making the average or less than the average. See Alexandra Chasin, *Selling Out: The Gay and Lesbian Movement Goes to Market* (New York: St. Martin's Press, 2000), 35–38, 267.

146. "Annual Report on Lesbian, Gay, Bisexual, Transgender Domestic Violence," National Coalition of Anti-Violence Programs (6 October 1998). <http://www.vaw.umn.edu/FinalDocuments/glbtdv.htm/>. This report suggests that this rate is similar to that found in heterosexual households. No data is presented to support this claim, and Department of Justice figures suggest a heterosexual rate of less than 1% for married couples and perhaps as high as 6% when including all intimates (i.e., husbands, wives, boyfriends, girlfriends, live-in lovers, etc.). For more on the link between homosexuality and violence see, Paul Cameron, "Violence and Homosexuality," Family Research Institute <http://www.familyresearchinst.org/FRI_EduPamphlet4.html>.

147. Callie Marie Rennison and Sarah Welchans, U.S. Department of Justice, Office of Justice Programs, "Bureau of Justice Statistics Special Reports: Intimate Partner Violence (17 July 2000) <http://www.ojp.usdoj.gov/bjs/pub/pdf/ipv.pdf>.

148. Garry Wills, "Bill Bennett Might Work On Improving His Own Virtues," *Sacramento Bee* (21 November 1997): B9.

149. K. Freund and R.J. Watson, "The Proportions of Heterosexual and Homosexual Pedophiles among Sex Offenders against Children: An Exploratory Study," *Journal of Sex and Marital Therapy* 18.1 (1992): 34–43. See too, Paul Cameron, Kay Proctor, William Coburn, Jr., Nels Forde, Helen Larson, and Kirk Cameron, "Child Molestation and Homosexuality," *Psychological Reports* 58.1 (1986): 327–337.

150. Paul Cameron et al. "Child Molestation and Homosexuality," *Psychological Reports* 58 (1986): 327–337.

151. Paul Cameron, *Child Molestation and Homosexuality* (Colorado Springs, CO: Family Research Institute, 1993), 4.

152. This figure varies from study to study, with most suggesting between 1–3%. The lack of an agreed upon number for the proportion of male homosexuals to male heterosexuals accounts for much of the variance of the percentages of homosexual pedophiles, in other words, "25% to 40%."

153. Freund and Watson.

154. Jeffrey Satinover, *Homosexuality and the Politics of Truth* (Grand Rapids, MI: Baker Books, 1996), 64–65.

155. Burtoft, 106. Burtoft provides specific examples in his end note 16.

156. Ibid., 64.

157. Kurt Freund, Gerald Heasman, I.G. Racansy, and Graham Glancy, "Pedophilia and Heterosexuality vs. Homosexuality," *Journal of Sex and Marital Therapy* 10.3 (1984): 197. See too, Robert K. Dornan, "Interview with Dr. Jeffrey Satinover," *Congressional Record* (Extensions) (8 May 1996) <http://wais.access.gpo.gov/>.

158. Joyce Howard Price, "Is Clinton Seeking Gay-Rights Legacy?" *Washington Post* (10 November 1997): A4.

159. The original report is found in Edward O. Laumann, Stuart Michaels, John H. Gagnon, and Robert T. Michael, *The Social Organization of Sexuality: Sexual Practices in the United States* (Chicago: University of Chicago Press, 1994). Quote from Sarah Boxer, "Truth or Lies? In Sex Surveys, You Never Know," *New York Times* (22 July 2000): B7.

160. Lewin.

161. A.P. Bell and M.S. Weinberg, *Homosexualities: A Study of Diversity Among Men and Women* (New York: Simon and Schuster, 1978), 308–309. Bell and Weinberg focused primarily upon the San Francisco Bay area.

162. Lever, 22.

163. Satinover, 55.

164. Ibid., 54. Also contained in Edward O. Laumann, Stuart Michaels, John H. Gagnon, and Robert T. Michael, *The Social Organization of Sexuality: Sexual Practices in the United States* (Chicago: University of Chicago Press, 1994). Satinover reports that these statistics "are quite conservative."

165. Marshall Kirk and Hunter Madsen, *After the Ball: How America Will Conquer Its Fear and Hatred of Gays in the '90s* (New York: Doubleday, 1989).

166. Satinover, 54. Satinover was citing D. McWhirter and A. Mattison, *The Male Couple: How Relationships Develop* (Englewood Cliffs, NJ: Prentice-Hall, 1984).

167. L. Corey and K.K. Holmes, "Sexual Transmission of Hepatitis A in Homosexual Men: Incidence and Mechanism," *New England Journal of Medicine* 302.8 (1980): 435–438. Other studies confirm the same: V. Beral et al., "Risk of Kaposi's Sarcoma and Sexual Practices Associated with Faecal Contact in Homosexual or Bisexual Men with AIDS," *339 Lancet* (1992): 632–635; Corey and Holmes, G.E. Hastings and R.W. Weber, "Inflammatory Bowel Disease: Psrt I. Clinical Features and Diagnosis," *American Family Physician* 47 (1993): 598–608.

168. *American Adolescents: How Healthy are They?* American Medical Association (1990).

169. Lever, 22.

170. Center for Disease Control, "HIV/AIDS Surveillance Report," 9.2 (May 1998). A similar figure is reported in Burtoft, p. 33. See too, Reuters, "One in 10 Urban Gays Have HIV, Study Finds," (5 February 2001) <http://dailynews.yahoo.com/htx/nm/20010205/sc/aids_prevalence_dc_1.html>.

171. For example, 1993 *New York Times/CBS News* poll data reveal that when believing homosexuality is a choice, only 30% of Americans felt that homosexuals needed more laws to ensure equal rights compared with 90% of those who say it cannot be changed. Only 18% felt homosexuality to be an acceptable alternative lifestyle when considering homosexuality changeable, whereas 67% who thought it unchangeable felt it acceptable. Jeffrey Schmalz, "Poll Finds an Even Split on Homosexuality Cause," *New York Times* (5 March 1993): A14.

172. James O. Goldsborough, "Lott, Armey, and Politics of Ignorance," *San Diego Union-Tribune* (22 June 1998): B7. Goldsborough does cite two researchers, from the Salk Institute and the American Psychological Association, who "suggest" that genetics is the cause.

173. Editorial, "Oblivious to the Facts," *Courier-Journal* (17 June 1998): A12.

174. Richard L. Tafel, "Does GOP's Tent Have Room for Gays?" *The Record* (23 June 1998): L09

175. William Endicott, "Lott Throws a Big Stone," *Sacramento Bee* (20 June 1998): A3.

176. "Lott: Homosexuals Need Assistance, 'Like Kleptomaniacs,' " *Des Moines Register* (16 June 1998): 5.

177. Editorial, "Sen. Lott's Tolerance Issues," *Times Picayune* (18 June 1998): B6.

178. Editorial, "Lott's Views Spawn Hate," *Seattle Post-Intelligencer* (19 June 1998): A12.

179. Satinover, 35.

180. Satinover, 32.

181. Simon LeVay, *Queer Science* (MIT Press, 1996) 224.

182. Allan Medinger and Tom Bisset, "More Acceptance of Gays if They See Possible Change," *Baltimore Sun* (26 June 2001): A17.

183. Frank Newport, "Americans Attitudes Toward Homosexuality Continue to Become More Tolerant," Gallup News Service (4 June 2001). Prior to President Clinton taking office the figures suggested that only 19% of Americans believed homosexuality as something homosexuals are born with. <http://www.gallup.com/poll/releases/pr010604.asp>.

184. W. Byne and B. Parsons, "Human Sexual Orientation: The Biological Theories Reappraised," *Archives of General Psychiàtry* 50.3 (1993): 228–239. Emphasis mine.

185. <http://www.narth.com/>.

186. Cal Thomas, "Politics, Not Science," *Baltimore Sun* (8 August 1995): A15.

187. A. Dean Byrd, Shirley E. Cox, and Jeffrey W. Robinson, "The Innate-Immutable Argument Finds No Basis in Science in Their Own Words: Gay Activists Speak about Science, Morality, Philosophy," *Salt Lake City Tribune* (27 May 2001). See too <http://www.narth.com/docs/innate.html>.

188. <http://www.narth.com/docs/bornway.html>.

189. I provide below a few of the examples given by NARTH. For the full list, see <http://www.narth.com/docs/bornway.html>. "From Dr. Dean Hamer, the 'gay gene' researcher, and himself a gay man: 'Genes are hardware . . . the data of life's experiences are processed through the sexual software into the circuits of identity. I suspect the sexual software is a mixture of both genes and environment, in much the same way the software of a computer is a mixture of what's installed at the factory and what's added by the user.' " P. Copeland and D. Hamer, *The Science of Desire* (New York: Simon and Schuster, 1994.); "William Byne, a psychiatrist with a doctorate in biology, and Bruce Parsons . . . carefully analyzed all the major biological studies of homosexuality. They found none that definitively supported a biological theory of causation." W. Byne and B. Parsons, "Human Sexual Orientation: The Biologic Theories Reappraised," *Archives of General Psychiatry* 50.3 (1993); "From sociologist Steven Goldberg, Ph.D.: 'Virtually all of the evidence argues against there being a determinative physiological causal factor and I know of no researcher who believes that such a determinative factor exists . . . such factors play a predisposing, not a determinative role. . . . I know of no one in the field who argues that homosexuality can be explained without reference to environmental factors.' " S. Goldberg, *When Wish Replaces*

Thought: Why So Much of What You Believe Is False (Buffalo, NY: Prometheus Books, 1994); "The American Psychological Association says: 'Various theories have proposed differing sources for sexual orientation. . . . However, many scientists share the view that sexual orientation is shaped for most people at an early age through complex interactions of biological, psychological and social factors.' " (From the A.P.A.'s booklet, "Answers to Your Questions About Sexual Orientation and Homosexuality"); "The national organization P-FLAG ('Parents and Friends of Lesbians and Gays') offers a booklet prepared with the assistance of Dr. Clinton Anderson of the American Psychological Association. Entitled, 'Why Ask Why? Addressing the Research on Homosexuality and Biology,' the pamphlet says: 'To date, no researcher has claimed that genes can determine sexual orientation. At best, researchers believe that there may be a genetic component. No human behavior, let alone sexual behavior, has been connected to genetic markers to date . . . sexuality, like every other behavior, is undoubtedly influenced by both biological and societal factors.' "

190. Donn Esmode, "Lott's Ignorance Apparent in Remarks About Homosexuals," *Buffalo News* (18 June 1998): B1.

191. <http://www.exodusintl.org/>.

192. Christianity and Homosexuality Homepage: <http://www.messiah.edu/hpages/facstaff/chase/h/index.htm>. For the list of ministries go directly to the "Organizations" page: <http://www.messiah.edu/hpages/facstaff/chase/h/helplis.htm>.

193. Stanton L. Jones and Mark A. Yarhouse, "Contemporary Scientific Research on Homosexuality: A Critique of Its Relevance to the Contemporary Moral Debate," unpublished manuscript, Department of Psychology, Wheaton College, Wheaton, Il 60187. Quote found in Burtoft, 44. Similar information can be found in Stanton L. Jones and Mark A. Yarhouse, *Homosexuality: The Use of Scientific Research in the Church's Moral Debate* (Downers Grove, IL: InterVarsity Press, 2000).

194. Emily Gest, "Gays Going Straight? Study Disputes View That Orientation Is Fixed," *Daily News* (9 May 2001).

195. Ibid.

196. Burtoft, 9. Emphasis in original.

197. Editorial, "Oblivious to the Facts."

198. Burtoft, Emphasis in original. Paul Cameron and Kurt Cameron state, "homosexual individuals produce too few children to sustain adequately replacement [sic] levels of homosexuals in future generations. The incidence of homosexuality varies directly as a function of its acceptance or condemnation both by societies and various social groups within society. Homosexuals claim that they can and do recruit. Homosexuals tend *not* to have close contacts with their genetic lineage and therefore would have difficulty advantaging those of their relatives carrying similar genes. *These facts would seem to point away from genetics and toward learning as a basis for homosexuality.*" In "Does Incest Cause Homosexuality?" *Psychological Reports* 76.2 (1995): 619–620.

199. Robert M. Entman, "How the Media Affect What People Think: An Information Processing Approach," *The Journal of Politics* 51.2 (1989): 366.

200. Soloman E. Asche, "Effects of Group Pressure upon the Modification and

Distortion of Judgments," *Groups, Leadership, and Men*, ed. H. Guetzkow (Pittsburgh: Carnegie, 1951).

201. Elisabeth Noelle-Neumann, *The Spiral of Silence: Public Opinion—Our Social Skin* 2nd ed. (Chicago and London: University of Chicago Press, 1993), 201–202.

202. Ibid., 150.

203. Ibid., 201.

204. Carolyn A. Lin and Michael B. Salwen, "Predicting the Spiral of Silence on a Controversial Public Issue," *The Howard Journal of Communications* (1997): 138, 140.

205. Wiliam P. Eveland, Jr., Douglas M. McLeod, and Nancy Signorielli, "Actual and Perceived U.S. Public Opinion: The Spiral of Silence During the Gulf War," *International Journal of Public Opinion Research* 7.2 (1995): 105.

206. Ibid., 106.

207. Elisabeth Noelle-Neumann, "The Spiral of Silence: A Theory of Public Opinion," *Journal of Communication* (Spring 1974): 51.

208. Marc Egan, "Heflin Chastises Sate Senator in Speech at ASU," *Montgomery Advertiser* (12 May 1996): B1.

209. NNSP: Alabama/Capstone Poll Survey, Institute for social Science Reserach, University of Alabama (IRSS Study Number: NNSP-AL-023), 1995.

210. NNSP: Alabama/Capstone Poll Survey, Institute for social Science Reserach, University of Alabama (IRSS Study Number: NNSP-AL-014, June 1987.

211. Editorial, "Slavery Defender Senator Embarrases State, Party," *Montgomery Advertiser* (12 May 1996): F2.

212. Editorial, "Oblivious to the Facts."

213. Editorial, "Sen. Lott's Tolerance Issues," *Times Picayune* (18 June 1998): B6.

214. Editorial, "Senator, Put Prejudice Aside," *St. Petersburg Times* (22 June 1998): A8.

215. Editorial, "Lott's Views on Gays Poison Confirmation," *Albuquerque Journal* (18 June 1998): A18.

216. "What of GOP Leaders' Views about Gays?" *The Tennessean* (21 June 1998): D2.

217. Rowan, "The Devil & Dick Armey."

218. Editorial, "Senator, Put Prejudice Aside."

219. Richard L. Tafel, "Does GOP's Tent Have Room for Gays?" *The Record* (23 June 1998): L9.

220. Editorial, "Hormel-Bashing," *San Francisco Chronicle* (23 June 1998): A18.

221. Editorial, "The Sin's in the Senate," *Los Angeles Times* (24 June 1998): B6.

222. Editorial, "Hating Gays GOP Intolerance."

223. Price, "Republican Leadership Has Forgotton Inclusiveness."

224. Editorial, "Some Straight Talk about the GOP," *Daily News* (27 June 1998): 16.

225. J.A. Adande, "White Crosses the Line and Is Ruled Offside," *Los Angeles Times* (27 March 1998): C1.

226. Bob Wolfley, "Remarks May Cost White Job in TV," *Milwaukee Journal Sentinel* (27 March 1998): Sports 1.

227. Bruton.

228. John McClain, "Speech Illustrates Double Standard on Racial Issues," *Houston Chronicle* (29 March 1998): 22.

229. Jonathan Rand, "White's Controversial Remarks Aren't Surprising," *Kansas City Star* (29 March 1998): C8.

230. Editorial, "On Race: Replace Stereotypes with a Must Do Agenda," *Wisconsin State Journal* (29 March 1998): B2.

231. James T. Campbell, "When a Good Guy Puts His Foot in His Mouth," *Houston Chronicle* (30 March 1998): A16.

232. Frey. Emphasis mine.

233. Tom Oates, "Will White Pay for Comments?" *Wisconsin State Journal* (27 March 1998): B1.

234. Dave Hyde, "Reggie White Deserves to Be Grilled for Comments," *Sunday Gazette Mail* (29 March 1998): D9.

235. Mike Fisher, "White Shows Why Athletes Shouldn't Be Role Models," *Fort Worth Star-Telegram* (30 March 1998): Sports 2.

236. Greenhut.

237. Rhonda Chriss Lokeman, "Clinton Right on Race: President Uses Office to Issue Call for Healing," *Kansas City Star* (18 June 1997): C8.

238. Medinger and Bisset.

239. Frank Newport, "Americans Attitudes Toward Homosexuality Continue to Become More Tolerant."

240. Deb Price, "Clinton Addresses [*sic*] a Grand Day for Gays and Lesbians, a Great Day for America," *Detroit News* (14 November 1997): E2. Emphasis mine.

241. Dominic A. Infante, Andrew S. Rancer, and Deanna F. Womack, *Building Communication Theory* 2nd ed. (Prospect Heights, IL: Waveland Press, 1993), 338.

242. Allan Rachlin, *News as Hegemonic Reality: American Political Culture and the Framing of News Accounts* (New York: Praeger, 1998), 4.

Bibliography

GENERAL

Bagdikian, Ben H. *The Effete Conspiracy.* New York: Harper and Row, 1972.

Barone, Michael. "The Return of Partisan Journalism." *The American Enterprise* 7.2 (March–April 1996): 30.

Bateson, Gregory. *Steps to an Ecology of Mind: Collected Essays in Anthropology, Psychiatry, Evolution, and Epistemology.* San Francisco: Chandler Publishing Company, 1972.

Behr, Roy L., and Shanto Iyengar. "Television News, Real-World Cues, and Changes in the Public Agenda." *Public Opinion Quarterly* 49 (1985): 38–57.

Benoit, William L. "Genesis of Rhetorical Action." *Southern Communication Journal* 59.4 (1994): 342–355.

Bitzer, Lloyd F. "Functional Communication: A Situational Perspective." *Rhetoric in Transition: Studies in the Nature and Uses of Rhetoric.* Ed. Eugene E. White. University Park: Pennsylvania State University Press, 1980. 21–38.

———. "Political Rhetoric." *Handbook of Political Communication.* Ed. Dan D. Nimmo and Keith R. Sanders. Beverly Hills, CA: Sage Publications, 1981. 225–248.

———. "Rhetoric and Public Knowledge," *Rhetoric, Philosophy, and Literature: An Exploration.* Ed. D.M. Burks. West Lafayette, IN: Purdue University Press, 1978. 67–93.

———. "The Rhetorical Situation." *Rhetoric: A Tradition in Transition.* Ed. Walter Fisher. East Lansing: Michigan State University Press, 1974. 247–260.

Black, Edwin. "A Note on Theory and Practice in Rhetorical Criticism." *Western Journal of Speech Communication* 44 (1980): 331–336.

Branham, Robert J., and W. Barnett Pearce. "Between Text and Context: Toward a Rhetoric of Contextual Reconstruction." *Quarterly Journal of Speech* 71 (1985): 19–36.

Brock, Bernard L., Robert L. Scott, and James W. Chesebro. *Methods of Rhetorical Criticism: A Twentieth-Century Perspective*. 3rd ed. Detroit: Wayne State University Press, 1989.

Bystrom, D.G., T.A. Robertson, and M.C. Banwart. "Framing the Fight: An Analysis of Media Coverage of Female and Male Candidates in Primary Races for Governor and U.S. Senate in 2000." *American Behavioral Scientist* 44.12 (2001): 1999–2013.

Cheney, Lynn. "Press Bias in the '92 Election." *The American Enterprise* 7.2 (March–April 1996): 37.

Cobb, Roger W., and Charles D. Elder. *Participation in American Politics: The Dynamics of Agenda-Building*. Baltimore: Johns Hopkins University Press, 1983.

Cohen, Bernard C. *The Press and Foreign Policy*. Princeton: Princeton University Press, 1963.

Comstock, George, ed. *Public Communication Behavior*. Vol. 1. Orlando, FL: Academic Press, 1986.

Cornwell, Elmer E., Jr. "Presidential News: The Expanding Public Image." *Journalism Quarterly* 36 (1959): 275–283.

Corwin, Edward S. *The President: Office and Powers*, 3rd ed. New York: New York University Press, 1948.

Dalton, Russell J., Paul Allen Beck, Robert Huckfeldt, and William Koetzle. "A Test of Media-Centered Agenda Setting: Newspaper Content and Public Interests in a Presidential Election." *Political Communication* 15 (1998): 463–481.

Day, Louis A. *Ethics in Media Communication*. Belmont, CA: Wadsworth Publishing Company, 1991.

Dearing, James W., and Evertt M. Rogers. *Agenda-Setting*. Thousand Oaks, CA: Sage Publications, 1996.

Denton, Robert E., Jr. "Rhetorical Challenges to the Presidency." Paper presented at the annual convention of the Southern States Communication Association, New Orleans, 1 April 2000.

Denton, Robert E., Jr., and Gary C. Woodward. *Political Communication in America*. 2nd ed. New York: Praeger, 1990.

Edelman, Murray. *Politics as Symbolic Action*. Chicago: Markham, 1971.

———. *The Symbolic Uses of Politics*. Urbana: University of Illinois Press, 1964.

Entman, Robert M. "Framing: Toward Clarification of a Fractured Paradigm." *Journal of Communication* 43 (1993): 51–58.

———. "Framing U.S. Coverage of International News: Contrasts in Narratives of the KAL and Iran Air Incidents." *Journal of Communication* 41.4 (1991): 6–27.

———. "How the Media Affect What People Think: An Information Processing Approach." *The Journal of Politics* 51.2 (May 1989): 367.

———. *Democracy without Citizens: Media and the Decay of American Politics*. New York: Oxford University Press, 1989.

Entman, Robert M., and B.I. Page. "The News before the Storm: The Iraq War Debate and the Limits to Media Independence." *Just Deserts: The News*

Media, U.S. Foreign Policy, and the Gulf War. Ed. W. Lance Bennet and D.L. Palentz. Chicago: University of Chicago Press, 1994.

Entman, Robert M., and Andrew Rojecki. "Freezing Out the Public: Elite and Media Framing of the U.S. Anti-Nuclear Movement." *Political Communication* 10.2 (1993): 155–173.

Fedler, Fred, Mike Meeske, and Joe Hall. "*Time* Magazine Revisited: Presidential Stereotypes Persist." *Journalism Quarterly* 62 (1985): 66–73.

Gamson, William A. "News as Framing: Comments on Graber." *American Behavioral Scientist* 33 (1989): 157–161.

German, Kathleen M. "Invoking the Glorious War: Framing the Persian Gulf Conflict through Directive Language." *Southern Communication Journal* 60.4 (1995): 292–302.

Ghanem, Salma I. "Notes on Recent Dissertations—Media Coverage of Crime and Public Opinion: An Exploration of the Second Level of Agenda: A Dissertation Completed at the University of Texas at Austin," *Political Communication* 14.4 (1997): 514.

Gilberg, Sheldon, Chaim Eyal, Maxwell E. McCombs, and D. Nichols. "The State of the Union Address and the Press Agenda." *Journalism Quarterly* 57 (1980): 584–588.

Goffman, Erving. *Frame Analysis: An Essay on the Organization of Experience*. Cambridge, MA: Harvard University Press, 1974.

Graber, Doris A. "Framing Election News Broadcasts: News Context and Its Impact on the 1984 Presidential Election." *Social Science Quarterly* 68 (1987): 552–568.

———. *Mass Media and American Politics*. 3rd ed. Washington, D.C.: Congressional Quarterly Press, 1989.

———. *Media Power and Politics*. Washington, D.C.: Congressional Quarterly Press, 1984.

Graham, Tim, and Jim Naureckas. "Q: Does Media Coverage of President Clinton Reveal a Liberal Bias?" *Insight* (22 July 1996): 24–27.

Green, Barbara, and Leon Hurwitz. "Press Views of Executive vs. Senatorial Powers." *Journalism Quarterly* 55 (1978): 775–778.

Grossman, Michael Baruch, and Martha Joynt Kumar. *Portraying the President*. Baltimore: Johns Hopkins University Press, 1981.

Hahn, Dan. *Political Communication: Rhetoric, Government, and Citizens*. State College, PA: State Publishing, 1998.

Infante, Dominic A., Andrew S. Rancer, and Deanna F. Womack. *Building Communication Theory*. 2nd ed. Prospect Heights, IL: Waveland Press, 1993.

Iyengar, Shanto. *Is Anyone Responsible?: How Television Frames Political Issues*. Chicago, IL: University of Chicago Press, 1991.

Iyengar, Shanto, and Donald R. Kinder. "More than Meets the Eye: TV News, Priming, and Public Evaluations of the President." *Public Communication Behavior*. Ed. George Comstock, Vol. 1. Orlando: Academic Press, 1986. 136.

Iyengar, Shanto, and Adam Simon. "News Coverage of the Gulf Crisis and Public Opinion: A Study of Agenda-Setting, Priming, and Framing." *Communication Research* 20.3 (1993): 365–383.

Johnston, Anne. "Trends in Political Communication: A Selective Review of Research in the 1980s." *New Directions in Political Communication: A Resource*

Book. Ed. David L. Swanson and Dan Nimmo. Newbury Park, CA: Sage Publications, 1990. 329–362.

Kegley, Charles W., Jr., and Eugene R. Wittkopf. *American Foreign Policy: Pattern and Process.* 4th ed. New York: St. Martin's Press, 1991.

King, Andrew A. *Power and Communication.* Prospect Heights, IL: Waveland Press, 1987.

Kristol, Irving. *Neoconservatism: The Autobiography of an Idea.* New York: Free Press, 1995.

Kuypers, Jim A. *Presidential Crisis Rhetoric and the Press in the Post–Cold War World.* Westport, CT: Praeger, 1997.

Kuypers, Jim A., Marilyn J. Young, and Michael K. Launer. "Of Mighty Mice and Meek Men: Contextual Reconstruction of the Iranian Airbus Shootdown." *Southern Communication Journal* 59.4 (1994): 294–306.

Lang, Gladys Engel, and Kurt Lang. "The Media and Watergate." *Media Power in Politics.* Ed. Doris A. Graber. Washington, DC: Congressional Quarterly Press, 1984. 202–209.

Liebler, Carol M., and Jacob Bendix. "Old-Growth Forests on Network News: News Sources and the Framing of an Environmental Controversy." *Journalism and Mass Communication Quarterly* 73 (1996): 53–65.

Lopez-Escobar, Esteban, Juan Pablo Llamas, Maxwell McCombs, and Federico Rey Lennon. "Two Levels of Agenda Setting among Advertising and News in the 1995 Spanish Elections." *Political Communication* 15 (1998): 225–238.

McAdams, Katherine C. "Power Prose: The Syntax of Presidential News." *Journalism Quarterly* 67 (1990): 313–322.

McCombs, Maxwell. "The Future Agenda for Agenda Setting Research." *Journal of Mass Communication Studies* 45 (1994): 171–181.

McCombs, Maxwell, and Taara Bell. "The Agenda Setting Role of Mass Communication." In Michael Salwen and Don Stacks, eds., *An Integrated Approach to Communication Theory and Research.* Mahwah, NJ: Lawrence Erlbaum Associates, Publishers, 1996. 93–110.

McCombs, Maxwell, and George Estrada. "The News Media and the Picture in Our Heads." In Shanto Iyengar and Richard Reeves, eds., *Do the Media Govern? Politicians, Voters, and Reporters in America.* Thousand Oaks, CA: Sage, 1997. 237–247.

McCombs, Maxwell E., and Sheldon Gilberg. "News Influence on Our Pictures of the World." *Perspectives on Media Effects.* Ed. Jennings Bryant and Dolf Zillman. Hillsdale, NJ: Lawrence Erlbaum Associates, Publishers, 1986.

McCombs, Maxwell E., and Donald L. Shaw. "The Agenda-Setting Function of Mass Media." *Public Opinion Quarterly* 36 (1972): 176–187.

———, eds. *The Emergence of American Political Issues: The Agenda-Setting Function of the Press.* St. Paul, MN: West Publishing Co., 1977.

McCombs, Maxwell, Donald L. Shaw, and David Weaver. *Communication and Democracy: Exploring the Intellectual Frontiers in Agenda-Setting Theory.* Mahwah, NJ: Lawrence Erlbaum Associates, Publishers, 1997.

"Media and Communication Clips." *The American Enterprise* 7.2 (March–April 1996): 17.

Miller, Carolyn R. "Genre as Social Action." *Quarterly Journal of Speech* 70 (1984): 151–167.

Nacos, Brigitte Lebens. *The Press, Presidents, and Crises*. New York: Columbia University Press, 1990.

Nelson, Thomas E., Rosalee A. Clawson, and Zoe M. Oxley. "Media Framing of Civil Liberties Conflict and its Effects on Tolerance." *American Political Science Review* 91.3 (1997): 567–583.

Nimmo, Dan, and James E. Combs. *Nightly Horrors*. Knoxville: University of Tennessee Press, 1985.

Novak, Robert. "Political Correctness Has No Place in the Newsroom." *USA Today* 123.2598 (March 1995). Proquest, no day given <http://pro quest.umi.com/>.

"Our Delicately Balanced Media." *The American Enterprise* 7.4 (July–August 1996): 13.

Pan, Zhongdang, and Gerald M. Kosicki. "Framing Analysis: An Approach to News Discourse." *Political Communication* 10.1 (1993): 55–75.

———. "Priming and Media Impact on the Evaluation of the President's Performance." *Communication Research* 24.1 (1997): 3–30.

Patterson, Thomas. "Bad News, Bad Governance." *Annals of the American Academy of Political and Social Scientists* 546 (July 1996): 97–108.

———. "The News Media: An Effective Political Actor?" *Political Communication* 14 (1997): 445–455.

———. *Out of Order*. New York: Vintage, 1994.

Patterson, Thomas, and Wolfgang Donsbach, "News Decisions: Journalists as Partisan Actors," *Political Communication* 13 (1996): 455–468.

Rachlin, Allan. *News as Hegemonic Reality: American Political Culture and the Framing of News Accounts*. New York: Praeger, 1998.

Rogers, E.M., and J.W. Dearing. "Agenda-Setting Research: Where Has it Been and Where Is It Going?" *Communication Yearbook 11*. Ed. J.A. Anderson. Beverly Hills, CA: Sage, 1988.

Rosemarin, Adena. *The Power of Genre*. Minneapolis: University of Minnesota Press, 1985.

Rossiter, Clinton. *The American Presidency*. New York: Mentor Books, 1962.

Ryan, Michael. "Journalistic Ethics, Objectivity, Existential Journalism, Standpoint Epistemology, and Public Journalism." *Journal of Mass Media Ethics* 16.1 (2001): 3–22.

Salwen, Michael B. "Effect of Accumulation of Coverage on Issue Salience in Agenda Setting." *Journalism Quarterly* 65 (1988): 100+.

———. "Four Theories, Three Decades Later." *Florida Communication Journal* 15 (1987): 12–24.

———. "News Media and Public Opinion: Benign Agenda-Setters? Opinion Molders? Or Simply Irrelevant?" *Florida Communication Journal* 18.2 (1990): 16–23.

Scheufele, Dietram A. "Framing as a Theory of Media Effects." *Journal of Communication* 49.1 (1999): 102–122.

Scheufele, Dietram A. "Framing as a Theory of Media Effects." *Journal of Communication* 49.1 (1999): 102–122.

Severin, W.J., and J.W. Tankard. *Communication Theories*. 2nd ed. New York: Longman, 1988.

Siebert, Fred S., Theodore Peterson, and Wilbur Schramm. *Four Theories of the Press*. Urbana: University of Illinois Press, 1956.

Smith, Carolyn. *Presidential Press Conferences*. New York: Praeger, 1990.

Smith, Craig Allen. *Political Communication*. San Diego, CA: Harcourt Brace Jovanovich, Publishers, 1990.

Smith, Craig R., and Scott Lybarger. "Bitzer's Model Reconsidered." *Communication Quarterly* 44.2 (1996): 197–213.

Smith, Ted J., III, S. Robert Lichter, and Louis Harris and Associates, Inc. *What the People Want from the Press*. Washington, DC: Center for Media and Public Affairs, 1997.

Sniderman, Paul M., Richard A. Brody, and Philip E. Tetlock. *Reasoning and Choice: Explorations in Political Psychology*. Cambridge, England: Cambridge University Press, 1991.

Stephens, Mitchell. *A History of News: from the Drum to the Satellite*. New York: Viking Penguin, 1988.

Straitmatter, Roger. "The Impact of Presidential Personality on News Coverage in Major Newspapers." *Journalism Quarterly* 62 (1985): 66–73.

Trent, Judith S., and Robert V. Friedenberg. *Political Campaign Communication: Principles and Practices*. 2nd ed. New York: Praeger, 1991.

Vatz, Richard E. "The Myth of the Rhetorical Situation." *Philosophy and Rhetoric* 6 (1973): 154–161.

Wanta, Wayne, Mary Ann Stephenson, Judy VanSlyke Turk, and Maxwell E. McCombs. "How President's State of the Union Talk Influenced News Media Agendas." *Journalism Quarterly* 66 (1989): 537–541.

Watkins, S. Craig. "Framing Protest: News Media Frames of the Million Man March." *Critical Studies in Media Communication* 18.1 (2001): 83–101.

Weaver, David H., Doris A. Graber, Maxwell E. McCombs, and Chiam H. Eyal. *Media Agenda-Setting in a Presidential Election: Issues, Images, and Interest*. New York: Praeger Publishers, 1981.

Wimmer, R.D., and J.R. Dominick. *Mass Media Research*. 2nd ed. Belmont, CA: Wadsworth, 1987.

Windt, Theodore O., Jr. *Presidents and Protesters: Political Rhetoric in the 1960s*. Tuscaloosa: University of Alabama Press, 1990.

Windt, Theodore O., Jr., and Beth Ingold, eds. *Essays in Presidential Rhetoric*. Dubuque, IA: Kendall/Hunt Publishing Company, 1983.

Woodward, Gary C. "Narrative Form and the Deceptions of Modern Journalism." *Political Communication Ethics: An Oxymoron?* Ed. Robert E. Denton, Jr. Westport, CT: Praeger, 2000. 125–146.

Yagada, Aileen, and David M. Dozier. "The Media Agenda-Setting Effect of Concrete versus Abstract Issues." *Journalism Quarterly* 67 (1990): 3–10.

Young, Marilyn J. "When the Shoe Is on the Other Foot: The Reagan Administration's Treatment of the Shootdown of Iran Air 655." *Reagan and Public Discourse in America*. Ed. Michael Weiler and W. Barnett Pearce. Tuscaloosa: University of Alabama Press, 1992. 203–224.

Young, Marilyn J., and Lloyd F. Bitzer. "Rhetorical Situation, Public Knowledge, and Audience Dynamics." In Jim A. Kuypers and Andrew King, eds. *Twentieth-Century Roots of Rhetorical Studies* Westport, CT: Praeger, 2001. 275–301.

Young, Marilyn J., and Michael K. Launer. *Flights of Fancy, Flight of Doom: KAL 007 and Soviet-American Rhetoric.* Lanham, MD: University Press of America, 1988.

———. "KAL 007 and the Superpowers: An International Argument." *Quarterly Journal of Speech* 74 (1988): 271–295.

———. "Superpower Role Reversals: Political Rhetoric Following the Destruction of KAL 007 and the Iranian Airbus." Paper presented at the annual meeting of the World Communication Association. Singapore, 1989.

CHARLES DAVIDSON: "THE CONFEDERATE BATTLE FLAG: A SYMBOL OF RACISM?"

"Alabama State Senator: Slavery Good for Blacks." *Orlando Sentinel* (10 May 1996): A12.

"Bible Backed Slavery, Says a Lawmaker." *New York Times* (10 May 1996): A20.

"Candidate Cites Bible on Slavery." *Austin American-Statesman* (10 May 1996): A5.

"Candidate Ends Bid Over Slavery Issue." *Los Angeles Times* (12 May 1996): A10.

"Candidate Uses Bible to Defend Slavery." *Milwaukee Journal Sentinel* (10 May 1996): 4.

"Candidate Withdraws After Slavery Defense." *Washington Times* (12 May 1996): A2.

"Candidate Who Backed Slavery Quits." *Commercial Appeal* (Memphis) (12 May 1996): A2.

"Candidate Who Upheld Slavery Quits Race." *South Bend Tribune* (12 May 1996): A7.

"Defense Knocks Out House Hopeful." *The Hill* 15 May 1996: 15.

Egan, Marc. "Heflin Chastises State Senator in Speech at ASU." *Montgomery Advertiser* (12 May 1996): B1.

"Elections." *The Record* (12 May 1996): A13.

Ferris, Gerrie. "Around the South: Candidate Praises Slavery." *Atlanta Journal and Constitution* (10 May 1996): C7.

Hochstedt Butler, Diana. "Does the Bible Justify Slavery: Yes, it Does—And Therein Lies the Pitfall of Mixing the Bible with Politics." Insight. *Austin American-Statesman* (26 May 1996): D1.

Hughs, Ina. "Food for Thought Gives Bellyache and the Giggles." *Knoxville News-Sentinel* (Knoxville, TN) (3 July 1996): A2.

Ingram, Bob. "Wasted Davidson Donors Should Get Refunds." Editorial. *Montgomery Advertiser* (14 May 1996): A6.

"In the News." *Arkansas Democrat-Gazette* (12 May 1996): A1.

Kleinberg, Howard. "In Biblical Terms, An Abomination." *Tampa Tribune* (15 May 1996): 11.

———. "Modern Biblical Blasphemy." *Chattanooga Times* (15 May 1996): A6.

"Lawmaker: Bible OKs Slavery." *Sacramento Bee* (10 May 1996): A31.

Liefer, Richard. "Candidate Quits after Speech on Slavery." *Chicago Tribune* (12 May 1996): 20.

"Out of His Cotton Pickin' Mind." *Hotline* (13 May 1996).

Owens, Gene. "Bible's 'Slaves' Were a Far Cry From South's." Editorial. *News &*
Record (Greensboro, NC) (14 May 1996): A7.

Page, Clarence. "It Defies Common Sense, Decency to Justify Slavery." Editorial.
Orlando Sentinel (14 May 1996): A9.

———. "Revisionist History of Slavery Reveals a Pervasive Racism." Editorial.
Seattle Post-Intelligencer (14 May 1996): A9.

———. "Senator's Denial of Slavery's Harm, Racism Is Absurd." *Fresno Bee* (16
May 1996): B7.

———. "Slavery: Southern Denial Defies Decency." Editorial/Opinion. *Phoenix*
Gazette (14 May 1996): B5.

Payne, Les. "What Does Koch Think Is a Sin?" *Newsday* (2 June 1996): A44.

Perkins, Al. "Wrong to Imply Christianity Condones Slavery." Perspective. *Mont-*
gomery Advertiser (19 May 1996): F1.

"Potpourri." Editorial. *Charleston Gazette* (20 May 1996): A4.

Rawls, Phillip. "Candidate Uses Bible to Justify Blacks' Slavery: Alabamian Seeks
U.S. House Seat." *Chattanooga Times* (13 May 1996): B3.

———. "House Candidate Uses Bible to Defend Southern Slavery." *Associated*
Press (10 May 1996).

———. "Senator Not Just Whistlin' 'Dixie' with Speech Defending Slavery."
Montgomery Advertiser (10 May 1996): A1.

Ross, Gary Earl. "Times Are Right for the Return of a Tradition: Slavery." Viewpoints. *Buffalo News* (2 June 1996): F9.

Saunders, Jessica. "Davidson Drops Out of GOP Contest." *Montgomery Advertiser*
(12 May 1996): A1.

"Slavery Defender Senator Embarrasses State, Party." Editorial. *Montgomery Ad-*
vertiser (12 May 1996): F2.

"Slavery Defense Derails Candidacy." *Times Union* (Albany, NY) (12 May 1996):
A8.

"Slavery Stance Draws Fire." *Montgomery Advertiser* (11 May 1996): A1.

"U.S. House Candidate Uses Bible to Defend Slavery." *Columbus Dispatch* (10
May 1996): A11.

Watson, Rod. "American Education Distorts and Devalues Black History To the
Point of Ignorance." Viewpoints. *Buffalo News* (16 May 1996): B3.

WILLIAM J. CLINTON: "INITIATIVE ON RACE"

Adubato, Steve Jr. "Affirmative Action? Yes, but Based on Need, not Race." Review & Outlook. *The Record* (22 June 1997): 4.

Ahearn, James. "Bradley Was There before Clinton in Trying to Heal U.S. Racial
Divide." *Asbury Park Press* (Neptune, NJ) (18 June 1997): A11.

———. "Opinion." *The Record* (18 June 1997): L9.

"A Letdown on Race." Perspective. *Times Union* (Albany, NY) (22 June 1997): B4.

Anderson, Mickie. "Memphians Cheer Clinton Race Focus; 'Ought to Be Some
Soul Searching.' " *Commercial Appeal* (Memphis, TN) (15 June 1997): A15.

"A New Racial Dialogue; Talk, but Let's Be Honest." Editorial/Opinion. *Arizona*
Republic (20 June 1997): B4.

"A President Confronts Race." Editorial. *St. Louis Post-Dispatch* (18 June 1997):
B6.

Arrn, Larry. "California Focus: Lincoln Beats Clinton Hands Down on Race." Editorial. *Orange County Register* (18 June 1997): B8.

Baker, Peter. "Clinton Calls for National Dialog to Heal Racial Divide." *Commercial Appeal* (Memphis, TN) (15 June 1997): A1.

———. "Clinton Kicks Off Campaign to Improve Race Relations." *Palm Beach Post* (15 June 1997): A4.

———. "Clinton Open to Idea of Apologizing for Slavery." *Austin American-Statesman* (16 June 1997): A2.

———. "Clinton Sounds Call for Dialogue On Race: President Argues for Affirmative Action." *Washington Post* (15 June 1997): A1.

———. "President Mulls National Apology for Slavery; Proposal Called 'Not a Bad Thing' as Racial Issues Gain Attention." *Washington Post* (16 June 1997): A4.

Baker, Peter, and David S. Broder. "The Final Word." *Washington Post* (17 June 1997): A4.

Baker, Russell. "Observer; We've Got to Talk." Editorial. *New York Times* (17 June 1997): A21.

Basu, Rekha. "An Experiment in Race Relations." *Des Moines Register* (16 June 1997): 1.

Baye, Betty Winston. "Heed Clinton's Race Initiative." Editorial. *Cincinnati Enquirer* (23 June 1997): A11.

———. "Race Debate Won't Be Picnic." Op Ed. *Montgomery Advertiser* (24 June 1997): A7.

———. "Time to Face Racial Truths." Forum. *Courier-Journal* (Louisville, KY) (19 June 1997): A11.

Beaulieu, Lovell. "What Bill Clinton Could Do about Race Relations in America." Opinion. *Des Moines Register* (15 June 1997): 1.

Bey, Lee. "Jackson: Action Must Follow Words." *Chicago Sun-Times* (15 June 1997): 28.

"Beyond Symbolism." *Las Vegas Review-Journal* (21 June 1997): B10.

Billingsley, K.L. "Clinton's Race Speech Delivered Where Preferences Issue Is Hot." *Washington Times* (16 June 1997): A6.

Biskupic, Joan. "Call to Renew Preferences Faces Resistance: Courts, Many White Voters Skeptical about Affirmative Action at Colleges." *Washington Post* (15 June 1997): A8.

Bivins, Larry. "Apology Seen as Way to Further Race Plan: Black Leaders Support It: President Would Consider Idea, Not Reparations." *Detroit News* (17 June 1995): A5.

———. "Clinton Tells America to Destroy Racism's Final Walls—'In Our Hearts.' " *Detroit News* (15 June 1997): A1.

Boren, Jim. "All Levels of Society Must Help Improve Our Racial Relations." *Fresno Bee* (17 June 1997): B5.

"Break Through Race Cynicism." Editorial. *Capital Times* (Madison, WI) (17 June 1997): A10.

Broder, David S. "Civil Rights, Minority Advancement Require More Than Presidential Lip Service." Opinion. *South Bend Tribune* (16 June 1997): A8.

———. "Clinton Must Maintain Vigilance on Race, Beyond the Speech." *The Plain Dealer* (15 June 1997): E3.

————. "Diversity Issue Is Too Complex to Be Solved as Clinton Hopes." *Idaho Statesman* (16 June 1997): A7.

————. "Nation Must Adapt to Diversity." Editorial. *Montgomery Advertiser* (15 June 1997): F2.

————. "On Race Issues, America Has Work to Do." Viewpoints. *Buffalo News* (16 June 1997): B3.

————. "Reaching across the Racial Divide." Opinion. *The Record* (16 June 1997): A12.

————. "The Racial Divide." *Times-Picayune* (15 June 1997): B7.

————. "What Talk Can Do." Op-ed. *Washington Post* (15 June 1997): C9.

Brownstein, Ronald. "Clinton Continues Attack on Prop. 209 with TV Interview; Race: President's Call for Dialogue Touches Off a Round of Reaction from Liberal and Conservative Critics." *Los Angeles Times* (16 June 1997): A3.

————. "Clinton's Speech Confirms Leftward Shift on Race Issues." *Los Angeles Times* (15 June 1997): A18.

Burgess, Philip. "Positive Progress on Race Relations." Editorial. *Denver Rocky Mountain News* (17 June 1997): A35.

Cannon, Carl M. "President Urges 'One America'; In College Address, Clinton Opens Discussion of Race; 'Challenge Your Parents'; Tone-Setting Speech Does Not Offer Specific Programs." *The Sun* (Baltimore) (15 June 1997): A1.

Capehart, Jonathan. "Black & White: Three Views, Bill Gaining Spot in Black History." Editorial. *Daily News* (New York) (14 June 1997): 31.

Carlson, John. "Candor Missing from Clinton's Speech on Race." Editorial. *News Tribune* (Tacoma, WA) (18 June 1997): A9.

Chavez, Linda. "Clinton Muddies Race Waters." *Denver Post* (18 June 1997): B9.

"Clinton Attacks Racism." *Pantagraph* (Bloomington, IL) (15 June 1997): A1.

"Clinton Focuses on Racial Divide." *Tampa Tribune* (15 June 1997): 1.

"Clinton Looks to Talking as Ethnic Understanding Step." *Central Maine Morning Sentinel* (Waterville, ME) (15 June 1997): A8.

"Clinton: Offering Apology for Slavery 'Is Not a Bad Thing' but a Top Republican Senator Says He Probably Would Not Vote for the Legislation." *Des Moines Register* (16 June 1997): 2.

"Clinton Opens Fight against Racism in U.S." *Des Moines Register* (15 June 1997): 1.

"Clinton Picks the Right Subject for Dialogue on America's Future." Editorial. *Buffalo News* (18 June 1997): C2.

"Clinton Praised for Speech, Told Real Work Lies Ahead." *The Plain Dealer* (15 June 1997): A16.

"Clinton Race Initiative Offers Nothing New." Editorial. *Atlanta Journal and Constitution*. Journal edition. (17 June 1997): A8.

"Clinton: Racial Barriers Breakable; He Says the United States Can Become the First Truly Multiracial Democracy in the World." *Des Moines Register* (15 June 1997): 8.

"Clinton Starts Reach Across Lines of Race; A Year of Words Must Produce Results to Have Any Meaning." Editorial. *Portland Press Herald* (17 June 1997): A8.

"Clinton Timing Apt in Resuming Dialogue." Editorial. *Albuquerque Journal* (18 June 1997): A8.

"Clinton Urges Nation to Bridge Racial Divisions." *San Antonio Express-News* (15 June 1997): A1.

"Clinton's Call for Talk on Race Might Be Good for the Nation." Editorial. *Idaho Statesman* (21 June 1997): A12.

Cohen, Richard. "America's Race Issues: Clinton's Speech Was No Help." *Des Moines Register* (20 June 1997): 15.

———. "An Empty Speech on Race." Op-Ed. *Washington Post* (17 June 1997): A17.

———. "Can We Replace Affirmative Action?" *Denver Post* (17 June 1997): B9.

Coleman, Trevor W. "Clinton Picks a Strong Leader for His Racial Advisory Board." Opinion. *Detroit Free Press* (16 June 1997).

"Conversation about Race." Editorial. *Washington Post* (17 June 1997): A16.

Delguzzi, Kristen. "Clinton Plan Applauded: Focus on Racial Divide Pleases Local Leaders." *Cincinnati Enquirer* (15 June 1997): A19.

"Dialogue on Race Begins." *News and Observer* (Raleigh, NC) (15 June 1997): A1.

Dionne, Jr., E.J. "Rational Discussion of Race Could Lead to Better Policy." Editorial. *Montgomery Advertiser* (23 June 1997): A6.

———. "The Keys to Successful Pluralism." Perspective. *Denver Post* (22 June 1997): D3.

———. "What If We Had a Serious Conversation?" Op-Ed. *Washington Post* (20 June 1997): A23.

Dobrin, Arthur, and Warren Payton. "The Path to Racial Justice Is Via Education." Viewpoints. *Newsday* (18 June 1997): A40.

Douglas, William. " 'One America'/Clinton Outlines Need to Transcend Ethnic Prejudice." *Newsday* (15 June 1997): A3.

"Dubious Apology; Perilous Sidetrack in Race Debate." Editorial. *Cincinnati Enquirer* (17 June 1997): A10.

"Empty Words on Race." Editorial. *Boston Herald* (17 June 1997): 20.

Eversley, Melanie. "Gulf Separating Races Still Wide, Survey Says; Young Blacks More Upbeat Than Elders." *Houston Chronicle* (18 June 1997): A10.

"Excerpts From Clinton's Speech on Race in America." *New York Times* (15 June 1997): 16.

Feder, Don. "Honest Dialogue on Race Impossible." Editorial. *Boston Herald* (18 June 1997): 29.

Foster, Shawn. "Would Apology for Slavery Help the Blacks of 1997?; Blacks May Hear 'Sorry,' but Will It Help?" *Salt Lake Tribune* (19 June 1997): A1.

Freedberg, Louis. "GOP Trying to Ban Affirmative Action; Bill Introduced in Response to Clinton Initiative on Race." *San Francisco Chronicle* (18 June 1997): A1.

———. "President Clinton's Ultimate Challenge." Editorial. *San Francisco Chronicle* (15 June 1997): 9.

Freeman, Gregory. "Clinton Does Nation a Favor by Talking on Race Relations." *St. Louis Post-Dispatch* (17 June 1997): B1.

———. " 'Unfinished Business' of Race Spurs Clinton." *St. Louis Post-Dispatch* (15 June 1997): B5.

Gaouette, Nicole. " 'Honesty' Key to Racial Harmony." *Christian Science Monitor* (16 June 1997): 3.

Gingrich, Newt. "Clinton's Clinging to a Harmful Past." Editorial. *Orange County Register* (17 June 1997): B9.

———. "Face the Failure of Racial Preferences." *New York Times* (15 June 1997): 15.

Glassman, James K. "The Divide Is Narrowing." Op-Ed. *Washington Post* (17 June 1997): A17.

———. "The Real Race Division Is in Education." Viewpoints. *Buffalo News* (19 June 1997): B3.

Glavin, Matthew J. "Crossing the Color Line." Editorial. *Atlanta Journal and Constitution* (15 June 1997): F5.

Griego, Linda. "Perspective on Race Relations; Share Tools to Build Opportunity; Correct the Economic Inequalities and Watch Attitudes Change from Divisiveness and Fear to Tolerance and Hope." *Los Angeles Times* (17 June 1997): B7.

Hamblin, Ken. "Clinton Exploits Race for Votes." Perspective. *Denver Post* (15 June 1997): E3.

"Healing the Wounds." Editorial. *Austin American-Statesman* (22 June 1997): H2.

Herbert, Bob. "In America: Racism's Nine Lives." *New York Times* (20 June 1997): A29.

Holmes, Steven A. "Gingrich Offers Program to Promote Racial Healing." *The Plain Dealer* (19 June 1997): A15.

———. "Gingrich Outlines Plan on Race Relations." *New York Times* (19 June 1997): B12.

———. "Many Uncertain about President's Racial Effort." *New York Times* (16 June 1997): B10.

"In 'Building One America, All Citizens Must Serve.' " *Washington Post* (15 June 1997): A8.

"Inclusion, Not Rejection, Will Spur Racial Harmony." *USA Today* (16 June 1997): A18.

Jackson, Derrick Z. "Clinton's Rosy Approach to Race." Op-Ed. *Boston Globe* (20 June 1997): A19.

———. "To Improve Race Relations, Close the Gap On Pay Day." Op-Ed. *Boston Globe* (18 June 1997): A15.

———. "To Improve Race Relations, Close Gap in Pay Disparity." Editorial. *Austin American-Statesman* (20 June 1997): A11.

Jacoby, Jeff. "Mr. President, You're No Racial Healer." Op-Ed. *Boston Globe* (17 June 1997): A19.

———. "Mr. President, You're No Racial Healer." *Des Moines Register* (21 June 1997): 9.

Johnson, Carrie. "Virginians: It's First Step; Words Need to Give Way to Concrete Action, They Say." *Richmond Times Dispatch* (15 June 1997): A18.

Kasindorf, Martin. "Little Rock Likely Site of First Forum." *USA Today* (16 June 1997): A14.

Kennedy, Randall. "Clinton Must Take Risks on Race Issue." Viewpoints. *Newsday* (19 June 1997): A51.

———. "OK, Let's Talk about Race. For Real; Will Clinton's Call Lead to Understanding? Or More Chat?" Editorial. *Pittsburgh Post-Gazette* (18 June 1997): A13.

———. "Race Relations Conversation Must Be Candid, Broad." Outlook. *Houston Chronicle* (18 June 1997): A27.

———. "Unlock Pandora's Box: Is Clinton Prepared to Ask Tough Questions?" Editorial/Opinion. *Arizona Republic* (18 June 1997): B5.

———. "Where Do We Go from Here? Clinton Must Resist the Impulse to Control the Race Debate to Come." Outlook. *Washington Post* (15 June 1997): C1.

Kilborn, Robert, and Lance Carden. "The News in Brief." *Christian Science Monitor* (16 June 1997): 2.

King, Colbert I. "A Long Walk on New Hampshire Avenue." Op-Ed. *Washington Post* (21 June 1997): A21.

Krauthammer, Charles. "Clinton Contributed Zilch to Race Discussion." Opinion. *Houston Chronicle* (21 June 1997): A23.

———. "Clinton Speech a Failure: He Misrepresents Opponents Views on Affirmative Action." Op Ed. *Dayton Daily News* (22 June 1997): B11.

———. "Clinton's Fuzzy-Wuzzy 'Candor.' " Editorial. *Cincinnati Enquirer* (20 June 1997): A14.

———. "Race Speech Touch-Feely Pap." *Las Vegas Review-Journal* (23 June 1997): B7.

———. "Racial Politics II: Clinton Begins Conversation on Race with a Whopper about Affirmative Action." Editorial. *Pittsburgh Post-Gazette* (23 June 1997): A9.

"Launching a 'Third Revolution.' " Perspect. *The Tennessean* (15 June 1997): D1.

"Let's Talk: Silence Surely Won't Reduce Racial Tensions." Editorials. *Houston Chronicle* (17 June 1997): A18.

Lockman, Norman. "Pollyanna Approach Better Than Hiding from Problem." Op Ed. *Montgomery Advertiser* (15 June 1997): F3.

Lokeman, Rhonda Chriss. "Clinton Right on Race: President Uses Office to Issue Call For Healing." Opinion. *Kansas City Star* (18 June 1997): C8.

Malone, Julia. "Clinton Says Race Programs Needed: He Uses California Speech to Defend Affirmative Action." *Atlanta Journal and Constitution* (15 June 1997): A1.

———. "Clinton Warns against Return to Segregation: Campaign against Racism." *Austin American-Statesman* (15 June 1997): B1.

Mancini, Francis. "Clinton's Rapid Racial Dexterity." Editorial. *Providence Journal-Bulletin* (19 June 1997): B7.

Marelius, John. "President Addresses Racial Healing." *State Journal-Register* (Springfield, IL) (15 June 1997): 3.

Matthews, Christopher. "A Peculiar Apology for Slavery." *San Francisco Examiner* (22 June 1997): D7.

Mathis, Nancy. "President May Back Apology for Slavery." *Houston Chronicle* (16 June 1997): A1.

———. "Clinton Calls for Dialogue on Race; Despite Raw Emotions, President Insists, 'We Must Begin.' " *Houston Chronicle* (15 June 1997): A1.

McClellan-Copeland, April. "Clinton Pleads for an End to Prejudice: President Comes Out Strongly in Support of Affirmative Action." *Plain Dealer* (15 June 1997): A1.

McFeatters, Ann. "Clinton Calls For Racial Unity; Who Will Listen?" *Denver Rocky Mountain News* (15 June 1997): A57.

McGrory, Brian. "Clinton Sets a Dialogue about Race; Pledges to Draft Specific Plan Over Next Year." *Boston Globe* (15 June 1997): A1.

Mecoy, Laura. "Clinton: Cast Off Racism." *Sacramento Bee* (15 June 1997): A1.

Milloy, Courtland. "White House Entertains Black Voices." *Washington Post* (18 June 1997): B1.

Mitchell, Alison. "Clinton Goes to California to Launch Initiative on Race." *Arizona Republic* (15 June 1997): A19.

———. "Defending Affirmative Action, Clinton Urges Debate on Race." *New York Times* (15 June 1997): 1.

Morris, Phillip. "Clinton Offers Only Platitudes to Heal Racism." Editorials & Forum. *The Plain Dealer* (17 June 1997): B9.

Navarrette, Ruben, Jr. "Clinton Must Extend Talk on Race Relations Past Affirmative Action." Editorial/Opinion. *Arizona Republic* (20 June 1997): B5.

Ness, Carol. "Cheers, Boos for Clinton on Race: Call for Unity in San Diego Fails to Charm All Hearers." *San Francisco Examiner* (15 June 1997): A17.

"News Summary." *New York Times* (15 June 1997): 2.

"Opening a Conversation on Race." Editorial. *New York Times* (16 June 1997): A14.

Overholser, Geneva. "Headlines and Objectivity." Op-Ed. *Washington Post* (22 June 1997): C6.

Page, Clarence. "Will Dialogue on Race Ever Get Beyond the Usual Rhetoric?" Opinion. *The Record* (Bergen County NJ) (24 June 1997): L13.

Page, Susan. "Dialogue on Race Hits First Snag." *USA Today* (16 June 1997): A1.

———. "Starting the National Discussion." *USA Today* (16 June 1997): A14.

Payne, Les. "It's a Strange Time for a Race Revolution." *Newsday* (15 June 1997): G6.

Perez, Miguel. "Clinton's Call for Dialogue Left Out Much of America." Opinion. *The Record* (Bergen County, NJ) (20 June 1997): L9.

Peterson, Jonathan. "Clinton Calls for 'National Effort' to End Racism." *Los Angeles Times* (15 June 1997): A1.

"Plain Speaking on Race." Editorial. *Atlanta Journal and Constitution* (17 June 1997): A8.

"Preaching about Diversity." Editorial. *Detroit News* (17 June 1997): A8.

"President Clinton Is Wrong about Affirmative Action." *Asbury Park Press* (Neptune, NJ) (23 June 1997): A11.

"President Kicks Off Anti-Racism Campaign: Defends Affirmative Action, Opens 'Conversation' for Next Century." *St. Louis Post-Dispatch* (15 June 1997): A1.

Raspberry, William. "Beyond Black and White." Op-Ed. *Washington Post* (20 June 1997): A23.

———. "Having Dialogue on Race Can't Hurt." Editorial. *Cincinnati Enquirer* (22 June 1997): D4.

———. "It's Something to Talk About." *Tampa Tribune* (19 June 1997): 15.

———. "Look Forward and Broaden Issues in Race Dialogue, Dorn Suggests." Editorial. *Austin American-Statesman* (18 June 1997): A15.

———. "Push Racial Talk beyond Black, White." *Times Union* (Albany, NY) (20 June 1997): A11.

———. "Right Parameters Vital for Racial Discussion." *Fresno Bee* (20 June 1997): B5.

————. "Talking about Racial Issue Viable Option." Editorial. *San Antonio Express-News* (20 June 1997): 5.

"Repairing the Breach: A Word or 1,200 about Race." Editorial. *Arkansas Democrat-Gazette* (22 June 1997): J4.

Reynolds, Gerald. "An Alternative Plan to Help the Downtrodden." Opinion. *The Record* (Bergen County, NJ) (23 June 1997): A11.

————. "History Key to Solving Racial Problems." Editorial. *Cincinnati Enquirer* (22 June 1997): D4.

Rich, Frank. "Racial Politics II: Go Ahead and Apologize and Talk, but How about Some Actions to Back It All Up." Editorial. *Pittsburgh Post-Gazette* (23 June 1997): A9.

Riley, Rochelle. "Bridging Gap Benefits Blacks and Whites. *Courier-Journal* (Louisville, KY) (19 June 1997): E1.

Roche, Walter F., Jr. "Warnings Accompany Praise for Speech: President Is Lauded, but Action Is Sought on Economic Matters." *The Sun* (Baltimore) (15 June 1997): A7.

Ross, Sonya. "First Steps on the Path to Harmony; Clinton Sets Agenda on Race." *The Record* (Bergen County, NJ) (15 June 1997): A1.

————. "Clinton Attacks Racism." *Chattanooga Free Press* (Bergen County, NJ) (15 June 1997): A1.

————. "Talk, but Little Action, Critics Say: Clinton Defends Speech on Race." *The Record* (Bergen County, NJ) (16 June 1997): A8.

Rowan, Carl. "Clinton's Race Stance Is a Huge Gamble." Viewpoints. *Buffalo News* (17 June 1997): B3.

Samuel, Terence. "Americans Already Talking about Search for Harmony." *St. Louis Post-Dispatch* (15 June 1997): A12.

Saunders, Debra. "Clinton Says Little." *Chattanooga Times* (20 June 1997): A9.

————. "Clinton Says Little about Racism." Editorial. *Idaho Statesman* (19 June 1997): A12.

————. "The Let's-Talk President Says Little." Editorial. *San Francisco Chronicle* (17 June 1997): A21.

Scanlon, Leslie. "Race Relations Always a Focus of Louisville-Area Pastors." *Courier-Journal* (Louisville, KY) (15 June 1997): A15.

Shepard, Scott. "A 'Conversation about Race'; Analysis; Affirmative Action Divide Is Apparent." *Atlanta Journal and Constitution* (15 June 1997): A12.

————. "Clinton's Talk Seen as Risky Rescue of Affirmative Action." *Palm Beach Post* (15 June 1997): A4.

Snow, Anita. "Clinton Attacks Racism." *Las Vegas Review-Journal* (15 June 1997): A1.

"Some in GOP Oppose Racial Preference; Measure Would Bar Government from Giving Weight to Race or Gender." *Milwaukee Journal Sentinel* (18 June 1997): 8.

"Speech Gets Conditional Praise." *Orange County Register* (15 June 1997): A16.

"Speech Highlights." *Austin American-Statesman* (15 June 1997): A13.

Stancavish, Don, and Matthew Mosk. "Can the Rhetoric, Observers Say: Effort Should Focus on Youth." *The Record* (Bergen County, NJ) (15 June 1997): A14.

"Start Talking; President's Idea for Candid Conversation on Race Has Merit." Editorial. *Daily News of Los Angeles* (18 June 1997): N16.

"Talk and Action on Race: Clinton's Jawboning on Racial Matters Is Welcome—If a Trifle Late." *San Francisco Examiner* (18 June 1997): A16.

"Talk First Piece of Racial Puzzle." Editorial. *San Antonio Express-News* (17 June 1997): A17.

"Talking about Race: Clinton Initiative: President Must Go Beyond Commission to Lead Interracial Discussions." Editorial. *Baltimore Sun* (17 June 1997): A10.

"The Great Debate: Clinton Challenges the County to Address the Racial Divide." Editorial. *Pittsburgh Post-Gazette* (17 June 1997): A10.

Thernstrom, Abigail. "The Overlooked Story." Editorial. *New York Times* (18 June 1997): A23.

"Timing of Clinton's Initiative on Race Relations Praised." Question. *News and Observer* (Raleigh, NC) (22 June 1997): A27.

"Valley Must Join Dialogue on Race." Comment. *Morning Call* (Allentown NJ) (17 June 1997): A14.

Walters, Dan. "Clinton Makes Desperate Bid." *Sacramento Bee* (15 June 1997): A3.

———. "Connerly and Clinton Clash." *Sacramento Bee* (17 June 1997): A3.

———. "It's Connerly vs. Clinton on Race Issue." *Fresno Bee* (17 June 1997): A3.

Wattenberg, Ben. "Mr. Clinton's 'Silly Little Boxes.' " Editorial. *Baltimore Sun* (19 June 1997): A17.

"We All Need to Take Part in Racial Dialogue." *South Bend Tribune* (17 June 1997): A9.

Wickham, DeWayne. "Blacks Should Seize Lead in Clinton Race Initiative." *USA Today* (17 June 1997): A13.

Will, George. "Affirmative Action Feeds Bloat of Obese Government." Editorial. *Chicago Sun-Times* (21 June 1997): 17.

———. "Clinton Defines Problems of Race in 1950s Terms: Speech Illustrates the Liberal Mindset." Editorial. *Seattle Post-Intelligencer* (19 June 1997): A19.

———. "Clinton's Overlooking Nation's Racial Change." Opinion. *The Record* (19 June 1997): L9.

———. "Clinton's Speech Akin to Carrying Coal to Newcastle." *Times-Picayune* (20 June 1997): B7.

———. "Clinton's Words on Race Indeed Illuminating." *Fresno Bee* (19 June 1997): B9.

———. "Don't Blame Minority Woes on Racism." Editorial. *Deseret News* (Salt Lake City, UT) (19 June 1997): A27.

———. "Expansive Government Ineptly Deals with Race." *Tampa Tribune* (19 June 1997): 15.

———. "From California, Here It Comes." Op-Ed. *Washington Post* (18 June 1997): A17.

———. "Less, Not More, Government Can Bridge the Racial Divide." Editorial. *Idaho Statesman* (19 June 1997): A13.

———. "Liberal Surrealism Frame Race Issue." Editorial. *San Antonio Express-News* (19 June 1997): 7.

———. "National Conversation about Race Misframes the Issue." *Times Union* (Albany, NY) (19 June 1997): A11.

——. "President Clinton Is Trodding a Slippery Slope." Opinion. *South Bed Tribune* (19 June 1997): A10.

——. "Problem of Race Is Racial." Editorial. *Austin American-Statesman* (18 June 1997): A15.

——. "There's More to It Than Just Black and White." Editorial. *Baltimore Sun* (18 June 1997): A11.

Yeager, Holly. "GOP Bill Goes after Affirmative Action; in Slap at Clinton, Measure Would Halt Federal Preferences." *San Francisco Examiner* (18 June 1997): A1.

LOUIS FARRAKHAN: "REMARKS AT THE MILLION MAN MARCH"

"Accuracy In Media: Journalists Puff Farrakhan Despite His Bigotry." *Chattanooga Free Press* (29 October 1995).

Addis, Dave. "Day of Commitment and Unity: One of D.C.'s Largest-Ever Assemblies Creates a Bond." *Virginian-Pilot* (17 October 1995): A1.

Apple, R.W., Jr. "Men on Mall Push Race Issue to the Fore." *Austin American-Statesman* (17 October 1995): A1.

——. "The March on Washington: News Analysis." *New York Times* (17 October 1995): 1.

"Black Men Hear Call for Unity: Farrakhan Leads Throng in Exuberant March." *The Plain Dealer* (17 October 1995): A1.

"Black Multitude Sends Message of Hope, Pride." *Des Moines Register* (17 October 1995): 1.

Blomquist, Brian. "Farrakhan to Support Candidates Accepting 'Third Power' Agenda." *Washington Times* (19 October 1995): A1.

Buckley, William F. "Evaluating Farrakhan and the March." Viewpoints. *Buffalo News* (21 October 1995): C3.

——. "Farrakhan's Goal Is Separatism." Editorial. *Cincinnati Enquirer* (19 October 1995): A22.

——. "Farrakhan's Ideas, Actions, Word are Cause for Concern." *Fresno Bee* (20 October 1995): B11.

——. "Leader's Words Plot Perilous Path." Editorial. *Arizona Republic* (20 October 1995): B7.

——. "The Battle for the Hearts and Minds of Young Blacks in Farrakhan, We Have the True Fanatic." Opinion. *The Record* (18 October 1995): AE.

Butler, LaChrisha, and John Manchette. "Rally Inspires Unity, Rival." *USA Today* (17 October 1995): A1.

Cass, Connie. "Day of Unity, Self-Respect: Thousands of Black Men Vow to Make Better World." *Chattanooga Times* (17 October 1995): A1.

Clines, Francis X. "The March on Washington: Overview; Black Men Fill Capital's Mall in Display of Unity and Pride." *New York Times* (17 October 1995): 1.

Crockett, Kimberly. "Black Men Took Positive Message without Anointing Farrakhan." Editorial/Opinion. *Phoenix Gazette* (18 October 1995): B5.

——. "March Leader, Message Are Kept Separate." *Fresno Bee* (19 October 1995): B5.

Dahl, David, and Jennifer S. Thomas. "The Million Man March// 'I Pledge.' " *St. Petersburg Times* (17 October 1995): A1.

Dokes, Jennifer. "Don't Let Farrakhan Overshadow Marchers' Earned Respect, Pride." Editorial/Opinion. *Arizona Republic* (18 October 1995): B4.

Douglas, William, and Monte R. Young. "Strength in Numbers: Largest-Ever Rally of Blacks in the Capital." *The Record* (Bergen County, NJ) (17 October 1995): A1.

Dowdy, Zachary R. "Black Men Hear Appeal to Action; Farrakhan Asks Throng to Atone, Take Control Million Man March." *Boston Globe* (17 October 1995): 1.

Dwyer, Jim. "Jesse: Now Work Begins." *Daily News* (New York) (19 October 1995): 6.

Eagleton, Thomas. "The March Others Could Not Produce." Editorial. *St. Louis Post-Dispatch* (22 October 1995): B3.

Ely, Jane. "Clinton Had a Powerful Message, Too." Opinion. *Houston Chronicle* (18 October 1995): 22.

"Excerpts from Farrakhan's Speech." *San Francisco Examiner* (17 October 1995): A14.

"Excerpts from Their Speeches." *St. Petersburg Times* (17 October 1995): A7.

"Farrakhan's Message Tainted." *Wisconsin State Journal* (17 October 1995): A7.

"Farrakhan Plots National Agenda on Heels of March." *Phoenix Gazette* (18 October 1995): A6.

"Farrakhan, Others Urge 400,000 to Act Morally." *Chattanooga Free Press* (17 October 1995).

Fletcher, Michael A., and Dan Balz. "Farrakhan Seeks Wider Role; Some Black Leaders Are Conciliatory, Others Cautious." *Washington Post* (18 October 1995): A1.

Fletcher, Michael A., and Hamil R. Harris. "Black Men Jam Mall for a 'Day of Atonement': Fiery Rhetoric, Alliances, Skepticism Mark March." *Washington Post* (17 October 1995): A1.

Freedberg, Louis, Teresa Moore; and Aurelio Rojas. "A Display of Unity and Peace." *Post and Courier* (17 October 1995): A1.

Freedberg, Louis, Teresa Moore, and Aurelio Rojas. "Black Men Heed Unity Call Hundreds of Thousands Gather in Washington." *San Francisco Chronicle* (17 October 1995): A1.

Fulwood, Sam, III. "Blacks Ponder Next Steps after Historic Rally." *Los Angeles Times* (18 October 1995): A1.

Gibbs, Jewelle Taylor. "Farrakhan Stepped Into a Vacuum." Editorial. *San Francisco Chronicle* (24 October 1995): A19.

Goldschlag, William, Dave Eisenstadt, and Raphael Sugarman. "Farrakhan Foes Quick to React Minister Should Atone, They Say." *Daily News* (New York) (17 October 1995): 23.

Goldstein, David. "March Heralds Racial Unity: Estimates of the Crowd in Washington Range from 400,000 to 2 Million." *Kansas City Star* (17 October 1995): A1.

Greene, Leonard. "Millions Gained Respect from This Show of Pride." *Boston Herald* (17 October 1995): 1.

Hallow, Ralph Z. "Many Believe Event Anointed New Leader." *Washington Times* (18 October 1995): A1.

Hanson, Christopher. "Black Men Make a Stand: Hearts Are Joined in a Mass Pledge of Responsibility." *Seattle Post-Intelligencer* (17 October 1995): A1.

Haynes, Jim. "AWOL at Million Man March." Perspective. *Arizona Republic* (29 October 1995): F3.

Hinckley, David. "Power & Glory in Unity." *Daily News* (New York) (17 October 1995): 42.

———. "Power & Glory in Unity." *Daily News* (New York) (17 October 1995): 42.

Holmes, Steven A. "After March, Lawmakers Seek Commission on Race Relations." *New York Times* (18 October 1995): A1.

Hoversten, Paul. "Some Whites Are Skeptical of March's Positive Effects." *USA Today* (17 October 1995): A2.

Ingraham, Laura. "Mr. Farrakhan's Message . . . and the Message of the Men." *Washington Times* (18 October 1995): A21.

Kaplan, Bill. "Return to '20s No Roaring Success for Society, Blacks." Opinion. *Wisconsin State Journal* (25 October 1995): A11.

Kifner, John. "The March on Washington: The Reaction; with Farrakhan Speaking, A Chorus of G.O.P. Critics Joins In." *New York Times* (17 October 1995): A18.

Kusnet, David. "Re-Examining Race, History, Beyond the Fringe: Is Coughlin a Model?" Opinion. *Los Angeles Times* (22 October 1995): 1.

Lacey, Marc, and Sam Fulwood III. "News Analysis: Blacks Hear the Farrakhan behind the Extremist Words; African Americans: Supporters Dismiss Abhorrent Parts of Rhetoric and Embrace His Message of Pride." *Los Angeles Times* (22 October 1995): A1.

Lambrecht, Bill. "The Minister, The March, and The Mission; One a Big Stage, Louis Farrakhan Stood in the Spotlight." *St. Louis Post-Dispatch* (22 October 1995): B1.

Loftin, Michael. "Good Message, Divisive Messenger." *Chattanooga Times* (18 October 1995): A6.

Loury, Glenn. "The Men, the March, the Message; Event Helps a Social Critic Find Himself." Opinion. *San Diego Union-Tribune* (22 October 1995): G1.

Magida, Arthur J. "A Day of Black Atonement?" *Washington Times* (19 October 1995): A19.

Maraniss, David. "A Clear Day, A Cloud of Contradictions; At Event Designated for Reconciliation, Its Organizer Stresses White America's Sins." *Washington Post* (17 October 1995): A19.

Maranto, Robert A. "The Farrakhan-Duke Parallels." *Times-Picayune* (24 October 1995): B5.

"March Marred by Racial Separatism Talk Farrakhan's Dream." *Chattanooga Free Press* (28 October 1995).

"March Nourishes Hope of a Transformation Across America." *Tampa Tribune* (18 October 1995): 11.

March, William. "March Meaning: Enormous Turnout Raises Questions about Political Direction of Blacks." *Tampa Tribune* (19 October 1995): 1.

Matthews, Christopher. "Farrakhan's Rhetoric Echoes Hitler's." *San Francisco Examiner* (22 October 1995): B11.

Matthews, Richard. " 'Million Man' Mishmash: Vain Hunt for Meaning in Farrakhan's Message." Editorial. *Atlanta Journal and Constitution* (19 October 1995): A18.

Maxwell, Bill. "Farrakhan as Seen from the Inside." Perspective. *St. Petersburg Times* (22 October 1995): D1.

———. "Power Abhors a Vacuum: Post-King Generation Likes Farrakhan Style: Older Blacks Attracted to Part of His Message." Spectrum. *The Ledger* (Lakeland, FL) (29 October 1995): G1.

———. "Separated by Time and Ideology." Editorial. *St. Petersburg Times* (18 October 1995): A12.

"Men in March Promise to Shun Violence, Uplift Lives Crowd Size Is Put at 400,000 by Park Police." *Knoxville News-Sentinel* (17 October 1995): A1.

Miga, Andrew. "On the March!: Black Unity Rally Draws Thousands to Nation's Capital." *Boston Herald* (17 October 1995): 1.

"Million Man March Largest Black American Gathering Since 1963." *Asheville Citizen-Times* (17 October 1995): A1.

"Minister Me Holds Court." Editorial. *Daily News* (New York) (17 October 1995): 32.

Morris, Phillip. "On the March: A Split Head." Editorial. *The Plain Dealer* (24 October 1995): B9.

Mueller, Alice. "Accept March's Message but Beware of Messenger." Opinion. *Wisconsin State Journal* (21 October 1995): A9.

Muwakkil, Salim. "White America Helps Give Rise to Farrakhan." Editorial. *Chicago Sun-Times* (24 October 1995): 31.

Nelson, Lars-Erik. "Farrakhan Preached a Positive Message . . ." Editorial. *Daily News* (New York) (18 October 1995): 31.

Ness, Eric. "Word for Word/Intolerance on the Internet; Dueling Bigotries: Nation of Islam vs. White Racists." *New York Times* (22 October 1995): 7.

Page, Clarence. "Race Card: Will Voters Pass if GOP Plays It?" Editorial/Opinion. *Phoenix Gazette* (24 October 1995): B5.

Pereira, Charles, Doug Mills, Mark Wilson, and Brian Jackson. " 'We Are One': 400,000 Black Men Join Show of Atonement, Unity." *Chicago Sun-Times* (17 October 1995): 1.

Raspberry, William. "The Battle for the Hearts and Minds of Young Blacks: The Rank and File Basked in Their Joy." Opinion. *The Record* (Bergen County, NJ) (18 October 1995): N7.

"Resonance Across an Entire Nation: March Sounds a Message to All Americans and Their Leaders." Editorial. *Los Angeles Times* (17 October 1995): B8.

Rowan, Carl. "Racism Inflamed by Media." Editorial. *Chicago Sun-Times* (20 October 1995): 35.

———. "The Media and Our Racial Divide." Opinion. *San Diego Union-Tribune* (21 October 1995): B8.

Schnur, Dan. "The March Wasn't Really Necessary." Editorial. *San Francisco Chronicle* (18 October 1995): A23.

Shear, Michael D. "Messages of Anger, Atonement." *Washington Post* (17 October 1995): A21.

Starr, John R. "Farrakhan Is One Sorry Leader." Editorial. *Arkansas Democrat-Gazette* (19 October 1995): B9.

Stern, Marcus. "Black Men Answer Call for Atonement; Farrakhan Leads Historic Gathering in Nation's Capital." *San Diego Union-Tribune* (17 October 1995): A1.

"Sum-up of the Million Man March." Kup's Column. *Chicago Sun-Times* (18 October 1995): 64.

Talbott, Basil. "Simon Criticizes Farrakhan Over Speech at March." *Chicago Sun-Times* (29 October 1995): 7.

Taylor, Stuart, Jr. "An Omen of Hate, Not Hope." Closing Argument. *Connecticut Law Tribune* (23 October 1995): 11.

———. "Filling the Vacuum: In a Nation Thirsting for Leadership, How Does the Hate-Filled Speech of Louis Farrakhan Become a Mobilizing Force?" Commentary. *The Record* (Bergen County, NJ) (23 October 1995): 6.

———. "Using Demagoguery to Fill a Vacuum of Leadership." *New Jersey Law Journal* (23 October 1995): 27.

Teepen, Tom. "Lapse Into Baffling Nonsense: Farrakhan's Talk the Sort You Hear on the Ward." *The Ledger* (Lakeland, FL) (23 October 1995): A7.

———. "Separating Message from Messenger at the Million Man March." *Star Tribune* (21 October 1995): A18.

"The Washington March." *Chattanooga Free Press* (17 October 1995).

" 'This Is a New Beginning': Black Men Vow to Carry the Spirit of Washington March Back to Their Homes and Communities." *The San Francisco Examiner* (17 October 1995): A1.

Thomma, Steven. "Powell Tempted to Join March: Found Farrakhan's Speeches Offensive." *The Record* (Bergen County NJ) (17 October 1995): A6.

"Thoughts on Race." *USA Today* (19 October 1995): A12.

Tilove, Jonathan. "A Wave of Humanity, A Sea of Tranquility and Hope." Opinion. *San Diego Union-Tribune* (22 October 1995): G6.

———. "March Seems a Holiday after Summer of Tension." *The Plain Dealer* (17 October 1995): A1.

Tucker, Greg. "An Inspiring March Leaves Crucial Questions Behind." Editorial. *The Capital* (Annapolis, MD) (22 October 1995): A11.

"Voices." *San Diego Union-Tribune* (17 October 1995): A14.

" 'We Must Accept the Responsibility That God Has Put upon Us.' " *Washington Post* (17 October 1995): A24.

Wilgoren, Debbi. "Farrakhan's Speech: Masons, Mysticism, More." *Washington Post* (22 October 1995): A1.

Witham, Larry. "Long Speech Draws on Tenets with Roots in Three Traditions; Nation of Islam Leader also Draws Heavily on the Bible." *Washington Times* (17 October 1995): A13.

Yeager, Holly. "Leaders May Make Amends; Farrakhan Is Ready to Talk." *Times-Picayune* (17 October 1995): A4.

REGGIE WHITE: "SPEECH BEFORE THE WISCONSIN LEGISLATURE"

Adams, Dwight. "Briefly Sports." *Indianapolis Star* (3 April 1998): C5.

Adande, J.A. "Reggie Spells Out Misguided Notions in Black and White." *Buffalo News* (28 March 1998): B2.

———. "White Crosses Line and Is Ruled Offside." *Los Angeles Times* (27 March 1998): C1.

"Anti-Gay Remarks Draw Some Boos, Support; While Some Twin Cities Evangelicals Dispute Football Star Reggie White's Comments, Others Side with Him." *Star Tribune* (Minneapolis, MN) (27 March 1998): B2.

"Arena: Sports Briefing." *Denver Rocky Mountain News* (26 March 1998): C2.

Baggott, Andy. "A Rush to Comparisons: Reggie's Remarks Stand Out in Crowd of Celebrity Gaffes." *Wisconsin State Journal* (31 March 1998): D2.

Borges, Ron. "White's Point Shouldn't Be Missed; Question: How Do You Know When Your Speech Was not Well Received?" *Boston Globe* (29 March 1998): D8.

Borsuk, Alan J. "Response to Reggie Statement Is Mixed." *State Journal-Register* (Springfield, IL) (5 April 1998): 61.

———. "Response to White Still Mixed: Latest Statement Given to Clarify March 25 Speech Is Both Accepted, Derided." *Milwaukee Journal Sentinel* (4 April 1998): 1.

Borsuk, Alan J., and Meg Kissinger. "White Stands by His Remarks: Reaction Mixed, as Some Criticize Him, Others Say He was Right to His Views." *Milwaukee Journal Sentinel* (27 March 1998): 1.

"Briefly: Gay Group Still Upset after White's Apology." *Atlanta Journal and Constitution* (4 April 1998): G4.

"Briefly: Report: DeBartolo Returns as 49ers' Chief." *Atlanta Journal and Constitution* (27 March 1998): E9.

Bruton, Mike. "Reggie Manages to Insult All." *Ventura County Star* (Ventura County, CA) (29 March 1998): B6.

Callender, David. "Reggie Speech Stirs Up Storm." *Capital Times* (Madison, WI) (26 March 1998): A1.

Campbell, James T. "When a Good Guy Puts His Foot in His Mouth." *Houston Chronicle* (30 March 1998): A16.

Carroll, Jon. "The Poison and the Antidote." *San Francisco Chronicle* (31 March 1998): F8.

"CBS Has White Out Correction." *San Francisco Examiner* (27 March 1998): B8.

"CBS May Reject White, but He Stands by Message." *Wisconsin State Journal* (28 March 1998): A1.

"Church Colleagues Not Upset by White's Comments." *Stuart News/Port St. Lucie News* (Stuart, FL) (28 March 1998): C3.

Clarke, Liz. "Packers' White Stands by Remarks: His Comments on Races Draw Reaction." *Washington Post* (27 March 1998): D1.

"Controversial Remarks Not Costly for White." *Austin American-Statesman* (3 April 1998): C4.

"Criticized White Stands by Comments." *Times Union* (Albany, NY) (28 March 1998): C2.

Cronin, Don. "Eagles Advance." *USA Today* (3 April 1998): C1.

Cuprisin, Tim. "White's Words Fill Talk Radio." *Milwaukee Journal Sentinel* (27 March 1998): 7.

"Expect White to Retain Sponsors." *Des Moines Register* (3 April 1998): 1.

Fisher, Mike. "White Shows Why Athletes Shouldn't Be Role Models." *Fort Worth Star-Telegram* (30 March 1998): 2.

Flaherty, Mike. "Don't Let Unfortunate Words Obscure White's Message." Opinion. *Wisconsin State Journal* (20 March 1998): A5.

———. "Packers' White Tackles Politics: Says Legislature Needs to Be More Compassionate Toward Poor." *Wisconsin State Journal* (26 March 1998): A1.

———. "Packers' White Tackles Politics: Says Legislature Needs to Help Poor, Lashes Out at Gay and Lesbian 'Sin.' " *Wisconsin State Journal* (26 March 1998): A1.

"Football Hero's Speech Shocks Lawmakers." *Patriot Ledger* (Quincy, MA) (26 March 1998): 36.

"Football; Uproar Continues Over White Comments." *Seattle Post-Intelligencer* (28 March 1998): E6.

"Free Speech; Scaring the Far Left." *Florida Times-Union* (Jacksonville, FL) (6 April 1998): A12.

Frey, Jennifer. "White's Opinions Laced with Ignorance, Arrogance." *Washington Post* (27 March 1998): D1.

"FYI; Packers' White Says He Asks for Forgiveness." *Star Tribune* (Minneapolis, MN) (3 April 1998): C1.

Gaddis, Carter. "Bucs 'Hit the Big Time' on MNF." *Tampa Tribune* (3 April 1998): 1.

Gilbert, Bob. "White's Comments Divisive, Lack Facts." *Knoxville News-Sentinel* (Knoxville, TN) (29 March 1998): BC7.

Graves, Gary. "White's Views on Race, Gays Stun Legislators." *USA Today* (26 March 1998): C3.

Hart, Joe. "Reggie Flagged for Illegal Use of Mouth." *Capital Times* (Madison, WI) (27 March 1998): B1.

"He Applauds Reggie White's Stand." Letters to Editor. *News & Record* (Greensboro, NC) (6 April 1998): C6.

"He Has God on His Side." *Palm Beach Post* (3 April 1998): C2.

Hoffmann, Bill. "Fury Over Green Bay Yakker: Grid Great Reggie Stands by Ethnic and Gay Swipes." *New York Post* (27 March 1998): 5.

Huston, Margo, and Tom Heinen. "Opinion Divided on Reggie White's Speech; Talk to Wisconsin Assembly Prompts Both Cheers and Jeers." *Knoxville News-Sentinel* (Knoxville, TN) (30 March 1998): A4.

———. "Religious Leaders Divided Over White's Comments: Opinions Differ on Tolerance, Biblical Readings." *Milwaukee Journal Sentinel* (28 March 1998): 4.

———. *Ventura County Star* (Ventura County, CA) (4 April 1998): C12.

———. *Stuart News/Port St. Lucie News* (Stuart, FL) (4 April 1998): D8.

Hutchinson, Earl Ofari. "A Diminished View of Manhood Underlies Black Fears of Gays." Commentary. *Pacific News Service* (31 March 1998).

Hyde, Dave. "Reggie White Deserves to be Grilled for Comments: Analysis." *Sunday Gazette Mail* (29 March 1998): PD9.

Imrie, Robert. "Comments May Cost White Job." *Chattanooga Times* (28 March 1998): F3.

———. "Fiery Words Land White in Hot Water." *Chattanooga Times* (27 March 1998): E1.

———. "Gay Group Not Pleased with White's Plea." *Commercial Appeal* (Memphis, TN) (4 April 1998): D1.

———. "Rights Groups Bash White." *Dayton Daily News* (27 March 1998): D7.

———. "White's Apology Draws Gay Scorn." *Chattanooga Free Press* (4 April 1998): A1.

———. "White's Comments about Race, Homosexuality under Fire." *Telegraph Herald* (27 March 1998): B9.

———. "White's 'Sermon' Provokes a Blitz." *Commercial Appeal* (Memphis, TN) (27 March 1998): D1.

"In Brief." *Las Vegas Review-Journal* (3 April 1998): C1.

"In Reggie's Words." *Knoxville News-Sentinel* (29 March 1998): C2.

Kane, Eugene. "Constant Game of Gotcha' Seems Hypocritical." *Milwaukee Journal Sentinel* (7 April 1998): 1.

Kelley, Steve. "Insensitive Speech Made White Serious Laughingstock." *Seattle Times* (27 March 1998): E4.

Knott, Tom. "White Drops Ball on Subject of Race." *Washington Times* (27 March 1998): B1.

Lupica, Mike. "White and Wrong." *Daily News* (New York) (29 March 1998): 90.

McClain, John. "Speech Illustrates Double Standard on Racial Issues." *Houston Chronicle* (29 March 1998): 22.

McLaughlin, Tim. "Reggie's Critics Here Give Him an Earful." *Capital Times* (Madison, WI) (27 March 1998): A2.

Martzke, Rudy. "White's Talk Sinks TV Job Bid." *USA Today* (27 March 1998): C1.

"News in Brief: Packers' White Stuns Wisconsin Legislature with Speech." *Detroit News* (26 March 1998): D2.

"NFL." *Houston Chronicle* (3 April 1998): 9.

"Notebook." *Knoxville News-Sentinel* (4 April 1998): C6.

Oates, Tom. "Will White Pay for Comments?" *Wisconsin State Journal* (27 March 1998): B1.

"On Race: Replace Stereotypes with a Must Do Agenda." Opinion. *Wisconsin State Journal* (29 March 1998): B2.

"Packer's Talk Produces Shock, Anger." *The Record* (Bergen County, NJ) (27 March 1998): S7.

"Pack's White Apologizes for His Stinging Sermon." *Palm Beach Post* (27 March 1998): C2.

"Packers' White Blasted for Stereotyping Races." *San Antonio Express-News* (27 March 1998): C1.

"Packers' White Gives Views to Wisconsin Legislature." *Washington Post* (26 March 1998): E2.

"People—TV Future Uncertain After White's Words." *Commercial Appeal* (Memphis, TN) (28 March 1998): D2.

Power, Tom. "Reggie White Seen Suffering for Beliefs." Editorial. *Chattanooga Free Press* (3 April 1998): A6.

"Pro Football: Remarks by Packers' White Draw Criticism in Wisconsin." *New York Times* (26 March 1998): C3.

Rand, Jonathan. "White's Controversial Remarks Aren't Surprising." *Kansas City Star* (29 March 1998): C8.

"Reggie White Accused of Gay-Bashing." *Providence Journal-Bulletin* (27 March 1998): D3.

"Reggie White Speaks on Race, Homosexuality." *Dayton Daily News* (26 March 1998): C5.

"Reggie White Speech Stirs Controversy." *Buffalo News* (26 March 1998): C2.

"Reggie White's Speech Met by Sharp Replies." *St. Petersburg Times* (27 March 1998): C11.

"Remarks by Packers' White Stun Wisconsin Legislators." *Star Tribune* (Minneapolis, MN) (26 March 1998): C1.

"Remarks Could Damage White's Hopes for TV Job." *News and Observer* (Raleigh, NC) (28 March 1998): C3.

Rinard, Amy. "Speech by White Upsets Assembly with Views on Race, Homosexuality." *Milwaukee Journal Sentinel* (26 March 1998): 1.

Robinson, Theotis, Jr. "Reggie White's Speech Deserves Criticism." Comment. *Knoxville News-Sentinel* (30 March 1998): A10.

"Some Lawmakers Get Cheesed Off at Speech." *Charleston Daily Mail* (26 March 1998): B2.

Spaulding, Ed. "Sports Notebook." *Houston Chronicle* (26 March 1998): 10.

"Speech by Packers' White Turns into Sermon on Race." *Chicago Sun-Times* (26 March 1998): 95.

"Sponsors Keep White." *St. Petersburg Times* (3 April 1998): C10.

"Sponsors Not Ditching White." *News and Observer* (Raleigh, NC) (3 April 1998): C7.

"Sports Brief." *Austin American-Statesman* (27 March 1998): D2.

"Sports Briefs." *Telegraph Herald* (4 April 1998): B2.

"Sports Digest." *Dayton Daily News* (3 April 1998): D6.

Stapleton, Arnie. "White Apologizes for Offensive Speech." *Chattanooga Free Press* (3 April 1998): E4.

Theimer, Sharon. "White Speech Makes Him 'Minister of Offense.' " *Chattanooga Free Press* (26 March 1998): F4.

———. "White's Remarks on Homosexuality, Race Shock Lawmakers. *Austin American-Statesman* (26 March 1998): C1.

Vecsey, George. "Pro Football: White Rejects Criticism for Remarks." *New York Times* (27 March 1998): C5.

Weisman, Larry. "NFL Community Quiet On White." *USA Today* (27 March 1998): C2.

"White Apologizes." *St. Petersburg Times* (3 April 1998): C10.

"White Apologizes for Fiery Speech." *Chattanooga Times* (3 April 1998): E4.

"White Apologizes for 'Inappropriate, Clumsy' Remarks." *Buffalo News* (3 April 1998): B2.

"White Criticized, but He's not Backing Down. *Fresno Bee* (27 March 1998): D5.

"White Doesn't Back Off from His Remarks." *Star Tribune* (Minneapolis, MN) (27 March 1998): C3.

"White Fumbles on Tolerance." Editorial. *Capital Times* (Madison, WI) (26 March 1998): A12.

"White: No Harm Meant." *Washington Post* (4 April 1998): B2.

"White Pays the Price for Controversial Talk." *San Diego Union-Tribune* (28 March 1998): D3.

"White Remarks May Have Been Wrong." *Fresno Bee* (3 April 1998): D5.

"White Says Comments not Meant." *Des Moines Register* (4 April 1998): 3.

"White Sorry for 'Clumsy' Race Examples." *San Francisco Examiner* (3 April 1998): D8.

"White's CBS Job in Doubt." *The Plain Dealer* (28 March 1998): D9.

"White's Church Friends Not Upset by Remarks." *Palm Beach Post* (28 March 1998): C2.

"White's Comments Draw Fire." *Tampa Tribune* (26 March 1998): 3.

"White's Remarks Could Cost Him." *Des Moines Register* (28 March 1998): 4.

"White's Remarks Criticized." *Ventura County Star* (Ventura County, CA) (26 March 1998): B2.

"White's Remarks on Homosexuality, Race Stun Lawmakers." *Austin American-Statesman* (26 March 1998): C1.

"White's Remarks on Race, Homosexuals Stun Lawmakers." *Cincinnati Enquirer* (26 March 1998): D01.

"White's Remarks Shock, Offend. *Fresno Bee* (26 March 1998): D5.

"White's Speech Shocks Wisconsin Lawmakers." *Columbian* (Vancouver, WA) (26 March 1998): C2.

"White's Strengths Lie Elsewhere." Opinion. *Wisconsin State Journal* (27 March 1998): A9.

"White's Talk Targets Racial, Ethnic Groups." *Sacramento Bee* (26 March 1998): D2.

"White's Words Reverberate." *Washington Post* (29 March 1998): D12.

Williams, Michael Paul. "There's No Monopoly on Ignorance." *Richmond Times Dispatch* (6 April 1998): B1.

Williams, Walter. "Generalizing about Race Is no Crime; Reggie White Was not Offside." Editorial. *Cincinnati Enquirer* (5 April 1998): B02.

———. "Reggie White's Generalizations Have Statistical Support." *Richmond Times Dispatch* (3 April 1998): A29.

Wineke, William. "He Doesn't Have It All, and That's OK." *Wisconsin State Journal* (28 March 1998): C1.

"Wisconsin Speech Dishonors Reggie White." Letter to Editor. *USA Today* (31 March 1998): A14.

Wolfley, Bob. "Remarks May Cost White Job in TV Network Spokespersons Hint His Prospects Dim." *Milwaukee Journal Sentinel* (27 March 1998): 1.

Zaleski, Rob. "Reggie Teaches Us Some Lessons." *Capital Times* (Madison, WI) (6 April 1998): D1.

TRENT LOTT: "ARMSTRONG WILLIAMS SHOW INTERVIEW REMARKS"

Abrams, Jim. "Lott Sets Off War of Words About Gays." *The Record* (Bergen County, NJ) (17 June 1998): A7.

———. "Vote Pushed on Gay Nominee." *Chattanooga Free Press* (17 June 1998): A9.

"A Lott of Sense." Editorial. *Augusta* (GA) *Chronicle* (18 June 1998): A4.

"Bible Cited as Proof Being Gay Is Sinful." *Times-Picayune* (17 June 1998): A4.

"City's 'Tolerance' Is a One-Way Street." Editorial. *Idaho Statesman* (19 June 1998): A13.

"Civic Sin; Lott Seems to Favor Blind Prejudice." Editorial. *Star Tribune* (Minneapolis, MN) (17 June 1998): A20.

Costello, Michael. "Lott Right; Homosexuality Really Is a Sickness." Opinion. *Lewiston Morning Tribune* (20 June 1998): A8.

Dahl, David. "It's His Religion; You're Welcome to It." *St. Petersburg Times* (21 June 1998): A3.

Dao, James. "Chiding G.O.P., D'Amato Pushes for Vote on Gay Nominee for Envoy." *New York Times* (19 June 1998): B4.

Davidson, Keay. "Texas Hate Slaying Spurs Ally in S.F.; Outraged Activists Decry Intolerance." *San Francisco Examiner* (22 June 1998): A4.

Davidson, Lee. "Hatch Looks Uncomfortable Standing By Gay Nominee." Opinion. *Deseret News* (Salt Lake City, UT) (24 June 1998): A15.

DeFrank, Thomas M. "AL: Anti-Gay View Stalls Envoy Bid." *Daily News* (New York) (19 June 1998): 48.

Dunleavy, Steve. "Rights, Schmights . . . Mayor Is Wrong on This." *New York Post* (25 June 1998): 5.

Endicott, William. "Lott Throws a Big Stone." *Sacramento Bee* (20 June 1998): A3.

———. "To Delete, or Not to Delete." *Sacramento Bee* (27 June 1998): A3.

Esmonde, Donn. "Lott's Ignorance Apparent in Remarks about Homosexuals." *Buffalo News* (18 June 1998): B1.

Forth, David. "Founders Intended Church-State Separation." *Bismarck Tribune* (29 June 1998): A4.

Fram, Alan. "Stance on Homosexuality Draws Criticism of Lott." *Buffalo News* (16 June 1998): A9.

Frank, Jackie. "White House Rips Lott For 'Backward' Views on Homosexuality." *Buffalo News* (17 June 1998): A11.

"Frank Lashes Out at Anti-Gay Comments." United Press International (22 June 1998).

Freda, Ernie. "On Washington; GOP Senator Decries Delay on Gay Envoy." *Atlanta Journal and Constitution* (19 June 1998): A12.

"Gay Church Invites Armey, Lott." *United Press International* (19 June 1998.

"Gay Congressman Counters GOP 'Appeal to the Haters.'" *St. Louis Post-Dispatch* (22 June 1998): A8.

Goldsborough, James O. "Lott, Armey and Politics of Ignorance." Opinion. *San Diego Union-Tribune* (22 June 1998): B7.

"GOP's Armey Renews Homosexuality Debate." *Palm Beach Post* (17 June 1998): A14.

Greenhut, Steven. "Criticism of the Gay Agenda Is Not a Hate Crime." *Las Vegas Review-Journal* (26 June 1998): B15.

Gunnison, Robert B., and Marc Sandalow. "Lungren Plays Down Lott's Remarks on Homosexuality: He Says Matter Was Overblown by the Media." *San Francisco Chronicle* (18 June 1998): A9.

Hamburger, Tom. "Wellstone Tries Again to Force Vote on Hormel Nomination." *Star Tribune* (Minneapolis, MN) (17 June 1998): A10.

"Hating Gays GOP Intolerance." Editorial. *Charleston Gazette* (26 June 1998): A4.

Holland, Judy. "D'Amato Decries GOP Effort to Block Gay's Bid for Ambassadorship." *San Diego Union-Tribune* (19 June 1998): A15.

———. "Debate Over Homosexuality Follows Armey's Comments." *San Antonio Express-News* (17 June 1998): A13.

"Hormel-Bashing." Editorial. *San Francisco Chronicle* (23 June 1998): A18.

Horowitz, Rick. "Speaking off the Top of His Head . . ." *Milwaukee Journal Sentinel* (20 June 1998): 10.

Huffington, Arianna. "A Leadership Void on Capitol Hill." Opinion. *San Diego Union-Tribune* (24 June 1998): B6.

———. "Take Us to Some Leaders." PostOpinion. *New York Post* (23 June 1998): 27.

———. "That Giant Sucking Sound Is the GOP Vacuum." Editorial. *Chicago Sun-Times* (24 June 1998): 45.

"In Fairness to Gay People." Editorial. *Boston Globe* (29 June 1998): A16.

"In Washington." *Commercial Appeal* (Memphis, TN) (17 June 1998): A6.

Javers, Eamon, Laura Dunphy, Jock Friedly, Mary Lynn F. Jones, and Robert Schlesinger. "Gay Pride?" *The Hill* (17 June 1998): 15.

Kelly, Michael. "Lott's Comments on Gays Sparks Clash of 'Illiberals.' " Editorial. *Denver Rocky Mountain News* (25 June 1998): A49.

———. "Lott's Sodom and the Righteous." Op-Ed. *Washington Post* (24 June 1998): A17.

———. "Politics Increasingly a War between Cultures." *Milwaukee Journal Sentinel* (26 June 1998): 16.

———. "The Indecent Culture Wars." PostOpinion. *New York Post* (24 June 1998): 29.

———. "The Politics of Moral Aesthetics." Editorial. *Arkansas Democrat-Gazette* (26 June 1998): B10.

Kennedy, Bud. "Armey Adds Moral Smugness to His Ego Trip." *Fort Worth Star-Telegram* (18 June 1998): 1.

Koch, Wendy. "Lott Accused of Playing Both Sides, Majority Leader Defended as Simply Representing a Divided Senate Debate." *USA Today* (19 June 1998): A6.

Lacey, Marc. "GOP Wins, Loses Votes with Its Comments on Gays; Politics: Senate Majority Leader Lott's Remarks Equating Homosexuals with Kleptomaniacs Point Up Pitfalls. Many Would Rather Avoid Stating Position." *Los Angeles Times* (17 June 1998): A19.

———. "Lott's Words Expose Fundamental Split in Party's Base." *Buffalo News* (18 June 1998): A3.

Lawrence, Jill. "Lott's Comments on Homosexuals Touch Off Furor." *USA Today* (17 June 1998): A7.

"Let Him Go: James Hormel's Homosexuality Should Not Prevent His Confirmation for Ambassadorial Post." Editorials & Forum. *The Plain Dealer* (27 June 1998): B10.

"Let Them Vote On Mr. Hormel." *New York Times* (22 June 1998): A18.

Lochhead, Carolyn. "Lott Interviewer Faces Sex Harass Suit: Ex-employee Claims Gay Advances." *San Francisco Chronicle* (18 June 1998): A2.

"Lott." *Las Vegas Review-Journal* (22 June 1998): A5.

"Lott Enters Fray, Says Homosexuality Is a Sin." *Star Tribune* (Minneapolis, MN) (16 June 1998): A6.

"Lott: Homosexuals Need Assistance, 'Like Kleptomaniacs': The Senator Believes Homosexuality Is a Sin, and Gays Should Be Helped in Dealing With It." *Des Moines Register* (16 June 1998): 5.

"Lott in Sodom." Editorial. *St. Louis Post-Dispatch* (20 June 1998): 34.

"Lott Says Homosexuals Sin, Need Treatment." *Milwaukee Journal Sentinel* (16 June 1998): 8.

"Lott's Comments on Homosexuals Stir Controversy." *Des Moines Register* (17 June 1998): 3.

"Lott's Views on Gays Poison Confirmation." Editorial. *Albuquerque Journal* (18 June 1998): A18.

"Lott's Views Spawn Hate." Editorial. *Seattle Post-Intelligencer* (19 June 1998): A12.

McCain, Stacy. "Still a Sin." *Washington Times* (22 June 1998): A6.

"Ministry Leader Dobson Suffers Stroke." United Press International (17 June 1998).

Mitchell, Alison. "Controversy Over Lott's Views of Homosexuals." *New York Times* (17 June 1998): A24.

———. "Debate Erupts over Homosexuality, Armey Defends Lott Remarks." *Austin American-Statesman* (17 June 1998): A6.

———. "Homosexuality a Sin, Senate GOP Chief Tells Talk Show. *San Diego Union-Tribune* 16 June 1998): A2.

———. "Lott Says Homosexuality Is a Sin and Compares It to Alcoholism." *New York Times* (16 June 1998): A24.

Morse, Rob. "A Case of Agenda Confusion." *San Francisco Examiner* (23 June 1998): A2.

Myers, Jim. "Nickles Asserts Homosexuality One of Many Sinful Behaviors." *Tulsa World* (22 June 1998.

"Nebulous Future for Tobacco Bill." Editorial. *San Francisco Chronicle* (17 June 1998): A22.

"News Briefs." *Dayton Daily News* (16 June 1998): A2.

"Newsline—National; Officials Trade Barbs Over Gays." *Patriot Ledger* (Quincy, MA) (17 June 1998): 4

"Nickles: Gays Shouldn't Be Ambassadors." United Press International (21 June 1998).

"Not a Lott to Get Upset About." Editorial. *Indianapolis News* 18 June 1998: A12.

"Oblivious to the Facts." Editorial. *Courier-Journal* (Louisville, KY) (17 June 1998): A12.

O'Rourke, Lawrence M. "Support Growing For Gay Nominee." *Sacramento Bee* (27 June 1998): A1.

"Personal Shift." *Chicago Sun-Times* (21 June 1998): 22.

"Policy and Morals." Editorial/Opinions. *Fort Worth Star-Telegram* (24 June 1998): 14.

Price, Deb. "Republican Leadership Has Forgotten Inclusiveness." *Detroit News* (27 June 1998): C5.

———. "To Survive, GOP Needs Big Top Tent." *Times-Picayune* (27 June 1998): B7.

"Religion in Brief: White House Gives, Gets Flak." *Atlanta Journal and Constitution* (20 June 1998): F4.

Rich, Frank. "Journal; The Fire Next Time." Editorial. *New York Times* (20 June 1998): A11.

Roberts, Cokie and Steven V. Roberts "Gay-Bashing Divides GOP and the Nation." Editorial. *Daily News* (New York) (24 June 1998): 31.

Robinson, Theotis, Jr. "Cynics Cite Scripture for Own Purposes." Comment. *Knoxville News-Sentinel* (22 June 1998): A10.

Roman, Nancy E. "McCurry vs. Lott on a Point of Theology: Is Homosexuality Sin, Sickness, or Choice?" *Washington Times* (17 June 1998): A1.

Roth, Bennett. "Senate Debate on Gay Nominee Turns Increasingly Nasty." *Houston Chronicle* (27 June 1998): A2.

Rowan, Carl T. "Beware of Politicians Quoting the Bible." Editorial. *Chicago Sun-Times* (20 June 1998): 20.

———. "Casting the First Stone in Washington." Opinion. *San Diego Union-Tribune* (19 June 1998): B7.

———. "Finding Whatever One Wants in the Bible." *Houston Chronicle* (19 June 1998): A42.

———. "The Devil and Dick Armey." PostOpinion. *New York Post* (22 June 1998): 23.

Sandalow, Marc. "Firestorm Over Lott Remarks on Gays; White House Calls His Views Backward." *San Francisco Chronicle* (17 June 1998): A1.

Saunders, Debra. "City of Tolerance Intolerant Toward Salvation Army." Editorial. *St. Louis Post-Dispatch* (19 June 1998): C19.

———. "The Special City." Editorial. *San Francisco Chronicle* (21 June 1998): 7.

Scales, Ann. "GOP Resists Gay Nominee; White House Pushes; Lott Remarks Galvanize Supporters; *Globe* correspondent Estella Duran Contributed to this Report." *Boston Globe* (24 June 1998): A11.

"Senate No Place For Gay Bashing." Editorial. *Atlanta Journal and Constitution* (23 June 1998): A8.

"Sen. Lott's Tolerance Issues." Editorial. *Times-Picayune* (18 June 1998): B6.

"Senator Opposes Ambassador Pick." *Chattanooga Times* (22 June 1998): A6.

"Senator, Put Prejudice Aside." Editorial. *St. Petersburg Times* (22 June 1998): A8.

Shepnick, Philippe. "Helms Says D'Amato Woos Gay Vote." *The Hill* (24 June 1998): 6.

Sobran, Joseph. "Playing Safe by Observing Current Etiquette." *Las Vegas Review-Journal* (28 June 1998): E2.

"Some Straight Talk about the GOP." Editorial. *Daily News* (New York) (27 June 1998): 16.

"Speaking to Homosexual Congregation, Frank Assails Remarks by Lott, Armey." *Buffalo News* (22 June 1998): A4.

Stone, Andrea, and Edward T. Pound. "Lott Fears Issues Won't Be Dealt with on China Trip." *USA Today* (16 June 1998): A8.

Stoner, Justin. "Gay Parents." City News Service (17 June 1998).

Sutton, Larry. "Homosexuals Are Afflicted, Senate Big Sez." *Daily News* (New York) (17 June 1998): 26.

Tafel, Richard L. "Does GOP's Tent Have Room for Gays?" Opinion. *The Record* (Bergen County, NJ) (23 June 1998): L9.

"The Issue Now: Can Lott Learn?" Editorial. *Dayton Daily News* (22 June 1998): A6.

"The Sin's in the Senate." Editorial. *Los Angeles Times* (24 June 1998): B6.

"This Week in Washington." *Idaho Statesman* (21 June 1998): B4.

"Trent Lott: Senator Calls Homosexuality a Sin." *State Journal-Register* (Springfield, IL) (16 June 1998): 2.

"Trent Lott's Gay Theory: Senate GOP Leader Sees Sin and Sickness in Homosexuality, but He Must Not Bend Public Policy to Serve His Bias." Editorial *San Francisco Examiner* (18 June 1998): A18.

"Western Empire." *Denver Post* (19 June 1998): B8.

"What of GOP Leaders' Views about Gays?" Perspect. *The Tennessean* (21 June 1998): D2.

WILLIAM J. CLINTON: "REMARKS BY THE PRESIDENT AT HUMAN RIGHTS CAMPAIGN DINNER"

Anderson, Lee. "Clinton's Distressing Choice." Editorial. *Chattanooga Free Press* (10 November 1997): A4.

Baker, Peter. "Attention by Clinton Has Brought Gay Rights into the Political Open." *Buffalo News* (8 November 1997): A3.

———. "Clinton Addresses Gay Rights Gala; Speech Echoes Truman's Remarks to NAACP in '47." *Commercial Appeal* (Memphis, TN) (9 November 1997): A2.

———. "Clinton at Gay Rights Gala Will Be a Presidential First." *Washington Post* (8 November 1997): A1.

———. "Clinton Equates Gay Rights: Civil Rights: Making Historical Link, President Echoes Truman's Speech That Broke Color Barrier." *Washington Post* (9 November 1997): A18.

———. "Clinton Says Campaign Money Undermined Public Confidence; Both Parties to Blame for Stretching Rules Too Far, President Tells NBC." *Washington Post* (10 November 1997): A23.

Bakst, M. Charles. "Clinton and Gays: His Tardy Message Can Still Be Helpful." *Providence Journal-Bulletin* (20 November 1997): B1.

Bedard, Paul. "Clinton Promises Gay Rights in Workplace." *Washington Times* (9 November 1997): A1.

———. "Clinton Urges School Diversity Training; Can't Trust Parents to Teach Tolerance of Gays, Minorities, He Says." *Washington Times* (11 November 1997): A1.

Bennet, James. "Clinton Is Greeted Warmly as He Speaks to Gay Group." *New York Times* (9 November 1997): 30.

————. "In Milestone, President Will Address a Gay Group." *New York Times* (8 November 1997): A11.

"Clinton Addresses Gays but Meets 'Ellen' in Private." *St. Petersburg Times* (9 November 1997): A3.

"Clinton Simply Endorses Equal Rights." Editorial. *Atlanta Journal and Constitution* (11 November 1997): A14.

"Clinton to Address Gay Rights Group: Plan Draws Criticism from Conservatives, Praise from Human Rights Campaign." *Milwaukee Journal Sentinel* (7 November 1997): 6.

"Clinton to Address Gay-Rights." *Des Moines Register* (7 November 1997): 5.

"Clinton to Address Gay Rights Group." *Palm Beach Post* (7 November 1997): A16.

"Clinton Speaks at Homosexual Group's Fund-Raiser." *Augusta (GA) Chronicle* (9 November 1997): A3.

"Clinton Speech to Gays' Group to Set Precedent." *Commercial Appeal* (Memphis, TN) (8 November 1997): A2.

"Clinton to Address Gay Political Group." *Stuart News/Port St. Lucie News* (Stuart, FL) (8 November 1997): A6.

"Clinton to Deliver Address at Gay-Rights Event." *News and Observer* (Raleigh, NC) (8 November 1997): A8.

"Clinton Will Be First President to Speak at Gay Rights Event." *Fort Worth Star-Telegram* (7 November 1997): 11.

"Clinton Will Make History in Address at Gay-Rights Gala." *Las Vegas Review-Journal* (7 November 1997): A11.

Colbert, Chuck. "All Americans Means Gay Americans, Too." *New America News Service* (13 November 1997).

"Differences Count." Editorial. *Indianapolis Star* (17 November 1997): A10.

Enda, Jodi. "Clinton Reaches Out to Gays: Saturday Speech a Presidential First." *Cincinnati Enquirer* (7 November 1997): A7.

————. "Clinton to Address Gay-Rights Event, 1st Sitting Chief to Do So." *Arizona Republic* (7 November 1997): A16.

————. "Clinton to Address Gay-Rights Gala: Will Be First President to Do So." *Charleston Gazette* (7 November 1997): C4.

————. "Clinton to Address Gay-Rights Gala: Will Be First President to Do So." *Charleston Daily Mail* (7 November 1997): C4

————. "Clinton to Speak at Gay-Rights Gala." *Times-Picayune* (7 November 1997): A10.

Galvin, Thomas. "Clinton on Gays: Teach Tolerance." *Daily News* (New York) (10 November 1997): 24.

"Gays Get a Historic Pep Talk: Clinton Tells Them That Their Dream Is the American Dream." *Des Moines Register* (9 November 1997): 7.

"Goals 2000 Is About Indoctrination, not Education." Commentary; Editorials, Letters. *Washington Times* (14 November 1997): A22.

"He's President of Everyone." Editorial. *Providence Journal-Bulletin* (17 November 1997): B4.

Kiely, Kathy. "Prez Gets a Big Welcome at Gay Rights Fund-Raiser." *Daily News* (New York) (9 November 1997): 4.

Lewis, Kathy. "Speech to Gay Group a First; Clinton Draws Praise and Fire." *Times-Picayune* (9 November 1997): A1.

Malone, Julia. "Clinton Plans Speech for Backers of Gay Rights." *The Plain Dealer* (8 November 1997): A8.

———. "Clinton to Address Gay Activists, Outraging Some Conservatives." *Atlanta Journal and Constitution* (7 November 1997): A9.

———. "Clinton to Address Gay Activists; Saturday Speech Called 'Historic Step' by Some, 'Disgraceful' by Critics." *Atlanta Journal and Constitution* (7 November 1997): A1.

———. "Clinton to Go Address Gay Rights Group; 'Bold, Historic Step.' " *Austin American-Statesman* (7 November 1997): A18.

———. "Clinton to Speak to Gays." *Dayton Daily News* (7 November 1997): A4.

———. "President to Address Gay Rights Gathering: Unprecedented Decision by Sitting President Draws Praise, Fire." *Fresno Bee* (8 November 1997): A8.

Mathis, Nancy. "President to Address Gay Rights Group: Speech Shows Human Rights Campaign Clout, Fuels Policy Debate." *Houston Chronicle* (8 November 1997): A1.

Matthews, Christopher. "Clinton's Historic Gay Rights Speech." *San Francisco Examiner* (13 November 1997): A23.

———. "Lobbying Triumph Brought Clinton before Gay Rights Group." Editorial. *Seattle Post-Intelligencer* (14 November 1997): A15.

McCaslin, John. "Plain Jane and Patti." *Washington Times* (11 November 1997): A5.

McFeatters, Ann. "Clinton is Asked to Omit Anti Gays as Hate Topic: President Schedules 1 Day Conference at White House on Monday." *Denver Rocky Mountain News* (8 November 1997): A57.

"National Digest." *Star Tribune* (Minneapolis, MN) (7 November 1997): A4.

Nichols, Bill. "Clinton Criticized for Gay Group Talk." *USA Today* (10 November 1997): A7.

———. "Gay Gathering Takes Gauge of a President Clinton Lauded, Warily, as Would-Be Heirs are Warned." *USA Today* (7 November 1997): A11.

"No Risk, But Something Gained." Editorial. *Des Moines Register* (14 November 1997): 14.

Pierce, Greg. "Inside Politics." *Washington Times* (17 November 1997): A7.

Powell, Stewart M. "Clinton Talk at Gay Event a Milestone." *San Francisco Examiner* (9 November 1997): A1.

Price, Deb. "Clinton Address Great Day for America." *Times-Picayune* (15 November 1997): B7.

———. "Clinton Addresses a Grand Day for Gays and Lesbians, A Great Day for America." Accent. *Detroit News* (14 November 1997): E2.

———. "President's Speech Means He's Finally Delivering on Promise to Reach Out to Gays." *Detroit Times* (8 November 1997): C1.

Price, Joyce Howard. "Is Clinton Seeking Gay-Rights Legacy? Bennett Poses Truman Comparison." *Washington Times* (10 November 1997): A4.

Rios, Delia M. "Clinton to Address Gay Rights Activists." *Atlanta Journal and Constitution* (8 November 1997): A10.

Sandalow, Marc. "Tonight's Speech to Gays a Presidential Precedent." *San Francisco Chronicle* (8 November 1997): A1.

Scales, Ann. "President Takes Stand on Gay Rights: White House Links His Speech to Larger Equality Movement." *Boston Globe* (9 November 1997): A1.

Shogren, Elizabeth. "Clinton, in Historic Speech, Urges Acceptance of Gays." *Los Angeles Times* (9 November 1997): A20.

———. "Clinton's Speech to Gays, Lesbians Will Be a First." *Los Angeles Times* (8 November 1997): A1.

Sobieraj, Sandra. "Clinton's Address to Gay and Lesbian Rights Group Is a First." *Buffalo News* (9 November 1997): A12.

———. "Clinton Addresses Gay Group's Fund-Raiser Steers Clear of Ellen Issue." *The Record* (Bergen County, NJ) (9 November 1997): A13.

———. "Clinton Addresses Gays, Avoids 'Ellen' Controversy." *Sunday Gazette Mail* (9 November 1997): A1.

———. "Clinton 1st President to Address Gay Group." *Chattanooga Free Press* (9 November 1997): A1.

———. "Clinton Pushes Fight against Hiring Bias." *Dayton Daily News* (9 November 1997): A3.

———. "Clinton Speaks to Gays, but Meets 'Ellen' Backstage." *Austin American-Statesman* (9 November 1997): A2.

———. "U.S. Must Broaden Idea of Equality, Clinton Tells Gays." *Sacramento Bee* (9 November 1997): A10.

Teepen, Tom. "Clinton Action Pressures Successors." *Dayton Daily News* (11 November 1997): A1.

———. "Clinton Adds Weight to Gay Rights Debate." Editorial. *Atlanta Journal and Constitution* (12 November 1997): A13.

———. "Clinton Brings Issue out of the Closet." Editorial. *Austin American-Statesman* (14 November 1997): A15.

———. "Clinton Gives What Could be a Lasting Boost to Gay Civil Rights." *Star Tribune* (Minneapolis, MN) (12 November 1997): A19.

———. "Clinton Put New Spin on Old Subject." Opinion. *South Bend Tribune* (13 November 1997): A14.

———. "Clinton's Boost for Gay Civil Rights." Commentary. *Cox News Service* (10 November 1997).

———. "Clinton's Boost for Gay Rights." *Chattanooga Times* (12 November 1997): A6.

———. "President Boosts Gay Civil Rights." *Tampa Tribune* (14 November 1997): 15.

———. "President's Boost for Gay Civil Rights." *Times-Picayune* (12 November 1997): B7.

Thomas, Cal. "Clinton's Evolutionary Morals." Viewpoints. *Buffalo News* (12 November 1997): B3.

———. "Bill Clinton's Evolving Morals." *Tampa Tribune* (12 November 1997): 13.

———. "Clinton Loses Moral Standing." Editorial. *Montgomery Advertiser* (17 November 1997): A4.

———. " 'Evolutionary Morals' Goes a Freedom Too Far." *Augusta (GA) Chronicle* (18 November 1997): A4.

———. "Evolutionary Morals of Bill Clinton: We Can't Base Standards on Public Opinion." *Des Moines Register* (15 November 1997): 13.

———. "Gay Dinner Celebrates Revolt against Creator: Clinton 'Redefines' Sexuality." Editorial. *Chattanooga Free Press* (11 November 1997): A4.

———. "Morals: Evolving or Mutating?" Editorial. *Cincinnati Enquirer* (13 November 1997): A22.

———. "Tolerance, Approval Not the Same Thing." Editorial. *San Antonio Express-News* (17 November 1997): A11.

Thurman, Skip. "Clinton to Openly Advocate Gay Rights." *Christian Science Monitor* (7 November 1997): 4.

Wattenberg, Ben. "Clinton Courts Gay Lobby: Sex And Character." *Chattanooga Free Press* (15 November 1997): A5.

White House, Office of the Press Secretary. "Interview of The President by NBC'S 'Meet The Press' " (9 November 1997). Available from the White House) at <http://www.whitehouse.gov>.

Wills, Garry. "Bill Bennett Might Work on Improving His Own Virtues." Editorials. *Sacramento Bee* (21 November 1997): B9.

Index

About the Author

JIM A. KUYPERS is Senior Lecturer and Director of the Office of Speech at Dartmouth College. He is the author of *Presidential Crisis Rhetoric and the Press in a Post-Cold War World* (Praeger, 1997) and co-editor, with Andrew King, of *Twentieth-Century Roots of Rhetorical Studies* (Praeger, 2001). He is a former editor for the *American Communication Journal*.